Writing Feature Articles

Writing Feature Articles

A practical guide to
methods and markets

Third Edition

Brendan Hennessy

FOCAL PRESS

For Ann and Caitlin

Focal Press
An imprint of Butterworth-Heinemann
Linacre House, Jordan Hill, Oxford OX2 8DP
A division of Reed Educational and Professional Publishing Ltd

R   A member of the Reed Elsevier plc group

OXFORD   BOSTON   JOHANNESBURG
MELBOURNE   NEW DELHI   SINGAPORE

First published 1989
Reprinted with revisions 1990
Second edition 1993
Reprinted 1994 (twice), 1995
Third edition 1997
Reprinted 1997 (twice)

British Library Cataloguing in Publication Data
Hennessy, Brendan
   Writing feature articles: a practical guide to methods
   and markets – 3rd rev. ed.
   I. Title
   808.06607021

Library of Congress Cataloguing in Publication Data
A catalogue record for this title is available from the Library of
Congress

ISBN 0 240 51471 8

Typeset by Florencetype Ltd, Stoodleigh, Devon
Printed and bound in Great Britain by
Hartnolls Limited, Bodmin, Cornwall

CONTENTS

ILLUSTRATIONS

ACKNOWLEDGEMENTS

I am grateful to the editors of the following publications for allowing me to reproduce articles in entirety – *The Times*, for 'The Great Utility Scandal' in the issue of 8 February 1995, © Simon Jenkins/Times Newspapers Limited 1995; *The Mail on Sunday's You Magazine* and Val Hennessy for 'Let your fingers to the nicking' in the issue of 1 June 1986; and *The New Yorker* for the review of William Dieter's novel *Beyond the Mountain*, © The New Yorker Magazine Inc. 1985.

Special permission was given to reproduce extracts from Irving Wardle's review of Shaw's *Misalliance* in the issue of 10 October 1986, Times Newspapers Limited 1986; and extracts from 'Pig heart swap for human patients' and 'Survival before sentiment' in *The Daily Telegraph* of 13 September 1995, © The Telegraph plc 1995. Freelance Press Services allowed me to reproduce two pages from *Freelance Market News*.

Extracts were taken with permission from the following newspapers: *The Guardian, Daily Mirror, Daily Star, The Independent* and *The Independent on Sunday, The Daily Telegraph, Financial Times, Daily Express, The European, The New York Times*, and *The International Herald Tribune, The Irish Times*, the Picture Sales and Syndication Department of *Today*, now no longer with us, *The Oban Times, South London Press, Kentish Times, Croydon Advertiser, The Sunday Times, The Sunday Telegraph, The Observer, The People, The Mail on Sunday, The News of the World* and *Sunday Express*.

Extracts were taken with permission from the following magazines: *Private Eye, Bella, Sunday Times Magazine, Loaded, Marie Claire, New Statesman & Society, Reader's Digest, The Face, Esquire, Life (The Observer Magazine), Arena* (with special thanks to Tony Parsons), *The Spectator, Vogue, Sunday Express Magazine, Woman's Own, Sight and*

Sound, Films & Filming, Empire, Time Out, Mojo, Gramophone, GQ and *Environment Now*.

The following authors and publishers allowed me to print extracts from their books: A & C Black, *Writers' and Artists' Yearbook*; Macmillan Publishers Ltd, *The Writer's Handbook* (ed. Barry Turner); Writer's Digest Books, *Writer's Market*; Dorling Kindersley Ltd, *The Good Housekeeping Step-by-Step Cookbook*; Peter Benchley and André Deutsche, *Jaws*; Jessica Mitford and Michael Joseph Ltd, *The Making of a Muckraker*; Penguin Books for a page from *The Economist Style Guide*.

I am indebted to the following publications for permission to reproduce pages containing illustrations: *The Times* and *You Magazine* for those relating to the articles mentioned in the first paragraph; *Bella* magazine's guidelines for freelances; *Press Gazette* and Naomi Marks for the page containing computer-designed graphics; *The European* and Chris Duggan for the page with a line drawing projecting two sides of a debate; *The Guardian* for the page presenting wider perspectives to a topic in Chapter 16; *The Mail on Sunday* and *The Sunday Telegraph* for their presentations of statistics; Caroline Marshall and *Campaign* for letting me reproduce the briefings to writers in Chapter 19; and *The Sunday Times* for a page showing how display techniques project an article.

Permission was kindly granted for the reproduction of the marks for copy preparation and proof corrections by the British Standards Institution; of their leaflet on copyright by the Society of Authors; of the NUJ Code of Professional Conduct by the National Union of Journalists.

The staff of the Reading Room of the British Museum were unfailingly helpful. Friends and colleagues among journalists to whom I am indebted are numerous, as are my students over the years. Paul Burlison in particular advised on word processors. Finally, I must specially thank Freddie Hodgson, my editor, whose advice and encouragement have been invaluable at all stages. The final shapes of Chapters 19 and 20 owe much to his efforts.

PREFACE

This book is aimed at everybody who wants to write feature articles –
including students on journalism courses; practising journalists, staff or
freelance; people in trades and professions who have the need or occasion to write articles and are not sure how to go about it; people in PR
and advertising; and people looking for a new hobby.

But I am optimistically casting my net much wider. Some of the discussion in the book refers to writing skills in general, so I believe that people
who need to improve the writing quality of their correspondence, business or personal, reports and memos, or of any other writing assignments
they are regularly faced with, can derive benefit from it.

Too much advice given in books on writing, while appearing practical,
is actually vague when you try to apply it to specific purposes. The differences in markets, requiring different treatments, lengths and language,
tend to be ignored. I have therefore drawn examples from, and made
references to, as wide a spectrum of articles as possible. I have devoted
a fair amount of space to showing how the principles of effective writing
work out in practice in the articles and pieces chosen for dissection.
I have tried to get inside them, tried to show what they look like from
the inside.

Markets come before methods, and that is a message beginners can be
reluctant to learn. They tend to worry only about *how* to write. The professional writer knows that the priorities are content (having something to
say) and audience. Once the content is understood and shaped, and the
audience identified, the writing will follow and will adapt. Keeping in mind
the different markets, I have examined the merits of the best of 'popular'
as well as of 'quality' journalism, in the sense of newspapers and magazines.

I think of journalism as a hybrid between a profession and a trade-and-
craft. Of course there is professionalism in the air that journalists breathe

in their efforts to develop and improve skills, meet obligations and deadlines, and keep standards. But the term 'craft' reminds us that the job needs cunning. It is a matter of watching the more practised, picking up tricks where you can, learning as much from the mediocre as from the brilliant – because you can see more clearly what is being attempted, and how it can be done better.

The third edition of *Writing Feature Articles* has been completely revised, with many updates and additions to the text and more illustrations. I now include assignments with each chapter, with some suggested responses given in Appendix 1, and a new chapter on the features department.

These revisions have taken note of ideas and comments made by my own students working through the book at the University of Westminster and elsewhere during the past few years; and also those made by journalism lecturers, students and practising journalists who have written to me.

The new Chapter 16 gives attention to the special requirements of in-house feature writing including team investigations and to the organization of daily and weekly news features.

Ways of adapting some of the end-of-chapter assignments to group work are given but tutors and readers working on their own will see how to adapt and extend the assignment ideas for their purposes. The suggested responses are not, needless to say, intended to be definitive. In preparing the assignments I have kept in mind the requirements of the National Vocational Qualifications (NVQs) in news journalism and periodical journalism and of the NCTJ and other training courses.

Suggestions from readers based on their experience of using the book are welcome, and should be addressed to me, c/o the publishers.

Brendan Hennessy
South Norwood
London, 1996

1 FROM AUTHOR TO ARTICLE

Are you curious about your fellows, about the human condition? Do you want to communicate with others by writing? Are you eager to tell them what they need to know? If it is yes to all three questions you already sound like a feature writer.

Whatever writing skills you are lacking can be developed by practice and persistence, as long as you are driven by those three urges.

Getting the approaches right for your subjects and audiences, however, is vital. Some beginners say there is no mystery about it. They write articles, send them off, and are then increasingly paralysed by rejection. Others do not know how to get started in any organized way. Writers in particular fields want to move to others, but are not sure how to acquire the new skills.

I believe this book will help all these groups to succeed in writing and selling articles if the urge to express themselves is there and they are prepared to work at it. Happily, you can start your writing activity at any time: before reaching your teens, at 50, 60, 70 and 80. Writing, because it is a form of self-expression, can be therapeutic and life-enhancing for the sick and the disabled. It can restore dignity and self-esteem to the unemployed and the retired; it can set up career prospects for the young.

Of course a basic talent has to be there but more people possess it than are conscious of the fact. It is the kind of talent that has to be identified and goaded into action.

The difference between successful and unsuccessful writers of non-fiction for newspapers and magazines is mainly a matter of application. Many would-be writers give up when they discover writing is hard work, on the whole, sometimes requiring much hard thinking and revision until it comes right.

A CHECKLIST FOR SUCCESS

Writing an article is something of a juggling act. You have to be aware of several aspects and you have to be using different skills at the same time. Thoughts and words present themselves in an unruly fashion and have to be pacified and put into order. While getting it right, six questions will help:

1 Is there an overall *purpose*? (Why am I writing the article? What do I hope to achieve with it?)
2 Is there an *audience* (market, readership) in mind?
3 Can I develop enough suitable *content*? (Is the information readily accessible?)
4 Have I got a good *idea*? (Do I know exactly what I want to say?)
5 Does the *form* (structure) match the content?
6 Is there an *individual contribution* to the subject (some originality, something only I could have put in, some particular knowledge, experience, contact)?

For those who like code words, you have *PACIFIC*.

This book aims to make you better prepared to answer these questions, and to show how writing skills can be adapted to a growing number of specialized interests.

The aim of this chapter is to map out the ground to be covered.

GETTING STARTED AND DEVELOPING SKILLS

'Something to say.' There is a two-way process between a writer's ideas and his/her markets: sometimes an idea suggests a market and sometimes it is the other way round. If you are a jackdaw with many interests that do not go too deep, you may need to select some to develop, at least initially, a few deep interests you may need to add to them. You could start by listing your interests, reminding yourself what they are by going through several issues of the newspapers and magazines you regularly read, and thinking about your main activities, your 'lifestyle' and so on. You could then make a selection – a short list – of subjects you think you could write about, and alongside them a list of which papers or magazines might be interested in articles.

This activity should give you some insight into your character/personality. Writing a 300–500 work 'biog' of yourself will give you more. Sum up your likes and dislikes, beliefs and political views. Whatever you are going to write about will start from yourself, and the most objective-looking writing reveals the person behind it. Understanding yourself will help you to write truthfully, and communicate better.

Keeping a journal

You may prefer to do this kind of thing continually in a journal, where among other things you may note how your attitude to the world changes. Some of your thoughts, even apparently idle ones, or descriptions of events in your life, may turn themselves into good article ideas. Your journal may be entirely devoted to noting ideas for articles, and developing them, and to experiment with structures, styles and themes. A journal can also provide a safety-valve when you are frustrated or temporarily blocked in other endeavours: it can help you relax and enable the writing to start flowing again.

In your journal write about anything that has captured your attention, engaged your mind, roused your feelings or stirred your imagination. When you read back over it, ask yourself whether the experience has been rendered vivid or memorable by the writing.

Does it come over as vague? Is that because there is too little fresh, concrete imagery to engage the reader's attention? If one word only is allowed to describe what is good writing, then that word is *precise*. There is no difference here between the poet and the journalist. To sum up, use your journal for various kinds of experiments in words and ideas and see how that can help in the production of articles.

FROM IDEA TO TEXT

A subject for an article is not enough: you need an idea. An effective title or headline can make it clear how good an idea it is. 'Giving doctor a taste of his own medicine', a *Guardian* article, is a study of how barriers to communication between doctors are being broken down. 'The Education of Doctors' would have indicated the general subject only.

An idea is a specific angle or approach to a subject. Ideas for articles tend to deal with a specific problem, tension, drama, struggle, conflict, question, doubt or anxiety. The subject 'Police in Britain Today' may become the idea 'The Police: Are they Racist?'

Ideas may come at any time – on a bus, in a pub or restaurant, while watching TV. This means that you should carry a notebook and pen wherever you go, or have them placed at strategic points in the house – in the bathroom, kitchen, sitting room, on your desk, on your bedside table.

Before an idea reaches its final form, you will have done some subject/idea testing. You will have answered such questions as 'Is it of particular interest at the moment?' or 'Has it been over-exposed recently in the media?' You will also have done some market research. This means analysis of newspapers and magazines to discover what their editors' requirements are and what kind of readerships they have.

You will then find it easier to shape the appropriate content. You will avoid gathering too much information and getting bogged down. It is probably best to concentrate at first on subjects you know something about, gradually including topics that need more research – whether this constitutes legwork (visiting places such as prisons, or scenes of disasters, where first-hand observation is appropriate), interviews or printed sources. Collect from newspapers and magazines cuttings of articles that deal with your interests and also those that are useful models of approach, language, construction, or research.

Professional writers are often working at various stages of several articles at a time. They develop a habit, and a rhythm, and have got themselves well organized. Thus certain parts of the day are devoted to scouring publications for ideas, doing subject research, market research, planning/writing an article, telephoning or corresponding with editors, interviewees and other contacts, and developing the business, keeping records, accounts, and so on. They have discovered what time of the day they are freshest to do the writing and at which the tiredest, when they deal with the humdrum tasks.

LOOKING AT MARKETS

Of these tasks it is the market study that tends to be neglected by the beginner. Failure to work at this will bring discouraging rejections. Analysing the papers and magazines to be aimed at prevents you wasting your time – for instance, offering book reviews to markets that have well established lists of reviewers regularly commissioned. (Offering such markets *samples* in an attempt to get on a list is, of course, another matter.) Market research saves you from such gaffes as sending articles that are too long or of unsuitable style or subject matter for a publication, or sending speculative articles dealing with the scientific, technological or political themes to newspapers that have their own specialist writers in these areas. That having been said, clearly your best chance of regular freelance work for a newspaper is by proving yourself as a specialist of some kind. In fact much of the magazine world is specialist.

Watch your timing. When you have followed up in an article a controversy that has been raging in a publication, and your effort has been politely rebuffed, it may be because you have noticed that, while you have been writing, interests have shifted to other matters. This should teach you to stay closely tuned to the market.

A word at this point about organizing and presenting yourself: produce a correctly typed script as described in Chapter 2, and keep clear records. Send a stamped addressed envelope with contributions, or, with those sent abroad, International Reply Coupons. If not on disk keep at least two 'blacks' (carbon copies), photocopies or printouts of all articles and other contributions. Give a daily paper two weeks to consider your work, a weekly about six weeks and a monthly about three months before sending a reminder to the editor, and have a list of other possible markets prepared, so that rejected work is immediately sent somewhere else (rewriting or improving it first if necessary). When work is sent off, start something new immediately: the best consolation for a rejection is new work progressing well.

The markets to start with

If you are a beginner, start modestly and develop crucial skills as you go. Here are a few practical suggestions. Write letters to friends – a good way of experimenting in a relaxed frame of mind. Write for amateur publications, your college or university newsletter or magazine, the house magazine of the company you work for, your parish magazine – or start your own magazine. Write for your local paper or for specialized papers on your wavelength. Choose among the political ones, for example, or consider *The Jewish Chronicle* or *The Catholic Herald* or whatever fits your religion. Study such markets, even if you do not belong to a particular religion, to consider what kinds of non-religious contributions you might send to religious publications.

Rather than try to break into highly competitive, well staffed areas such as the national papers or high-powered national magazines, look for outlets for any specialized knowledge or special insights you may have about your particular job, trade or profession. If you are doctor, lawyer, teacher, accountant, or architect, aim at the specialized journals for these careers.

When something happens in your village or town that may have national implications – wildlife is dying of a mysterious disease in alarming numbers, for example – write about it. Conversely, relate national issues – growing drug addiction, increase in car accidents – to your local area, pointing out how its efforts to deal with such problems compare with other places or the national average. Markets for such articles might be either national or local, or both.

You may find it useful to subscribe to authorship magazines which will keep you up to date with markets, and may provide a stimulation and fruitful suggestions (see Bibliography). Going to meetings of a local writers' circle might help. Your local library may know of one nearby:

if not, see Appendix 5. Authorship magazines and writers' circles are particularly useful for the ideas being shared about new markets for different kinds of feature, especially for the shorter kind, and they may provide training ground and source of income at the same time. You will obtain information for the 'letters to the editor' page which are paid for, news 'fillers', competitions of various kinds, advertising slogans, greetings card messages, and so on. Such information would otherwise be quite difficult to gather.

Letters and fillers

Writing letters to editors of newspapers and magazines is good training and practice. You become familiar with the readership, you keep up to date with the latest controversies, and you make your name familiar to the editor.

Many letters to magazines tend to comment on, or follow up, articles or letters that have appeared. If you have a specific interest, hobby, trade or profession that is covered by one or more magazines, writing letters will keep you thinking and writing on that subject. Certain controversial topics are rarely out of the news, and you may have a point worth making on the current crime wave, on test-tube babies, or the abuse of children, especially if there is something in your own experience that you can use to illustrate your remarks.

The more popular newspapers and magazines give scope for a wide variety of subjects and treatments, but you must study issues of the publication closely to assess the readership aimed at in different markets. If you are not following up a subject already aired, ask yourself whether your item is going to be of interest to those particular readers. Can you say why you believe it would?

Letters to publications often give useful information or tips, such as a new use for old things, or how you dealt with the vagaries of your word processor. Some remarks made by your children, or your ironic commentary on a politician's speech, might make an amusing letter. Complaints are conspicuous in the letters column: about people's annoying habits, for example, and what the law can and cannot do about it; about various injustices, including examples of sexism; about dishonesties that big companies get away with and the individuals do not; animals – cruelty to them, and the nuisances they are allowed to perpetrate.

In the popular papers there is room for views on television programmes, especially on the 'soaps' and others that attract mass audiences. If you have nearly fallen off a cliff, or drowned, and are thankful to have survived, some publication, somewhere, will print your letter about it.

Some of the fillers, the short news items used to fill up a gap in a page, are supplied by freelances. Local papers and popular magazines are the markets that immediately suggest themselves. Once again, think of the readers. Would your item help, amuse or instruct them in some way? *Reader's Digest* will pay well for anecdotes under various headings, including 'Life's Like That' and 'Humour in Uniform'. Recipes, jokes, interesting records (or 'Is this a Record)? make fillers in various market.

Letters and fillers are unlikely to be returned. If you get no response from an editor you have sent such pieces to, you may want to try other markets. Send a freshly typed or printed copy. Keep a record of where you send them.

You may want to enter writing competitions; prizes may be worth winning. Competitions to write advertising slogans – on such subjects as the tourist attractions of Britain or the merits of some food product, for example – can be fun, and can provide practice in using words economically.

WHAT IS AN ARTICLE?

An article is a piece of deliberately structured writing for publication, usually running from 600 to 2000 words, which aims to inform, comment, persuade or entertain. It might aim to inspire or to stimulate the reader to think, or to provoke to action. An article often includes the author's point of view, and sometimes develops an argument. Many beginners' efforts are rejected because they have not quite ended up as articles, whatever other merits they may have. The following is an attempt to clarify what the essential elements are.

Take newspapers first. Newspapers' feature articles, although they may not all relate directly to the news of the moment, normally have a topical peg of some kind. Many fill in the background to the news, explaining why events happened, sometimes speculating on future consequences. Such articles are written to order and have a particular point of view to put.

The topical peg, both in newspapers and magazines, can come out of people's special interests. For example, both cover such activities as gardening, cooking, athletics, do-it-yourself (DIY) and travel, with the seasons or the emergence of new fashions providing the topicality. Specialist magazines can assume a more knowledgeable readership. These and many other kinds of article benefit from illustrations.

In terms of structure, as will be shown, the feature article is unlike, for example, the personal letter which chattily rambles on, since it is partly a substitute for conversation, and discusses matters only of interest to the sender and the recipient. The letter may not be easily understood by anyone older than the person to whom it is addressed because of the particular knowledge and experience shared by writer and recipient. An article, on the other hand, aims to inform, persuade or entertain a large audience in a purposeful way.

The article has something particular to say. The something may take the form of a thesis, a message, a point, a question. If you cannot say in a few words what the article is *about*, what the controlling idea is, or if you cannot complete the following sentence, 'The article shows that. . . .', then there is something wrong. There is a beginning (or intro), a middle (or body), and an end. The body contains the main points to be made, lists the facts, reveals their significance, anticipates readers' questions and attempts to answer them.

What is normally meant by the term 'essay' needs to be distinguished from the feature article, too. The academic essay of learned journals attempts to bring its limited, highly specialized readership up to date with new discoveries in the field, and it contributes to the constant research and debate. The other kind of essay, the fine-writing kind, is usually too personal, too discursive and self-indulgent, and has too casual an approach to structure to be called a feature article. Nevertheless certain personal columns and commentaries, particularly in weekly reviews covering politics and the arts, keep this personal essay form alive outside the school-room.

You may have got high marks for your discursive school essays and be awaiting the summons to take over a newspaper column. In that case you should be warned that rambling reflections are not in great demand. A close study of columns reveals that most are firmly anchored to topical pegs, however free-wheeling they may appear to be. Furthermore, those columnists are generally well established writers who have earned the right to some self-indulgence. They have often spent years in other departments of journalism, as reporters, subeditors or feature writers. Even so, there are opportunities for new columnists in local papers and in specialized magazines, if that is where your interests lead.

News and features contrasted

News generally has the qualities of conflict, human interest, importance, prominence, proximity, timeliness and unusualness. Features, as this book will amply show, reflect these qualities. Structures differ. A straightforward news story often has an inverted pyramid shape, the most important point coming first. Readers short of time can quickly gather the main news from the first paragraphs, and read on only to find the details. This form is useful if the story has to be cut because of demands on space, as more stories arrive at the news desk. The story tends to be cut from the end, which is where the least important bits are, or should be.

Articles, on the other hand, take various shapes, dictated by their content, and a common shape is the pyramid right way up, with the weight of the conclusion at the end. While reporters have to 'kiss' (keep it short and simple), there is generally a more relaxed approach to the writing of the article (though not wasting words), some literary skill and some originality of content and style.

The differences between a news story and a feature article are recognized by newspaper editors, special pages being allocated to news and others to features. The news story is considered to be 'straight' or 'hard', but precisely what these terms mean can vary from paper to paper. In general it means reporting of an event that sticks to the facts, though when the story is very dramatic, 'colour' (description) and, more controversially, the author's feelings and opinions are sometimes allowed to creep in.

Conversely, the depth, imagination and sensitive handling of the human interest in a feature article will go for nothing if the writer does not have the basic reporting skill to build on a framework of facts, details and names as accurate as they would be in a news story.

The crucial distinction between reporting and feature writing is the inclusion in the latter of viewpoint and opinion, commonly under a byline, that serves to make the attribution of the viewpoint clear.

Subediting a feature

While reporters might suffer their words being decimated, pieces reordered, tested against new facts, feature writers are expected to fill the space and to need light subbing. They must give editors what they want, or find another editor who wants what they write. The more creative/more subjective feature writer is valued for opinions, based on facts. 'Make them laugh, make them cry, make them wait' is a precept for the fiction writer that can sometimes be adapted for the feature writer (though the intro must make it clear why the reader should wait).

As a result of competition from television, there has been a shift from news towards feature treatment in newspaper content. When the main news is televised at night, the morning paper has to try to add something – more background, more analysis, extra angles, and, most commonly, more human interest. It is a two-way breeding process, for TV programmes follow up newspaper stories. Middlebrow papers have articles reflecting on the social issues underlying television's situation comedies. Popular papers give much space to the private lives of the stars of TV 'soaps', sometimes blurring the distinction between these and their lives as fictional characters.

The variety of newspaper features

For convenience, then, newspaper editorial matter, whether daily, evening or weekly, is generally labelled either 'news' or 'features'. Features include background or 'current situation' articles, on politics, the economy and social questions, closely pegged to current events; plus human interest stores, investigative features, opinion formers, 'think pieces', colour pieces, celebrity interviews and profiles. Then there are the specialist Parliamentary sketch writers, lobby correspondents and arts reviewers, columns ranging from law and science, through education, to gardening and cooking. There are many kinds of service columns, giving no-frills advice on shopping, holidays, DIY, and so on. The features department is also responsible for such miscellaneous non-news items as readers' letters, comic strips, crossword puzzles and horoscopes.

Human interest stories ('people journalism') are rated high in most newspapers; they deal with people being abused, people getting into trouble, or people struggling against illness, misfortune or oppression rather than with the statistics of social problems, because that is the way to get readers' interest. Similarly it is usually more interesting to read about people being successful than organizations being successful; even specialized business magazines constantly hunt out the human angles. Sometimes on thin nights popular papers will blow up items about TV or film celebrities or royalty which are short on facts.

The 'investigative' feature, such as the *Sunday Times* Insight column, can be very influential. The aim is to explore behind the news, particularly the kind of news that is of public concern: dangerous drugs put on the market with insufficient testing, aeroplane accidents due to negligence at trial stage are examples. Investigative articles are often linked with a hard-hitting campaign to obtain better compensation for victims. Such features are usually produced by a team of reporters, feature writers and research assistants, and are an example of how reporting and feature-writing techniques are sometimes combined in the modern newspaper.

Colour pieces are descriptions of such events as the Oxford–Cambridge boat race or an account of a visit to a woman's prison. Their effect depends on an imaginative use of language to create atmosphere, and on qualities such as humour and pathos.

Planning ahead

A newspaper features department plans well head for features that can be based on important anniversaries (the end of the Second World War, the Queen's accession), and for seasonal articles to do with Christmas, Easter, and the start of the grouse-shooting season in Scotland. The feature writer is likely to have a copy of the *Dictionary of Dates*, and to keep a notebook in which to jot down seasonal events and ideas.

Illustrated features are valued by newspapers and magazines. An article can often be written round an interesting picture or two: if these are worth a good deal of space, the words may be limited to an extended caption. 'News features' may depend largely on the effectiveness of the pictures that accompany them. These pieces are hybrid forms. An example is the piece accompanying the news report of an inner city riot and adding descriptive colour and explanatory background. There may be pictures of, and interviews with, policemen, rioters, and spectators, and shots of looted shops or burning motor cars. A new cure for baldness might be dressed up as a feature by getting pictures of, and quoted comments on it from, two or three bald celebrities.

Much sports writing is of a hybrid kind in which news-writing and feature-writing techniques merge. It is not easy to decide whether to call a detailed and vivid description of a football match that is interlaced with critical commentary a report or a feature.

MAGAZINES FOR EVERYTHING

Magazines have to settle for a more general topicality than newspapers (although the weekly review is close behind the news). The magazine article is allowed greater space and a more leisurely approach: much time and care can go into the writing and the research, and it can be planned further ahead. The newspaper feature is generally urgent in tone, with information being used to work out solutions. The magazine article is inclined to spread itself, giving more attention to colour and readability. It may tend to deal in questions and doubts rather than in providing solutions.

Newspapers are mostly for large general audiences. Magazines are aimed at particular sections of the community, and the writer has a more precise picture of the readers: young men on the town, old people slowing down, travellers, film buffs, teenage girls. The scope for writers is vast in magazines: a complex world is producing more and more specialization, and new magazines appear in response to this. Sometimes, as with computer magazines in the UK, the newcomers increase at an alarming rate until the competition begins to bite and the weakest go out of business.

A successful magazine depends on a successful recipe or formula, meeting the expectations of a carefully built up readership. The magazine's identity is maintained, while ideas and treatments are subtly varied, taking care to adjust to changes in the world around and in readership tastes. The latter changes can reflect population shifts (for example, an increasing number of under-20s or over-70s).

The subject matter of the bigger general magazine can have a wide net and might include science, medicine, politics, economics, social questions, sport, adventure, family life, business success and travel. The treatment might vary from 'think pieces', investigative or exposé features, to humorous or how-to-do-it pieces or question-and-answer interviews. When market-researching, you will notice how different topics tend to be treated, and you will note any specialized vocabularies that might be worth learning.

Full-time freelance writers faced with this variety in newspapers and magazines need to be versatile in their approach to different readerships if they stick to one or two subjects. For instance, writers on biogenetic issues will increase their satisfaction as well as their income if they can reach the bigger audiences of popular markets as well as the audience for specialized journals and quality papers, even though effective popularizing may require greater thought and writing effort. If the desire to communicate is strong enough, and the material is there, these skills can be fostered.

The emphasis of this book is firmly on developing writing skills. For career opportunities in journalism, including staff feature writers and sub-editors, and freelances, see Peter Medina and Vivien Donald, *Careers in Journalism*, Kogan Page, current edition.

ASSIGNMENTS

1 Study the current issues of the *Daily Telegraph* and *The Sun*. Reply to one letter to the editor in each, in the appropriate style (300 words, 200 words).
   Agree or disagree with the opinions expressed. Add to the content if you agree.

2 Indicate (200 words for each) how you would develop your letters into 800 word feature articles for those markets. Give a summary of the proposed content and suggest someone you might interview in each case.

3 You died in 1960 aged 30 but were deep frozen. You left a husband or a wife aged 28 and a son or daughter aged 10. You were discovered and brought back to life by Professor Ulrich at

Cambridge University last Monday. You are very confused and have mixed feelings about the resurrection. A glossy monthly magazine asks you to describe what you find. Although you are a one-off (there are unkind references to 'a freak'), an increasing number of people in this country are opting to be deep frozen at the time of death in the hope that they can at some time in the future be brought back to life. You have therefore been asked to include in your piece some advice for such people. Write 300 words and indicate the target publication.

Assess yourself

Journalists, as well as physicians, need to know themselves. Readers want to know what you think, but not to be caught up in your ego trip or bombarded by your unconscious prejudices. Knowing yourself means that you can more easily work out where you stand on a given subject or where your leanings are, so that you can focus on the needs of your readers.

Here is an assignment that will help you to know yourself:

4 (a) Try to stand outside yourself and see yourself as others see you. Write an account of yourself in the third person. Include your appearance, family background and education, character (strengths and weaknesses), main interests, what attracts you to journalism as a career, what your ambitions are (freelance writer?, editor of a newspaper?, editor of a magazine?). List the skills (keyboarding, etc.) that you possess that are necessary for feature writing and those that you need to develop further.

List the newspapers and magazines that you read regularly and some of the books that you have read recently. Consider whether your reading could be widened/deepened, considering your ambitions (250 words, 40 minutes).

(b) Reduce the above to 100 words (10 minutes).

(c) Reduce the 100 words to 50 words (5 minutes).

2 DEALING WITH EDITORS

John Steinbeck, author of *Of Mice and Men* and *The Grapes of Wrath,* and Nobel Prize winner, looked over his writing class at its first meeting. 'Why are you here?' he said. 'Why aren't you sitting at home writing?'

The first lesson a prospective writer needs to learn is that a lot of time needs to be spend *doing* it. The suggestions of such a book as this need to be adapted to your own experience.

The next two chapters will describe the process of producing articles from start to finish. They are key chapters, since they will provide a frame of reference for the varieties of subjects and activities explored in subsequent chapters.

THE STAGES IN ARTICLE WRITING

Here, for guidance, is a list of the activities that occur in writing articles:

1 Formulating ideas (preliminary subject research).
2 Collecting and filing cuttings and other materials for possible use.
3 Testing their market feasibility (market research).
4 Selling: the query letter.
5 The preliminary outline
6 Subject research: legwork.
7 Subject research: library, background reading and note-taking.
8 Subject research: interviewing.
9 The final outline.
10 The first draft.
11 The final typescript.
12 Following up, and checking for spin-offs.

It is likely that about a fifth to a quarter of the time taken over an average article of 1500 words will be actual writing. But allotting of time can vary considerably, depending on the length and complexity of the article. You need to organize your time carefully, and this theme is taken up in Chapter 6.

FROM IDEA TO MARKET

Ideas are tender plants: some you've just got to let grow, others you've got to feed and watch over. The way you develop ideas is a personal matter, depending on your own kind of creativity. What this book can do is suggest the atmosphere, moods, thought processes, raw material, triggers and techniques that might help your ideas grow. In this chapter we are concerned with the overview of the process by which ideas turn into articles and articles turn into a writing career; a process in which satisfying the needs of editors and their readerships is as important as satisfying your need to express yourself. In Chapters 3, 4 and 5 we shall plunge deeper: into the world of ideas and into the world of their markets.

Finding an idea

After reading a letter about transcendental meditation (TM) in a national paper, let's assume you become interested in the cult/religious organization that at the time of writing is turning a former American airbase in Suffolk into a Natural Law University. The movement was founded by Maharishi Mhesh Yogi in 1958. The Beatles flirted with it, the President of Mozambique believes it has saved his country from the destruction of war. Collective meditation, it is believed, can solve the world's problems.

You want to find out more about cults in general, and TM in particular. You therefore consult in a good reference library an index to articles published (see pages 406–7). The Clover Index, the British Humanities Index (BHI) and the *American Reader's Guide to Periodical Literature* are probably good ones to start with. You will note articles and obtain the publications from the librarian or access through microfilm or CD ROM, whichever is available. You may have your own cuttings on the subject, and there may be a useful book.

Suppose you come across a series of three articles on cults in successive issues of Life, the *Observer* magazine. The first contains a list of cults/groups, including TM. Here there is a quote from the Toronto *Globe and Mail* when in 1993 TM announced its programme of building a dozen universities in the country: 'What is TM, a religion or an off-shore multinational selling breathing techniques and psycho-twaddle?'

You divide and subdivide the question and ideas begin to suggest themselves. You find different ways of grouping the cults: those confined to the UK, and those that are international; those that are big business and those that have limited funds; those that have brainwashing techniques and those that don't; those whose members can be debriefed easily and those whose members cannot; those that are hostile to the family unit and those that are not. And so on.

You select on or two ideas that seem to have potential. One might be a case study of how a cult established in a large Victorian house in a London suburb succeeded (or failed) to win local support. Another idea might be based on the long process of debriefing normally required of members who leave such cults, and the different methods of debriefing to be explored through interviews with debriefers and those being debriefed and the debriefed, as well as printed sources. But before spending much more time on reading, you will want to know if you'll be able to sell the idea to an editor.

Pre-testing the idea

Here are some questions that will help you to decide whether your idea has marketable qualities, based on your preliminary subject research:

- Is there a clear theme/angle/point of view?
- Is there a market? Who is likely to be particularly interested?
- Is the idea fresh? Make sure your information and approach will be different from the articles you've located through the indexes or that you've seen very recently, or at least that you can make it different by updating it (see below).
- Can the published information be updated? Is there enough information about new developments? Is it readily available? Where from?
- Is the idea timely?
- Is it a good time for you to handle it? Why?
- Are there any dangers of libel, or other legal or ethical considerations?

You decide what you would aim to do in such an article. You would inform, explain and entertain undoubtedly. You would give a few words of warning, too. Your attitude to far-out cults is amused without being scornful, fairly tolerant if highly sceptical of their aims. You are establishing the angle. You decide, perhaps, that a chatty treatment, with quotes and anecdotes would work, at about 1000 words. You consult the pages of a writers' guide such as *Writers' and Artists' Yearbook* (A. & C. Black),

Figure 1 Page from *Writers' and Artists' Yearbook*

£24.00 per annual volume. Journal of the Royal Numismatic Society. Articles on coins and medals. Memoirs relating to coins and medals are unpaid, and contributions should reach a high academic standard.

Nursery World, Ruth Beattie, The School House Workshop, 51 Calthorpe Street, London WC1X 0HH *tel* 0171-837 7224 *fax* 0171-278 3896.
90p. W. For all grades of primary school, nursery and child care staff, nannies, foster parents and all concerned with the care of expectant mothers, babies and young children. Authoritative and informative articles, 800 or 1600 words, and photos, on all aspects of child welfare and early education, from 0-8 years, in the UK. Practical ideas and leisure crafts. *No* short stories. *Payment:* by arrangement. *Illustrations:* line, half-tone, colour.

Nursing Times and Nursing Mirror (1905), John Gilbert, Macmillan Magazines Ltd, Porters South, 4-6 Crinan Street, London N1 9SQ *tel* 0171-833 4000 *fax* 0171-843 4645.
95p. W. Articles of clinical interest, nursing education and nursing policy. *Illustrated* articles not longer than 2000 words. Contributions from other than health professionals sometimes accepted. Press day, Monday. *Illustrations:* photos, line, cartoons. *Payment:* NUJ rates; by arrangement for illustrations.

The Observer (1791), Andrew Jaspan, 119 Farringdon Road, London EC1R 3ER *tel* 0171-278 2332.
90p. Sun. Ind. Some articles and illustrations commissioned. *Payment:* by arrangement.
The Observer Life Magazine, Michael Pilgrim *tel* 0171-713 4175 *fax* 0171-713 4217. Free with paper. *Commissioned* features. *Length:* 2000-3000 words. *Illustrations:* first-class colour and b&w photos. *Payment:* NUJ rates; £150 per illustration.

Office Secretary (1986), Jayne Belcher, Trade Media Ltd, Brookmead House, Thorney Leys Business Park, Witney, Oxon OX8 7GE *tel* (01993) 775545 *fax* (01993) 778884.
£9.50 p.a. Q. Serious features on anything of interest to senior secretaries/working women. *No* unsolicited MSS; ideas only. *Illustrations:* colour transparencies, cartoons. *Payment:* by negotiation.

Oldham Evening Chronicle (1854), Philip Hirst, PO Box 47, Union Street, Oldham, Lancs. OL1 1EQ *tel* 0161-633 2121 *fax* 0161-627 01905.
26p. Mon.-Fri. News and features on current topics and local history. *Length:* 1000 words. *Illustrations:* colour and b&w photos and line. *Payment:* £20-£25 per 1000 words; £16.32-£21.90 for illustrations.

The Oldie (1992), Richard Ingrams, 45-46 Poland Street, London W1V 4AU *tel* 0171-734 2225 *fax* 0171-734 2226.
£1.80. F. General interest magazine reflecting attitudes of older people but aimed at a wider audience. Welcomes features (500-700 words) and ideas on all subjects. No interviews but profiles (900 words) for *Still With Us* section. Would prefer not to have to return MSS. *Illustrations:* welcomes b&w cartoons. *Payment:* approx. £80-£100 per 1000 words; minimum £30 for cartoons.

Opera, Rodney Milnes, 1A Mountgrove Road, London N5 2LU *tel* 0171-359 1037 *fax* 0171-354 2700. Seymour Press Ltd, Windsor House, 1270 London Road, London SW16 4DH.
£2.35. 13 p.a. Articles on general subjects appertaining to opera; reviews; criticisms. *Length:* up to 2000 words. *Payment:* by arrangement. *Illustrations:* photos.

Opera Now (1989), Graeme Kay, 241 Shaftesbury Avenue, London WC2H 8EH *tel* 0171-333 1740 *fax* 0171-333 1769.

Everywoman

9 St Alban's Place, London N1 0NX
☎0171 704 8440/359 5496 Fax 0171 226 9448
Editor *Louisa Saunders*
Circulation 15,000

Feminist magazine providing general news and features geared towards women's interests in current affairs and practical concerns, such as health, employment and relationships, rather than traditional consumer lifestyle pursuits. No short stories please. Contributors must study the magazine, show an understanding of its point of view, and indicate which section submissions are intended for. Approach in writing with a synopsis, not by phone.

Executive Travel

Reed Travel Group, 6 Chesterfield Gardens, London W1Y 8DN
☎0171 355 1600 Fax 0171 355 9630
Owner *Reed Travel Group*
Editor *Mike Toynbee*
Circulation 41,444

FOUNDED 1979. MONTHLY. Aimed specifically at frequent corporate travellers.

The Expatriate

175 Vauxhall Bridge Road, London SW1V 1ER
☎0171 233 8595 Fax 0171 233 8718
Owner *FMI Publishers*
Editor *Vera Madan*
Circulation *c.* 2000

FOUNDED 1977. MONTHLY. Serves the expatriate community. Unsolicited mss welcome.

Features Special features on working in particular countries, and international travel. Also psychological problems for spouses, education difficulties, pensions, investment and taxation features, health matters.

News Information on special facilities for expatriates, e.g. mail-order presents, financial services, relocation agents, etc.

The Face

3rd Floor, Block A, Exmouth House, Pine Street, London EC1R 0JL
☎0171 837 7270 Fax 0171 837 3906
Owner *Wagadon Ltd*
Editor *Sheryl Garratt*
Fashion Editor *Ashley Heath*
Circulation 100,000

FOUNDED 1980. Magazine of the style generation, concerned with who's what and what's cool. Profiles, interviews and stories. No fiction. Acquaintance with the 'voice' of *The Face* is essential before sending mss on spec.

Features *Richard Benson* New contributors should write to the features editor with their ideas. Maximum 3000 words.
Payment £150 per 1000 words.
Diary No news stories.

Family Circle

King's Reach Tower, Stamford Street, London SE1 9LS
☎0171 261 5000 Fax 0171 261 5929
Owner *IPC Magazines Ltd*
Editor *Gilly Batterbee*
Circulation 310,000

FOUNDED 1964. THIRTEEN ISSUES YEARLY. Little scope for freelancers as most material is produced in-house. Unsolicited material is rarely used, but it is considered. Prospective contributors are best advised to send written ideas to the relevant editor.

Fashion and Beauty *Janine Steggles*
Food and Drink *Sally Mansfield*
Features *Deborah Murdoch* Very little outside work commissioned. Max. 2500–3000 words.
Fiction *Dee Remmington* Short stories of 1000–1500 words. 'No fiction for the moment.'
Home *Caroline Rodriguez*
Payment not less than £100 per 1000 words.

Family Tree Magazine

61 Great Whyte, Ramsey, Huntingdon, Cambridgeshire PE17 1HL
☎01487 814050
Owner *J.M. & M. Armstrong & Partners*
Editorial Director J.M. Armstrong
Circulation 38,000

FOUNDED 1984. MONTHLY. News and features on matters of genealogy. Unsolicited mss considered. Keen to receive articles about unusual sources of genealogical research. Not interested in own family histories. Approach in writing with ideas. All material should be addressed to *Michael Armstrong.*

Features Any genealogically related subject. Maximum 3000 words. No puzzles or fictional articles.
Payment £20 per 1000 words (news/features).

Fancy Fowl & Turkeys

Andover Road, Highclere, Newbury, Berkshire RG15 9PH
☎01635 253239 Fax 01635 254146
Owner *Fancy Fowl Publications Ltd*
Editor *Shirley Murdoch*
Circulation 3000

The Writer's Handbook (Macmillan) – Figures 2.1 and 2.2 – or *Willing's Press Guide* (see page 305 for other guides). You might also have your own market research notes to help you choose. You pick out three or four popular to middlebrow publications that might be interested.

STUDYING THE MARKETS

This brings us to market research. It is needed to provide you with several possible markets for each article idea. But choose carefully. If you have collected some horrific cuttings on train accidents, do not suggest an article to the free magazine sold on railway stations. If your first choice of publication rejects the idea, or if it accepts the idea but later rejects the article, all may not be lost. You are ready to aim at other targets. It is also possible to sound out one or two selected targets simultaneously.

But what exactly does market research mean? It means keeping yourself familiar with different readerships by regular reading of newspapers and magazines. Subscribe to a few that are important for you, and also look through many more, on the bookstalls and in your local library, making notes on ideas and trends.

On the whole you should write articles that are closely tailored to fit a particular market. Experienced freelance writers might be producing many articles speculatively and yet finding markets for them easily, but their sense of direction and marketability will be built into their work almost unconsciously. A beginner ignoring the need to aim at particular markets is like someone driving a car through busy streets ignorant of the meaning of road signs and traffic lights. Early in your career it is essential to give market analysis much attention: it will greatly reduce the number of rejection slips.

Market research enables you to find out who your potential readers are, what interests are being covered in different areas, at what level, with what kinds of language, and using what kinds of treatment. Having studied these aspects in a particular publication, you look at the material you have to offer and decide what sort of article you could produce for it.

Access to the various writers' guides to markets provides a good starting-point; the most useful of these should be on your shelves, unless they are available in a nearby library.

Writers' Market (Writer's Digest Books), the equivalent in the USA, gives much more detail on editors' requirements and shows how the sort of hints that UK guides give should be interpreted and followed

Figure 2.2   Page from Macmillan's *The Writer's Handbook*

up. Gordon Wells's *The Magazine Writer's Handbook* (Allison & Busby) devotes a page of analysis to each of some eighty UK magazines.

Magazines' own guidelines

The guidelines to writers supplied by some magazines – more common in the USA than in the UK – will provide further information. Add your own notes to any such information, including any based on discussions, verbally or by letter, with editors, and keep a file. Figure 2.3 shows part of the magazine *Bella*'s guidelines. These go on to describe requirements for their other slots, entitled 'Families' (11,000 words), 'My Own Story' (1400 words), 'Scales of Justice' (1100 words) 'The Secret I Must Share' (1000 words), 'Talking Point' (800–900 words), 'Blushes' (brief anecdotes) and 'Others: Royals, Relationships, That's Life, Love Crimes' ('these tend to be specifically commissioned from specialist writers. Style and content will be discussed in detail beforehand'). *Bella* says that it works approximately twelve weeks in advance.

The information in these market guides must be updated of course. It may be a year or two old. Check by looking at current issues for names of current commissioning editors. Telephone the switchboard if necessary.

Producing good ideas for various publications, and following them through to the production of competent articles, can be demanding in time and energy. It is better to make a careful selection of a few subjects from which to generate ideas and articles. Some of these articles it should be possible to write quickly, with little research; some, with additional research, can be rewritten as spin-offs for other markets. Hold a second league of subjects in reserve so that you are ready to change direction when markets dry up.

Formula for market study

A simple exercise in market analysis can be based on the following headings:

Type of publication: Popular paper . . . general interest magazine . . . trade journal.
Frequency: Weekly, monthly, quarterly, etc.
Price.
Prospects for freelances: Note, as far as you can, which areas are covered by staff and which by freelances. Study the by-lines. The contents page

Figure 2.3 Part of the weekly magazine *Bella*'s guidelines for freelance feature writers

FREELANCE FEATURE GUIDELINES

BELLA stories slot into a set format using tried and tested writing styles. The following detailed guidelines explain what is needed for each category and should be used as a checklist for commissions. Please note that the word counts given tend to be near the maximum. Writers should endeavour to be within 200 words of the upper limit.

General guidelines:
All commissioned features require certain facts which must always be included. The following checklist should ensure no omissions are made: Christian and surname (check spellings), ages (give dates of birth), addresses, occupations, dates of important events, marital status, number and names of children, and precise legal details of court cases.

In addition:
■ Always write names, addresses and telephone numbers of interviewees at the end of copy.
■ Please write word count at foot of copy.

Report (1500 words)
Newsy, well-researched and authoritative double-page feature on trends, social issues and syndromes. Can be light, heavy or off-beat.

Guidelines:
Use three strong case histories with details to illustrate different aspects of theme. Back up with experts' comments, facts, figures, statistics and boxes of information. Those quoted must give a proper insight into the causes, problems, how people feel and how they can be helped. Include telephone numbers of information helplines where relevant.

Note: Cross-check case histories with commissioning editor before writing report. Do NOT use examples straight from old cuttings without speaking to source and updating.

Real life (1000 words)
Lively, true drama. Can be triumph-over-tragedy, adventure or off-beat. Can involve individuals, families, even animals. Usually about extraordinary events in the lives of ordinary people.

Guidelines:
Establish good chronological order. Do not be vague about time-scale; for example, 'over the years' or 'weeks later' isn't good enough. Ask interviewees how they felt at the time, what emotions they experienced then and now. Make ample use of first person quotes, reporting both facts and feelings. If story involves more than one person, get everyone's point of view. Small details, personality traits and raw, fresh emotion are very important.

of magazines give clues to which writers are staff and which freelancers, so compare the by-lines with the names of any staff members listed beside job titles on mastheads.

Readership: By sex, age, range, class, occupation, spending power, lifestyle. (Use the National Readership Survey, see below.)

Main kinds of article: Travel, personal experience, think piece, nostalgia, do-it-yourself, interview, profile, expository argument.

Style: Abstract, vivid, thoughtful, chatty . . . .

Treatment: Factual, instructional, humorous . . . use of quotes, anecdotes, illustrations.

Average lengths: Of article, of paragraph, of sentence. You can work out the level of difficulties, as shown below.

Titles/intros/endings: Note policy, and any striking ones.

Formula of magazine/feature articles policy of newspaper: Try to sum up. For 'formula' – think in terms of recipe. What does the editor aim at in the particular mix that you have been examining?

Analysing the style

An average length of sentence in today's journalism, where the writing is on the whole tightly structured, muscular, with few subordinate clauses, is twenty words – more for the qualities, fewer for the pops. To work out more precisely the level of difficulty of the styles of different publications, you can calculate what is called the Fog Index of a typical extract of 100 words, and compare the figure with the Fog Index of a representative 100-word extract of your own writing. This will give you clues on how to adapt to a publication that is pitched at a higher or lower level than your average.

The Fog Index is calculated in this way. Take an extract of 100 words that finished at the end, within a word or two, of a sentence. Divide 100 by the number of sentences, to get *average sentence length*. Add up the number of long words (three syllables or over) leaving out capitalized words and verbs with prefixes and suffixes. Add SL to NLS and multiply by 0.4. The answer is the Fog Index. Do a few examples to get a fair average. A Fog Index of 10 is the level of the average 15-year-old secondary school pupil, 11–13 for senior school, 14–16 for university and over 18 is becoming too difficult for newspapers. *The Daily Mail* averages 9.5, *The Times* 18.

Readership information

What the marketing guidebooks I have referred to lack is an account of the readers. This gap can be filled by studying the advertisements and exploiting the research the advertisers themselves have used to make sure they are on target (this includes various compilations of circulation and readership statistics, and specially commissioned surveys).

The Audit Bureau of Circulations (ABC) publishes quarterly the circulation of numerous publications owned by member publishers. The National Readership Survey (NRS), now a private company, calculates readership figures, which are generally two to three times circulation figures, on the basis of the number of readers per copy, though they can be much higher for some magazines. Readership is socially described by a combination of letters from the group ABC_1C_2DE, representing kinds of occupation (and by implication spending power), from the top company chairman to the lowest earners and non-earners. These categories are used to provide a rough social differentiation between publications.

The advertising agency that fails to reach the target audiences desired by its clients, for whom it designs and places adverts, will be out of business, so much time and expense is devoted to the task. Whether or not the adverts in a publication individually succeed or fail to sell the product or the image, they give a collective indication of the readership.

Consider the adverts in the *Daily Star*, such as TV licensing for £7.00 a month, OdorEaters insoles, 400g Sainsbury's strawberries £1.19, Sleeprite mattresses from £18.95; and in *The People* for pet grooming gloves £7.95 a pair, Sport'n'Leisure RX1 shoes, £9.95, answering machines £23.99. Contrast these with the typical *Sunday Telegraph* adverts for the Jaguar XJ6 3.2 Automatic for £31,083.75 or £371 a month, and solar watch £395. Readership pictures begin to emerge.

Media packs

The advertising departments of many publications send out 'media packs' to prospective advertisers, and prospective freelance writers will find them just as useful. These packs normally include a recent copy of the publication, the advertising rate card, a statement of the policy or 'philosophy' and an analysis of the readership by age, class and profession.

Some magazines are very generous with readership information. You may discover how many cars are owned by the average family subscribing, the average number of plane flights a year, the level of education of the average reader, and the estimated number of single, married and divorced readers.

There are other indications in newspapers and magazines of what the readers are like. Consider the letters page, the service columns, the agony aunt (advice on love life) and other advice columns, the editorials, plus the assumptions made about the readers that underlie the various articles.

You could summarize what the readership surveys say about particular publications by using an A4 sheet or a catalogue card for each. File them and keep your market information up to date with each new survey by noting any developments from your own regular perusal of the publication and from your dialogue with it.

Target publications

Suppose you have decided that a weekly newspaper published in your area is a likely prospect for a cult article. You have studied a dozen issues or more. You have noted that what they do not want from freelances at the moment are things already covered by their regular columns on such subjects as cooking, gardening, theatre reviews and political commentary. These appear under regular names in the publications. So also are the main new topics regularly covered by staff reporters. 'Puffs', or supplements, for various kinds of services and entertainments are not normally contributed by freelances either but by staff writers, often using publicity material. Such pieces can be found supporting adverts for the products and services mentioned.

Having done your market research, you are able to approach the editor of your chosen weekly newspaper confidently, professionally. You suggest a title: 'When Bingo Bored, They Turned to Witchcraft'. There will be some pegging to recent local events and to local history, and the point of view will be light-hearted but informative.

Before sending off the query letter discussed below with your idea, you have made market notes on two other weekly papers in the same geographical area. If the first editor rejects your idea, you scrutinize both idea and letter carefully to see if there is anything wrong with either, reshape as necessary, and approach the second editor. If the first editor accepts the idea but rejects the article, you then carefully check the article, and, if still happy with it, approach the second.

Finding freelance opportunities

Meanwhile you have perhaps done some market study of magazines. Identify the work of regular writers. US magazines tend to be much more forthcoming in these staff details. Regular contributors are often listed in them, together with staffers with such titles as Associate Editor, Arts Editor, Travel Editor and Economics Editor. British magazines are increasingly following this example.

Not all writers on mastheads are staff; some are freelances under special contracts or retainers to cover particular areas. Note these areas.

It occurs to you that with some adaptation your article might appeal to a popular weekly magazine ('Strange Rites in Backwoods England'). For this purpose you extend the subject a little, taking on other manifestations of the cult in the UK or similar cults, adding to the number of anecdotes and quotes.

You might discover a new monthly magazine dealing with the occult. Off goes another enquiry. The treatment you suggest here makes much greater use of notes made from book sources; the article will go deeper, examining international cults. You detect that this magazine is concerned to expose dubious cults. You may propose 'Sects Can Easily Damage Your Health', or an investigation into some cults that are hostile to the family, and that use brainwashing techniques; or that claim association with charities where no connection exists, or where cult or charity produce no proper accounts.

By the time you are regularly writing for two or three publications the strategy outlined here may not be necessary. But for the beginner trying to get established, and making early approaches to editors, it is a valuable, practical way of becoming knowledgeable about markets.

From market to idea

Instead of moving from ideas to markets, you may find that ideas suggest themselves readily while you are looking through publications. You find the monthly magazine *She* interesting, so you take a closer look. (You have got to the stage when every time you pick up a publication you have at the back of your mind the question 'What could I contribute to this?')

You have noted what sort of articles are written by *She* staff: regular columns, pieces that are clearly set up by the magazine. Articles contributed by freelances include a fair number of interviews, fairly thickly quoted ones. Many of these are with women, not celebrities but interesting because of their unusual experiences or jobs. Articles run at between 800 and 1400 words. You go through a dozen issues. You now work out a plan for an article based on a story you noted in your local paper about a woman who built up a mail order business from home after being struck down by multiple sclerosis.

So, one way or the other you have a good idea, you have pre-tested it, gathered some information, market-researched the publication(s) you have in mind for it and worked out what sort of article you want to write. Where do you go from here?

WHETHER TO QUERY OR SPECULATE

It is usually better, as a freelance writer, to sell your idea to an editor by telephone or by letter than to write articles speculatively and send them in. You explain to the editor or features editor what the point of your article is, what information you will use and where you will get it from, emphasizing any sources exclusive to you, how you are going to develop it, what treatment you have in mind, and convincingly put across why you think you are the best person to do it.

If editors are interested in seeing articles proposed, they are likely to make valuable suggestions about the sort of things they would like, the angle and the treatment. If you then do your best to meet the requirements of particular publications, you stand some chance of being published.

Even if editors say no to the ideas, they may have time to tell you what is wrong with them. If they do not, you will have to scrutinize the ideas and the markets again. Either way, you may have saved yourself a great deal of time and energy producing and sending off unsaleable articles.

There are some kinds of articles, however, that should be written speculatively. We shall now consider them:

- First, the idea may be of the kind that is difficult to define and the resulting shape of article impossible to predict. It is best to write it and see what happens. Many humorous articles are like this: their point is in the skilful way in which they are written and in the projection of the writer's personality.
- Second, if you are starting out, writing an exceptionally good and original article straight off, after studying the market thoroughly and making sure you have something to say, can be a good way of breaking through the barrier. Some editors, it has to be said, are reluctant to respond positively to beginners' queries, even when they sound promising. They may have found that such articles have proved unsatisfactory in the past. Or it may simply be that they are overstocked. Such editors can be delighted to find a new talent beaming up at them – an article unexpectedly well researched and well written, in tune with everything in the publication and yet having a distinctly fresh voice – and they will make room for it.
- Third, you need to experiment sometimes and not be always guided by the rules, even if it means some of the wilder 'specs' do not come off. You will have learnt valuable lessons on the way and it will help you to find a distinctive voice.
- Fourth, there may be certain types of article you can write with little or no research, either because you are an expert in a particular field or because you have the flair and style to produce pieces for which there is a ready market.
- Fifth, if you have reached a stage in your career when you are not constantly chasing ideas and shaping them for markets, but are getting regular commissions from specific types of publication, you may have

engineered a working relationship with an editor in which a commission is based on little more than a nod and a wink. You will then be trusted to make all the right decisions about how to develop the idea and your work will be favoured.

The telephone approach

A fairly urgent topic in which a daily, weekly or Sunday newspaper, or weekly magazine, might be interested will justify a telephone query, at least as a starter. Make sure you are talking to the right person. This is probably the features editor on a newspaper. If, however, the piece you have in mind is really hard news – a report, through a personal connection, on an important science fiction writers' conference about arms control rather than an article about the contribution science fiction writers might be making to the art of the novel – then the news editor might be the person to talk to. Job titles vary greatly on magazines: the authority to commission may be invested in the editor alone, or in a deputy or assistant editor.

Your market research will help you decide how to project yourself and the idea. Vagueness will irritate the busy executive you are talking to and, apart from losing you the commission you are aiming at, might leave an unfavourable impression. It is often valuable to jot down the points you intend to make in a logical order, before telephoning.

Phone call number 1 to a daily paper: 'Good afternoon, I'm Joan Marsden and I'm going on holiday to St Petersburg for two weeks. I wonder if you'd be interested in a feature when I get back.'

'What do you want to say about St Petersburg?'

'I don't know really until I get there.' Pause. 'I thought you might suggest something I could look into while I was there.'

'Not really, but if you think you've got something that might interest us, write it up and send it in.'

The journalist you have been talking to has to be vague because you have been vague. The journalist dare not say anything that sounds like a commission in the midst of so much vagueness. In any case, it is not expected that you will produce any article about St Petersburg.

Phone call number 2 to a women's magazine or a Sunday colour supplement: '. . . I have an idea for a feature about how parents push their children to win at various sports. It's often an ego-trip for the parents, and it can do children damage when they really have to be driven. Title perhaps: 'Champion Children – But is the Price Too High?' I thought a composite piece, interviews with four or five children and their coaches or parents. The Sports Council has just published some research on effects on children of different ages. I specialize in sports background pieces.'

This is better, especially since it is aimed at a general interest magazine rather than a newspaper. Sports writers would be asked to deal with such a subject on a newspaper. The writer has looked at several issues of the magazine to check on how it deals with sport, and has decided it is a likely bet. She has three or four of the magazines in mind to try if this one does not take it.

A word of warning. Market-study *before* phoning. Alex Renton, Features and Arts editor of the London *Evening Standard* was quoted in *UK Press Gazette* as saying that hours are spent daily fielding calls from PR companies and freelances. Time-wasters include 'endless people offering you interviews with people you interviewed in the previous night's paper'.

COMMISSIONING POLICIES

Here are summaries of some samples of commissioning editors' policies I gathered in July 1995. Almost all will want to see cuttings. Failing cuttings, send one or two of your best samples.

What kind of approach from writers do you prefer?

Newspapers (mainly national): Writers whose work is known may be encouraged to telephone with ideas, but on the whole a concise query letter is preferred, posted or faxed. You will normally have a news peg and be able to say when publication of your proposed article would be timely.

Local newspapers tend to have staff feature writer(s) to fulfil all needs. Get in by filling a gap in the news coverage.

Magazines (national): Query letter as above. Timeliness: find out how far in advance they work (*Bella*, a weekly, works twelve weeks ahead.) Careful consideration of timeliness of your idea should be based on this. Pictures: note that many magazines (Sunday supplements, the glossy monthlies) are picture-driven, and your pictures or your proposals for pictures might sell an idea. You might want to work with a photographer or become a writer–photographer. *You* Magazine (*The Mail on Sunday*) says: 'We will consider ideas which are addressed to us in written form, containing a full outline and an indication of the writer's experience and background. But, by and large, we work with a regular team of highly experienced national journalists of our choosing and tend not to venture outside the group.'

What sort of query letter?

Newspapers: A concise outline of proposal rather than a detailed outline.

Magazines: As above, but some magazines like a full outline. Emphasize why your idea will interest the targeted readers.

What information about writer?

Newspapers: Some like to see a cv (but concise) from a writer not known. Many prefer a brief paragraph on qualifications for doing the proposed piece.

Magazines: As above; cv's probably even less wanted.

Cuttings as samples of published work?

Newspapers: Yes: two or three of your best cuttings of published work.

Magazines: As above. Magazines are more likely to be looking for the undiscovered talent who has only a few (good) but unpublished pieces to show. Specialist titles want evidence of knowledge of the subject. *Mojo* (the rock 'n' roll magazine) says: 'If we are unfamiliar with a writer we need to see evidence of detailed knowledge in the subject or access to good contacts.' Dealing with editors of specialist publications is dealt with in Chapter 19.

What other preferences make acceptance more likely?

Newspapers: The reply tended to be 'good ideas'.

Magazines: Good ideas.

How is a follow-up briefing done?

Newspapers: Often by telephone, so give your phone numbers and time of availability.

Magazines: Varied. You may be asked to drop in and talk about your proposal.

Are ideas taken up but given to another writer?

Newspapers: The commission normally goes to the proposer, if the evidence of ability is convincing. This is how the *Sunday Express* put it: 'If I liked the idea I would normally commission the originator, subject to status as a bona fide journalist, but sometimes I would pay for the idea and get the piece done in-house.'

Magazines: It does happen. The advice is given elsewhere that you don't give too much away when proposing magazine ideas: there may be other likely markets if your first choices reject a proposal. Nevertheless, you must make sure you're selling it effectively, and when sending out proposals more than once, make sure you adapt it to the new market.

Fees

See pages 102–3 for reference to the NUJ Freelance Guide.

FACE TO FACE

If you have had a fruitful telephone conversation with a commissioning editor and impressed with an idea or two, or if you have written one or two good articles, you might be asked up to the publications offices. Take along a *curriculum vitae* (cv), including educational qualifications and record of employment, but make it brief and highlight relevant experience such as writing published. Take along a portfolio of any published work.

You can use a cuttings book to make a portfolio, pasting up photocopies of your printed articles, heading them with publication and date, alongside the title page of the newspaper or magazine. Don't use original cuttings, which will soon fade. Any front cover of a magazine that features or mentions your article, even going back to school or college magazines, could be pasted opposite. Some writers prefer a display book of the kind used by travelling salesmen, with cuttings inserted above a back-up sheet in a transparent plastic envelope. The cuttings may then be moved or replaced with better ones. Another kind of portfolio is loose-leafed, so that reordering of the content is easier.

At a fairly advanced stage of a writer's career, several thin portfolios might be useful. If you are to meet a literary editor, you take your reviewing portfolio, and so on.

Do not overload a portfolio with boring or short, insignificant material. Work out the best way to present your achievements so far. Leave your card, which should be well designed and practical and should give only essential information – probably 'freelance writer' or 'journalist' – with name, address and phone numbers.

Writers do not necessarily spend much time talking to editors across their desks. It is difficult to find the time if you live far from London or

New York or other publishing centres, and difficult too for editors to find time. In addition, if you become too fond of the idea of lunching or drinking with editors or their executives, it can make serious inroads into writing time.

But *some* fraternization in this way is desirable. Faces stick in the mind better than letters, especially if you have prepared well for the meeting. Preparing well means having two or three good ideas, with some reading and thinking behind them, put together in such a way as to suggest saleable articles, along with an account of yourself that aims to show you have the credentials to write the articles.

If you are already writing for a publication regularly it is useful to meet your editor anyway. Depending on how far you live from the publishing centre and whether you need to visit the place (to buy books and equipment or do research), allot days for the purpose in your timetable, once a month or even once a year. Plan your visits well so that you go with several ideas to discuss for the particular market, having perhaps broached them in a letter or telephone call. You will thus not be starting cold.

THE QUERY LETTER

Query letters to editors look more businesslike on headed notepaper with your name and address (if you do not move too often) printed elegantly. Your name should not be too large and the presentation should be crisp and discreet, not fanciful. As with the telephoned query, make sure you address the right person, the commissioning editor, by name. Check this in the current issue or obtain it from the switchboard or the editor's secretary.

There are many kinds of query letter. Their main function is to sell an idea or ideas, and to see yourself as the person best fitted to write the article. If the letter follows up a telephone conversation or meeting with the editor, you will not need to say much more about yourself, but you may be expected to give more elaborate descriptions of ideas already discussed.

If you send a brief cv, you can underline parts of it that are relevant to the ideas being proposed and to the subject areas covered by the publication. Your cuttings of work should, if possible, be an indication of how you can do what you propose.

Exactly when to query varies. You normally query when you have done some preliminary research so that you have something interesting to say about the subject. Do not query too soon for you may find you cannot perform – there may be too little information available, or it may be too expensive to obtain, for example. Do not query too late, when you have spent days on research, only to discover no one is interested or that the idea has been overtaken.

Do not say to an editor: 'Here's an idea. If you like it, I'll find out more.' Be more forthright.

Samples analysed

Here, for example, is a potentially fruitful idea presented without enough preliminary subject research to the editor of a magazine covering ecological/environmental issues:

> Dear ——
>
> I believe I have an excellent idea for an article that would appeal to your readers. It will be about a new social movement that has been called the 'DIY Culture'. An increasing number of people, mainly young, are working out an alternative lifestyle outside the mainstream of conventional commercial culture.
>
> I am not sure, before I have done some research, what my own attitude to these people is or whether they will succeed or not. I shall describe the ways in which they are opposed to the conventional culture of 'economic growth' after interviewing those practising this different lifestyle. I will also look into LETS (Local Exchange and Trading Schemes) used as an alternative to money in places where this is carried on. Have you heard of this? If so, and you have some information, I'd be grateful if you'd send it on to me.
>
> Yours sincerely

Something lacking, isn't there? It would have been better to suggest that you had at least an initial attitude to 'these people' and that you knew a little more about LETS, including whether or not the magazine has covered it, and if not, whether it's likely to have information not readily available.

Your letterhead will indicate your home telephone number but you may need to give one or two other numbers. State times when you can be contacted.

A brief but to-the-point letter to the leisure section of a national newspaper (early 1994) succeeded, I would guess, out of its sheer enthusiasm:

> Dear--
>
> A new leisure pursuit is sweeping Britain – walking! Everyone is getting into it and there are all kinds of snazzy gear to do it in – so it could prove a bit of an 'ad-get' for the paper t'boot. I am an experienced hiker

and journalist and feel that a walking feature would be just right for your Weekend Leisure Section. About 1500 words.

Here is a suggested intro:

Walking is fast eclipsing fishing as the number one leisure pursuit in Britain today. Britons are taking to the hills in vast numbers each weekend and the sport is getting so popular that some of the favourite routes, like the Pennine Way and the Coast to Coast are beginning to be so well trodden you hardly need a map. They join the Ramblers Association or ad hoc groups, or they like to do it in pairs, or they strike off on their own, but however they do it, they are like to be well and truly togged.

How about a stand-first:

Manufacturers are cashing in on the walking boom with all kinds of expensive kit on offer in a growing number of High Street stores. —— took to the hills to investigate.

If this sounds interesting to you, please give me a call on the above number.

Yours sincerely

The writer then went on to suggest another article to several of the dozen or so specialist walking and outdoor pursuits magazines, this article more to do with gadgets – computer digitization of maps and navigational aids. He had discovered that these magazines had not covered much in this area.

A commission having been obtained, a publication may make suggestions for approach, content and treatment. The more specialized the publication, the more likely it is that there will be discussion with the writer as the work progresses. Figures 19.1 and 19.2 give a sample of such discussion.

The five essentials

There are five essentials in a query letter:

1 *It should contain,* first, *a good idea* or several good ideas that are fresh, timely and important. You should not be telling the editor what he or she knows, but what you know he or she would like to know. The start should immediately whet the editor's appetite. Your task should be like that of someone standing at a window and calling to someone in the room, 'Come and look at this!'.

If you want to suggest several ideas at the same time, it will probably be best to write a short covering letter with a separate ideas sheet.

Each description of an idea should include provisional title, the angle, a brief summary of the content and subject research. Do not give away too many vital contacts, but give one or two selling points that the ideas possess. These points, if possible, should include something along the lines of 'Your readers will be particularly interested in this at the moment because. . . .'

2 It should show that *you have studied the publication*, that you know why the readers will be interested, and that you know how to shape the article to fit. (Do not waste time saying now wonderful you think the publication is or, even worse, how incompetent it is.)

In every way show that you have studied the market thoroughly. Soak in the style and general attitude of the publication you are addressing before you write the letter, and make a conscious effort to fit into these, without losing your individual tone. Failure to study the market is the most conspicuous defect noted by editors in beginners' approaches.

3 A query letter should show that *you have the ability to do the job* well, including the writing ability. If you're not sending samples of your published or unpublished writing, it may be a good idea to include a sample intro for the proposed article.

4 You should mention such specifics as *title, length, treatment and illustration* for the work you propose.

5 You should mention any *unique selling points* – for example, any exclusive material or contacts you have managed to obtain.

It might be best to introduce as many of these attributes as you can in the first paragraph, expanding on them in subsequent paragraphs.

The more thorough your preliminary work has been (though within the limits mentioned), the more persuasive your query letter will be. You will not make the mistake of proposing an idea that was dealt with in the publication recently. You may be able to show that though your subject has been neglected for a long time, it is due for an airing. You should try to avoid suggested ideas covered recently in competing publications. If something similar to your proposal has appeared, you may be able to show how your article should upstage it in some way, perhaps by sending it up, perhaps by going into greater depth. There will be something to indicate your idea's timeliness: some kind of topical peg.

You will have borne in mind how far ahead a magazine has to prepare its issues: your Easter idea will be submitted weeks or months before Easter. You can ask for a publication's time-scale. Such awareness will satisfy the editor that you know what you are doing.

Do not become over-ambitious in your query letters. Choose the ideas carefully, and try to convince editors that you are genuinely interested and knowledgeable. Some writers find they are good at spilling out ideas, but are daunted when faced with the hard work that has to follow. Ask yourself if you really want to do this particular article. Are you capable of producing what is wanted or is it too far outside your field? Would you be able to do it within the deadline required? Some writers produce promising query letters, are given the go-ahead, and are never heard from again.

Some editors (especially in the US) prefer a more detailed outline of your proposal than I have suggested. Or you may feel that a particular idea needs plenty of build-up to win acceptance. See pages 127–8 for the 'query plus outline'.

Multiple queries

You may want to send the same ideas to various non-competing markets, in different cities perhaps, or different countries. If you receive an embarrassing number of acceptances, be sure you have prepared plans to adapt the ideas in different ways for the various markets. If you do send out identical articles, make sure you are not breaking copyright laws. There is no problem about selling first British rights only to a magazine in Britain, retaining world rights, and selling the same article to markets elsewhere in the world.

If your query letters/idea sheets are not working, scrutinize them for specific detail. Do they contain enough important information on ages, descriptions, mannerisms, colours, weights, anecdotes, quotes etc.? A shortage of detail can give a general air of blandness.

Beware, however, of sticking rigidly to any formula given here or in any similar text. Formulas are guides, to be adapted to your own purposes, whether they are for query letters, outlines or articles. Every query letter is different, just as every article is different.

ORGANIZING THE ASSIGNMENT

At the moment you are commissioned to write an article you may be in the middle of several other assignments. It is advisable to write down the main instructions clearly, so that when you start the new assignment, you will not be trying to decipher yet another illegible note.

You can use your desk diary or a special telephone logbook for notes of phone conversations at home. Keep a note of the time on the phone; the cost will be allowable for income-tax purposes. Above all, note the deadline.

If you received your assignment verbally, you should note it down, adding anything that occurs to you while the adrenaline is flowing and the discussion is fresh in your mind. You may, of course, get an assignment letter containing clear instructions on what kind of article and content is wanted, and you should certainly get a letter confirming the terms. If you do not, and if you are not quite sure of the instructions, compose a letter that sets out the agreement as you have understood it and send it off. Some writers use a specially prepared form for this. If need be, telephone first.

Starting an article file

On being commissioned, immediately open a document (wallet) folder for the article. Use different colours of folders for articles in progress and articles published. Put any material you already have into the folder, including cuttings and the letter or note containing the assignment. If your head is full of it, you could exploit all that mental energy by typing a first short draft. Use the points or brief paragraphs from your query letter or outline, expanding them, and leaving gaps where you might develop with interviews, anecdotes, quotes from experts, pithy quotations, or other researched material. This ensures that the points you have put up will be covered. Work out as soon as you can what time you will have to spend on the article, make any necessary phone calls to arrange interviews, and note these particulars in your desk diary.

Every writer produces a dud occasionally, and it should have a lesson to teach. You will avoid producing them too frequently by being as clear as you can at every stage about what you are doing. A dud teaches you to plan more carefully, to achieve greater control over the information you are gathering, to get right in your own mind what it is you are trying to say.

If you have any doubt about the editor's requirements or about what you are aiming at, clear this up before you start researching in earnest, so that you get your line of enquiry right. Some articles fail because despite apparent agreement between writer and editor about the assignment, there has been a failure in communication. The best of editors and the best of writers can end up with the wrong idea of what the other has in mind.

A wise editor judges which writers need a lot of guidance and which little: it is a delicate balance. Flexibility in the commissioning policy is necessary: there must be scope for imagination, second and third thoughts may turn out to be best, and some writers do not work well feeling hamstrung or over-briefed. On the other hand, new writers might prefer a fairly detailed briefing.

NOTE-TAKING SYSTEM

Once you are clear about the assignment, you can tackle the job of information gathering. You need a well organized system of note-taking.

A desk piled with dog-eared cuttings, scraps of paper with illegible scribbles on them, and odd leaflets and pamphlets can be daunting if you are sitting down to write. So be tidy. Notes are best made on A4 sheets or catalogue cards, which can easily be shuffled into different arrangements.

Use one side only, with headings, so that the material can be quickly sorted. Having put the notes in order (perhaps guided by an outline), number them consecutively to help you as you write.

It is frustrating to know that you have notes made on something but don't know where they are. The order in which they are taken will not necessarily follow any plan, but will depend on circumstances. Thus one afternoon you may take notes at a library from a book on your subject, and then move on to other books or to magazine articles. Using an exercise book for all this makes the ordering of the information difficult.

In your own words

Paraphrase when making notes so that you do not repeat other writers' words and risk being accused of plagiarism. Do a complete job of this immediately. You may be tempted to think, 'I'll change the wording when I write the notes up', but at the later stage you will probably not have the original source available to check which words to change. Put quotation marks round significant statements that you may want to use as quotes because the point is being expertly expressed, or because you want to show that the manner of expressing it is revealing of the writer.

You may have useful thoughts about the points you are noting. If so, put them under the notes in square brackets. Note the source at the end of each note, so that you can return to it later, if necessary, to check: author, title of book or article, publisher or title of publication, date, page number; or name of interviewee with date of interview; or event attended, with date.

Some notes may be taken on the move, perhaps in a reporter's hard-backed notebook. Try to transfer all such notes to sheets, cards, or computer file regularly. It is worth standardizing the style and method of your note-taking, especially when you are writing long or complex articles.

If you have not learned shorthand, work out some system. Many journalists find the Teeline system easy to learn from a book and/or evening classes, and more convenient than the more elaborate traditional systems. Figure 2.4 shows the Astbury abbreviation system, a useful basis

Astbury's Abbreviation System

the	/		been	bn
-ever	-r		brought	brot
-ing	-g		chairman	chn
-ment	-nt		committee	comme
-ion	-n		could	cd
-sion	-n		different	dift
-tion	-n		evening	evg
-ance	-ce		every	evy
-ence	-ce		extraordinary	extry
according	acc		faithfully	ffy
advertise	ad		from	fm
affectionate	aff		general	genl
America	Amer		generally	geny
book	bk		good	gd
England	Eng		government	govt
English	Eng		great	gt
especially	esp		had	hd
excellent	exc		important	impt
for	f		might	mt
Friday	Fri		morning	mg
large	lge		notwithstanding	notwg
manuscript	MS		objection	objn
manuscripts	MSS		occasion	occn
Monday	Mon		opinion	opn
necessary	necy		opportunity	oppy
o'clock	o'c		particular	partr
of	o		query	qy
page	p		question	qn
pages	pp		said	sd
popular	pop		should	shd
quotation	quot		there, their	thr
reference	refce		together	togr
Saturday	Sat		truly	ty
shall	sh		very	vy
specially	spec		whether	whr
Sunday	Sun		without	wt
that	t		would	wd
though	tho		yesterday	yesty
through	thro		your	yr
Thursday	Thurs			
Tuesday	Tues		affectionately	affly
very good	vg		against	agst
Wednesday	Wed		because	bec
which	wh		circumstance	circe
with	w		difference	difce
you	y		importance	impce
			meeting	mtg
about	abt		yours	yrs
account	acct			
afternoon	aftn		between	btwn
again	agn		difficult	difclt
among	amg			
amount	amt		difficulty	difclty

Figure 2.4   Astbury's abbreviation system

for building a system of your own. If you do decide to do this, record plenty of samples, so that you use it consistently and efficiently.

If you need to increase your note-taking speed, practise at lectures, meetings, or from radio talks. Practise editing in your mind as you go, so that the most important points are recorded. If necessary, jump ahead, returning when you have a moment to spare to record the bit you missed.

Purposeful notes

Don't make too many notes, or make them too indiscriminately, or they will overwhelm you and delay your work or even confuse the issue. Read and digest background material so that it is at the back of your mind and write down only those things that are central to your purpose. Over-researching suggests a lack of confidence, which encourages procrastination – the feeling that you don't know enough and must examine further. As expert follows expert into your sights, your gloom and self-doubt may deepen. If this happens, re-examine your original purpose, remind yourself that after all the article is a business arrangement and that you, and perhaps a family as well, have to eat.

Whether working from an outline or not (see Chapter 3), once you have decided what aspect of the subject you are dealing with, you can label for notes fairly complex – 1A, B, etc., 2A, B, etc. (1–2–3–4, etc. for aspects, and A–B–C–D, etc. for sources), so that you can easily shuffle them into the order that you want. Unless you are doing a feature based entirely on interviews and points of views, it is the topics that determine the logical order of the article and not where you get the information from, nor from whom.

RESEARCH METHODS

There are four way of getting (and updating) information: from your own knowledge and experience; by legwork; by library research, and by interview. Of course there is constant interaction and cross-checking going on.

Personal experience

Personal knowledge and experience are unique and therefore a valuable basis for any writing. Mostly it will be unconsciously employed. Occasionally it will be essential to any treatment of the subject (anorexia, alcoholism). Even here, make sure that what you say will be of value to your readers and not merely an exercise in self-expression therapy. Bring in plenty of other knowledge and experience (via library and interview) as a commentary on your own. On the whole, recognize that it's what you find out that's interesting, rather than what you know.

Legwork

You go and find out for yourself: that is the basic legwork activity of the reporter. You visit a fire, a factory, a mental hospital, a prison, a café or a pub, and you note what you see there and you interview. The basis of feature writing is reporting skills, and if you write much about yesterday's demo, you should have been there. See pages 167–8 for comments on first-hand and second-hand sources.

Library

Library research means studying all kinds of printed sources. Some articles can be written off the top of your head, but most need library research of some kind. Don't overload yourself with notes. Nevertheless, time allowing, saturate yourself with information from books, newspapers, magazines, handouts, brochures and other material.

The more you read, depending on the time available, the easier it will be to select information that is significant and striking for your purpose, and the more convincing and strongly grounded will be the argument in your article. Don't be tempted to think that the quality of the writing is the important thing. It avails little if you do not have enough of interest or relevance to say. Readers who are interested in the subject will notice if you have left out something important or have adopted a superficial approach. There is an evasiveness and blandness about the writing, signs of the writer mentally papering over cracks. The more you know about your subject, the easier it is to leave out the right things, and to know what omissions will not leave a gap.

Readers new to researching techniques will find Kenneth Whittaker's *Using a Library* (André Deutsch) and Ann Hoffman's *Research for Writers* (A. & C. Black) useful. To start into a subject, consult a good encyclopaedia as well as articles' indexes. Also consult organization indexes such as the *Directory of British Associations* (DBA) for pressure groups of all kinds which will provide you with literature. Put yourself on the mailing list of organizations in whose activities you are interested, and which are potential sources of material. PR companies, PROs and press contacts are listed in *Hollis Press and Public Relations Annual.*

Some of the effects of new technology on writers' methods are covered in Chapters 9 and 21. As far as the freelance writer is concerned, the possessor of a wordprocessing computer can call up databases (computerized libraries) for information. Some of the biggest libraries have a database and they are increasing in number rapidly. The operation is done through a modem, an electronic circuit linking up your word processor to a telephone line. You then simply dial the number you want.

Interviewing

Even for the briefest interview during legwork or for the five-minute phone call, try to find time to prepare good questions (those that elicit useful answers), beforehand. A little library research first?

More generally, the oldest idea can be given fresh impetus by carefully chosen interviewees: the interview is a unique event, whether it is five minutes on the phone or thirty minutes face to face. It will give special point if the interviewee is a renowned expert on the subject who is difficult to corner, or who has not discussed the subject for some time, or is an unusual choice.

Reference books for useful names you might need to interview include *DBA*; *Who's Who*; the various extensions of *Who's Who* (*Who's Who in the Theatre*, etc.); the Central Office of Information's directory of press and PR officers in government departments and public corporations; film and TV annuals; *Spotlight*, for agents of showbiz/film/TV theatre celebrities; *Willing's Press Guide*, whose back pages list hundreds of specialized magazines; *Keesing's Record of World Events*; and *The Statesman's Yearbook*.

There is more on interviewing in Chapters 9 and 13. A final point here about research: be careful to give in the article sources of official figures or of unusual information, especially things that might be queried. Editors appreciate a separate list of key sources attached to an article in case there is checking/updating to be done in the office.

ASSIGNMENTS

1 Rewrite in 250 words the following query letter proposing an article on ageism. Do some preliminary research on the subject, give a better idea of the proposed content (including a few facts and figures, and, include an intro. Address a targeted commissioning editor by name:

Dear—

Many companies today specify the age limit of applicants when advertising a job vacancy within their company. Such a practice is illegal in countries such as Australia and America, so why is it perfectly acceptable in Britain?

Even at the age of 30 I have already noticed job advertisements requiring only people between the ages of 23 and 28 to apply. In this day and age we have sexism, racism, and now ageism.

I plan to write an article of about 1000 words. The intention is to prove that ageism does exist and for what reason. Do people feel threatened by employing someone with more experience than themselves? Is any of it to do with the company image? Or maybe they believe that once you reach a certain age you are unable to do the job? There is no medical proof that says that age affects everybody's mental abilities. There is in fact more proof to the contrary.

I will discuss the possibility of making ageism illegal in this county and the experience and expertise that is going to waste in the country due to the narrow minds of employers. I will also cover the medical proofs, for both sides of the argument.

I feel this is a subject your readers will be interested in no matter what their age as it is a prejudice that will affect all of us at some stage. I will start my article with this opening paragraph:

'Two men apply for one job. The first man has the right qualifications and the right experience. The second man does not possess all the required qualifications and has only half the experience of the first man and yet he is offered the job. Why? He is eighteen years younger of course.'

I hope you will consider this article for your paper and I look forward to hearing from you.

2   Following the format recommended on pages 20–1, do market studies of these magazines: *Arena, Cosmopolitan, Esquire, GQ, The Spectator, Loaded, Marie Claire, She, Woman's Own.*

3   Select three of the above magazines and find a suitable article idea for each. Summarize them in paragraphs of 100 words.

4   Select the most likely idea and propose it in a query letter addressed to the features editor of the targeted magazine (250 words).

5   Write three query letters proposing the same idea, varied to appeal to three different markets.

3 THE WRITING PROCESS

Most good writing has been rewritten, so you should not be dismayed by the shortcomings of a first draft. Saturate yourself in the information to be used, read it over and over again, think about it, until the urge to start communicating it is irresistible. Then write it, probably quickly but anyway giving yourself time to rewrite, and perhaps rewrite again. Be clearer about idea, content, form, audience and purpose (ICFAP, see pages 1–2) with each draft. Leave a day or so between drafts, so that you see them with fresh critical eyes. Avoid constantly mulling over what you have written, while the piece is in progress: it can make you bored with your subject.

Often, the easier a feature article is to read, the harder it has been to write. It should come across as a whole, with all its elements related, the words and sentences working towards that purpose. Consider the elements to be these:

1 Introduction.
2 Premise or point to view.
3 Thesis or theme.
4 Body – the core of points/facts/arguments/explanations.
5 Supporting material – anecdotes, quotes, etc.
6 Conclusion.

You will notice in the articles you read varied techniques for making the facts/material of the body (points 4 and 5) readable. Early on, it can help to have tantalizing snippets or pictures (giving the feeling of being in a fast train). The pace has to slow down for description, explanation, or argument, but the supporting material can keep it vivid. Then perhaps the pace speeds up again, with shorter sentences, as the article gets into the homeward stretch.

Sometimes when an article does not come off, there is nothing obviously wrong; it just reads boringly. Just as jokes told by one comedian may not raise a titter, but told by another have sides splitting. It is a matter of timing, and pace: keeping information back, keeping up suspense or provoking curiosity, *making* the reader want to know more.

Collect a few models. Paste cuttings of well written articles on A4 sheets. You could use a highlighter to pick out material that denotes premise or thesis, the core of argument and the supporting material, including interview quotes. You can also colour in such stylistic elements as figurative language. Draw a line under the intro, and above the ending, so that the core of the article can be isolated at a glance. In the margins of the sheet make your comments.

A fairly short article – up to, say, 600 words – may be written without much planning beforehand on paper.

You may find, as a beginner, that the first draft of your article reads disjointedly and yet you cannot see exactly what is wrong. Make an outline of what you've got and the fault may be revealed as structural. Prepare outlines of what you want to write, following one of the patterns described below.

Let the content dictate the form, as a foot dictates the shape of the shoe. Don't persist in imposing a form that doesn't seem to fit. Experiment with mind maps (see pages 65–6) and drafts until your idea and the content built on to it are clear. Be prepared to make false starts, to start again.

WHEN OUTLINES HELP MOST

With an outline you can tackle your worries one at a time. Once you've used your analytical powers to think out the overall shape, your creativity can be released.

Any article longer than about 600 words really needs some kind of outline, even if only a list of points. A 600-word article on the London homeless might be planned as follows:

1 Intro: set the scene.
2 Thesis: solutions must include restoring sense of community.
3 Background, definitions and law.
4 Past attempts to solve.
5 The various social problems in the chain.
6 Likely solutions.
7 Conclusion.

The more experienced you are, the more likely it is that you'll be able to work from an outline in your head, if you prefer not to be too regimented for your first draft. A more detailed outline helps when there is some complexity of material and a fair number of points that need putting across in order. An article of 1500 to 3000 words on such a social problems theme as the homeless may need the kind of detailed schematic outline shown on pages 126–7 and 129–32.

For unity and coherence

An outline brings unity. You can work out exactly where the information gathered will fit in, how much of it you need, and how much you can discard (provided you know pretty well what you want to say).

An outline brings coherence. It forces you to work out relationships: what is the best order? Where should the emphasis lie? What are the best links to lead the reader through the material? How can the anecdotes, quotes, examples be used for maximum impact?

Look through your notes or rough draft and let a pattern emerge.

FINDING THE RIGHT ORDER

The pattern will be found among the following arrangements – or will be a combination of two or more:

1 List order.
2 Chronological order.
3 Climax order.
4 Anti-climax order.
5 Logical order, for example, problem followed by solution, cause and effect, origin and development (or the other way round).
6 Readers' interest order.
7 Repetitive structure.

List order

A 500 to 600-word piece for a tourist magazine or the children's page of a newspaper on the Science Museum in London or similar place to visit works perfectly as a list of selected attractions (to appeal to the readership aimed at), with a brief hello and goodbye at start and finish. Some travel pieces at greater length, of the service kind (holiday recommendations, etc.) may be mainly organized as: places to see, places to avoid; or things to do, things to see; or day life, night life; or combinations.

For such simple structures it's often a good trick to put your (well ordered) points in a summary paragraph to make your intro, and then to give a paragraph or two to each point or to two or three points, keeping the points in the same order as in the initial paragraph – as, in fact, I'm now doing in this account of the different structures.

Chronicle order

This means that by the time you've finished narrating an event, an experience or a life story, the chronology is clear.

A profile of Christina Foyle by Jeremy Lewis in *The Oldie* is organized as follows:

1 At 83 (in 1994) she still supervises the running of the famous London bookshop, on a weekly visit taking back all the post since her last visit to her stately home in Essex.
2 Her father opened a second-hand bookshop in London in 1904.
3 Her parents' liking for rogues was inherited; one of her literary lunches was devoted to ex-cons who had written their memoirs.
4 She started in the bookshop at 17, and started the literary lunches at 19.
5 Anecdotes from the lunches, and quotes from a few famous people over the years (three paragraphs).
6 The setting of the interview: her rooftop flat, shared with fifteen cats and other animals and a Maltese maid.
7 Her equanimity about the new bookselling chains surrounding her shop.

You can see that this is mainly chronological, but in the reading, because of the numerous anecdotes, it is not obtrusively so. The odd date sprinkled in, a careful link or two and keeping the interviewee centre stage (several repetitions of 'Miss Foyle') serve to avoid getting lost among so many years.

Climax order

Simply meaning from least to most important, climax order requires, for example, that you get across your points in the best order for appreciating the significance of each.

A climax order (adding drama to the concept) helps the writer to keep the reader engaged, like a novelist; the information is played out with a little suspense. In the Miss Foyle article, her appearance and personality are delayed until the final paragraph, which is strong and vivid, so that the article doesn't tail off. If the important point has to be made early to avoid irritation, a typical shape (as has already been said) is to have it both ways: anticipate the main point in the intro and then echo it or underline it somehow in the ending.

In a how-to article, importance order will mean the necessary order for understanding: from the preparation to the completion, from the simple to the complex – the order that the reader will have to follow to learn the skill.

Anti-climax order

The news story (see pages 8–9) normally has to get across the most important points first, whereas the feature writer has to avoid tailing off. The list type of article works best with an anti-climax order for each separate list, so there are plenty of landmarks to see you through.

Logical order

This usually requires careful analysis of the subject-matter. You will probably move from problems to solutions, from causes to effects, from origins to developments.

But there are many variations. You can divide an article into two – all the problems followed by the solutions – or you can divide each aspect of the subject into problems and solutions.

Consider the following outline for an article entitled 'Should All Police Be Armed?' The article obviously didn't work, so the student was asked to outline it as it was, as follows (I have added the for and against labels later):

1   Intro – in favour (F).
2   There are armed response vehicles (ARVs), but they can't get to the scene quickly enough (F).
3   Arming police will encourage villains to arm (A).
4   Police not now part of the community (F).
5   It's up to the police to remain friendly, with arms or without (F).
6   The traditionally friendly attitude to the police would be destroyed (A).
7   Unarmed, the police are at the mercy of increasingly violent (and armed) criminals (F).
8   With police armed, more police and more innocents get shot (A).
9   The answer to the danger of more people getting shot is good training of police and clear rules of engagement (F).
10 The UK police are the only unarmed police in Europe. European villains come here (F).

It's hard to see much logic in this order. The against arguments should be followed by the relevant for arguments. Number 9 should surely be the conclusion: it answers several of the objections, and on this condition the success of the argument for arming rests. Number 3 has not been answered. Number 6 should come before 4 and 5, and should include some reference to the question: how far are the police part of the community? Numbers 4 and 5 should follow, and be brought together (how strong is the argument that the police are not now part of the community?). Then a better order would be 10 (is there any answer to this?), then 8 followed by counter-argument 7, followed by further counter-argument (and supposedly a clinching argument) 9.

Consider therefore the following order: 2, 3, 6, 4/5, 10, 8, 7, 9.

Readers' interest order

The best approach to many topics is to list the questions you would like answers to. Make sure that they are the same as the questions your readers will want answers to.

The order in which readers would ask the questions can provide you with the best order for your feature. What is the first question they would ask? What would they ask then? And so on. . . .

A good example of an article where this concern must have been important is 'Let your fingers do the nicking' (pages 115–20).

Repetitive structure

The typical form is that you take a strong argument and make your main point as soon as possible. You then build round it, adding facts as evidence, a deepening argument rather than an analytically linear one. The repetition of the theme in a classical symphony, in different varying forms, is an analogy. Key words or synonyms are repeated to maintain the thread throughout. See the illustration of this in an extract on page 147.

WRITING UP METHODS

Those writers who prefer to write first and worry about it afterwards go straight to a handwritten or typed first draft: then, if necessary, cut it up and reorder the pieces by pasting or stapling them on to other sheets in the required sequence. From this a second draft that is sufficiently polished can be written.

A word processor makes this approach easier, since editing and reordering of material can be carried out effortlessly as you go along, giving second, third and even fourth thoughts; but you may prefer to make a few print-outs and compare them.

You may find that some of your best writing is done when you are 'in overdrive' – when, having digested your material, the unconscious is let off the rein and you sit back and allow the sentences to flow. Welcome any thoughts that spill out, as if from nowhere; collect from the shores of your consciousness like a river picking up debris as it runs. You can easily remove any rubbish later. With luck, you will have surprised both yourself and your readers once or twice with treasures. Occasionally those treasures will bring a shiver of revelation.

When such a flow of words has subsided and you seem to have come to a halt, compare the results with your outline and put things in order. Thoughts that the unconscious drive yields up may sometimes be so valuable that you will revise the outline to include them.

Writers who prefer to sort out structural problems in the course of writing drafts rather than by carefully thought out plans may find that they have to produce several drafts of an article before they are satisfied.

Editing tasks

Rewriting drafts or editing on screen mainly entails the cutting out of verbiage. A lot depends on a writer's work methods. Some work like those sculptors who build up from nothing by adding and moulding; others like to have as much material as possible so that they can hack away until they discover the shape and meaning hidden within it. Some can be likened to painters in that they first get something down over a large part of the canvas, and worry about details later. Whatever the method tends to be, the first draft generally needs tightening up, and in that process there should be an increase in clarity and precision. The article should be made, in revising, livelier, more readable, more entertaining or thought-provoking, and the tone of voice should be made unmistakable throughout. Figures 3.1 and 3.2 show the process at work in an article of my own (written when the Soviet Union was still the Soviet Union), reproducing the typescript.

The other essentials of subediting – the double-checking of all facts, figures and doubtful spellings (especially names) must be done before submitting the script: they must not be left to the subeditors of the publication. The subs do their own checking, of course, but they have to rely on your accuracy on many points, not having your research sources at hand.

In the use of words make sure you follow the house style of the publication you are contributing to. If it uses 'recognize', put this, even if you

In theory, ①

~~W~~ho does not believe in human rights? / *Are* ~~They are~~ *not*, as the Universal Declaration of Human Rights of the United Nations proclaims, the foundation of freedom, justice and peace in the world? Amnesty concentrates on ~~a clear, simple programme. It works~~ *working* for the release of prisoners of conscience / ~~who have been~~ *— those* deprived of liberty for political or religious beliefs, ~~and~~ who have not used or supported violence. / ② *Amnesty demands* ~~Early~~ and fair trials for all prisoners, *and it opposes* ~~are demanded.~~ ~~And by Amnesty~~ |in all circumstances| the death penalty, torture, and any cruel or degrading treatment ~~are opposed.~~ ③

Internationally, ~~In the international arena, there is a great deal of fear and hypocrisy blocking the~~ securing ~~of~~ human rights *is blocked by fear and hypocrisy,* ~~for all, and also propaganda that aims~~ *and by obfuscating propaganda.* ④ *The United States* ~~to cloud the issues or create a conspiracy of silence. To take some examples.~~ *condemns* ⑤ ~~Although the~~ aggression against the people of Afghanistan and Poland, ~~meets with condemnation by the United States~~, yet~~,~~ it, |on the grounds that the area must be kept free of Communism| helps the governments of El Salvador and Guatemala to maintain repression ⑥ ⑦ ~~The Communists are labelled as 'terrorists'.~~ ⑧ The Soviet Union condemns *the* ~~Chile's~~ human rights record *of Chile, with* ~~but it is noteworthy~~ *which* ~~that~~ it has no diplomatic relations, *but not that* ~~with the country. On the other hand, the human rights record~~ of Argentina, ~~is not attacked,~~ with which it has the largest volume of trade in Latin America after Cuba. ⑨ ~~Although~~ The British government *speaks out against* ~~condemns~~ torture in a great many of the world's prisons, *yet* ~~nevertheless it~~ is forced by the European Court of Human Rights to change its own ~~unacceptable~~ detention regimes in Northern Ireland. ⑩ In practice, where are human rights not violated?

272 words

Figure 3.1 The process of editing

Points

1 Neater balance of first sentence of extract with last on addition of 'In theory'
2 Tightening up: such words as 'programme' and 'procedure' are unnecessary when the verb already expresses the meaning adequately
3 Best to continue with Amnesty as subject and join with next sentence. Switching of subject too often makes a passage hard to follow. The distancing of agent ('Amnesty') from 'opposed' means that the meaning of the last sentence of the first paragraph was unclear until the end.
4 One precise adjective ('obfuscating') in place of twelve words (with two cliché phrases)
5 Simple word 'condemns' preferred to 'meet with condemnation' – the meaning is best put into verbs rather than abstract nouns where possible

In theory, who does not believe in human rights? Are they not, as the Universal Declaration of Human Rights of the United Nations proclaims, 'the foundation of freedom, justice and peace in the world'. Amnesty concentrates on working for the release of prisoners of conscience -- those deprived of liberty for political or religious beliefs who have not used or supported violence. Amnesty demands early and fair trials for all prisoners, and it opposes the death penalty, torture, and any cruel or degrading treatment, in all circumstances.

Internationally, securing human rights is blocked by fear and hypocrisy, and by obfuscating propaganda. The United States condemns aggression against the people of Afghanistan and Poland, yet helps the governments of El Salvador and Guatemala to maintain repression on the grounds that the area must be kept free of Communism. The Soviet Union condemns the human rights record of Chile, with which it has no diplomatic relations, but not that of Argentina, with which it has the largest volume of trade in Latin America after Cuba. The British Government speaks out against torture in many of the world's prisons, yet is forced by the European Court of Human Rights to change its own detention regimes in Northern Ireland. In practice, where are human rights not violated?

213 words

Figure 3.2   The edited version

---

6   The topic of the paragraph (first sentence) is now clearly threaded through: see the starts of next two sentences. Each sentence gives the practice of a particular country, in the simplest way (subject, verb, object). This kind of list is much easier to follow when each sentence starts in a similar way. The repetition of 'condemns' obviates the need for any other kind of link between sentences. 'Speaks out' in the last of the series prevents monotony.

7   Subject 'it' was too far from its verb 'helps'. In reshaped sentence 'it' hardly necessary

8   Sentence removed as it weighs the balance of the argument against the USA. It was a comment of my own that crept in among the facts. The point about Amnesty is that it tries to be even-handed in criticism

9   Notice how tightening up reveals the argument more clearly in a sharp focus, and the way that joining the two sentences removes repetition. In the second of the two sentences, the relative pronoun 'which' was too far removed from its antecedent 'record', making it read awkwardly

10   'Nevertheless' was redundant after 'although'. 'Yet' more appropriately echoes 'but' and 'yet' of previous sentences

prefer 'recognise'. Give the subeditors as little work as possible. For points of word style in general, useful sources are *Hart's Rules for Compositors and Readers,* and *The Oxford Dictionary for Writers and Editors* (both Oxford University Press). Buy either *The Economist* or *The Times Style Guide.*

Double checking

Accuracy and reliability (which means, above all, keeping to deadlines) are top priorities when an editor assesses contributors' merits. Double checking, especially of figures, should become second nature to a writer who wants to be free of problems, and to please editors. If you have extracted some figures from a newspaper report, for example, you should check them with the government department or local authority or statistical publication from where they originally came. When figures do not look quite right, a check with the original source might reveal the figures themselves to be right, but that the omission of other factors or figures necessary in order to make sense of them has robbed them of context. The figures for certain crimes, we often learn, are increasing. But does this mean that the committing of the crime is increasing or that more people are reporting it, or that police activity and success in bringing offenders to count are increasing?

Revising your first draft

You should revise your article thoroughly at a first draft stage to ensure that it effectively does what you want it to do. It is best to put it aside for an hour or two or even a day or two if there is time to spare: you then see it freshly, more objectively. There are certain key questions you should ask yourself. Does the opening grab the attention? Is there sufficient pace to keep the reader hooked? Have you done enough research, and if you have not, where is the lack of it obvious? Are alternative points of view noticed? Are your arguments well supported by evidence? Are all explanations clear?

Does the article tend to 'tell' instead of 'show'. Does it need more quotes, anecdotes, descriptions and people to humanize it?

Revising can suggest more ideas for spin-offs, which should be noted.

PRESENTING YOUR SCRIPT

All full pages of script should have wide margins, left and right, top and bottom.

Left and right margins are used for instructions to the printers. Lines should be double-spaced, to allow room for subeditors' corrections. On the first page of the article put the title about 89 mm from the top, centred, with your name (or a pseudonym) under this. Start the article about 126 mm from the top. Don't indent the first word of the first line, but indent the first word of every subsequent paragraph five spaces. Within the top margin of page 1, indicate rights being offered (for example, first British serial rights, FBSR). Within the top margin from page 2 onwards, put author's name underlined on the left, and the catchline on the right (for example, homeless 1, homeless 2, etc.).

You may want to put 'mf' (more follows) in the bottom right-hand corner of each page except the last. Don't underline any works in the text unless they are to be printed in italics.

At the end of the article put 'ends' immediately underneath. In the bottom left-hand corner put the word count, or if your machine hasn't got one, give the approximate number of words. To do this, take the average number of words in a line and multiply by the number of lines on a page, and then by the number of pages. In the bottom right-hand corner put your name (not any pseudonym), address and telephone number. Add any contracts the subeditor may need for checking purposes with telephone numbers.

Publications that have slightly different requirements from the above will let you know (for example, they may require a title page and no indenting).

A title page precedes the first page of text. The title, byline and rights offered are in the same positions as on page 1. At the bottom left, put the number of words; bottom right, name, address, and telephone number, as on the last page.

A script should be accompanied by a covering letter and, if not commissioned, a stamped addressed envelope (international reply coupons if sent abroad). Keep the letter as brief as possible. Remind the editor, if necessary, about any verbal or written discussion there has been about the article, and point out any changes to the original plan that you found necessary.

Figure 3.3 shows a summary sheet format for indicating research. This, or a modified version of it, may be welcomed by college lecturers.

PROOF READING

If you are sent galley or page proofs, you may be charged for any correction you may make if they are second thoughts, additions or deletions, or reorderings. Be sure to use British Standard Institute (BSI) proof marks for copy preparation and proof correction (see Appendix 1). Printers'

SUMMARY SHEET FOR ARTICLES

GENERAL
Reference number/invoice number
Author
Title
Number of words
Deadline
Date submitted
Publication aimed at
Published in (with date)

BACKGROUND
Lead
Briefing

RESEARCH
With addresses, telephone numbers and dates

Primary sources
Legwork
Interviews by telephone
Interviews face to face
Interviews - correspondence
Original correspondence
Number of questionnaires sent
Number of questionnaires returned
Printed sources

Secondary sources - printed
Books consulted in libraries
Press cuttings from libraries
Own library and press cuttings
Current newspaper/magazine articles
Campaign literature from organizations
Other publicity materials

Illustrations
Reference number
Content/caption
Copyright
Source if different, for example picture agency or publication

Figure 3.3 A specimen summary sheet/checklist for longer articles errors or errors attributable to the publication will be charged to the publication. Changes made by the writer that are second thoughts may be charged to the writer.

Feature articles are generally subbed lightly; an established writer may expect any alterations to be discussed on the phone first. If the proofs show that your copy has been heavily edited, you may want to complain if you don't like the result, particularly if you were not warned.

But before complaining, look at the proofs or final version and work out why the changes were made and assess how far the article has been improved. You may find that you're being educated and that your submissions for that market will improve as time goes on, needing fewer and fewer adjustments.

You will have learned how to look at your work, in these final stages, with the eye of an editor. You will have recognized that while the writer's role is as subject expert, the editors are readership experts. You're burning to tell what's important about your topic. There's sometimes smoke along with your fire. The editor is coming from the other direction. Why should *my* readers want to read it? Some smoke may have to be removed, to let the readers see the article's value at once.

RESPONDING TO REJECTION

If an article is rejected, any comments by the editor should be considered carefully and compared with the script. Work out why your article has not appealed to that particular publication. You may see what other market it might fit, with or without some rewriting.

Beginners tend to be too discouraged by rejection. Pieces that do not work for one market may be just what is wanted by another. If you are getting too many rejections, make sure you are doing sufficient market research. If too many of your 'spec' articles in particular are failing to find a home, concentrate more on getting commissions through query letters/outlines.

How many is too many? Highly professional freelance writers can be content with a rate of 60 per cent acceptances from 'specs' You may be content with fewer if you are a beginner or if you readily sell second time out. On the other hand, you might expect more acceptances of 'specs' if you customarily spend a great deal of time rewriting and polishing work before submitting.

Chapter 6 expands on such matters. Meanwhile here are an extra thought or two about rejection in general. Far from doing too little market study, it is possible that you have followed its pointers too closely. Remember, the same formula, but something different. A fresh editor may be injecting new ideas (however gradually) into the publication you so carefully analysed a month or so ago, and your product looks too much like the old regime. The former editor might have loved it.

Three or four articles on the same theme as yours may have arrived at the same time: yours was good, but one of the others was better. Or two articles on the same theme arrived: yours was twice as good as the other, but the other was commissioned and yours was not.

Consider all the possible reasons for rejection, and if you still decide not to send it out again or rewrite it, file it away. From time to time, you might have cause to look through your unpublished articles, and immediately see new possibilities in one. Something in it may be echoed by a headline in that morning's paper, and a new peg may restore life to your material. You may also see, at this distance, exactly why it was rejected, and how it can be improved.

Don't let responsive editors escape when they move to other publications. Follow them.

ASSIGNMENTS

1   Take three articles (approximately 500 words, 800 words and 1500 words) from different publications. Produce clear outlines of the content of each by listing the main points in note form (not sentences), one point for each paragraph.

2   Change each of the above to *sentence* outlines.

3   Rewrite the following paragraphs, the intro to an article 'Mercy Killing or Murder? – A Nursing Perspective'. Reduce by half, into one paragraph. Improve the structure and make it less academic. (For a popular woman's magazine.)

> Whatever area of nursing nurses find themselves in, from geriatrics to hospice or intensive care, as nurses, they are confronted by patients whose condition is so severe, or whose quality of life so questionable, that thoughts of euthanasia inevitably cross their minds. These thoughts can throw into turmoil all that their training has taught them about the preservation of life, and cause them to confront their most deeply cemented ethical beliefs. This article attempts to explore the differing opinions on euthanasia, from a nursing perspective. The primary question is whether it is in our society's interest to change the current law against euthanasia in Britain. This has far-reaching implications, outlined later in the

article. I have spoken to Philippa, a senior nurse with several years experience working with terminally ill, who remains unconvinced that causing the premature death of a patient is a viable option in the ongoing quest to relieve suffering. I have also spoken to Anne, a retired nurse who endorses 'active euthanasia'. From these opposing viewpoints, I hope this article will provide the basis for further discussion and research into this very difficult and emotive subject. It is my personal belief that 'active' euthanasia goes against the very grain of nursing standards of practice, which endeavour to provide dignity, comfort and support to those suffering long-term and terminal illness.

4 Write an essay of 1000 words entitled 'The Roles of Writer and Editor: How they Differ'. Re-read Chapters 2 and 3 to pick up any points. Find other reading. Talk to one or two feature writers and one or two editors if you can, to gather anecdotes and quotes. Use any relevant experience of your own in dealing with editors.

4 THE WORLD OF IDEAS

Louis Macneice, the poet, spent twenty-five years learning to write poetry, then suddenly one day realized he had poems flying past his right ear. All he had to do was move his head a little bit sideways and they would fly in. There are connections between writing poetry and writing feature articles.

From one angle, this anecdote illustrates the first point made about feature writing. The most important thing to start with is something to say.

The story also reminds us that the generation of ideas is an intensely personal process. Sitting at your desk with your head cocked to one side may not do much for you. Nor may having rotting apples in a drawer do as much as they did for the great German poet Schiller, who believed that the smell aided composition.

But you may have your own strange but effective ways of getting in the mood. Ideas certainly do come to those who learn how to be receptive to them; to those in a relaxed, open but alert, state of mind.

There has to be a feeling behind ideas. They should move you, excite you in some way. Avoid if you can writing about something that does not stir some interest in you. Look for elements of development, change, conflict in your subject – things that annoy or elate you – things that get you thinking.

The staff writer is already living in a world of ideas that has built up round the publication. There may be editorial meetings where feature writers can bounce their ideas off each other; or this may happen informally. Press releases and other literature are arriving daily, which suggest possible topics. Ideas come from freelances, and if they are good they may be paid for, even when staff writers are asked to develop them.

The freelance writer should recognize that against the disadvantage of not being part of a publication's little world, and the further disadvantage of there being no copyright in ideas (only in the words used to express them), there is the advantage of being more likely to come up with the more unusual idea.

A FERTILE NOTEBOOK

In a pub you overhear two men in the tiling business discussing how they avoid the tax man. You may get some ideas for an article on moonlighting. You may be able to make some surreptitious notes on the newspaper you are carrying, since using a notebook might rouse suspicions. You may get into conversation with them – if you don't look too much like an income tax inspector, or if they are not too big, and if you choose your words carefully.

There are many personal experiences that can form the basis of saleable articles, and you need to be on the alert for them, and to make notes as they happen. Articles can be written about the domestic upheavals of moving house, about a change of career, your operations or your wife's or child's, your failure to make friends with the local dogs, your experience of 'office politics', your conversion to Buddhism, or about how you have found the strength to cope with a disability.

Radio phone-in programmes, like newspaper and magazine letter pages, are natural homes for the cranky and the quirky, and can be a fertile source of ideas. Child abusers should be castrated, you may hear someone say, or everyone should be sterilized, or nothing at all should be open on Sundays. Whether such remarks make you smile or make you angry, they usually make you think. Radio and TV documentaries on drug addiction or the prison system, or immigrants or a reviving industry, may start you off on an article, or help you with one you are writing.

They may, in effect, be doing some of your interviewing for you, or at least be suggesting contacts, but if you are going to follow them up with articles, be careful to check when the programmes were made, and to update. Tonight's documentary could have been made a year ago.

Printed sources

For freelances, many ideas are likely to come from reading – books, magazines, newspapers, publicity material, telephone directories. Lots of ideas, for example, might be extracted from *Chambers Dictionary of Dates*. Take the section 25th March: '1843 – The 1300 foot Thames tunnel, from Wapping to Rotherhithe, was opened. 1867 – Arturo Toscanini born. 1975 – King Faisal of Saudi Arabia assassinated by his nephew'. Some library research into these subjects will generate more ideas about these and other famous tunnels, musicians, assassinations.

Anniversary dates are a convenient starting peg.

Leafing through encyclopaedias and yearbooks can produce a rich harvest, including of course the writers' yearbooks mentioned. Looking through the London South East telephone directory I find the following intriguing entries: chimney sweeps, diamond sawing, fallout shelters, gold blockers, hairpiece manufacturers and importers, naturopaths, noise and vibration consultants, pawnbrokers, portable buildings, robots, ship breakers, toastmasters.

Newspaper and magazine articles that you read might add something new to one of your subjects, or may suggest further articles, or be good models of particular kinds of articles: a celebrity interview, a political background feature, a humorous column, film review, or whatever. Cut, paste on an A4 sheet, photocopy (to preserve them) and file the most likely. Date them so that you will know how to update them when the time comes. Make comments in the margin so that you won't wonder several months later why you cut them. To avoid overloading yourself with such material, clear out cuttings regularly, replacing them with better and updated material.

A cutting containing a useful idea can be filed in a special 'current ideas' folder for more urgent attention. Otherwise file the sheets of cuttings, under subject headings. If you find this time-consuming, put cuttings straight into old envelops or wallet folders but with some means of reference.

Thumbing through old magazines can generate ideas. You should sub-scribe to useful magazines. *Press Gazette*, for example, will keep you in touch with news about the journalism business, and a writer's trade magazine will keep your techniques in trim and your market information up to date. Use libraries that take the magazines that cover your special interests.

Even the contents pages of discarded magazines can suggest new ideas in themselves. Hoarding whole magazines, however, even as market guides, can take lots of space, and it is better to spend a morning or after-noon hunting ideas and studying the market in a fair-sized reference library, where you will find the photocopier useful.

Another source of ideas is the newsletters, pamphlets and handouts that come from government departments, pressure groups and academic insti-tutes, and from companies and PR and advertising organizations whose mailing lists you are on.

The imagination at work

You read that a country horse event is to take place next Saturday, so you decide to attend and write an account of the event as seen by a man who cleans out the stables. You are angered by a shop assistant's lack of interest and courtesy, and you decide to write an article comparing English shopkeepers with their counterparts in Europe.

An advert for a special luxury object catches your eye: 'Two fine examples of Chinese lacquer. The larger can be found in the British Museum, the smaller in the High Street'. What are the other uses of lacquer today, you wonder. Who else uses techniques over 2000 years old? Is there an article in it? Who would be interested in such an article?

An advert for unit trusts in *The Financial Times* is headed 'Why the Meteorological Office Should be Staffed by Giraffes'. That is a good title. It makes you wonder what other animal habits, as well as those of giraffes, signify changes in the weather, and what angle could be given to that. Or you may be more interested in pursuing the idea in the advert: you may ask yourself how reliable are the predictions of stock market movements made by financial analysts who believe they come in foreseeable cyclical patterns.

A nose for future news

Some news stories don't break in newspapers but in trade magazines and professional journals. If you keep in touch with some of these periodicals, preferably those that relate to your specialized knowledge, you could corner ideas worth wider dissemination.

You read in a catering magazine, for example, that a famous hotel company in its bid to take over another accuses the latter of various management faults, including the failure to use efficiently technology new to hotels. You have noted that the newspapers, concentrating on the financial side of the conflict, have not found room for this aspect. You check the main business magazines and find that they do not cover these arguments either. You can see that there are various names in the catering magazine article that should help you to pursue the story. You could be on to a national story that highlights new technology, or the lack of it, in hotels, or at least a consumer magazine might be interested.

Such ideas frequently revolve around new products or new technology. The information about a new kind of computer for use in schools, or about a court case concerning an accident caused by a department store escalator breaking down, may have wider implications following its first mention in a trade or technical journal, and the news media may not at first realize the news value of such stories or see how to interpret them to a wider audience. Freelances with the expert knowledge, or at least a specialized interest, are a useful source of articles in these areas.

A part-time freelance whose main job is in hotels or computer technology, or in store management, could be the person to explore the ideas mentioned, but any specialized knowledge can set you off on this track. Examine your own interests and see which are worth cultivating.

Other merits of trade magazines as sources of ideas are that they are mostly national in scope, and are responsible organs within an industry or profession. They therefore tend to be accurate sources of information, and a useful source of essential contacts; and there are trade magazines for almost every occupation you can think of.

WHAT MAKES A GOOD IDEA?

I have emphasized method and initiative in formulating ideas. Exploiting them successfully means first shaping them for the appropriate market.

Chapter 2 showed that a good idea is not just a matter of a catchy title. It must have the potential to be developed into a good article. Ideally, when you read an article in this morning's *Times* or in the current issue of *19*, you should feel that it is perfectly fitted to the publication and the date, and would not fit well anywhere else. That appropriateness to the market should be revealed as soon as you begin to develop an idea and should determine the way you target it.

Beginners often find it hard to hit on good ideas because they are not sufficiently attuned to markets. Once they have published several articles in a particular market, ideas for that or similar markets come more readily to mind.

Some may be misled by confusing ideas with subjects. 'Racism in London' they feel is important, but it is a subject, not an idea. Beginners have to learn to distinguish between subjects and ideas, and the notion of the 'importance' of certain subjects can obscure the issue. 'Relevance to readers' is a more appropriate phrase.

The *Concise Oxford Dictionary* says that an idea is a 'conception ... of thing to be aimed at, created, etc ... way of thinking. ...' You should, in fact, take a subject and extract an idea from it. You must find a particular way of looking at the subject, you must have something particular to say about it, a point of view, a focus on one aspect of the subject, an attitude, an angle, a slant. The synonyms and near-synonyms for this essential element are many. 'Why there are Fewer Jobs for London's Blacks', or 'London's Classrooms: Where the Racial Lessons Start', would be promising titles for articles based on the subject 'Racism in London'.

The young approach

A piece of advice sometimes given to beginners is to write about what they know. Taking this too literally, beginners may be dismayed by the thought they have too little experience of the world to have anything significant to say.

In fact young people have some keen advantages in idea-hunting in a fast-changing world. Their receptiveness to new trends, and enthusiasm for new behaviour patterns and for new fashions in clothes and music, their awareness and curiosity about the changes going on around them, are assets to journalism. Stimulating articles can be produced by such minds, provided the writing ability is there. Furthermore, there are many publications aimed at a young readership, and they may prefer the fresh approach of a young writer to a tired-sounding veteran.

In the long run, however, the wiser advice is to write about what other people want to know rather than about what you happen to know. If you are young now, you won't remain young, nor will your readers, and it is almost certain that you will have to appeal to markets containing wide age ranges as your career progresses. You will become motivated more by what you know you can find out than by what you know.

I am not ignoring, in saying this, the value of specialized knowledge, which tends to increase over the years. Newspaper and magazine editors look for freelances who possess it, and specialized magazines provide limitless opportunities. The principle still holds good that the readers' needs come first, even though a freelance naturally develops special interests.

Formulas and 'creative thinking'

If we are to assess the importance of subjects, as opposed to ideas, we could say that they are those things that appeal to people's basic drives: self-preservation (food and shelter, and physical needs such as sports and recreation), reproduction (love and sex), spiritual needs (beliefs and self-improvement goals), and worldly ambition (power, money, possessions). It is useful to think in these terms when evaluating an idea.

Thinking about subjects in this way reminds us that many of them, and the ideas they produce, are perennial, however topically dressed up. A perennial subject such as old age might produce the idea 'How Old is Old Age?' – and it will be pegged on to news about pensions or jobs for retired people, or perhaps some new figures indicating there are now four out of ten people over 65 in this country. Such pegs lend topicality and prevent an article from becoming an essay.

Word associations

Sometimes an idea begins with a word that lodges in the mind for no apparent reason. 'Animal' becomes 'Animals Anonymous', and that might suggest animals ganging together mysteriously or genetic experiments that have produced the shoat (sheep-and-goat) and other hybrids.

There are formula ideas, hundreds of them, that work well for popular markets: 'What Your ... Should Tell You About Yourself' (hand, hand-writing, earlobes ...), 'What is the Best ...?' (age, diet, education ...), 'The ... of the Future', 'Behind the Scenes at the ...', 'How to ...', 'Make the Most of Your ...', 'What makes a ...?' (best-seller, good party ...), 'The World's Biggest ...', 'The World's Smallest ...', 'The Art of ...', The Cult of the ...', 'Why You Should ...', 'Can ... Survive?' (person-ality, conversation ...), 'The Truth About ...', 'The Facts Behind ...', 'These Practices are Dangerous', 'How to Succeed in ...', 'Coping With ...' (loneliness), 'The ... Game' (dating, party ...), 'Recovering from ...'. Variations on such formula ideas are seldom missing from the popular media and, handled well, they can produce good reading.

Some intriguing lists can be turned into articles. The great bars of the world, the best hotels, haunted houses, famous railway engines ...

Putting two subjects together can make an idea. The police by itself is a subject. Ideas are: the police and arms, or the police and race, or rape, or TV, or interrogation techniques, or the law, or football hooliganism, or politics. Looking at a subject's contrary can make a possible idea: for example, 'Fortunate Accidents', Unhappy Millionaires', 'Ingenious Mishaps', 'Tragic Trifles'. Such phrases at least start you thinking.

Free association and lateral thinking

Any stimulation to think in an unusual way can be valuable. 'Free asso-ciation' and the workings of the unconscious have been mentioned in the context of letting ideas flow in the course of an article. Free association applied to words may result in interesting associations.

More calculatedly, 'lateral thinking' may be fruitful. Since our educa-tional system has trained us to think logically and systematically, from origins through developments to conclusions, and from causes to effects, we can find a liberation of the imagination in crashing through the barriers.

Suppose surgery is our subject. Logical or linear thinking takes us perhaps to such a pattern as:

Medical training
Priorities in budgeting
Criteria?
Cutbacks in the Health Service
Ethics
Law
Errors
Compensation
Insurance

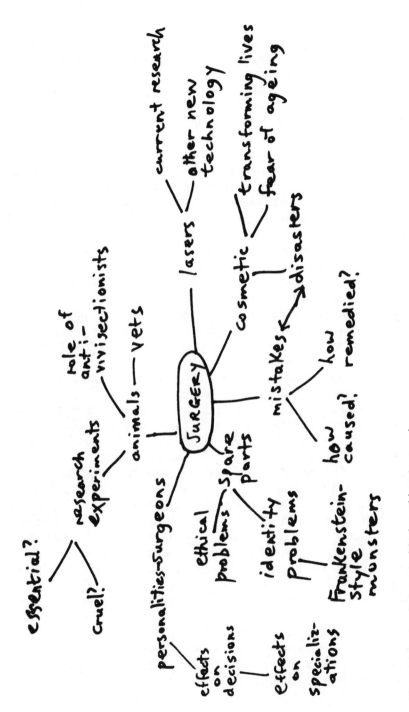

Figure 4.1 A mind map with the subject 'surgery'

All very important, but this way of thinking can be restrictive, if you want to be sure that you have a comprehensive picture to select from. Your thinking at each stage tends to be limited, for example, by the word(s) you have just written.

MIND MAPS

Try putting 'surgery' in the middle of an A4 page and fan out the aspects and associations as they come into your mind: make a mind map. Keep a measure of control. Then compare the result with Figure 4.1. You will find that the words and phrases will work on each other, and you will soon see you have various possible directions. When you have filled a large part of the page, you will be able to suggest the direction and aspects you want with more confidence, and at least some of your thinking on the subject is more likely to be more original. You will have a kind of map of the subject, and you will be able perhaps to make some surprising and fruitful conjunctions without losing your way.

Similar games, without immediate purpose, of what might be called 'creative doodling' might be played with what comes in your daily post, or with any mix of materials that comes to rest on your desk, or with a dictionary, encyclopaedia or similar reference work. My subject is surgery again. I open a dictionary and write down words at random: candle, cry, danger, fence, again, left-handed, meeting, nerve, pact. 'Candle' makes me wonder about lack of equipment, 'cry' what proportion of victims of errors complain? What would a list of recent surgical errors suggest are the most likely dangers – what is being done to circumvent them, and what else should be done? Are many errors hushed up? 'Left-handed' – how often do physical weaknesses contribute to errors, such as poor eyesight, hand tremors? What screening is made of surgeons? Do they have to undergo tests periodically? Are the tests rigorous enough? After a mishap, what meetings take place, who are present? What pacts are made? 'Nerve' – how often does the anaesthesia go wrong, what are the main dangers? Once you have gathered points in this way and decided on the direction you want to go, allow logic back again to outline your article.

TWISTING INTO AN ANGLE

What turns a subject into an idea, it will be seen, is twisting it so that you have an angle. For example:

Subject	*Idea*
The Police in Britain today	The British Police: When Should they be Armed
The reasons for rape	Can a Rapist Talk to His Mother?
The danger of noise	Discos can make you deaf
English teaching in the schools	The appalling level of school leavers' grammar and spelling

The first three ideas have come, as can often happen, in the shape of acceptable titles: they are probably effective enough to put at the head of the article finally produced. The publication they are sent to may not use these titles for a variety of reasons. They may not harmonize with other titles, or they may not fit the space allotted. Nevertheless editors like to see good provisional titles. They are convenient labels until the final title is chosen, and they may need little change to turn them into good titles. A good provisional title or headline is a selling point. If you have an eye and an ear for a good title, you will find that ideas come along with it more readily.

Of the four ideas above, the one derived from English teaching still needs working on. 'Why School Leavers Can't Spell' or 'Come back Grammar, come back Spelling!' could well be the outcome. They are notions that will help focus the reader's attention.

A final word of warning. Don't ruin a good idea by leaving it inchoate. Back it up with facts, develop it with more facts, and with thought and feeling. In these information-hungry times, readers want authority rather than more cleverness.

ASSIGNMENTS

1 Try a mind map (as shown in Figure 4.1) with one of the following subjects: noise, dyslexia, nursery schools, students, the Criminal Justice Bill.

2 Use the pattern to work out an outline for a 1000-word article targeted at a specific publication.

3 Write the article.

5 ARTICLE TYPES AND THEIR MARKETS

An idea will start growing once it is linked with an article type or category. Here are a few tips about how to deal with some of the commonest and most enduring types and subjects. You get a sharper insight into markets when you find the same or similar topics treated in different publications, so there are a few comparisons of this kind.

Types come and go with fashion, as do different kinds of magazine, so keep up to date with market trends by watching the bookstalls. Subscribe to such writers' guides as *Freelance Market News* and *Writers' Monthly*, which try to keep up with news of future launches of publications as well as of those just launched, and also with news of staff and policy changes in established ones.

THE TYPES IN DEMAND

How-to

There are hundreds of subjects for how-to articles. They are in great demand, and fall into three main classes: how to make things, how to deal with the practical problems of life, and how to deal with psychological and social problems.

The first group includes do-it-yourself (DIY) about the house, making quilts, knitting, cooking, and gardening. The second group includes how to choose a career, or a dentist or a lawyer, how to buy or sell a house, how to start a small business. Third, articles explain how you, or others, gave up drink, made the most of being in hospital, dealt with the problems brought by divorce, etc.

What is common to all how-to articles is that you are teaching. It is essential to get the instruction across clearly, taking care to present it at the right level for the readership. Since you have no immediate feed-back, as the classroom teacher has, you must ensure that your content can be grasped at first reading. Try to get feedback by showing the article to someone who would represent its average reader. The content must be authoritative as well as clear, so make an outline – a checklist of points in the right order. Faulty instructions about cooking, car maintenance or sailing can be dangerous. Information about prices of materials and where to get them, and about the names and functions of essential parts of machinery you are describing, must be accurate. Photographs or other illustrations, such as sketches and graphs, may be necessary. 'How to Make a Bookcase' will not get far without some illustration.

A typical shape of a how-to article is the following: objective/problem; reasons for doing it; steps or solutions indicated in order; and conclusion, which should not fail to show the satisfaction waiting as a reward for successful achievement.

To write how-to articles you do not have to be an expert, but you must top up your information with an expert's knowledge and explanation, if necessary through an interview. You do not need to feel guilty about this: the expert carpenter or orchid grower might be quite incapable of imparting his or her own knowledge in writing, and the journalist is often cast in the role of interpreter.

If you think of the good teachers you have known, almost certainly what comes to mind first in writing such a piece is a positive and enthus-iastic approach. Along with this should go a lack of preaching and pretentiousness, and a down-to-earth manner. Humour can help, too: the odd joke against yourself, an anecdote showing how you learned from your mistakes.

Language can present a few problems in a how-to article, as it does in this how-to book. Where the subject can be of either sex there is the his/her problem. I think my solution, using 'you' as often as possible, works sufficiently well. In the average-sized how-to articles it is normally possible to avoid the problem by addressing the reader directly throughout. Using the plural and passive forms are other solutions.

Humour

As an ingredient, humour is everywhere. Its effectiveness in how-to articles has been mentioned. It is especially effective where strong emphasis is required: when the reader is expected to remember the points being made, as, for example, in a point-of-view article. If you make your readers smile, you are halfway to persuading them, or to making them think about what you have said. If you pound at them like heavy waves on a beach, they are likely to remember the din rather than your words.

Many personal columns in newspapers and magazines can be labelled as humour. Humorous articles, such as those printed in the old *Punch* (before revival) and *Private Eye*, are delicately sprung: it is a difficult market, which comprises widely different outlets. Ex-*Punch* readers will say it was highly intelligent, subtly humorous, well written, and detractors that it was blandly bourgeois and self-regarding. *Private Eye* is described as sharp, outrageous, classless, hitting the mark; or as immature, full of public-schoolboy punning, with no direction. The following extracts can give only a taste of each, to illustrate their differences.

Punch: in 'Summer Stock' Alan Coren meets a couple on a coach trip in Aix-en-Provence:

> Excusez-moi, he was wondering if he might have a look at your *Daily Telegraph*.
>
> This is extremely odd. Does she have a dog? Can it read? Does it want the greyhound results?
>
> No, I now note that she has a male human being with her who is sort of- how can I put this? – trembling encouragingly at me, but it surely cannot be he who wishes to have a look at my *Daily Telegraph*, because he would ask me himself.
>
> Why on earth is she speaking on his behalf? It cannot be because she is the sole Francophone (*vide* 'Excusez-moi') and he is, therefore, unable to get a *Daily Telegraph* east of Dover, because anyone east of Dover with a *Daily Telegraph* presumably knows enough English to get it taken off him.
>
> He could be mute.

He turns out to be one of 'the new share-owning thatchocracy, worried about falls in some of his shares.

Private Eye: from 'I Weep With The Yorkshire Martyrs' by Lunchtime O'Dewsbury (sending up the tabloids):

> Today I saw with my own eyes the living hell that has been forced on the heroic Yorkshire parents whose only crime is that they want their kids to be British.
>
> I walked with the 'Dewsbury 36' as, with their heads held high, they marched into the mayor's parlour and punched him in the face.
>
> 'How can he do it to us,' said one concerned Dewsbury parent, 'when all we want is the right to have our kids brought up to hate darkies.'
>
> Make no mistake, these plucky British parents mean business.

They set fire to the headmaster's car at a predominantly Asian Church of England Primary School 'in a last desperate attempt to get him to see reason'.

> All these parents want is the natural, God-given right to bring up their kids to be as bigoted and unpleasant as themselves.

Beware the personal essay. You may think you have cooked a crepe suzette but it may taste like a month-old blancmange. It is better to take something serious or interesting in itself, and see it from a funny angle, or turn it upside down.

Similarly, domestic tiffs over the toast and marmalade provide a thin pretext for attempts to be amusing about the human condition. There is more potential in using wit and irony to analyse situations that are either more offbeat or more in need of exposition: how to survive the first day at a new job, for instance, or (as spoofs of practical advice columns) learning how to understand a word-processor manual, or how to decide which golf club to use.

Inspirational

This is mainly a popular market type where they are called TOTS (Triumph over Tragedy): a human-interest story about a person or a small group of people whose courage in the face of pain or misfortune readers can easily identify with. At their best such articles are uplifting and strengthen one's faith in human nature. At their most blatantly commercial they skirt around the realities in bland sentimentality, or they are sensational, exploiting with lurid description the tragic elements, with unconvincing attestations of concern.

Stories about the work of such exceptional people as Mother Teresa, who takes the sick and destitute off the streets of Calcutta so that they can die with dignity under her care, are straightforward examples. Typical titles are 'She Devoted Her Life to her Brain-Damaged Father', or 'Blind and Lame – But He Created His Home out of a Wilderness'. Some magazines – the American *National Enquirer,* for example – lift the life off the secret tragedies of celebrities. Further upmarket, the concerns tend to widen out-into self-improvement, into the 'art of living'.

That phenomenon of middlebrowdom, *Readers Digest,* the most successful magazine of all time, with 28 million copies sold in fifteen languages, makes its inspirational articles keynotes of its formula. Sub-categories within this formula are medical or scientific, business achievement, international politics, sport, recreation, travel and food, all covered in a wholesome, conservative manner. They often employ techniques more common in fiction:

He remembered his wife, dead of cancer two years before, at only 32. The long period of suffering. Christine's wonderful courage. *She never gave up.* . . .

Endings are typically upbeat:

> We shared an experience that pushed us both to our limits. It made me far more sensitive to life and the people around me – even to those I know only slightly. That's because total strangers risked their lives to save mine. This takes a rare kind of courage, and I'll always be grateful.

The credit side of the *Reader's Digest* technique is the magazine's devotion to getting the facts right and clearly told. The danger in fictionalizing the narrative so that the characters' thoughts so neatly fit the chosen theme is that the piece can seem contrived.

Standing up to bullies makes an inspirational theme for a popular magazine. *Bella* has 'Those bullies can't scare me' by George Dearsley, the story of a pub landlady who was subjected to a campaign of terror by thugs after she had ejected one from the pub for brawling. The windows were smashed, causing £1,000 worth of damage.

The landlady went to the police and the two men were charged with assault and criminal damage. They offered to pay £500 if she dropped the charge, but she refused. The subsequent terror included threats and damage to several cars of her and her son. It lasted for months before the Crown Prosecution Service brought the case to court. One of the men got three years and three months, and the other two and a half years. After the hearing the landlady put on a champagne celebration at her pub.

The article ends by quoting her saying:

> 'It was a victory for everyone who's prepared to stand up and be counted. The damage to the cars alone cost me £10,000, but I never thought of giving in. If I'd been scared off, those monsters would have destroyed me. I had to stand up for what was right – and prove that bullies don't always win!'

Note how this matches up to *Bella's* writers' guide (Figure 2.3).

Old age

An increasing number of magazines and feature pages cater for older readers, supported by advertisers' recognition that the old are more comfortably off than they used to be. Whether you are getting old, or want to write about the old, or the ageing, the first suggestion is: be positive. Old people can be bored, boring, grumpy or embittered. These are not promising states of mind either for writers or for the subjects of articles.

'We should never have behaved like that when we were at school', has been said by each generation about the one that follows it since the beginning of schooling. It is safer to assume that human nature does not change all that much (I should have said more interesting to assume), and it is more thought-provoking to find specific points to make in an article about different generations than to purvey stereotyped homilies. In any case it is your job as a journalist, more difficult though it may be as you get older, to understand previous generations and be able to communicate with them. Having children and grandchildren is strongly recommended; otherwise, get to know your nephews and nieces.

Old people can be wise and amusing, and may have great stories to tell, and the skill to tell them, without their having tried to get anything published. If you are this kind of old person, you might make a good writer, and even if your health and strength are not good, you can start now.

Accurate nostalgia

From nostalgia many ideas can be mined, but control your memory and work on it. To remember the pleasant episodes of the past and forget the bad times may be understandable. But if you want to make convincing comparisons between then and now, be specific and accurate. Do the necessary research. Get some names (who was prime minister at the time?) and dates to pinpoint periods exactly, and some prices. Make price comparisons only after you have calculated the effects of inflation. Make other useful comparisons – with the average wage, for example. A bicycle may now cost an average weekly income. There was a time when it probably cost an average fortnightly income. Yet people will bemoan that things are much more expensive than they used to be. Beer, you might find, is not dearer than it was many years ago.

Nostalgia can strike at any age. At 20, 30 or 40 you may well look back ten or twenty years with yearning, and there are plenty of subjects for articles that your contemporaries particularly respond to. This is especially so as the changes around us become so rapid. The 'hippies' or 'flower people' of the 1960s are already the stuff of history.

Watch for fashions and revivals of taste that stem from nostalgia. The death of actor Fred Astaire and a season of his dancing films on TV brought a burst of interest in the 1930s and 1940s, just as the 1950s revival was beginning to fade. The shifts in nostalgia fashions bring fresh ideas for articles.

Then there is a whole world of subjects related to old age as a social problem: the psycho-geriatric wards; the old people's homes, good and bad; senile dementia and other illnesses that old age is prone to; questions of euthanasia, early retirement and the longer evenings of life; the new careers, hobbies and recreations of old age.

More than 10 million people have, at the moment, reached retirement age. People are retiring early at 55 and living to 85, so you cannot lump all these together. Study carefully the age ranges and situations that different publications deal with.

Whatever age range you are writing for, talk to your readers about what interests them; but do not talk to them as if they were a fascinating tribe just discovered by an anthropologist – with rituals that we cannot help smiling at. The same mistake can be seen in articles written for teenagers, even when written *by* teenagers. Do not be saddled with preconceptions about how different age groups fill their time. Consider what writer/traveller Freya Stark was doing at 90, and Mozart at 6.

Personal experience

Using the first person is much more common that is used to be. The factual information so much in demand nowadays is given interest, drama and verisimilitude if attached to a flesh-and-blood participant in the experience/event. And if the information is funny, dramatic, or tragic in itself – mishaps, adventure, surgical operations – the first person narrator can add to the appeal and the effect.

The approach must not be: since most of you readers live such comfortable middle-class lives, you will be fascinated by my story. The approach must be: here is a fascinating story. It happened to me, but it can happen to anybody. Perhaps something similar will happen to you, reader, some day. If so, I hope reading this will help. In other words, readers should be seen as being interested in the event, the experience, for the excitement and the lessons it contains, not because it is you personally that it has happened to.

A typical article in the now defunct *Weekend* was 'Cast Adrift in Shark-Infested Seas'. Susan Docker, a skin-diver aged 30 in Sydney, Australia, tells of how, in escaping from a shark, she is swept by a current that takes her far out to sea. She clings to her tiny float (18 inches by 12) for 44 hours before being washed up on an island where she is rescued by a helicopter. She thinks about her husband and family. . . .

The language is quite ordinary, with a few clichés – 'such enormous force', 'the rain pelted down', 'a deep voice droning', 'awoke in a daze', a deafening roar'. But ordinary language, and even the odd selected cliché, can go convincingly well with extraordinary experience (as can the reverse combination) and the effect is satisfying. At under 1000 words the account has to keep moving: 'Those waves washed over me all night. By dawn I was exhausted. As the sun rose higher, its scorching heat seared my face'.

Freelance writers are on the whole too busy to find themselves in such places as shark-infested seas, but they can find survivors of the experience and ghost their accounts for them or put them into shape, or tell the story through an interview. The following actual stories may well have been ghosted, or 'assisted': 'Why I Decided to Emigrate' (by a nurse), 'Watching My House Burn Down', 'I was Lost in the Amazonian Jungle', 'Why I Sent the Father of My Child to Prison', and 'How My Family Reacted to my Sex Change'.

Slightly more common experiences that will interest specific readerships – learning to paraglide, or making a living out of street portraiture in the South of France – must be kept under control. Either your main purpose is to recommend the reader to take up these activities, or the occasion is the peg for something more deeply significant for you, which the readers will share to a degree.

Rambling personal reflections are unlikely to be wanted. Too many '*Is*' are likely to be irritating, especially at the start. Probably not: 'I flew! I flew! Can you believe it? I was airborne after less than an hour's tuition.' Rather: 'You can fly! You can be. . . .'

A personal account of anorexia, however moving, may help to explode some myths about the subject, and may incidentally be an indictment of the inadequacy of the average treatment on offer, but to become journalism it will probably need to be put into the context of others' experiences and of experts' views.

Service pieces

To write satisfactory, helpful accounts of various kinds of goods, services, and institutions often requires much legwork and research: poring over much printed material, such as handouts, leaflets and brochures; giving facts and figures and comparing them; checking and rechecking the information; and talking to people so that you can confidently select and recommend. Consider hotels, cameras, career decisions, for example, as typical subjects.

Although service pieces are in great demand, freelance writers have to work out whether they would be able to earn enough to recompense them for the time and effort expended. You cannot compete with the Consumers Association's *Which?*

For some articles – a survey of swimming pools in your area, for example – you may be able to gather the information you need on the telephone. It helps of course if you have visited or used most of the pools at some time, so that you can add genuine colour.

For other articles it may be easy to gather the information by studying the manufacturing or marketing publicity material, and then by filling in the gaps by questioning users. But some legwork is normally required.

There are many informative articles, from buying a house to choosing a dog, that are given authority, or at least authenticity, if the information is combined with personal experience. If you need to do a job at your home, you collect estimates from several firms before deciding which one will do it. If their carrying out of the work is interesting in some way, whether expert, lackadaisical or disastrous, you may then have material for both service and personal experience pieces.

An article comparing the journey to Paris by Eurostar train with that by air will need careful alignment of like with like: the prices of everything, the quality of the food, the times taken by the plane and train and also city centre to city centre – probably displayed in a box.

Think pieces

Local papers and popular magazines are markets for the numerous 'sounding off' ideas that might start or finish in the letters page. Poor service in post offices and shops, the inconsiderateness of the young, the tediously repetitive conversation of the old, thoughtless neighbours (but do not choose your own and be sued for libel), saloon-bar bores, office politics. But do not merely *grouse*. Be constructive.

How the BBC should be reorganized, parental choice in schools – how far it is possible?, is Britain on the way up or down again?, the current sexual morality, abortion – whose choice should it be?, the tameness of the lobby correspondents, the women who ask to be battered, the wastes of charity money, are subjects with more mileage.

National papers have think pieces that shed light on an important issue raised by a current event. It is often both background and polemical. Notable is Simon Jenkins in *The Times*. Among his titles (with standfirsts) in 1995 were 'The great utility scandal' ('Privatizations have enriched directors and ministers but enraged the public'), 'Triumph of tabloid TV' ('Having chosen to live by the ratings, television is doomed to be trashy'), and 'Just playing at Chequers' ('The cabinet will not cut taxes, because it cannot cut spending'.)

Some papers put their main think pieces alongside the leaders: for example, 'Let them swagger – and keep the peace' by Edward Pearce in the *London Evening Standard* (intro: 'Only one thing matters about Northern Ireland: in pursuit of the twin causes of becoming part of the Irish Republic or staying part of the United Kingdom, nobody has been murdered there for 369 days'); 'Streetwise or Gutter Politics' by Penny Wark in *Today* (standfirst 'Shadow Home Secretary Jack Straw says Labour will sweep away drunks and beggars. So what's become of compassion?'); and 'Why we lost our pride in being British' by Andrew Roberts (strap line 'As a government adviser calls for our national identity to be put on the school curriculum. . . .')

When the think pieces become 'investigative' – when established interests' noses are going to be put out of joint – you can quote John

Tusa, former Managing Director of the BBC World Service if asked to explain your impertinence: 'The media have no choice but to ask questions of the government of the day or the state of the moment, not because they are special, not because they are better, not because they are arrogant, not because they are self-appointed, but because if they do not do it, nobody else will.' ('A mission to be there', *British Journalism Review*, Vol. 3, No. X, 1992).

The in-house sort of backgrounds, think pieces and investigations (the greater and the lesser) are among other in-house, news-orientated features discussed in Chapter 16.

Travel

The trouble with travel is that the place you're writing about has probably been described many times, and the adjectives and adverbs are well worn. Ideally, choose an out-of-the-way place or an out-of-the-way treatment or angle. A completely honest account of a trip of the more adventurous kind, with a mixture of tedium, suffering, and exhilaration is a refreshing change. Here is Stephen Pile on an adventure holiday in the Peruvian jungle (*Sunday Times Magazine*):

> On arrival the Indians offered us beer which caused great excitement. However, it turned out that this was made from chewed yucca and women's spit. 'It's a cross between somebody's home-brew and gone off yoghurt', said the couple from Leicester, who adapted to the jungle best of all. When the chief came out with a plate of roast tapir, they tucked in. 'It's chewy, but quite nice.' 'I asked if there was anything they wouldn't eat and they paused for thought. 'Squirrels,' they said after some minutes.
>
> Within ten years a road is to be built into the jungle. The Leader asked the Indians how they felt about the 20th century coming in and sweeping away their culture, their eco-system, their traditional ways and superior non-mercantile values. Are you worried about this? he inquired. 'No,' came the reply. 'We're going to open a restaurant.' And no more rain dances. They couldn't wait.

The way travel articles talk gives a strong clue to the readership being addressed. Increasingly nowadays travel sections are looking for off-the-beaten-track content and style. Compare the above with *Loaded* of July 1995, for whom Trevor Ward had a look at the bars and brothels of South America. He begins:

'Belize City? You must be crazy, you'll be shot. Yeah well, I'd sooner be a crazy Englishman dying of shotgun wounds to the sounds of Shabba Ranks and the sweet smell of herb outside a Belize City tin-shack rum-shop than a yellow-bellied, earnest-eyed American tourist dying of boredom to the sounds of a tour guide and the smell of sunscreen factor 8 while queuing-up outside some ruin or other, so fuck you Elmer.'

If you have to write about Paris, or some equally well-known city, repeating the brochurespeak that has been churned out for decades is hardly likely to please editors or readers, even if no one takes it seriously enough to complain. The expectations readers have of travel pages are low on the whole: their eyes slide over the lubricating superlatives to pick out the useful facts – such as prices of hotels and meals, and the availability of sensual delights, such as night clubs and high-quality patisseries.

Do plenty of research in guide books, travel books, perhaps novels, then put your notes aside before you write. Dig out the unexpected. If you send up the tourists, include yourself among them. Be knowledge-able with a light touch, not pedantic. For nine out of ten markets snobbery is out. Avoid the tenth. Refer to your notes later to ensure you have got all the essentials in.

The travel specialist

The above remarks apply to both the occasional and the regular travel writer. The regular travel writer, to be successful, has to travel a great deal and not depend on guide books, which can rapidly become out of date. Give plenty of information about conditions and prices, and double-check.

Don't clog up your article with too many facts: use charts and tabulate or box information when appropriate, and select what your readers will need to know. Articles can then be updated for further sales with little more than new figures.

Indicate where readers can get further information, about trips, and so on. Eliminate from your first draft all know-all tones, while keeping space for romance and nostalgia.

Travel writers are offered a fair number of 'freebies' – free trips, including perhaps travel, accommodation, excursions laid on by a city's or a country's Department of Tourism, hotel, airline or other company. These should be treated warily. Your duty is to your reader, and if the city/resort is too expensive, the hotel dirty, the travel uncomfortable, you should say so. But the cost of a fare may be merely mentioning the airline.

Use a camera. Your photographs will help you to be precise in descrip-tion. But do not use the camera as a crutch. Note your impressions as they come, otherwise your photographs, a day or two later, may gaze back at you blankly, or freeze your imagination. Use them to complement what you have to say, to bring back to your mind precise detail.

If you are a good photographer, and the publication is interested, send your pictures with the article. Find out first whether a publication prefers to use its own pictures or photographers. (Whether you are a good or bad photographer, please read Chapter 10.)

If the place you are covering is familiar, you may find an original slant by getting there in an unusual way. In a balloon? By yak? (Be careful of the wild yak: when it gets bored with you, it is liable to jump off the nearest cliff.) If you are planning a trip to some far-off exotic place, try to get commissions from several publications before you go. Two or three of them might pay a third each of the fare, and then you can ignore the blandishments of 'freebies'.

Build a travel article round a theme. If you cannot find one, try to sum up the place in a short pithy sentence. Will that do as a theme? Try to turn a theme into action – a story with beginning, middle and end. Keep the description (unless it is for a glossy magazine, or unless it is brilliant) short. Spice the narrative with anecdotes.

A theme might be redolent of nostalgia: you return to the town where you grew up and meet old friends and an ex-sweetheart or two. But before you write it, ask yourself what makes you think anyone will be remotely interested in all this? A theme might be wider in scope: how tourism is helping a developing nation to progress rapidly, or how a culture will be destroyed by tourism unless action is taken fast.

Whatever the theme, be careful to keep the readers' needs uppermost. Why are they going to read your article? What will they particularly enjoy in the places described. What will they want to avoid?

MISCELLANEOUS SUBJECTS

Let's look now more closely at a few specific subjects and consider likely approaches.

Alternative medicine

While many alternative medicine practices such as hypnotherapy are recognized as valuable by the orthodoxy, the reader is warned in reputable publications of the dangers in going to people who are inadequately qualified. One or two dependable organizations which can supply the names of properly qualified practitioners make a reassuring addition to the article: they're often displayed in a box.

It is particularly advisable to make your angle clear to an editor, after studying the target publication to see how the subject has been dealt with in the past.

Bizarre

Include under this heading the occult and the paranormal.

Popular magazines commonly include one bizarre ingredient among their recipes. The past invading the present, as in poltergeist stories, or the present invading the future, as in an article in *Yes! Magazine* (with *The People*) on an American woman who has arranged to be mummified after her death. Sex-change stories have a fair amount of mileage: an involuntary change to a woman caused by a cancerous growth was the subject of a recent *She* article; after the growth's removal the beard went as well.

Such stores need plenty of facts, case-studies (one long interview or a few short ones), and an open, though not gullible, mind. Investigate any corruption, but steer clear of libel territory. Stories originate all over the world, so the temptation to heavy use of cuttings is understandable; but be careful to freshen them up by updating.

Sunday Magazine (with the *News of the World*) encourages readers to send in accounts of any supernatural experience they have had for their paranormal pages. Reincarnations figure frequently: a survivor of the sinking of the *Titanic* and 37-year-old Philip Corrigan's discovery that in Edwardian times he had been murdered – in the shape of a 26-year-old Lilian Bland – are examples.

Children

This is not such an easy subject to be interesting about as may be imagined. You should probably be a parent at least, and a child psychologist at most, with insight into children's worlds, an expertise in getting them to talk, and an ability to interpret what they say. Large themes are growing up in the wide world (temptations, delinquencies, lack of guidance, children's diseases) and the dangers that surround them in their immediate environment (child abuse, etc.). When aiming at obvious markets (*Nursery World* for example), you need to go back some way over past issues to make sure you've got a fresh idea or angle.

Child psychiatrists are plentiful among the experts interviewed by writers and among the writers – both on a professional level for the journals and broadsheets and on popular levels. An article in *She* by Paul Keers ('Hero today, gone tomorrow') analyses the effects on children of their heroes disgracing themselves (sports persons taking bribes or drugs, etc.) This was based on case studies with a large section in the middle containing the comments of a child psychologist at London's Tavistock Clinic. More about crashing the age barriers on page 309.

In the February 1995 *Tatler* Jonathan Margolis 'dispels the myth that a learning difficulty equals failure' in an article about dyslexia and associated conditions in children. (This is followed by an article about his own dyslexia by A. A. Gill, prolific columnist.)

Crime

Specialist writers find many welcoming avenues, including general interest magazines. *Cosmopolitan* of July 1995 has a well-researched article by Ann Lloyd on women in prison (full title 'The number of women in prison has risen by 46 per cent. What's their crime? Mostly, not paying a fine. Does that justify locking them up?' One box highlights the most common charges (extracted from a report by the National Association of Probation Officers (NAPO); another some cases (sources NAPO and the Howard League for Penal Reform), such as 'A part-time cleaner with five young children, who earned £42 a week, spent 20 days in prison because she couldn't pay a fine'. There are one or two brief case studies (names changed, as in the articles discussed below).

Ann Lloyd is author of *Doubly Deviant, Doubly Damned: Society's Treatment of Violent Women* (Penguin). Trudy Culross in *She* of July 1995 has an article that concentrates on human interest called 'Prisoners of the system'. Three case studies tell the detailed stories of three of the few lucky women prisoners who found themselves in the mother and baby unit of Askham Grange open prison. Some of the background figures of the *Cosmopolitan* article reappear, via Chris Tchaikovsky, founder and spokeswoman for Women in Prison.

Employment

The changes in the nature of employment and in attitudes to it are providing a rich seam of subject-matter. The decrease in 'jobs for life', the uncertainties, the tendency to move from job to job picking up the latest skills, the increase in working from home, whether as a staff member or a freelance – these are just a few of the many aspects.

Describing an unusual or especially interesting job is a perennial. A recent issue of the glossy quarterly *The London Magazine* – not to be confused with the bi-monthly literary *London Magazine* – contains 'Capital Door Nobs', based on interviews with the doormen ('linkmen') or several London hotels.

Health and fitness

The coverage is heavy, in all kinds of publications. Some particular expertise or unusual angle will make acceptance easier. Certain aspects, such as dieting, should be regarded as more specialist than others. Information and advice must be checked with the experts.

Where health (or lack of it) combines a topic with personal experience, we have seen that it's important to put the personal experience into perspective and to make it clear where expert help is available. *Marie Claire* with an article by Deborah Holder (July 1995) tackled the less exposed anorexia victims – a 12-year-old girl and a 42-year-old-woman rather than teenagers. The people spoke for themselves: the girl, her mother; the woman of 42, her husband. A panel of information explains the help available from the Eating Disorders Association.

Hobbies

An advantage of articles on hobbies and sports is that the basic information remains your capital for further articles. You can continue writing in the same vein for years, provided you keep up with new techniques and equipment. Seasons, as in gardening, are important, and you will soon have thick files of past articles and notes for all kinds of weathers to draw upon.

The danger is that you may become lazy about it. The lack of challenge can result in lack-lustre pieces on such subjects. Study all those warmed-up potatoes and cook something new: many editors are on the look-out for new approaches to familiar things. You might find, however, that there are still a few cynical editors who perpetuate the unethical practice of using the names of well-known experts above new writers' work – experts who it is hard to believe are still alive.

Human rights

Amid all the epicureanism of the glossies it is refreshing to find some of them joining battle in the war against social problems as in the above, with advice to victims, relatives, friends and carers. Even more gratifying to find the sights lifted on to such international concerns as human rights violations, as *Cosmopolitan* of July 1995 does with 'How telling the truth sentenced this woman to death' by Hilary Burden. The article gives the story, through interview, of Taslima Nasrin, a Bangladeshi writer in hiding in Europe who received the *fatwa* (death sentence) from Islamic militants for allegedly criticizing the Koran in an interview with a Calcutta newspaper.

'How You Can Help,' says a box: join Amnesty International's campaign, write a letter to Prime Minister Begum Khaleda Zia and send it via *Cosmopolitan*.

Relationships

Make sure you find fresh angles. Unusual people (or celebs) in a well-known kind or relationship? Average people in a most unusual relationship? The woman leaving home and family rather than the man? The woman 20 years older than the man? Or why do gorgeous girls go out with ghastly men? (an *Arena* article). 'What on earth can a top-drawer *wunderbabe* with peachy pert buttocks see in a man who exudes pure unadulterated cheese?'

The sizzling sex of sun-filled holidays still gets extraordinary mileage in the women's glossies: it may be the same story, but the articles depend on no interviewee being exactly the same as another, and/or the style being somewhat outrageous or overwritten. There are currently signs that some of the magazines are recognizing that their obsession with the subject is not being shared by their newer readers.

ATTUNING THE IDEA TO THE MARKET

The foregoing survey of subjects for articles and recommended approaches has brought us back to the market-place, but with our eyes a little sharper. Let's look more closely at what newspapers and different kinds of magazines want from freelances. Keep in mind that you need to update constantly your knowledge of the markets. If you're about to write an article for a monthly magazine as it was three or four months ago, because that is the most recent issue you have seen, look at the current issue first. It may have acquired a new, revolutionary editor.

Note from the miscellaneous subjects section that it is sometimes the unlikely match of subject and market that succeeds. So occasionally try listing ideas and markets in facing columns and experimenting with the possible combinations.

While the emphasis has to be on what the markets demand of you, make sure you make your demands of the markets, too, from time to time. As well as writing for the markets you find, sometimes find markets for the articles you have written. You need to impose yourself on your material now and again, to ensure that you develop your own style. Furthermore, your knowledge of your audience should be employed with courage on occasions, to put across truths you know it may find unpalatable.

NATIONAL NEWSPAPER MARKETS

A politician in the TV sitcom *Yes, Minister* said:

> *The Times* is read by the people who run the country.
> *The Guardian* is read by the people who think they ought to run the country.
> The *Daily Mail* is read by the wives of the people who run the country.
> The *Financial Times* is read by the people who own the country.
> The *Daily Express* is read by the people who think the country ought to be run as it used to be run.
> The *Daily Telegraph* is read by the people who still think it is.
> *The Sun* readers do not care who runs the country provided she's got big tits.

There is some truth in these labels, and they do give an idea of the vast differences in the national papers in Britain. There are the quality papers: *The Times, The Daily Telegraph, The Guardian, The Independent, The Financial Times; The Sunday Times, The Sunday Telegraph, The Observer* and *The Independent on Sunday.* There are the middlebrows: the *Daily Mail,* the *Daily Express,* and the *Mail on Sunday* and the *Sunday Express.* There are the populars: the *Daily Mirror, The Sun, The Star;* and the *News of the World, The People,* the *Sunday Mirror.* There are the special interest papers: *The Socialist Worker, The Catholic Herald,* etc.

The total of national newspapers sold in Britain (July 1995) is more than 14 million daily, with about 15.7 million on Sundays, and the readership is estimated at nearly three times this. The highest circulation qualities are *The Sunday Times* at about 1.2 million and the *Daily Telegraph* at 1.03 million. The top-selling pops are *The Sun* at around 4 million and the *Daily Mirror* at 2.5 million among the dailies, and among the Sundays the *News of the World* at 4.6 million. The *Daily Mail* (1.9 million) and the *Daily Express* (1.25 million) fight for the biggest share of the middle ground.

Those figures are extremely high for the size and population of the country – compared to other countries.

Features with topical pegs

Articles for newspapers must have topicality. A feature article tends to be pegged to a news event. Readers are interested to know more about it: the background to it, or the ramifications, or the possible consequences.

A feature writer scrutinizing a news item about a company collapse perhaps may notice something that does not quite get all about the facts as stated. There is something being held back, covered up. The writer digs further, finds more figures, finds the real story perhaps that the reporters, being busy, missed; some unexplained appropriations of funds ... some rapid and unreported changes of staff.

Specialist writers are naturally aware of trends in the areas they deal with. When the time is ripe for an analysis of the trend, they go to their, or their papers', cuttings libraries, among other sources.

Feature articles for newspapers thus tend to have their origins in news items. The following news story was followed up by articles in many papers. A 16-year-old youth was detained for life after attempting to rape a 10-year-old girl and leaving her bleeding and unconscious. His father blamed the sex and violence on video films the family watched. Among the questions raised by the articles were the following. Was the father right? Who is to blame? How should the blame be shared? What's going wrong with family life? What is the law about selling videos and hiring videos? What kind of censorship is in operation? Some of the articles stayed close to the story, whereas others took off into other aspects of censorship, pornography, rape, family life, using the story merely as a starter.

There are freelances who become experts in religious problems in general, or Jewish, or social, economic or scientific matters, and who are called on to provide background features in these areas for national papers, though under the tight budgets of modern newspaper management an editor will try to use staff writers whenever possible. The likeliest openings are for freelances with highly specialized knowledge that it is difficult for the staff writer to keep up with: the hobbies and the professions, about which there will be more in Chapter 18. Specialized articles sell on content, with quality of the writing, although this must also be high, taking second place.

Look for stories in your local papers that might have national implications, or be of interest outside the area. It might be a certain kind of pollution of river water, faulty building construction, nepotism and worse in the way local council contracts are awarded. You wonder why certain cases are not being investigated, what are the loopholes in the law, how widespread are the practices throughout the country.

It has to be said, however, that the practice of national papers working through accredited local correspondents, some of them freelances, reduces the likelihood of articles offered on spec from being considered if the area has already been allocated to a correspondent whose income it provides.

LOCAL NEWSPAPER MARKETS

About eighty local, also called regional or provincial, papers are sold daily, and about 1300 weekly, plus hundreds of free newspapers, or freesheets, almost all of them distributed weekly. The analysis of papers done by Ian Jackson in *The Provincial Press and The Community* (Manchester UP) in 1971 is still useful. He identifies four functions of local paper features: reflector, booster, watchdog and pump-primer.

The reflector function is carried out, says Jackson, by articles on local history that 'deepen the sense of community identity'. Booster features are stories of local heroes, champions of local causes, sports champions. Watchdog campaigns are frequently started off or sustained by public annoyance or concern. Attempts to stop a planned motorway spoiling a particular area is an example. Pump-priming includes those general environmental concerns over urban developments, local transport problems, lack of recreational facilities for children.

Samples of local topics

Here are a few examples of titles and subjects of features from specimen local papers:

1 'Author recalls bygone era of the old village', by Anne Leask, *Beckenham and Penge Advertiser* – about a book with illustrations of old Beckenham, on sale at the local bookshop (reflector function)
2 'Typhoid', by Dr Sydney Wright, *Croydon Advertiser* – about the last typhoid epidemic in Britain, which hit Croydon, Surrey, published on the 50th anniversary. The author was the borough's medical officer of health from 1948 to 1973.
3 'Luxuries in store for London rubber-neckers', by Anne Cowan, Glasgow *Herald* – aimed at 'London tourists', this guide to shopping reflects the growing confidence of Glasgow as a cultural centre (booster).
4 'The great north-south divide built with bricks and mortar', by Eric Baird, associate business editor, *Glasgow Herald* – about the problems caused by the vast differences in property prices between Scotland and England (watchdog aspect).
5 'Blockade threat over by-pass plan', by Kate Davey, *Bournemouth Evening Echo*. Locals are protesting about a proposed trunk road linking the Midlands and the South Coast (watchdog aspect).
6 'Josie flies home from Olympics', by Maria Croce, *Croydon and Purley Advertiser*. Interview with Mrs Jill Horton, on the welcome awaiting daughter Josie in Croydon who had gained world ranking of fifth in her judo class in the Barcelona Olympics (reflector/booster).
7 'No Room at the Inn', by Will Smith, *South London Press*. Foreign tourists avoid South London because the hotels are full of homeless families. This costs South London boroughs millions of pounds a year in lost tourism (watchdog).

If you want to get your articles accepted by your local paper, try to start by doing some reporting on the side for it: it is a good way of building up contacts. For example, make a note of groups, societies, associations, clubs and committees in the area, obtaining your information from friends and acquaintances, notice boards in libraries, town halls, church halls and other public places. Do not, however, get in the way of staff reporters by approaching their regular sources – the police station, local council, town hall, fire brigade, and so on.

Plugging the gaps

Find out which organizations and activities are not covered by the paper, develop convincing arguments for their inclusion and send those arguments to the editor with some samples. If you are taken on as a regular contributor (which could even lead to the offer of a staff job), not all your reports are going to be used, but you might be able to negotiate a retainer fee. Whatever payment you receive for this will not make you rich, but the experience and the connection are the things. Put yourself on the mailing lists of the organizations. Attend some meetings, and make yourself known to the chairmen, who will telephone you with the dates or results of any future ones. Having contributed news items to the paper on this basis for a while, you may find it easy to get space on the feature pages.

Let's note the feature ideas that can be developed out of local paper news items or articles. Take, for example, the articles in local papers in regional magazines that retell some local history: a location provides the context, and an anniversary the topical peg. An example might be:

Subject	*Idea*	*Title*	*Place/time peg*
The conjoined twins of Millingham	Their life story retold as a curiosity	Even death did not part them	To publish on the anniversary of the twins' death, in the village of Millingham, where they were born

You came across the strange story of Millingham twins, Mary and Peggy, by accident, while delving into local history to research another story. Suppose they lived from 1880 to 1930 and were joined at the hip throughout their lives. They became music-hall stars and toured Britain and the US. You write your article after going through the paper's cuttings on the twins (the last piece on them was written 20 years ago) and on aspects of life in the town when they were alive. You talk to a few people who remember them. The story throws up connections with London and other places where the twins spent many years, and you are able to rewrite the article for other publications.

Twins, in the course of your research, have become one of your subjects. After several months you have accumulated a bulky cuttings file, covering many aspects of twins, apart from conjoined or Siamese ones. Any event or controversy that concerns twins gives you the chance to produce an article that can be pegged to that event. You even have one or two articles in readiness for a topical peg to trigger them off. You have developed a specialism.

MAGAZINE MARKETS

There are about 6000 periodicals in the UK, so the young freelance may feel like a child in a sweet shop, dumbfounded by the possibilities. Consider as markets first the magazines you enjoy reading regularly, read more widely for ideas, and add to your target by market-studying others (as described in Chapter 2). Add to these the thousands of English-language publications in the US and many other parts of the world.

The fees paid by magazines for articles vary greatly, according to circulation, social-economic classification of readership, and the advertising rates charged. Freelances, on the whole, like to work towards the higher-paying markets, but it is not such a straightforward matter as it seems. It depends on your subject material, preferred level, and other factors. You may find that to write for a market that pays double your normal fee may require three times the number of hours with fewer articles accepted. Examples of fees are given in Chapter 6.

There is an almost infinite variety among magazines and periodicals. There are general interest magazines, trade magazines, technical magazines, hobby magazines, weekly reviews ('journals of opinion'), such as *The Economist, The Spectator* and *New Statesman and Society*; professional journals, numerous ethnic-minority magazines, house magazines, magazines for almost every conceivable subject, magazines for all social, religious, political and age groups.

The magazine article tends to go deeper and wider than a newspaper feature, since generally there is more space available, and more time. The subject of mental handicap might be covered in a local paper by a story about problems in a local home. A national paper might sum up with figures showing national prevalence of mental handicap, and might analyse the way the care-in-the-community policy is working, pegging the feature to yesterday's speech by the Health Minister in the House of Commons. A general interest magazine might follow up a fairly brief summary of the problem nationally with accounts of how several regional health authorities interpret the policy and put it in into effect, with descriptions of treatment in two or three examples of homes run by the authorities contrasted with the treatments outside them. A professional journal such as *Mental Handicap Research*, published by the British Institute of Mental Handicap, will publish an article under the heading 'Changes in life style for young adults with profound handicaps following discharge from hospital care into a 'second generation' housing project'.

Varying your style

You may quickly learn to work out what different magazines want in terms of content and style. Adapting your style, however, to different publications, readerships, formulas and personalities is not always easy. Writing for a very young age group, for example, is difficult for many writers.

For the specialized requirements of magazines, consider the comments made earlier about *Reader's Digest* and look at one or two current issues. There is something quite distinctive about the content and writing style. It is aimed at the broad middle-interest adult age band of readers.

Those million of readers, you imagine, feel safe and happy with the style. The content is also safe, and middle-of-the-road: health, optimism, happy family life, and patriotism shine through its pages. If you have some quirks, or strong minority views, you might not find it easy to adapt to *Reader's Digest* requirements.

The specialized requirements of a trade magazine are very different. If you have a fair amount of knowledge about say, computers, plus writing ability, you may find yourself in demand by computer magazines, because the combination is not too common. The technicians and programmers are not often writers. It is not necessary to be an expert in the field, though you may well have something to do with the industry and probably use a computer at work or at home. But you must have the skill to be able to translate what the technicians tell you into terms comprehensible to people who have to buy or use the equipment. It is especially important in this field to build up a reputation for accuracy: subeditors of trade and technical magazines don't have time to check all your facts. Once found to be sloppy or wrong, your connections could be at an end.

Even if you need to spend a month or two brushing up your trade/technical knowledge before aiming at specific targets, you might find the time fruitfully spent. You can find a niche on magazines and be hard to dislodge. Look for a trade magazine directory in a good reference library, and ask local tradesmen and professional people what magazines they subscribe to (and, while you're about it, what they think of them).

FREE PUBLICATION MARKETS

Despite some fall-out in 1995, there remains a strong market in free news-papers (called freesheets) and free magazines. By now you will have read several that are distributed in the areas where you live and work. Market-research those that seem good prospects. Try a good reference library for the Newspaper Society's *Reaching the Regions Regional Newspapers, Facts and Figures.*

Freesheets are local, so much that has been said about writing for local papers is relevant. Their dependence on advertising, however, gives them a different outlook. Some, like trade magazines, may have stories that are of national interest in reflecting the national scope of an industry or insti-tution. New-product pieces or other news items often have some connection with advertisers' businesses, although most local freesheets are trying to improve their news and feature content to compete with paid-for newspapers, often with a small staff, and offer a promising market for the local freelance.

Free magazines are born in the same way as any other magazine. A gap in the market is noticed, and someone plunges in with a free magazine to fill it. Targeting of the readership is careful so that adver-tisers are keen, and there are the minimum of distribution problems; this is the key to business success. *Ms London,* for example, led the way in London. With page after page of situations vacant, and a fair number offering pregnancy advice, it is aimed at 18-to-25-year-old secretaries, clerks and accountants pouring into London's railway and tube stations daily. The issues are handed out. Articles are on entertainments, fashion, pop stars, other celebrities, and on London life.

This was followed by *Girl about Town, 9 to 5,* and, among others, *Capital Magazine,* which was helped by an exclusive contract to be sold on railway platforms. British Airways' *Highlife,* and those who advertise in it, similarly recognized the advantage of such a captive audience passing through airports and travelling by plane. There are now many in-flight magazines. Each has its particular area of contents and reader-targeted style.

ASSIGNMENTS

1 Develop feature ideas from six news stories in a national broadsheet. Choose the shorter page 2 or page 3 stories rather than the big political ongoing stories on page 1. Include one or two 'nibs' (news in brief). Write a total of 200 words for each idea – and indicate target publications. Indicate length of proposed feature, summarize content and angle, interest to readership aimed at, and possible sources including at least one interview.

2 The lists of coming events published by local papers can suggest plenty of ideas other than a mere reporting of events. Here are a few from my local paper:

- Dead Poets' Society: evening of wine, candlelight and poetry
- Shiatsu (spiritual healing): free consultation (telephone number)
- Speakers Club: Improve and enjoy yourself, six basic lessons for £8
- Ferret racing
- Heritage Group meeting

Look for familiar events coming up in your area. Choose three, attend them, and write up three 500-word light-hearted features aimed at your local paper.

3 Write a how-to service article of 1000 words with the title 'To Complain is a Duty'. Use humour rather than bile but bring out the points forcefully. Use the following points and sources, but add to them:

- The English are not good at complaining. Why?
- Examples of services that need complaining about, but are not complained about often enough (for example, restaurant food, flat beer, faulty goods, overcharging, poor service, unfriendly sales assistants).
- Examples of companies that attach great importance to encouraging complaints and following them up.

Some sources

Advisory Committee on Telecommunications (Oftel)
Association of British Travel Agents (ABTA)
National Consumer Council
Office of Fair Trading. Publishers of a 60-page booklet. *A Buyer's Guide*
Office of Gas Supply (Ofgas)

4   Group assignment (can be done by two or three students). Each student writes a 200-word how-to piece on the same subject ('How to start a magazine' ... 'How to travel comfortably' are examples). Each piece is read out to the group; the reader is questioned about anything not clear. Notes are taken: after discussion it is decided which was the clearest exposition, and why.

5   Group assignment, a variation on 4, using different subjects ('How Government works' ... 'How to use a library'). Each piece is then exchanged for a fellow-student's and subbed down to 200 words. Several pairs then explain to the group:

  (a) How I decided on the reductions
  (b) The subbing I agree with, and the subbing I don't. A brief discussion by the whole group follows each pair's contribution.

6   Article for local paper or magazine: Describe a concert hall, theatre, entertainment complex, sports/recreation centre or similar. Give an idea of its place in the community, indicate its catchment area, describe the building and its amenities clearly, explain how it is administered and how it operates. Peg your piece to an anniversary (600 words).

6 GETTING ORGANIZED

Your goal in developing writing skills is to achieve the highest competence demanded by the markets you are submitting to. Without this you are unlikely to succeed in getting published, for selling articles is a competitive business. With this in mind, plus hard work and the adaptability to turn to different markets if need be, you have a good chance of success, whether writing full-time or part-time.

Even moderate success will bring you confidence. You will need confidence because even established writers receive rejection slips. Professional freelances find that as many as a quarter of submissions sent on spec might be rejected.

You must learn to recognize why a piece is being rejected. If the idea is worth rescuing, but the piece is rejected because it is the wrong market, try it on another market, perhaps with some improvements. By keeping records of your submissions and the results a picture will emerge of the kinds of work you are not succeeding with, and the kinds of work you are.

WORKING ROUTINE

Your family, or your household, might encourage you in writing but they are not a safe yardstick in measuring success. They might fail to understand why you write or what you write, and they can give few clues to how editors or readers may respond. The family can, however, affect work routines. A demanding family may make working outside the house easier: in a shed at the bottom of the garden, for example; in a rented office; or in a library. Some writers, in their early days, are glad to escape to bus or railway station waiting room or to cafés, or even park benches.

The constant fight for periods of quiet to work in can be debilitating. Yet some professional writers, including prolific novelists, can work guilt-free and effectively, surrounded by noisy children, nappies, a blaring television, and argumentative relatives. Such writers might be unnerved by quietness. There are likewise journalists who find it difficult to write unless there is electronic equipment bleeping, telephones ringing and people bustling past their desks.

Paradoxically, combating difficulties about space and time in which to work can provide the stimulus to do it, as any artist develops the skills to overcome the limitations of the medium worked in. What all this adds up to is that the space and time for working in must be carefully organized to fit in with your temperament and domestic situation.

Space and equipment

Try to establish a study in a quiet room, away from traffic, kitchen or television noises. Use a fairly large desk or table so that you can spread out papers. Your chair should be chosen for comfortable support rather than looks, and should encourage a straight rather than a hunched back. Another table or desk alongside, or at right angles, is useful to accommodate a word processor and printer or typewriter and other equipment.

A telephone and an answerphone are recommended. For telephone interviewing there are various useful devices – for example, a tapedeck that plugs into the telephone and can be used as a tape-recorder as well.

One or two filing cabinets will take your correspondence and cuttings library. Stationery should include A4 pads, lined and margined: yellow ones are easier on the eye. Typescript paper should be about 70 gsm for submissions, bank paper about 45 gsm for copies. Use headed notepaper, or if using a word processor, make a template for correspondence (don't have your name printed too big), business cards, address book for contacts, an accounts ledger, a book in which to record details of articles submitted, catalogue cards in boxes 6 in × 4 in for notes for layered projects and 5 in × 3 in for short notes/bibliographies/contacts.

Notepads, as mentioned, should be scattered round the house, including one on the bedside table. A reporter's notebook should be carried everywhere; ideas jotted down at random can be transferred to an ideas book or folder kept on your shelves and consulted regularly. The best ideas can be given room to develop in an A4 or foolscap folder, with a provisional title. In this folder cuttings, notes from books and other materials can be collected at your leisure until you feel the idea is ready to be tried on selected markets, or until you want to write an article speculatively.

Shelves will be needed for box files, folders, document wallets and essential reference books.

Many writers have now been won over to word processors, and new writers tend to start off with them. There are many sophisticated machines and software now, though you may be content with the simplest machine with its built-in memory. You may arrange to post disks or directly input articles via a modem to publications. If you travel frequently, you may find a laptop computer worth having. You can have, if your hardware is sophisticated enough, numerous writers' aids such as: spellchecks, dictionaries and thesauruses, databases for contacts etc., as well as layout formatting facilities. If you write about current affairs, you may want a satellite dish to pick up CNN's 24-hours news and Sky.

There is the temptation, however, to think that a word processor will solve your writing problems, a temptation to settle for what the machine does easily – re-ordering of passages, insertions and deletions – and to neglect to rewrite completely when that is what is needed. Although a wordprocessor will not turn a bad writer into a good one, however, it will speed up a good writer's production.

When a typewriter is used it should be tough, to stand up to a great deal of pounding. That means an office machine, not a light-weight one, whether manual, electric or electronic. It is worth looking at 'reconditioned' machines in typewriter repair shops because they are often very good value.

Consider buying or renting a photocopying machine once you have a reasonably large output since some word processing printers are slow. Technology brought us the fax (facsimile) machine. Again, you can use a fax service as required (see *Yellow Pages*) and some copyshops also provide the service. But Established freelances are increasingly turning to this method of delivery – exact copies of articles and photographs are sent to the publishing house's receiving machine in seconds. Consider also the advantages of a mobile telephone. Further information on new technology is given in Chapter 21.

ORGANIZING THE INFORMATION

A further word on article files, mentioned on page 36. Cuttings can be collected in envelopes, but it is worth pasting or stapling important ones on A4 sheets, with publication and date indicated, and occasionally comments of your own or ideas for possible use.

When an article is published, a copy of the final typescript and a tearsheet of the article can be filed in a document wallet with the research material in case, as time goes by, you want to update it or rewrite the material for another market.

Storing and retrieving

If you are young and aim to write prodigiously over the next twenty years or so, a more elaborate storage and retrieval system might be worth developing. Here is the system I use, which is equally suitable for the writing of articles or books.

I have two filing cabinets with suspended files in drawers containing correspondence and cuttings. I cut all Sunday papers and, on average, two or three magazines a week, and usually one paper a day. The cuttings are limited by the fact that they reflect my interests, the kinds of subject that I am likely to use for ideas for articles. When I am commissioned to do an article, or when I write one on spec, I normally find in my files sufficient cuttings to start me off. If I am trying to work out some ideas, I will then supplement my information with whatever I can quickly find out from other sources before working out an outline for the proposed piece.

Some of the material from my own cuttings files will go into folders started for articles, or into folders for each chapter of a book. The personal archive can be kept to manageable size by regularly weeding out cuttings that are out of date or have become uninteresting for one reason or another.

At such clearing out sessions I transfer those cuttings that have a more enduring value to a box file. Likewise, material used for articles published is put into box files if worth keeping. Lever-arch files can be used instead of box files with locksprings, but the advantage of the latter is that you do not need to punch holes in tear sheets and other materials.

Each box file can have a letter to identify it: for example, A, B, C. On the front of each file you could paste a sheet on which is listed the contents, or even keep a card-index system (5 in × 3 in) to locate the contents. This is useful where you are keeping a permanent record of material on subjects in which you are interested and which you are likely to write about. Here meaningful headings, subheadings and cross-references are necessary to make for easy retrieval.

A less elaborate system of storage/retrieval is using an envelope or folder for each aspect of a subject. Large document wallets/envelopes/ boxes allocated to a general subject heading such as, for example, Class, could have smaller envelopes or dividers on such aspects as accents, barriers, lower, middle, upper, politics, prep schools, public schools, rituals, Sloane rangers, snobbery, titles, upper, working, yuppies. Cross-references, perhaps to education, could be written on the envelopes or the dividers.

Beginners should experiment to see what sort of system works best for them. Useful though it is, it should not be so complicated that it takes too much time away from actual writing. If the nature of your writing means that you do not have a great deal of information gathering and storing to do, then the simplest filing system is best.

Keeping records

As a freelance, you need to keep a check on time spent on writing and money earned. Records are essential for tax purposes. I keep mine in a hard-backed exercise book spread over two pages, with titles of articles, and publications. At 4 April each year I draw a line across and total up the fees for the tax year.

A record of query letters sent out can be kept on 6 in × 4 in cards, one for each publication, with the name of editor/features editor/address/phone number at the top, and arranged alphabetically by publication in a box. Alternatively, a ring binder could be used, with an A4 sheet headed for each publication. You can see at a glance which ideas a publication has rejected and which it has accepted over the years. You can look through the record whenever you are thinking of sending a query or an article, if necessary turning up correspondence. Of course you can computerize this information.

Organizing the time

The main difference between an amateur and a professional writer is in attitudes to time. Amateurs tend to be dilettante, to be beguiled by the setting and the ancillary activities. They probably spend more time talking about writing, going to writing clubs, studying at night classes, or even teaching there, than in writing itself. They tend to be easily discouraged by rejection, are easily distracted, and tend to say, 'If only I had the time. . . .' They tend to push any writing they have in mind into an odd corner of the day when they have finished everything else. They tend to regard writing as a luxury activity.

The professional has to be single-minded. Writing is scheduled into the day *first*: other activities are slotted in round it. Freelance writers, like theatre performers, rarely admit they are too ill to work: the show must go on. They establish their own work patterns, refreshing their techniques perhaps by subscribing to a writing magazine (the American *Writer's Digest* is the best I have found for this purpose) and by careful reading of selected journalism.

You should decide how many hours you can devote to writing in a day, how many words you can expect to produce. When you fail for one reason or another to achieve that number, you should try to make them up later in the day or on the following day. If working to a carefully planned outline, decide how many words are required for each section, so that you have specific goals.

Beware the danger of time-consuming 'liquid' contacts and subjects. Try to sort out assignments on the telephone.

Writers who are not full-time freelances may choose to work early in the morning or late at night. I have three friends who regularly write books on their way to and from work. They have about 1½ to 2 hours' journey time each way, by train or coach. Other writers with full-time jobs spend a useful lunch hour or two in a library or at their desks with a sandwich.

Some writers, even full-time, find that a 3 or 4 hours' concentrated writing session a day is enough – that more than this will produce lower quality work, needing more rewriting. On the whole it is best to write when you are freshest.

However you do it, it is best to set aside blocks of time for writing daily, so that a rhythm is established.

Yet try not to concentrate too hard at your desk for too long periods, especially if you are using a word processor. The tension can make you hold your breath, and the brain functions badly when not getting enough oxygen. Get up occasionally and walk round the house, which gives you thinking time. Do some arm-stretching while still in your chair. Close your eyes for a minute or two occasionally. Circle your head slowly, drop your head on to your chest and raise it again several times. Do some deep breathing exercises. If you are at home all day, you may find it stimulating to get away from the desk altogether at times and do some manual work – anything for a change.

Reading into a subject can be done in an easy chair, or even in bed.

THE BUSINESS SIDE

As a writer aiming at sales you are a one-man (or woman) business, whether full- or part-time. You have capital invested in writing, and you constantly have to spend money on stationery, equipment, research materials, and other items. You are in business – yet many professional freelance writers fail to recognize that they are eligible for business advice or help.

Writers who aim to establish themselves as full-time businesses and who are unemployed should consider taking up the free training course provided by their local authorities. These are part of the business support schemes, mostly run by Training Enterprise Councils. The names of the schemes (and the duration of the courses) vary from place to place but they follow the same lines as the previous national one known as the Enterprise Allowance Scheme.

Typically, to be eligible you must have been unemployed for at least six weeks and perhaps several more. You will be shown among other things how to prepare a business plan, and if this is approved you may in some areas be granted a weekly allowance for the first six months of your business. Apply through your local job centre or unemployment office.

There are other possibilities of funding – co-operative development agencies, local-council funding bodies and private trusts. In the UK the small business section of the *Thomson Directory* for your area will give addresses, or details are available from your local Citizens Advice Bureau. Of course money does not rain down from these treasure chests, but it is worth exploring the possibilities.

If you are young and planning to live full-time off your writing, you would be advised to have six months' to a year's salary available to draw on during the first year of freelancing. It might take two years or more to build up to a reasonable income. Even when the year's total becomes adequate, cash flow can be a problem unless you keep plentiful reserves.

Freelances in the UK who get into financial difficulty can of course get Supplementary Benefit or, if you have dependants, Family Income Supplement. Expenses can be deducted from profits when calculating Supplementary Benefit, but the irregularity of freelance work and fees, and the difficulties of estimating exact numbers of hours spent on writing and research tasks, make the calculations complex. Family Income Supplement will be a small sum, but no deductions are made from the agreed amount for a year, after which you submit figures showing net profit and are reassessed for another year.

Trading as a company, which some years ago was a sensible arrangement for a freelance journalist, is at the time of writing complex and costly. There is the alternative of registering your one-man (or woman) business under the Business Names Act if you are using a trade name. If your business is on a commercial basis, you can carry losses forward and offset against profits – or against your wife's/husband's income. More advice on such matters is given in *Writers' and Artists' Yearbook*. See also the Miscellaneous section of the Bibliography (pages 412–14)

Claiming expenses

There is not an automatic allowance against income tax to freelance writers: all expense claims have to be supported, preferably with bills. If your situation is complex, use a tax accountant, whose fees can be claimed under expenses. Otherwise type and tick your items carefully. Try to justify everything. Annual expenses can include bank charges. If you work from home, you should be able to claim a quarter or more of the amounts paid for rates, rent, gas and electricity, cleaning, window-cleaning – even repairs. Add these to the other expenses incurred by your freelance work – the equipment, stationery, and so on and include them all in the Statement of Professional Income and Expenses that you send to the Inland Revenue with your tax return.

You must be meticulous about expenses. It is a fiddly, boring business to be constantly noting small items such as a few pencils or stamps; avoid it as far as possible therefore by buying such items in fairly large quantities. Small items can amount to a considerable sum over a year. It is also easy to forget the odd expenses that do not bring a bill with them, such as taxi fares and phone calls made outside your home. Carry a pad of petty cash expenses dockets or note them religiously in your pocket diary or reporter's notebook. Do not say. 'I'll remember that'. You will not!

You may claim expenses of entertaining overseas visitors. When entertaining others, claim from the company you got your assignment from, if you have previously come to some agreement about what is acceptable.

Your status as a freelance must be safeguarded. From time to time the Inland Revenue puts various kinds of jobs, traditionally regarded as self-employment under closer scrutiny. If you do most of your work for a sponsoring company, for example, and are given facilities at its offices, such as secretarial assistance, telex or phone, make sure you do at least 20 per cent of your business outside, or you may be regarded as drawn back into employee status. Then the various financial advantages of self-employed status, such as a sympathetic attitude towards expenses, will disappear. The expenses of the freelance are tax-deductible if shown to be 'wholly and necessarily incurred' and that extra word makes a lot of difference.

A word of warning. Some tenancy agreements and deeds of properties make it illegal to carry out business activities from your home address, and this should be checked.

Pensions

Do not neglect to think of pensions. Contribute to a self-employed scheme and take full advantage of the tax allowances. Payments are categorized as pre-tax expenditure. How much income qualifies for the allowance depends on your age. 1996 figures are: under 35, 17.5%; 36–45, 20%; 46–50, 25%; 51–55, 30%; 56–60, 35%; 61–74, 40%.

Operating methods

It is worth repeating here that you can make your aims in writing as lofty or philosophic as you like, but if you are not successfully operating a business, you will not get near to fulfilling them. You need to keep up a supply of ideas. You should be constantly looking for new markets to replace those that disappear, and diversifying to keep up with current trends and fashions. Follow up a successful sale immediately with new ideas.

You should take out a health insurance policy. Make sure help and advice on this and other matters is accessible by joining the National Union of Journalists or the Institute of Journalists.

To keep the commissions coming in, it is useful to advertise your services and look for freelance work being advertised. A place to advertise in is *Press Gazette*, on the Freelance Services page. In a typical issue freelances offer: astrology, general features. PR, books, industrial copy, crosswords, film reviews, and controversial and general features. The same issue contains a typical vacancy, under 'Freelances Wanted', for two freelances, one for trade and technical writing, the other for consumer features. 'A challenging prospect with a leading weekly which could lead to full-time employment', it concludes.

The first essentials in creating goodwill with editors are punctuality and accuracy. Journalism is about deadlines, and editors are, naturally enough, obsessive about them. Each issue has to be not just the best possible, but the best possible that can be put to press on publication day. At the same time it will be assumed that you have checked your facts and figures.

If your work is accepted, demand the proper price for it. This is at least the minimum rate that the publication should be paying for articles, which is based on the advertising rates per page. If you accept lower fees, you will be doing other freelances out of work.

Getting paid

Give firm estimates of expenses to be covered. Be certain the person commissioning the article has the authority to commission, and that the rights bought (first British, or world, etc.) are indicated.

If there is no definite publication date for ordered work, try to negotiate a date of payment – perhaps within a month of submission of the work. Send an invoice with your copy, or at least a few days afterwards.

A simple numbering method for invoices is to use your initials followed by the number of the month in which the invoice was posted and the last two digits of the year. You can then add your own number, the first invoice of the year carrying 1, and so on. The tenth 1995 invoice Tom Malpass sent was in August: TM 89510. National Union of Journalists' members can buy a personal rubber stamp having the NUJ logo to use on copy and invoices.

If you negotiate a regular contract to produce work, you should try to get an agreement for a severance payment – 'usually one month's expected earnings for every year of contributing' – and for some paid holiday time.

The magazine business is volatile: if the particular publishing firm is not well known, check on its payment record. If payment is not forthcoming for an article, try the accounts department. It may be possible, if you are a member, to get help from the NUJ organization at the firm, or from your own NUJ branch. As a last resort, there is the action of a summons at a small claims court.

Here is a final warning: in your dealings with editors, just as any other business person, do not give away all your ideas. Keep back vital contacts (phone numbers, for instance) as a safeguard before an article is written.

UNION MEMBERSHIP

Most journalists in the UK are members of the National Union of Journalists, and freelance membership in 1996 is about 6000. Before joining, you should ask for the Union's latest leaflet on conditions of membership. Members get protection, guidance and advice. The NUJ Rules of Conduct are listed in Appendix 2.

In general the NUJ promotes and defends the incomes and conditions of employment of journalists, and provides various benefits and legal assistance. It is the largest member of the International Federation of Journalists, which links journalists throughout the world.

Members of the NUJ Freelance Branch receive monthly the newspapers *The Journalist*, with its articles about trends and strikes, management problems and future prospects for the industry, and *Freelance*, a news sheet giving details about branch meetings, updated information on agreements about fees and conditions made with various publishing houses.

The annual NUJ *Freelance Guide* lists minimum rates for book royalties, radio and TV scripts, articles and news reporting, and casual work such as subbing. These are the rates agreed with various book publishers, newspapers, magazines, the BBC, the Association of Independent Radio Contractors (commercial radio) and Independent TV Contractors Association (commercial TV). Most freelance work is negotiated directly with editors, and once you are established, you should be obtaining rates higher than the minimum ones.

Some of the average minimum rates for 1000-word feature articles in 1996 are: national dailies £220; Sunday papers £260; colour supplements £300; special features (for example, centre spread), 50 per cent above.

Magazines' agreements are based on the cost of a page of advertising: Group A magazines charge over £5,000; and Groups B to E progressively less. Thus the 1000-word rate for Group A is around £300, negotiable, B £235 and C £200, D £145, E £120. If you sell world rights (English language) to a magazine, the fee should be doubled, and general world rights add 150 per cent. The booklet indicates that 50 per cent of the agreed is payable for work cancelled before it is begun. Delivered work which was commissioned must be paid for in full, whether it is used or not.

If you are a beginner in full-time freelancing, you may be happy to accept minimum rates and in general not to be too fussy about conditions. You are likely to produce a fair number of articles on spec, and if they are not used, you will not expect to be paid.

As you become established, your attitude to money will be more professional. It will become normal to negotiate above minimum rates.

The Institute of Journalists, a union describing itself as 'progressive and professional but not political', welcomes, as does the NUJ, journalists from all the media and from the public relations. Compare its literature with that of the NUJ before deciding which you should belong to.

Associate Membership of the Society of Authors is open to authors who have had articles published. The same annual subscription is paid, and the same benefits are enjoyed as by full members, who have had a full-length work published or have an established reputation in another medium. These benefits include advice on contacts and on legal matters generally.

The Writers' Guild of Great Britain (formerly the Screenwriters' Guild) gives similar protection and advice, and has national agreements with broadcasting and film industries on fee structures, etc. Particulars are given in the current *Writers' and Artists' Yearbook*. Addresses of these and other organizations writers may want to join are given in Appendix 5.

Literary agents (see the *Writers' and Artists' Yearbook*) are rarely interested in short scripts, unless from the clients whose full-length works they are handling. Dealing with articles is not likely to be profitable for them, though a series of articles for a high-paying market, or the serialization of a book, might be. On the whole, self-employed journalists need such a close knowledge of their potential markets that it is better for them to do their own marketing.

7 SHAPING TO THE PURPOSE

This chapter concentrates on structure – already discussed in Chapters 2 and 3 in a different context of much else. We consider the more detailed outlines that provide useful frameworks for longer or more complex articles. The best approach to this is first to analyse how published articles have been put together. Here are two in full, a backgrounder/argument from a broadsheet newspaper, and a profile from a magazine.

ANATOMY OF A BACKGROUNDER/ARGUMENT

'The great utility scandal' by Simon Jenkins, *The Times*, 8 February 1995. (Stand-first) 'Privatizations have enriched directors and ministers but enraged the public'.

1	(A) John Major has no feel for the public's outrage at the utility options scandal. His Government is chief shareholder in Britain's two electricity generating companies, National Power and
5	PowerGen. The bosses of these companies are believed to have accumulated shares and options worth up to £23 million, in utilities that are still 40 per cent in public ownership. The money is legally theirs. In every other sense it
10	belongs to the public. These share options discredit privatization. They ridicule legislation. They make a mockery of honest toil. They invite Labour to reintroduce supertax.

(B) When Gordon Brown speaks of the 'corporate
greed' of those running the water, gas and
electricity oligopolies he is speaking the
literal truth. This reaction is no criticism of
the effective management of the companies
concerned, or objection to the proper reward for risk
capitalism. To all these deities we may nowadays
pay obeisance. What enrages the public, the
utility users and energy workers facing the sack
is to see executives carting off barrowloads of
windfall loot.

(C) This money was fixed by non-executive
directors, usually in collusion with consultants.
They recommend salaries in line with other firms
of similar size. They do not consider the
'market price' of the executive concerned, let
alone put that price to the test. This is known
as the buddy system, and it is rotten. As for
the options windfall, it derives from the soaring
price of shares that were underpriced at the time
of privatization. The rise in share price
reflects an added value that should be returned
to past generations of taxpayers. Some of it is
now going that way through dividends to ordinary
shareholders. That millions of pounds should be
diverted into the bank accounts of the executives
is indefensible and plain wrong.

(D) I suppose the executives would claim they
are only milking a system set up for them by the
Thatcher Government. Successive Treasury
ministers should have spotted the time-bomb of
options when they underpriced their
privatizations. Afterwards they failed to use
their powers as minority or special shareholders
to call the boards to account. Both John Major
and Kenneth Clarke have recently declared that
the options deals are 'up to the shareholders'.
In the case of National Power and PowerGen, that
includes them. They have an obligation to see
that the boards are accountable.

(E) So far, merely so indolent. Now the picture
starts to darken. The Cabinet has not been
wholly idle in this matter. Yesterday it sent one

of its number, David Hunt, to the Nolan
committee. His purpose was to squash as
'outrageous' any ban on ministers going straight
60   from office on to the boards of, for instance,
privatized monopolies. He said that stricter
rules might 'discourage talented people from
accepting office'. He was supported yesterday by
a withering blast to *The Times* from Lord Young,
65   former Industry Minister and maestro of the
revolving door. Tighter rules, he implied, would
deprive industry of the immense talents possessed
by ex-ministers. They would also strip ministers
of that intuitive commercial sensibility that
70   comes from knowing a warm nest is ready outside
should disaster befall them. The Cabinet
Secretary, Sir Robin Butler, wheeled out the
'poor diddums' argument: that ministers get
sacked at short notice and must be allowed to
75   stagger to the nearest trough as quickly as
possible.

(F) Ministers and ex-ministers greet this
subject with a look of injured innocence.
Surely you are not suggesting, they protest, that
80   there is anything improper in jumping from a
ministry into a company that had received
ministry's recent favour? Lord Young
expostulated: 'The biggest insult is the
implication that moving from one to the other is
85   somehow corrupt, a job given as a reward for past
favours.' Anybody would think this was sleazy
Italy, not honest Britain. Yet the
qualifications of most former ministers for a
career in gas, electricity or water are not
90   instantly apparent. A reasonable person might
guess that they were to secure privileged
access to current ministers – or at least as an
example to current ministers that not rocking the
boat has its eventual reward. This is not an
95   insult, just a whisper of a suspicion of a hint.
We are all men of the world, Lord Young.

(G) Let us return to the utilities. Whatever
the Government says, these have not been truly
privatized. Ownership was sold by the Thatcher

100   Government to help to reduce taxes and free
       investment from Treasury control. There was
       little attempt to make the industries competitive
       or impose market disciplines. Regulators were
       put in to control prices and stop the companies
105   going mad or bankrupt. In his memories, Lord
       Lawson acknowledged that the Cabinet had
       concentrated 'too much on ownership and not
       enough on competition'.
           (H) The utilities boards claim that the rise in
110   their share values from which they are making so
       much money has been due to cost-cutting, not just
       to the original underpricing. But the cuts have
       been achieved largely by sacking staff whom these
       same executives featherbedded when in the public
115   sector. For the executives now to pay themselves
       large salaries for doing what they failed to do
       before privatization is bad enough. To claim
       capital gains which were formerly denied to
       taxpayers is truly rich. Ed Wallis of PowerGen
120   implies that he needs such incentives on top of
       his £350,000 pay – as Iain Vallance of BT
       explained last month that he needed his vast
       income because he worked so much harder than a
       junior hospital doctor. It is the sort of talk
125   that drives salaried employees screaming into
       Labour's arms.
           (I) Who is accountable for these goings on? The
       obvious answer is the electricity regulator,
       Professor Stephen Littlechild. He is reputedly a
130   tough customer. He wrote in the 1980s on the
       need to apply competitive disciplines to
       privatized utilities. He warned against
       regulations going native. But monopoly regulators
       do not 'go' native. They *are* native. They are
135   part of a framework in which the public is fast
       losing faith. Mr Littlechild last year told
       PowerGen and National Power to sell 10 per cent,
       or 6000 megawatts of their capacity to the
       private sector to provide competition. They have
140   not done so. Instead, electricity prices have
       risen and the option-hungry executives are able
       to offer new shareholders a 20 per cent rise in

dividend and presumably another boost in the
share price.

145   (J) Mr Littlechild has threatened to refer them
to the Monopolies Commission. They can laugh
in his face. The same happened last year with gas.
The commission recommended that British Gas be
properly privatized, that is, broken into

150   competitive units. Ministers took fright and
rejected this, overawed by a clever British Gas
advertisement about its soaring international
standing. As the 1980s showed, there is no touch
quite so soft as a British Government faced with

155   a utilities monopoly. As long as ministers are
timid, all the regulators in the world are paper
tigers.

(K) I am prompted to think that the Cabinet is
so unwise to the ways of business that it does

160   not see what is going on under its nose. As long
as utilities are not subject to market
disciplines, they are *de facto* in the public
sector. Their share price is determined by the
actions of legislators, regulators, commissions

165   and ministers. That is the case with water, gas
and electricity. That is why the share price of
these companies should not form the basis of any
options for directors, period.

(L) As for the revolving door, the Government's

170   complacency increases every suspicion that Mr
Hunt and Lord Young are seeking to deny. Of
course they are right that there needs to be more
interchange between politics and business. The
profession of politics is becoming ever narrower

175   in its career base. It would be good for
ministers to return to Government from business. It
would be equally refreshing if no Cabinet minister
took office without having held some
substantive job outside politics first. These

180   are matters for the Prime Minister to correct.

(M) What he cannot do is pretend that this goal
is promoted by former ministers taking jobs with
companies which they favoured in office. When a
defence minister goes to an arms contractor, an

185   energy minister to an electricity company or a

transport minister to a road haulier, the public
smells a rat. Ministers should find less suspect
jobs. They should get on their famous bikes. As
190   long as the rules remain lax, protests of
innocence will be greeted with a wink, a nod and
increasingly a jeer.

OUTLINE

Intro

Para A

- The public anger at the bosses' windfall from utility options and shares
  is justified.
- The utilities are still 40 per cent in public ownership.

Para B

- It is agreed that the managements are effective and that risk capitalism
  should be rewarded.
- But on this scale the rewards add up to greed.

Body

Para C

- Salaries have been arranged on the 'buddy system' (in line with companies of similar size) without considering 'market price' of executives.
- Options resulted from shares underpriced at privatization that have
  since soared.
- Taxpayers should have benefited, not merely bosses and shareholders.

Para D

- The Government should have anticipated the effects of the options
  system and made the boards accountable.

Para E

- Even worse, Government ministers walk straight out of office on to
  boards, including those of privatized monopolies.

- The justification has been that stricter rules would deprive industry of exceptional talent.
- Such talent deserves to face open doors when dismissal from Government comes: it can be unpredictable.

Para F

- Lord Young says it's natural to suggest such ex-ministers' moves are rewards for past favours.
- But mostly they don't have obvious qualifications for careers in the utilities.
- It's reasonable to suspect they have useful contacts with current ministers, or at least give them a message that favours will be rewarded.

Para G

- Thatcher sold the utilities to help reduce taxes and free investment from Treasury control.
- Regulators were established to control prices, but little was done to ensure competition.

Para H

- Bosses say their cost-cutting as well as underpricing caused rise in share prices.
- But the cost-cutting (mainly sacking) could have been done before privatization, and therefore the gains should have been the taxpayers'.
- Such talk as 'working harder than a junior hospital doctor' (Iain Valance of BT) turns salaried employees to Labour.

Para I

- Professor Stephen Littlechild, electricity regulator, has talked about competition, but it's all bark and no bite.
- He told PowerGen and National Power last year to sell 10,000 megawatts to the private sector and was ignored.
- Instead electricity prices have risen and shareholders have got the benefit.

Para J

- Threats of referral to the Monopolies Commission have been empty.
- Ministers rejected the commission's idea of dividing British Gas into competitive units.
- When ministers are timid, regulators are powerless.

Ending

Para K

- The Cabinet seems blind to the fact that without competition utilities are *de facto* in the public sector.
- Their share price depends on actions by government and regulators, etc.
- It should not therefore be the basis of options for directors.

Para L

- Moves between ministers and business would be good, but of a more meaningful kind.
- They could return to government from business, and business experience could be a requirement for a cabinet post.
- The Prime Minister should arrange for such interchange.

Para M

- Such benefits are not produced by ex-ministers moving to companies favoured in office (for example, a defence minister moving on to an arms contractor).
- Such moves will remain suspicious while the rules are not made stricter: there are other jobs to go to.

At the time of writing the rules have been made stricter:

ANALYSIS

Type and length   Backgrounder/argument. 1420 words.

Thesis/point of view   This is neatly summarized in the intro: 'These share options . . . toil.' The attack on the system widens to include over-generous salaries to utilities' bosses and the move of ex-ministers into these and other lucrative business posts.

Purpose   To expose the injustice in the rewards gained by the public utilities' bosses, to raise consciousness of this injustice generally, and to bring about a change in attitude and policies in business and government.

The great utility scandal

Privatisations have enriched directors and ministers but enraged the public

Simon Jenkins

John Major has no feel for the public's outrage at the utility options scandal. His Government is chief shareholder in Britain's two electricity generating companies, National Power and PowerGen. The bosses of these companies are believed to have accumulated shares and options worth up to £23 million, in utilities that are still 40 per cent in public ownership. The money is legally theirs. In every other sense it belongs to the public. These share options discredit privatisation. They ridicule regulation. They make a mockery of honest toil. They invite Labour to reintroduce supertax.

When Gordon Brown speaks of the "corporate greed" of those running the water, gas and electricity oligopolies he is speaking the literal truth. This reaction is no criticism of the effective management of the companies concerned, or with the proper reward to risk capitalism. To all these deities we may nowadays pay obeisance. What enrages the public, the utility users and energy workers facing the sack is to see executives carting off barrowloads of windfall loot.

This money was fixed by non-executive directors, usually in collusion with consultants. They recommend salaries in line with other firms of similar size. They do not consider the "market price" of the executive concerned, let alone put that price to the test. This is known as the buddy system, and it is rotten. As for the options windfall, it derives from the soaring price of shares that were underpriced at the time of privatisation. The rise in share price reflects an added value that should be returned to past generations of taxpayers. Some of it is now going that way through dividends to ordinary shareholders. That millions of pounds should be diverted into the bank accounts of the executives is indefensible and plain wrong.

I suppose the executives would claim they are only milking a system set up for them by the Thatcher Government. Successive Treasury ministers should have spotted the time-bomb of options when they underpriced their privatisations. Afterwards they failed to use their powers as minority or special shareholders to call the boards to account. Both John Major and Kenneth Clarke have recently declared that the options deals are "up to the shareholders." In the case of National Power and PowerGen, that includes them. They have an obligation to see

that the boards are accountable. So far, merely so indolent. Now the picture starts to darken. The Cabinet has not been wholly idle in this matter. Yesterday it sent one of its number, David Hunt, to the Nolan committee. His purpose was to squash as "outrageous" any ban on ministers going straight from office onto the boards of, for instance, privatised monopolies. He said that stricter rules might "discourage talented people from accepting office". He was supported yesterday by a withering blast to *The Times* from Lord Young, former Industry Minister and maestro of the revolving door.

Tighter rules, he implied, would deprive industry of the immense talents possessed by ex-ministers. They would also strip ministers of that intuitive commercial sensibility that comes from knowing a warm nest is ready outside should disaster befall them. The Cabinet Secretary, Sir Robin Butler, wheeled out the "poor diddums" argument: that ministers get sacked at short notice and must be allowed to stagger to the nearest trough as quickly as possible.

Ministers and ex-ministers greet this subject with a look of injured innocence. Surely you are not suggesting, they protest, that there is anything improper in jumping from a ministry into a company that had received that ministry's recent favour? Lord Young expostulated: "The biggest insult is the implication that moving from one to the other is somehow corrupt, a job given as a reward for past favours." Anybody would think this was sleazy Italy, not honest Britain. Yet the qualifications of most former ministers for a career in gas, electricity or water are not instantly apparent. A reasonable person might guess that they are there to secure privileged access to current ministers — or at least as an example to current ministers that not rocking the boat has its eventual reward. This is not an insult, just a whisper of a suspicion of a hint. We are all men of the world, Lord Young.

Let us return to the utilities. Whatever the government says, these have not been truly privatised. Ownership was sold by the Thatcher Government to help to reduce taxes and free investment from Treasury control. There was little attempt to make the industries competitive or impose market disciplines. Regulators were put in to control prices and stop the companies going mad or bankrupt. In his memoirs, Lord Lawson acknowledged that the Cabinet had concentrated "too much on ownership and not enough on competition".

The utilities boards claim that the rise in their share values from which they are making so much money has been due to cost-cutting, not just to the original under-pricing. But the cuts have been achieved largely by sacking staff whom these same executives featherbedded when in the public sector. For the executives now to pay themselves large salaries for doing what they failed to do before privatisation is bad enough. To claim capital gains which were formerly denied to taxpayers is truly rich. Ed Wallis of PowerGen implies that he needs such incentives on top of his £350,000 pay — as Iain Vallance of BT explained last month that he needed his vast income because he worked so much harder than a junior hospital doctor. It is the sort of talk that drives salaried employees screaming into Labour's arms.

Who is accountable for these goings on? The obvious answer is the electricity regulator, Professor Stephen Littlechild. He is reputedly a tough customer. He wrote in the 1980s on the need to apply competitive disciplines to privatised utilities. He warned against regulators going native. But monopoly regulators do not "go" native. They *are* native. They are part of a framework in which the people is fast losing faith. Mr Littlechild last year told PowerGen and National Power to sell or 10 per cent, or 6,000 megawatts of their capacity to the private sector to provide competition. They have not

done so. Instead, electricity prices have risen and the option-hungry executives are able to offer new shareholders a 20 per cent rise in dividend and presumably another boost in the share price.

Mr Littlechild has threatened to refer them to the Monopolies Commission. They can laugh in his face. The same happened last year with gas. The commission recommended that British Gas be properly privatised, that it be broken into competitive units. Ministers took fright and rejected this, overawed by a clever British Gas advertisement about its soaring international standing. As the 1980s showed, there is no touch quite so soft as a British government faced with a utilities monopoly. As long as ministers are timid, all the regulators in the world are paper tigers.

I am tempted to think that the Cabinet is so unwise to the ways of business that is does not see, what is going on under its nose. As long as utilities are not subject to market disciplines, they are *de facto* in the public sector. Their share price is determined by the actions of legislators, regulators, commissions and ministers. That is the case with water, gas and electricity. That is why the share price of these companies should not form the basis of any options for directors, period.

As for the revolving door, the Government's complacency increases every suspicion that Mr Hunt and Lord Young are seeking to deny. Of course they are right that there needs to be more interchange between politics and business. The profession of politics is becoming ever narrower in its career base. It would be good for ministers to return to government from business. It would be equally refreshing if no Cabinet minister took office without having held some substantive job outside politics first. These are matters for the Prime Minister to correct.

What he cannot do is pretend that this goal is promoted by former ministers taking jobs with companies which they favoured in office. When a defence minister goes to an arms contractor, an energy minister to an electricity company or a transport minister to a road haulier, the public smells a rat. Ministers should find less suspect jobs. They should get on their famous bikes. As long as the rules remain lax, protests of innocence will be greeted with a wink, a nod and increasingly a jeer.

Figure 7.1   A backgrounder in *The Times*

Links/transitions

His Government (2)
of *these* companies (5)
in every *other* sense (9)
These share options (10)
of *those* running (15)
This reaction (17)

To all *these* deities (20)
What enrages (21)
This money (25)
As for the options (31/2)
Some of *it* (36)
Afterwards (46)
So far (54)
Now the picture (54)
Yesterday it sent (56)
His purpose (58)
Tighter rules (66)
This subject (77/8)
Yet the qualifications (87)
guess that *they* were *there* (91)
Whatever the Government says (97/8)
But the cuts (112)
now to pay *themselves* (115)
It is the sort of talk (124)
Who ...? (127)
The obvious *answer* (127/8)
But monopoly regulators (133)
Mr Littlechild *last year* (147)
Instead (140)
to refer them (145)
The same happened *last year* (147)
rejected *this* (151)
As the 1980s showed (153)
prompted to think (158)
As long as utilities (161)
Their share price (163)
That is why (166)
As for the revolving door (169)
Of course (171/2)
ever *narrower* (174)
When a defence minister ... (183/4)
Less suspect jobs (187/8)
As long as the rules (189)

Treatment

The article is given the main pundit spot in the paper, centred on the page with other personal columns around it and in the largest type. A relentless logic, with much repetition of key terms (directors, bosses, ministers, options) and links (many appearances of 'this', 'these', etc.). Serious impassioned argument, with careful presentation of the evidence.

Style

Its calm arguing, with short sentences hitting the points firmly home, and the occasional ringing, memorable phrase, notably lines 10–12.
Fog index (see page 22).

Average length of sentences (LAS): 20 words
Number of long words (NLW): 19
$0.4 \times (20 + 19 = 39) = 15.6$

The subject-matter is fairly complex, and Simon Jenkins helps the reader by ensuring that the language is as clear and simple as possible.

Slant

Reflects the general outrage that has cut across party lines, but will certainly have given *Times* readers in government and in the city soul-searching to do.

Tone

Quiet, unfussily persuasive, with a highly moral undertone, the odd flare of passion, an urbane sincerity and irony keeping preachiness at bay.

Further comment

Unity is provided by the author's clear conviction throughout. Where he stands in relation to the claims of supporters of the utilities' bosses, to the claims of those bosses themselves, and to the claims of the regulators in thus never in doubt. He gives room to those viewpoints, so that readers can judge.

Note the teamwork of title, standfirst, intro and ending. The standfirst at once turns the subject flagged by the title into a thesis; the intro explains wherein the injustice lies (with a couple of striking figures), and grabs the attention with angry, stirring words; the ending echoes the indictment of the intro in other words ('they ridicule legislation' becomes 'as long as the rules remain lax'), much evidence of that laxity having now been given.

Abstract argument is made concrete by the examples of the behaviour over the past year or so of key figures (David Hunt and Lord Young, who are directly quoted, and of regulator Professor Stephen Littlechild), the emptiness of whose threats when it comes to practice are made clear.

In terms of language, what holds the article together is plenty of links and repetition of key terms. There is much dependence on pronouns as links (note how often 'this' is used), but the concentration on the thrust of the argument makes that dependence fairly unobtrusive. Key terms are repeated with subtle changes into synonyms ('bosses', 'directors', 'management', 'executives' . . .).

Note that a sentence outline suggested itself, to reflect the pattern of a well-structured argument. Compare this with the outline for the next piece analysed: a mix of sentences and brief phrases.

ANATOMY OF A PROFILE

'Let your fingers do the nicking', by Val Hennessy (no relation). Published in *You*, magazine of the *Mail on Sunday,* June 1986

(A) Old thieves never die. They simple steal
away. Take veteran pickpocket, 76-year-old
Rose Jones who, last spring, shuffled out of
a London court on her walking-frame and announced:
5 'I've had a good run for my money. Maybe it's
time to call it a day, though. Having to use
a walking-frame means I'm not as quick on my feet
as I used to be, which is a bit of a drawback in
my line of business'.
10 (B) The offence, on this occasion, had taken
place when Rose went 'on the binge' in Harrods
during the January sales and lifted three purses.
They had yielded £50 and Rose was just hobbling
gleefully into Harvey Nichols to pinch a handbag
15 or two for luck when the law caught up with her.
Faster than you can say 'electronic eye', two
store detectives were propelling Rose, and her
walking-frame, into the back room for a search.
(C) She drew herself up to her full 4 ft 5 in and
20 was about to let forth a volley of verbal but,
suddenly, her heart wasn't in it. She sensed
that the game was up. Harrods had been the
final fling in a 'line of business' that has
resulted in 30 convictions for pickpocketing,
25 dating back to 1926, and a total of 20 years in
prison. This time Rose got off with a
conditional discharge and strict instructions to

co-operate with her social worker.

30 (D) Nicknamed 'Yellow Pages' because she lets
her fingers do the walking. Rose Jones is living
affirmation of the adage that crime doesn't pay.
Her home is a damp bed-sit in a grimy East London
basement where filthy wallpaper has peeled from
the plasterwork, exposing mildew and cracks.

35 (E) There is a sink, a cooker, several cats and dogs
and a large colour television which flickers non-
stop to keep Rose company. There is no heating.
During the winter freeze she wrapped herself up in
a couple of malodorous blankets and cuddled up with

40 the dogs. 'Picking pockets is a mug's game, ducks',
says this Dickensian old lag, casting a disparaging
eye over her few pathetic possessions. 'I've got
nothing to show for it: I'd have done better to
stick to the straight and narrow'.

45 (F) Not that she's complaining. Far from it.
At least she's not in 'the nick'. Indeed,
she's planning to steer clear of 'the nick'
for what's left of her life. God willing.
'Trouble is, I've been a bit naughty since

50 Harrods. I got carried away at a supermarket
in Ilford. But they were very nice to me in
court. My grand-daughter went with me. I got
so scared in the dock that I went stone deaf, and
couldn't hear one solitary word they were saying.

55 I was afraid they'd put me in a mental home and I
burst into tears. Then I heard them say, 'Tell
your granny we're not sending her away, we're
sending her back home". I was so relieved I
promised never to be naughty again.'

60 (G) Mind you, says Rose, prison isn't the terrible
punishment it once was. Women's prisons have
changed considerably in the 60 years since she
took her first fearful steps through the clanging
door. She can remember Holloway when it resembled

65 a castle. 'In the old days you felt like you were
going into something straight out of *Grimm's Fairy
Tales*, it was so grand ... it's been modernized
outside now. All the cells have their own flush
toilets and there's even a swimming-pool, so I've

70 been informed by a girl who's just come out'.

(H) During twenty years of being detained at Her Majesty's pleasure. Rose has rubbed shoulders with suffragettes, drug-dealers, prostitutes and notorious villainesses. 'What used to stick in my gizzard

75 were those dreadful days when someone was hung. I was deeply affected when Ruth Ellis was hung – she was a very nice girl, always glad to give you a cigarette even though we weren't supposed to talk to her. She had beautiful flowers sent to

80 her every day. Armfuls of them.

(I) 'The first time I met her I'd booked to see the doctor in C wing and this sad-looking girl was sitting in the waiting room. I said "What are you looking so miserable for? Just thank God you're

85 not Ruth Ellis". She said " I am Ruth Ellis". I was ever so embarrassed and said, "Oh, I'm sorry, dear," and she just laughed and said, "That's all right. I've no regrets, I'd do it again".
'I was also in prison when Myra Hindley first

90 arrived. One of the girls had read about the Moors murders in the newspaper and when she recognized Myra on her way to the toilets she went for her like a she-devil. Myra tried to mix, but if the officers let their attention wander, the

95 other girls used to throw her out on her face'.

(J) Rose reckons that an instinct for self-preservation launched her into a life of crime. 'I used to cry a lot as a little girl. My mother died when I was four, you see, and I went for a

100 short time to a foster mother who was a wonderful, motherly woman. If I'd been left with her I'd never have turned out like I did. But the First World War broke out, my father married again and was called up. I was left with my stepmother,

105 Eva, who hated me.

(K) 'She was the original wicked stepmother. Although I was too young to understand what was going on. I realize now that she was a prostitute. She'd bring her soldier boys back to our house and

110 make me stay out in the street till past midnight. She never fed me. If it wasn't for the neighbours I'd have starved. One lady used to give me sheep's head broth and dumplings which doesn't sound very

nice but it was so delicious that I can still feel
115 it warming me. It was the only hot food I ever got.
     (L) 'A boy called Charlie Dobbs taught me how to
steal. It was always food I took at first – from
the market. It took me about six weeks to get the
knack of "dipping". I never used to open the
120 purses: I'd give them to Charlie who shared the
money out. The first thing I bought, other than
food, was a little dolly from Woolworth's with
clothes that came on and off and eyes that went
to sleep. I was six. I went independent after
125 that.'
     (M) At the age of 11 Rose began working as a drudge
in large houses. At the same age, she recalls,
she became a victim of child abuse. 'These men
would say "If you tell anyone, Rose, you'll be
130 locked up". I was terrified, I didn't know what
was going on. She was always hungry, always
cold.'
     (N) At one of the houses where she blacked grates
and lugged coal she remembers waiting until 'the
135 nobs' had departed for their afternoon stroll and
sneaking upstairs to take a look through their
luggage. She slipped a lipstick into her pocket
and took a five pound note which she hid under a
staircarpet. 'I swore black and blue I hadn't
140 taken it, and I didn't find a chance to slip the
note out from under the carpet for six weeks.
     (O) She was the first sent to Borstal at the age of
17. All the money she's ever stolen has been
given away, or frittered on inconsequential items.
145 She hates the idea of shoplifting. Pockets and bags
are her weakness. 'My biggest ever haul was £700.
I was meeting a boyfriend in the Tottenham Court
Road and I handed my haul over to him. Never saw
it again. We went to the dogs and lost every
150 penny.
     (P) 'Nowadays there's no point picking posh
pockets. They don't often carry money, just
stupid plastic cards. I've never attempted to
find out how to use them. I bumped into another
155 old friend several years back who said, "How's
business, Rose?" and I moaned, "I've only got these

two cheque-books and stupid cards. Give us a
fiver and you can have the blinkin' things". Well,
he got £5,000 worth of stuff using them before he
160 was picked up. But me, I stick to pockets and
bags.'

(Q) Speaking of which, even as we are conversing
in her gloomy room she suddenly remarks: 'Look,
ducks, I wish you'd do your bag up, right? You
165 don't want to put temptation in my way, do you?
These days I often go up to ladies in shops and
say "Watch your purse, dear". Of course they
don't realize that *I'm* the one who's likely to take
it. I'm not proud of being light-fingered, believe
170 me. No one else in my family is dishonest. My
daughter, who is very good to me, can't understand
me at all. She never reproaches me when I get
caught. She pulls a face and says "Oh Mummy, not
again".'

175 (R) Rose refused to divulge the tricks of her
trade. 'Practice makes perfect,' she says
evasively. 'You mustn't let the grass grow
under your feet.'

(S) After marriage when she was 34, Rose began
180 banking her money. 'I put away my pickings for
my daughter. My Bill, you see, was a good
father but no good at all as a husband. He never
gave me a penny for house-keeping. He didn't
even collect me when I came out of hospital with
185 our new baby. I stood in the snow waiting for
a bus. I had to go to my job next day which was
charring in a pub. During one of my spells
inside he dragged our daughter down to the bank
and made her draw out all the savings. I went
190 mad, didn't I, when I found out. He died while
I was in prison.'

(T) At this point, I suggest that we might venture
out for some lunch. Rose claps her hands, grabs
her coat – 'Posh isn't it, for 10p at a jumble' –
195 and expresses a preference for The Golden Egg.
Without her walking-frame she seems almost
sprightly, toddling along the street. Her small
stature makes her seem disconcertingly near pocket
level.

200   (U) At The Golden Egg we sit down and I discreetly
fasten my bag and place it out of Rose's reach.
'You needn't worry, dear,' remarks Rose, looking
hurt. 'I never steal from friends, never would,
never have.' She orders a cup of tea and a
205   scampi platter. No dessert, because of her
diabetes. 'Oooh, I love scampi' she grins.
          (V) 'Talk about living it up!
'I tell you this, ducks, in spite of all my
tribulations I do try to keep cheerful. I've got
210   a bad heart, bronchitis, kidney trouble and an
arthritic hip that plays up in the cold. I have to
take so many pills I rattle like a tin of marbles,
but I'm not letting it get me down. As for luck,
I've never had any.
215   (W) I've never won a prize in my life and don't
talk to me about raffles, bingo, football pools
or racing. Never mind, hey? As from today I'm
turning over a new leaf. There's a lot to be
said for going straight. I'm a good girl now.'
220   (X) She pauses. She taps her nose with a callused
thumb. And adds, with a roguish twinkle,
'Specially when the old fingers aren't as nimble as
they used to be.'

OUTLINE

Intro

Paras A–C

- 76-year-old Rose Jones said last spring after her court case: 'Maybe it's time to call it a day' (thesis/theme).
- Had stolen three purses at Harrods' January sales and handbags at Harvey Nichols: caught.
- 30 convictions since 1926, 20 years in prison.
- conditionally discharged (anecdotes).

Body

Paraas D–F: Current situation

- living in a slum: description
- few possessions

- 'crime doesn't pay'
- another court case: discharged.

Paras G–I: Recollections of prison (anecdotes)

- Holloway was a grim castle: now modernized
- she met the notorious, including Myra Hindley and Ruth Ellis, the last woman hanged in Britain
- the misery of hanging days.

Paras J–N: Recollections of childhood (anecdotes)

- mother died at 4
- wicked stepmother: prostitute who neglected her, gave her no food
- taught by boy to steal: started with food from market
- at 11, servant in large houses – sexually abused she stole money in the house.

Paras Q–R: Skill with pockets and bags (anecdotes)

- Borstal at 17
- developed skill with pockets and bags
- defrauded by boyfriend
- has honest, unreproaching daughter
- doesn't reveal tricks of the trade.

Para S: Marriage (anecdotes)

- marriage at 34
- banked money
- husband neglectful: drew out her savings
- husband died while she was in prison.

Ending

Paras T–X: A cheerful lunch

- scampi at the Golden Egg
- she tells of the various ailments
- but: 'I'm not letting it get me down'
- '. . . a good girl now . . . 'specially when the old fingers aren't so nimble' (thesis).

ANALYSIS

Type and length

Profile/interview Social problems/human interest. 1800 words.

Purpose To show how social problems beget social problems, with the story of a typical petty criminal. Slightly (or perhaps more than slightly) inspirational, describing an apparent nobody who cheerfully survives much adversity.

Premise/point of view Complete sympathy with the protagonist is supplied.

Thesis It is suggested that Rose's petty crimes are explained by the poverty and ill-treatment she has suffered; but no explicit judgements or solutions are proffered.

Links/transitions

Line numbers in brackets

> *On this occasion* (10)
> *This* time (26)
> *Not that* she's complaining (45)
> *But* they were very nice (51)
> *Then* I heard them say (56)
> *Mind* you (60)
> *The first time* I met her (81)
> *I was also* in prison when (89)
> *She was the original* (106)
> *At the age of 11* (126)
> *At the same age* (127)
> *These* men (128)
> At *one* of the houses (133)
> *She was first* (142)
> *Nowadays* (151)
> *Speaking of which* (162)
> *At this point* (192)

Treatment

Interview, with much quoting. The subject mainly tells her own story. Many anecdotes, revealing a cheerful, resilient character. Some background facts, descriptions and figures.

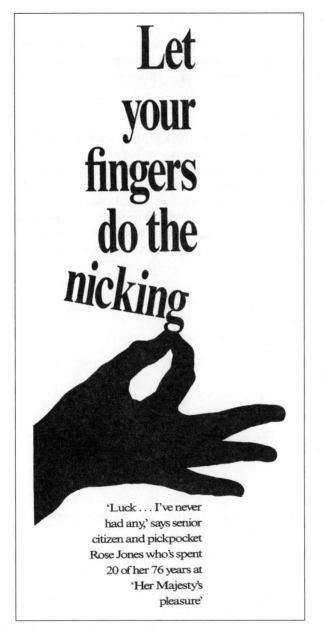

Figure 7.2   A profile in *You Magazine*

Illustration (printed with article)

Photograph by Tony Latham. Shows Rose sitting on a sofa in her bleak bed-sitting room, sparsely furnished. Caption: 'Rose Jones at home ... living proof that crime doesn't pay – "it's a mug's game, ducks".'

Style

Rose's prose, which is the major part of the article, has no doubt been a little straightened out, with sentences reshaped; but it obviously gives a very good idea of how she actually speaks. The author's present tense/tone of voice occasionally obtruding (for example, 'I suggest that we might venture out for some lunch') serves as useful punctuation/pause/variety. Conversely, the author integrated the transitions from Rose speaking to author's summarizing by leaving typical Rose-isms in indirect speech (for example, 'and was about to let loose a volley of verbal ...' and 'Mind you, says Rose ...').

Fog index.

Average length of sentences: 15 words
Number of long words: 3
$0.4 \times (15 + 3 = 18) = 7.2$ (very easy)

Because Rose is allowed to do almost all the talking the difficulty level is unusually low.

Slant

A piece relying on colour and character rather than ideas, preconceptions: realistic.

Tone

Unsentimental but sympathetic author: lets the character dictate the tone. Avoids being patronizing in this way.

Further comment

The article is only notionally topical, pegged to recent court appearances. Notice that, again, the intro contains topical peg, figures. Interest in aroused by a striking example of her exploits – Harrods – and just enough description of her (4 feet 5 inches with a walking frame) and taste of her personality to whet the appetite.

Notice the teamwork of title, intro and ending. 'Nicking' in the title, as well as giving the flavour of the whole piece, is echoed immediately by 'thieves' in the first line.. Rose's thoughts of retiring, connected with the hindrance of her walking-frame, in the intro are echoed in the ending, with a slightly different twist: it's 'the old fingers' this time she mentions as the hindrance. The title is also echoed in line 29 – 'Nicknamed "Yellow Pages" because she lets her fingers do the walking' [as the advert says]. In fact the point of the title is not fully understood till then, and such echoes/associations help to cement the piece.

Much of a person's life story can be boring, and even when it isn't an attempt to tell it chronologically, or account for it chronologically, very often is. Notice now the author selects the vivid episodes of Rose's life that will interest readers, taking them out of chronological sequence (for example, the references to the famous murderess), and reveal Rose's character (the doll, the naivety about credit cards). The first four paragraphs have to cover much background information. By slipping in the odd quote from Rose here and there, the author establishes the flavour of the whole, and by ending the information section with a longish quote ('Picking pockets is a mug's game . . .'), she links Rose's current situation with her past career.

The rest of the body of the article is mainly anecdotal, quoting Rose, but it is varied by the occasional bit of summarizing. It is possible to do an article of this kind almost entirely from quotes, but normally information to fill in the gaps of the story needs to be summarized. Avoid wasting space on material that turns the reader off. There may be three times as much talk on the tape or in the notebook as is needed; this should make it easy to find good copy in the course of editing. Rose, for example, may have spent some time describing how a friend's feet hurt just like hers do. This would have been irrelevant.

Readers' interest order

To put the pattern, easily seen in my outline, in closer focus, we can say that the order follows readers' interest rather than chronology. We have to get to know Rose well enough before wanting to know about her childhood. Since the striking facts about Rose in the intro are 76 years of age and 20 years in prison, the reader is likely to be asking what were the most interesting or traumatic aspects of life in prison? That having been described, the reader is likely to ask when it all started. The author, in fact, is so sure that this question is in the reader's mind that she answers it without bothering to make a link (96–7): 'Rose reckons . . . crime'.

When a necessary sequence does not suggest itself and there are various possibilities, a good way of shaping the outline is to put down the questions the reader is going to ask. Then either work out in which order the reader is likely to ask the question before you start, or get into the article and ask yourself at each stage what the reader would want to know next.

Whether or not the author of this kind of article has interesting information/quotes/anecdotes/atmosphere in the material that has been gathered has much to do with whether the questions at the interview were good, and whether the rapport with the subject was good. Did the questions bring interesting and revealing answers? Dull questions can produce dull answers, no matter how potentially interesting the subject of the interview is.

Careful preparation plus sharpness of reaction help. It is not as easy as the finished item might suggest either to get interesting answers or to shape them into an article. Notice how space and emphasis are given in the writing when Rose has been interesting and revealing.

OUTLINING TECHNIQUES

From this analysis of the structures of printed articles, let's tackle structure from the other end again. Chapter 3 discussed the simplest techniques. Let's explore further ways of structuring your own material.

If there are many aspects to be covered, you may want to list them first as they come into your head, and then give them a logical writing order by numbering them. Take the London homeless again, as the aspects come to mind (the numbers were added later).

The London homeless: what are the answers?

6 Economics background
2 Definition
2 Current legal situation (Act) – see Pritchard, *Penguin Guide to the Law*
4 Vagrancy – alcoholism, drug addiction
4 Unemployment – failure to pay rent or mortgage
3 Scarcity of accommodation for rental
4 Government's housing policy
4 Council-house sales – fewer to rent – fewer being built
6 Argument that it would be cheaper to build new council houses – needs examining
1 Anecdote/figures illustrating extent of current situation
4 Private housing – high rents
4 Break-up of families
4 Divorce
4 Increase of single people

5 Homelessness leading to crime, and other problems
8 Councils' points system – is it fair?
5 The road to Skid Row
8 Attempted solutions – the work of housing associations, pressure groups (SHAC, CHAR, Shelter).
8 Evidence of 'rip-offs' by landlords of B & Bs
8 Temporary solutions: bed-and-breakfast hotels
7 The political arguments (council-house sales, etc.) summed up
7 Political arguments – how far are homeless to blame?
9 Conclusion
9 Suggestions for future? For example, vetting of B & Bs and landlord.

The points were put down first, the numbers inserted later. From these points you evolve the following numbered order:

1 Intro: Thesis: efforts to solve problem inadequate without changes in housing policy.
2 Definition and law (Act of 1967).
3 Current situation and its causes.
4 Kinds of homelessness – specific causes.
5 The road to Skid Row.
6 Economic background.
7 Political arguments over (a) council-houses, sales, etc., (b) questions of responsibility – how fair are homeless to blame?
8 Attempted solutions: credits and debits.
9 Conclusion: summarizing evidence, to support thesis.

When the subject is complex or many-angled you could summarize each point in a few sentences or in note form. At drafting stage you could build on the above outline by working in figures and quotes from your source material. This building-up process is particularly effective when you find it difficult to get started, or you don't feel ready to write the complex article of 1500 words or more straight off.

QUERY PLUS OUTLINE

You might want to send such an outline together with a query letter, or you might want to combine them. Here is an example of how you could arrange such a letter in seven brief paragraphs after briefly introducing yourself:

1 *Suggested intro.* 'There are . . . homeless people in London. They shuffle through the streets despondent and weary. They keep moving so that

they do not have to be moved on. At night they creep under railway arches, motorway flyovers, building complexes. Homeless used to be considered synonymous with alcoholics, misfits, feeble-minded, feckless, useless, old and resigned. Many of them still are, but an increasing number are young, only very recently unemployed and desperate to find a way back. They probably could if they did not feel their family or society had rejected them.'

2 *Summary* of proposed article, with *thesis*. There are short-term answers – housing policy – but one long-term answer must be restoration of a sense of community to the homeless. (Compare treatment of mentally ill and mentally handicapped: shoving them into lodgings without adequate services is not enough.)

3 *Background.* How is homelessness defined? (Act of 1967). Who/what is responsible? – Government, central and local; housing policy: fragmentations of social structures? Are there many people who don't deserve the title of 'homeless'? Would building new houses be cheaper than local authorities paying for bed and breakfast accommodation (comparative figures)?

4 *Past attempts* to improve the situation. Views on housing policy (quote an economist and the pressure group Shelter). Views on improvement of hostel conditions: quote pressure group CHAR (Campaign for the Homeless and Rootless).

5 *The task ahead.* A chain of social problems: unemployment, break-up of family, no fixed abode, alcoholism, etc. One or two quotes from some homeless people. What is there to learn from how other countries deal with the problem.

6 *The ending.* Sketch in conclusions.

7 Indicate *what kind of article is intended* – anecdotal, analytical, action-provoking. Also the length and treatment.

Give *qualifications for writing such a piece,* including articles on similar subjects, if any, and any *special contacts*, though not in detail.

With the letter could go – if it is the first contact with the publication – a brief and relevant cv and samples of published articles.

If you have to send queries out several times, make sure you update such matters as the state of the law and government policy each time.

SCHEMATIC OUTLINES

'Bigger' ideas – that is, features running to thousands of words – need a more complex plan, perhaps a schematic outline. Many publications in the USA and Canada (see *Writers' Market* and *The Writer's Handbook*) are keen on outlines being submitted before they will consider commissioning articles. If the outline you have decided to submit is to be a page or more, it is better, when approaching an editor, to enclose it separately, with a short query letter.

Schematic outlines may be prepared in phrases or sentences. Here is a model of a detailed schematic outline in phrases that contains in its different sections all the patterns described above, and which could be simplified for a less complex article (in fact any single section could be developed into an article), or extended for a longer project such as a pamphlet or book:

Detailed schematic outline: alcoholism

Possible titles

> Never say drink, never say die
> One man's beer, another man's poison
> When another little drink does a great deal of harm
> VINO: Another four-letter word
> ALCOHOLISM: A disease without a cure?

Subject

The increase of alcoholism, especially among the young, is reaching alarming proportions.

Thesis

The attempts to stem the tide are looking desperate: there is a lack of attention to positive measures:

Outline

1 *Introduction: The nature of the problem.*
   (a) Anecdote illustrating a particular case, suggesting its tragedy in human terms and its repercussions socially and economically.
   (b) Figures illustrating the extent of the problem, for example, the cost of unwanted effects of alcoholism in Britain is over £2 billion p.a. Some contrast with other countries (figures).
   (c) Thesis stated – with the emphasis on increase – and the aim of this article.
2 *Historical background.*
   (a) Brief history to indicate it is a perennial problem.
   (b) Understanding of alcoholism as a disease rather than merely the result of character defects.

(c) Definition (*Directory of Psychology* and *Psychiatry Encyclopaedia*) – distinguished from 'heavy drinking'. Misconceptions removed.

3   *Causes*

(a) Physical, including heredity (Interview at King's College, London).

(b) Psychological:
  (i)   Family background.
  (ii) Upbringing.
  (iii) Environmental.
  (iv) Personal feelings of inadequacy, etc.
  (v)   Suicidal tendencies.

(c) Social:
  (i)   The 'this is a crazy world' syndrome – fear of nuclear war/lack of meaning to life/lack of religious and moral sanctions.
  (ii) The current recession/unemployment.
  (iii) Occupational:
    – lack of interesting employment.
    – stressful employment (for example, politicians, actors/entertainers, journalists: various articles).
  (iv) Climate of tolerance:
    – little restriction of advertising (why?).
    – little emphasis on dangers of drinking by parents and other authoritarian figures (why?).
    – the pub ritual of 'rounds', etc.
    – the GPs too overworked to tackle the problem?
    – public attitudes to overdrinking probably too tolerant.

4   *Economic aspects.*

(a) Production and sale of alcoholic drinks is big business (figures).

(b) Increase of sale outlets, for example, supermarkets, together with increase in 'secret drinkers' among housewives (figures).

(c) Important source of revenue for government (figures).

(d) Are adequate government funds given to research/medical facilities/voluntary organizations?

(e) 'Oiling the wheels':
    – expense-account lunches.
    – 'freebies' for journalists, etc. from PR departments.

(f) Lack of production/inefficiency at work.

(g) The cost – in treatment in rehabilitation, in drink-and-drive accidents (how many of these related to alcoholism?).

5   *Effects on the alcoholic.*

(a) Damage to brain (interview with Institute of Psychiatry).

(b) Sexual impotence.

(c) Other physical effects – heart disease, cirrhosis (liver disease), etc.

(d) Psychological effects.

(e) Behaviour (research at Reuters University, New York), shows that alcoholic hallucinations are indistinguishable from schizophrenia).

(f) Drink Watchers organization: 6 units of alcohol (for example, 3 pints of beer daily is enough: more is dangerous).

(g) But varied degrees of effect on different constitutions.

6 *Effects on others: on foetuses.*

(a) Damage to unborn children of women drinking during pregnancy (US research increasingly shows).

(b) Foetal alcoholic syndrome: oriental look, very small for age, very backward (the extreme cases). No 'safe amount' for pregnant women.

(c) Cf with smoking: pregnant women warned not to smoke, less urgent warnings given to drinkers (why?).

7 *Effects of others: psychological/social.*

(a) Breakdowns of marriage/damage to children's upbringing/other relationships.

(b) Inefficiency at work: lack of production (see also economic).

8 *Treatments.*

(a) Available in the National Health Service.

(b) Alcoholics Anonymous methods (legwork and interview).

(c) The work of other organizations: for example, The Carter Foundation (listed in DBA).

(d) Research and treatment at Edinburgh Unit (interview following up recent media coverage). Two methods of cure – controlled drinking and abstinence. Records of progress (based on TV programme).

(e) Economic problems – refer to 4(d).

(f) Sum up on present successes/failures in treatment. (Background from Edward Griffith, *The Treatment of the Drinking Problem*, Easett, 1982, and more recent books.)

9 *Other research.*

(a) In Edinburgh.

(b) In London.

   (i) Centre for Alcoholic Studies.

   (ii) National Institute of Alcohol Abuse and Alcoholism (tests showing even moderate drinking impairs memory and judgement: recent articles and broadcast coverage).

(c) At Ruttgers University, New York.

10 *Prevention.*

(a) Publicity of organizations aiming at prevention.

(b) Some success, for example, some restrictions on advertising on TV.

(c) Interviews with (or literature from) advertising organizations – Institute of Practitioners in Advertising (IPA), Advertising Standards Authority (ASA).

11   *The failure to act.*

(a) The power of the brewers – big business.

(b) Important source of revenue for government.

(c) Traditions die hard (of more rigid attitudes to other drugs).

(d) The currently renewed interest may help, but what effects so far?

12   *Conclusion.*

(a) The changes in attitude required:

   (i)   Governmental.

   (ii) Official/employers, etc.

   (iii) Of doctors.

   (iv) Public attitudes – need for more awareness of dangers of drink to be publicized.

   (v)   Positive values of good health:

   – living without stress.

   – 'organic' living.

   – living with purpose.

(b) The National Health Council's work.

(c) Work of other organizations.

(d) Further action required.

If you have prepared an outline of this kind for your own use only, then the names of those to be interviewed might conveniently be inserted, but to repeat a point already made – not necessarily if you are submitting it with a query letter, in case the commission is not forthcoming. Names of good contacts are hard won and should be treasured.

The number of words likely in each part of a long article may be estimated in a schematic outline, so that you don't get carried away. But it can only be a rough guide. In the course of writing the material is constantly being weighed in the balance and will fall into its own pattern of length within the total number of words permitted.

LINK WORDS

You can also insert link words into an outline. If you are laying out a sentence outline, which works especially well for logically developed arguments, linking matter suggests itself. Suppose, for example, you are devoting a 1000-word article to the aspect covered by section 6 of the alcoholism example above. A sentence outline would look something like this (the links are in italics):

Title: 'Warning: Alcohol Can Seriously Endanger Your Foetus'

1 There is much damage to unborn children of women drinking in pregnancy.
2 *This fact* has been evidenced by increasingly convincing research findings.
3 *Yet* it is only the extreme cases that attract attention of many health authorities.
4 *This is because* the damage is not very visible unless extreme.
5 *Then* such phrases as 'foetal alcoholic syndrome' are used for babies that are well below average size, or very noticeably backward.
6 *In fact* there is no 'safe amount' of alcohol for pregnant women.
7 *In spite of this,* the warnings given to drinkers among pregnant women are much less urgent than those given to the smokers.
8 *Some of the questions that arise* are the following. Is the government's slowness connected with the revenue from sales of alcoholic drink? How greatly is the government swayed by the brewing interests? By the fact that drinking is a 'socially acceptable' activity?
9 *And so* to the conclusions.

The link words are serviceable in that at the outline stage they help keep your thread of argument running, and you are less likely to produce non-sequiturs or faulty reasoning than with a phrase-outline.

ASSIGNMENTS

1 Analyse any published article of 1000 words in the same way as is done to the two models in this chapter.

2 After a tutor or colleague has cut out the paragraphs of a published article, and pasted them on sheets in the wrong order, re-order them.

8 MAKING THE ARTICLE COHERENT

This chapter concentrates on the teamwork that keeps an article together: the association of title, intro, body and ending; the key terms that keep the theme resounding; the links that keep the whole coherent. A fine title, a fascinating intro, an anecdote or two that illuminate an analysis, quotes that bring people to life on the page, endings that satisfy or stir emotions or thoughts – perhaps one or two of these things will linger in the mind, so that the article, provided it has something to say as well, is remembered some time after it is read.

THE TITLE

Even though your title might be changed by the subeditor, it still helps to have a good provisional title. It can provide the controlling idea, it can help give direction, and it helps editors to find a better one. Start with a label if nothing better presents itself, and you should be able to improve it once the article takes shape.

In arriving at a title or headline that satisfies you and helps to sell the piece, it might help to experiment with key words in the article. Try putting them in different combinations; you will find other, associated, words will suggest themselves. Take the feature article 'Let your fingers do the nicking', reproduced in Chapter 7. What other possibilities for titles are there? Some key words/phrases are 'steal', 'pickpocketing', 'pinch', 'handbags', 'crime', 'prison', 'dipping', 'independent', 'purse', 'dishonest', 'tricks of the trade', 'pickings', 'never steal from friends', 'turning over a new leaf', 'going straight', 'old fingers', and 'not so nimble'. You could come up with 'It was a fair nick, Your Lordship', 'The Old Lag who doesn't steal from friends', 'Pickpocket Rose – Keeping Cheerful and Going Straight'.

If you work for a publication as staff writer or subeditor, or write for one regularly, your feeling for titles that are appropriate for it will be finely tuned. Freelances should study the headlines of any publication aimed at, and the intros and endings as well, for guides.

Leaving aside market considerations, a title must first of all grab the reader's attention. It should charm, amuse, intrigue, or buttonhole the reader in some way. My suggestion is that the first title of each pair below, in italics, would send readers leafing through the publication to find something more interesting, whereas the second, in capitals, would make them pause and at least look at the intro.

1 *The Superiority in Russian Tanks*
   WHY RUSSIAN TANKS ARE BETTER
   Avoid long abstract words such as 'superiority'. Simple, direct words work best on the whole.

2 *Useful Information About Mortgages*
   WHAT YOU SHOULD KNOW ABOUT MORTGAGES
   'Wh' phrases get straight to the point, and it is easy to give them a smooth rhythm. The first title is awkward and doesn't stick in the mind.

3 *The Lack of Good Manners Today*
   WHERE ARE ALL THE MANNERS GONE?
   The tone of the first is too serious and preachy. The second is helped by its allusion to an old song, 'Where are all the flowers gone?' An example of how a question can sometimes make a good title – though of course any publication would ration their use.

4 *The Problem of Infant Nightmares*
   WHEN BABY WAKES UP SCREAMING
   Simply to say that there is a problem or a difficulty or a tragedy or a confrontation is heavy and irritating. It is better to indicate a point of view/plan of action, or translate the problem into human terms.

5 *Studying a Star*
   STAR STUDIED
   A typical example of *The Guardian* punning in the second, on an article about a new Hollywood star. Alliteration is a common ploy in titles.

6 *Does Repression Make Men Strong?*
   THE TEARS THAT STRONG MEN WEEP
   The direct approach saves the reader being landed with a puzzle head-line, and on having to try to find an answer to it.

7 *The Unemployed Who Are Happy As They Are*
   THE RISK OF FINDING A JOB
   The irony of the second gives it more resonance.

8   *How Deaf People Help Each Other*
    THE DEAF LEADING THE DEAF
    Repetition of a key word can be effective, especially if there is allusion, as here to a well known phrase.
9   *The Men who Went to the Moon*
    MOON STRUCK
    The second title was used for a *Texas Monthly* article by Al Reinert about the early astronauts and the effects of their experience: a neat pun in two words.
10 *What You Can Learn From Misfortune*
    THE LUCK OF THE LOSERS
    Contrast, as well as alliteration, helps here.

SUBTITLES

Some titles, while grabbing attention, need explaining immediately, and leaving this to the intro might create a gulf. 'The Risk of Finding a Job' could do with an explanation along the lines of 'The long-term unemployed can become work-shy. There is much talk about counselling and retraining. But the services available are far from adequate'.

Such explanations can be referred to as subtitles, though in newspaper production language they are called 'standfirsts', since they stand first above the intro.

'Thank You for the Music', an article in *You,* is backed up by 'It may look like fun and games, but to these handicapped children music therapy is the key to a more active life.' The article opens with an 11-year-old boy learning to play the cymbals, and your curiosity takes you to the end of the first paragraph, where you learn that he has cerebral palsy, epilepsy, and severe learning difficulties.

A subtitle, or standfirst, adds greatly to the effect of the title of a *Telegraph Sunday Magazine* article, 'A Tale of Two Cities'. The allusion to Dickens's novel about the French Revolution is intriguing, since the strapline, 'Money Matters', which is used above the headline, warns that it is an article about the financial world of the city of London. But the subtitle quickly brings out the force of the allusion and sharpens our curiosity: 'The City wants us to believe that the aristocracy has gone and that the meritocracy is here. But, as Charles Jennings reports, a subtle class war is still being fought inside the banks and brokers' firms'.

Significant questions from the article in special type, inserted between title and intro make effective subtitles.

THE INTRO

The main purposes of the intro are to continue the work of the title by holding the readers' attention, to give them a taster of what is to come and persuade them to continue reading, and to convey to the reader what the article is about. It establishes the writer's angle, as in the two specimen articles in Chapter 7. It can contain the writer's thesis, or the thesis may be delayed until the main body.

The intro should above all convince the editor that the article is worth reading through. To put this in another way, there should be a promise implicit in the intro that the article is worth offering to the readers aimed at: that it contains something of value or interest for them.

When you are writing your intro, think of cold, bored readers, perhaps giving the article only half their attention. How do you break through? How do you *talk* to someone about something you believe should be of interest to them? Intros, which in American practice are called 'leads', entice the reader into the article, teasing them to guess what is coming, deliberately awakening their curiosity.

With many newspaper articles it's the news pages that attract readers. After taking the news peg in, they will decide whether or not they find the subject to be of sufficient interest for them to read on.

By contrast, a magazine article tends to be written specifically to appeal to the tastes and expectations of the readers. A greater effort is made to speak directly to the readers, to indicate the article's value to them, considering the type of magazine it is.

If argument or exposition is the article's purpose, the intro may have to clear away any common misconceptions about the subject. It may need to express authoritative definitions of such things as alcoholism or mental handicap, to make sure that reader and writer are starting from the same premise; or it may start with what is familiar about the subject and build a bridge from that to the unfamiliar aspects that are to be the heart of the article.

Here are samples of several techniques.

Use of striking facts/figures

An interview with Denis Healey by Steve Platt in *New Statesman and Society* (16 June 1995) starts with dates that remind us of the significant parts of Healey's career, followed by a paragraph in which he produces figures that reflect the enormity of the problem to be discussed:

> It's eight years since Denis Healey left the shadow cabinet and three since he quit the House of Commons, but he's still as well-briefed as ever he was

as Labour's defence secretary (1964–70), chancellor (1974–79), or shadow foreign secretary (1980–87).

There are eighty-two armed conflicts occurring in the world today,' he says at the start of our interview, 'of which seventy-nine are taking place inside national frontiers.' This, he declares, is *the* big international security issue of today; and one of the big challenges of the international community is how it responds to problems within nation states for which most of the causes and potential solutions lie outside the control of national governments.

Anecdote

It was 5 a.m. when the fuse-box in the cupboard under the stairs in the Doherty family's house in Ilford, Essex, developed a fault. As it grew molten red, it set fire to plastic rubbish bags near by: acrid, poisonous fumes started to pour out towards the sleeping family.

Then suddenly a small, saucer-shaped object fixed to the ceiling of the landing above the cupboard emitted a piercing, 85-decibel shriek. It woke Olive Doherty, who shook her husband Jimmy. Together they grabbed their three daughters from their bedrooms and rushed down the stairs before the smoke and fumes, already spreading through the house, could engulf them.

So begins an article on 'Home Fire-Alarms', *Readers Digest.*

Atmosphere/description

She was small, bare-headed and wearing a brown poncho. Full face, it was the warmth of her eyes that you noticed; but in profile, the strong nose and lips gave her a decisive look. She walked slowly on the path above the mine. She was very pregnant. She said little. There was nothing in her manner to suggest that for several years Domitila Barrios has been a household name in her own country, Bolivia, and was now one of the best-known women leaders in South America (*The Guardian*).

Here the readers are made familiar with a situation. They should feel it must be as you have described it, that you are not straining for effect. Then you can take them from the familiar to the unfamiliar without protest.

You do not give too much at once in this kind of intro. You supply significant but tantalizing glimpses, promising more, doling out so much at a time to keep the reader with you.

Exposition/argument by analogy

> Ironically, the animal whose name is a synonym for everything contemptible in the human vocabulary is in many essential respects the most similar of all animals to man. The basis of this similarity is the fact that men and rats are the only omnivorous animals.

In this sample the analogy quickly builds a bridge from the familiar fact to the unfamiliar that will be the basis for the article.

Significant scene

Describing a scene or situation that symbolizes what the article is all about can make a good start. Here's the intro to a special feature 'Prophets of Da City' by Gavin Hills in *The Face,* the Cape Town rappers by that name being one voice of the continuing struggle for justice:

> Black man holds hand with white man as they march in protest down the street. People are chanting demanding justice. The protesters are reaching fever pitch, they start to *toyi-toyi* – make the traditional South African march of protest. The left leg lifts up, holds crook for a few seconds, then scuttles downwards while the right leg shoots up and repeats the action. A white man at the front of the march is hopelessly out of rhythm. The only thing that is swaying in time is his large pot belly, which flaps over his belt with each lumbering step. The scene is pretty ridiculous and the police are looking nervous. The police are looking very nervous, actually, because the protesters are the police. Low pay and bad working condition have sent them out into the streets they used to terrorize. This is the New South Africa, topsy-turvy land, where now even the police have the right to be shat on.

Significant quote

> 'You can be a 50-year-old anything except a 50-year-old actress,' Faye Dunaway said recently with some bitterness. In truth, ageism is a form of discrimination that does not only affect thespians and doesn't only affect 50-year-olds. Age discrimination in employment can affect everyone (*Ms London*).

A quote from a celebrity or a profound literary quote will get you into a serious subject but as with the above, deal briskly with its relevance to your theme. The *Ms London* article was about 1500 words.

For a longer article the quote may be intriguing as well as significant:

> 'It's a big story,' said the tobacco-chiselled drawl on the other end of the line. 'It's too big. It gets deeper and deeper. It grows and grabs people from all walks of life. It destroys history. It's the biggest story of the century.'

'I'm sitting by the phone in an apartment high above the fume-shrouded sprawl of Metro Manila, thinking: if this is the century's biggest story, then why has most of humanity never heard of it? The reason is almost too obvious. It is gold. Absurdly huge amounts of gold: enough to pay off national debts or buy Manhattan, enough to feed the world or destroy every economy in it, and more than enough to make men lie, cheat, steal, kill – and keep very quiet while they're doing it'.

Thus the intro of 'In Search of Yamashita's Gold' by Andrew Marshall (*Esquire*, June 1995). General Tomoyuki was executed after the Second World War for plundering South East Asia. In the Philippines the search goes on for his vast booty.

In a long article it's a long time before we discover that a Texas businessman, one of the searchers, was the owner of the voice and find out what he meant by 'it destroys history'.

Vivid, surprising, or shocking statement

There were four ways in which airmen used to come into Ward 3 of the Queen Victoria Hospital in East Grinstead during the war: boiled, mashed, fried and roast. 'Just like potatoes, really', said one of them (a *Mail on Sunday* article on plastic surgery).

Question

This can make an immediate contact with the reader; but be certain it does not irritate by being outside his/her experience, or cryptic, or silly, or of insufficient relevance to the rest of the article.

'What is the first thing you do when you arrive home after a holiday?' is an example of the routine approach.

'Curious, isn't it, that a man who hurtles through African swamps, Amazonian jungles and Arctic lakes for his living, should be "quite honestly, jittery", at having to navigate the one-way system of Reading, Berkshire?' is a question that is not really a question at all but a way of keeping you alert until a fair amount of information has been got across.

Digging behind the news

'One extraordinary effect of the recent storms, which so far seems to have attracted very little attention, is . . .' suggests you are more alert than other commentators so the rest of the article should prove it.

Celebrity peg

Dudley Moore has one in Beverly Hills. Peter de Savary, rich financier and yachtsman, has put one in his Paris club. And Flora Freeman keeps doves in hers, in a back garden near Peterborough.

All are players in British Telecom's new game, which is now perplexing buyers at an auction near you. It is the great telephone box challenge – the challenge being to find a use for an old phone box once you have hired a crane and got it home.

From an article by Tim Rayment in *The Sunday Times* on new uses for telephone boxes.

Humour

She is known as the best bottom in London, And since this year Bottoms Are Back, she is currently in great demand.

Irony

Some marriages may be made in heaven, but some are made by mail order.

Personal experience

Personally, I never cheat the Customs when returning to this country: not necessarily because I am any more honest than the next man; it's simply that, if you declare what you're bringing in, the Customs officer is generally so delighted with your frankness he minimizes your duty. And anyway, I don't like breaking the law. . . .

Cryptic/intriguing/dramatic

There is an unreported war in progress in Ireland. The island is in danger of being covered to a depth of ten feet by a vicious Turkish importation which eats everything in its path, swallows up whole oak trees, houses and entire colonies of the native inhabitants, and is insidiously and maliciously spread by Japanese immigrants. A vigorous counterattack has been mounted and armies of sturdy Irishmen and their valiant women are to be seen by the alert, North and South, conducting their lonely and arduous campaign as intrepidly they creep through the undergrowth in valley and hillside, up mountains and across the treacherous surface of boglands, their weapons ever at the ready, eyes peeled for the enemy (a gardening example, from Stan Gebler Davies's 'Day of the Rhododendrons' in *You*).

A 3000-word article 'Does he just love being in control?' on Cedric Brown, Chief Executive of British Gas by John Sweeney in *Life* (*The Observer Magazine*) succeeds in attracting our attention with the three qualities. At the same time Sweeney subtly summarizes some needed historical background:

> Pay attention. This story about greed and the backlash against greed; about eating sheep's eyes and boardroom intrigue; about slant drilling and class snobbery; about the cunning of PR men and the fecklessness of press and parliament. And about the custodianship of our nation's natural treasure. It starts 300 million years ago in the Carboniferous era when a bubbling gloop of primeval pondlife died somewhere west of Morecambe. The pond-life metamorphosed to gooey slime, then turned to rock, discharging a noxious fizz in the process. The fizz fizzled out into the atmosphere in most places. but just here, under a slab of rock the fizz couldn't bubble through, five trillion cubic feet of natural gas lay trapped down the ages.
>
> Dinosaurs, seas, woolly mammoths, ice ages, Celts, Romans, Vikings, Irishmen and Britons came and went, hither and yon. Then, 3000 million years after the pond-life passed on, came Cedric Brown.

Contrast

> On that June day nearly 50 years ago it was an inferno of chattering machine guns, whistling shells and exploding bombs. Many men were killed – in the boats, in the water, on the sand.
>
> Today little French children play happily on the beach. . . .

So begins a piece about the coast of Normandy.

Teaser–bridge–text

A common technique in intros is to make a pattern that has three elements, each in itself arousing curiosity. Look again at the intro to the phone box article. This is a typical example of pattern-making, which has been described as teaser–bridge–text. The first paragraph has a puzzle effect even though the title has already indicated that the subject is phone boxes. The bridge paragraph begins to get specific, but doesn't reveal completely what this stuff about phone boxes is really all about. What exactly is British Telecom doing ... ? Paragraph three finally begins hitting you with some figures. Notice how the emphasis changes if you put the three paragraphs in a different order: teaser–text–bridge, text–teaser–bridge, text–bridge–teaser. . . .

The intro is most important. If you find your ending would make a far better intro than the one you've got, transfer it and rewrite the ending.

THE ENDING

A good ending can be elusive to the writer, like a good beginning. It may be found hiding in another part of the article. It is usually easy to pull out with just a little changing of links. Just as a better intro may sometimes be found by removing the first paragraph or two of the first draft, so a better ending may be found by removing the last paragraph or two.

The ending should make you feel that the writer has achieved his or her purpose, whatever that was. It should be fulfilling, satisfying in some way, though some daily newspaper articles might tend to raise questions and worries that stem from the raw edges of news, while magazine articles within their slower process are more likely to answer questions and suggest solutions.

The writer's aim may have been to create an atmosphere, paint a portrait, to leave the reader something to think about, perhaps to move emotionally, as some magazine articles do; or it may have been to argue a case in order to persuade or provoke to action, as many newspaper articles do. The nature of the aim, and some kind of evidence that the aim has been followed through, should be present in the ending. Make sure your ending grows out of the context of the article, and does not appear to be stitched on as an afterthought.

Here are a few types of endings.

Summing up (often with restatement of thesis)

An article in *Choice*, about The Queen's Messengers, who are all over 50, and who deliver state papers to diplomats abroad:

> Such demanding work and hours ... engenders considerable loyalty and comradeship. No wonder the Colonel can point out with pride that ... the Corps has never had a traitor in its ranks in over 300 years and never knowingly failed in its duty.

Unexpected fact/'sting in the tail'

> Most of Marilyn's will is still the subject of long-drawn-out court proceedings in America. But in 1983, out of the blue, a London children's psychiatric hospital inherited one quarter of her estate (*Weekend)*.

Final quote

An article on the looting of ancient sites, using metal detectors, quoting an archaeologist:

'Our main hope,' says Gregory, 'is for landowners and police to take a greater interest in what goes on at local sites. It is vital if we are to prevent the small minority who detect illegally from inflicting damage out of all proportion to their number' (*Reader's Digest*).

Provocation to action – or at least to think again

An article advising parents how to deal with children's nightmares and night terrors:

> If your child suffers three or more night terrors a week over a period of months, you should ask your doctor for advice (*Living*).

Looking at future prospects or possibilities

A travel article on Yemen:

> One of Yemen's latest projects, now almost complete, is the building of a new dam here at Ma'rib, to restore the region's former glory *Country Life*).

The South African feature (see page 139) ends on an appropriately rapping let's-learn-the-lesson, note:

> Mandela's in charge now. He's there because international sanctions and boycotts crippled the evil apartheid regime into submission. Now the struggle continues. It's the struggle for justice. It's a struggle we should support. We should press for land rights, investment and justice for those for whom apartheid was a robber, a killer. . . . We should also look at ourselves, our own politics. Think of the Eighties, think of the lame arguments given by the sanction busters. Think of the heroic achievement of Mandela and think of the empty words of Thatcher, Tebbit, et al. Think of Mike Gatting and his cricket tour, of Status Quo and Queen playing Sun City. Think of the guilty that remain unpunished. Know in your heart that the struggle continues. We have few heroes left in this world, let's support the ones we've got.

Make sure you have arrived at as clear a view of things as you can get on the basis of your material. You may have too many points/aspects circling round each other that need to be pulled together in the ending.

Avoid preaching or begging the question. Make sure you have given the evidence throughout the article by which readers can come to their own conclusions as well as follow yours. A proposition can fail if you are seen to have imposed rather than argued your case from evidence.

THE BODY

The principles of unity, coherence and proper emphasis apply as much to feature articles as to any other form of writing.

Unity means that the main theme is threaded through the article and anything not relevant to it is removed. *Coherence* means that all material used is shown to be related to the theme, especially by skilful linking techniques and orderly arrangement, so that full understanding is achieved by the reader. *Emphasis* means that the main purpose of the article is identifiable throughout, so that it is distinguished from subsidiary themes.

Each paragraph should be shown to have a distinct contribution to make to the main theme, and the order chosen for paragraphs should bring out the relative importance of their topics. Similarly, within each paragraph there is normally a topic sentence, round which the others play a supportive role, like satellites. In intros the topic sentence is often last, or late in the paragraph, as in *The Guardian* intro (page 138); but it may be first if you want to stun the reader with the force of a point of view or with shock. In the body, topic sentence position will vary according to the flow of the argument.

Words within sentences are given emphasis in the same ways: by their position, and by the way they interact with one another. An article structured properly has a 'flow' – it 'reads well'.

The question of *which* order of sections, of paragraphs, of sentences within paragraphs, of words – is less rigid than it sounds when theorizing. Enough has been said about shaping your material in outline form to indicate that any article idea may suggest several possible shapes.

Tailoring to the reader

Where the subject matter is subtle (pickpocket), or complex (why the stock markets crashed), one particularly effective technique has already been suggested: that you put down the questions the average reader would ask, in the order in which they would be asked. Then answer them.

Notice, however, that in the pickpocket article in Chapter 7, narrative tricks are used to keep the reader hooked, so that the order is partly imposed by the author. She raises in readers' mind the questions she has the answers for. Furthermore, except for highly factual how-to pieces, with working subheadings, the structure of the articles should not be too obvious, too inevitable-looking. There may be no spare flesh on a good-looking human being, but you do not see what the skeleton looks like. You are talking to the reader, after all – there must be a naturalness in the flow, but with a few surprises, or shocks or twists if the relationship is to be alive. An article may *sound* inconsequential or teasing at various points; the reader should be confident, however, that by the end, when the threads are gathered together, all will be made clear.

There are, of course, types of article that break the rules, but work. You are more likely to succeed with the unorthodox, though, when you know exactly which rules you are breaking, and how far you can go without damaging your material.

LINKING TECHNIQUES

Links are, in effect, transition words or phrases. They provide a smooth passage from one point to the next, and special skill in linking is needed at the start of paragraphs. The devices can be identified as follows.

Pronouns, demonstratives, definite article and comparative words

These refer to words or statements further back in the text. Examples are 'he', 'she', 'it', 'they', 'this', 'these', 'those', 'the', 'equal', 'similar', 'such', 'bigger', 'smaller', 'the former', 'the latter'.

Words lexically related

In developing the theme of an article key words and their synonyms may need to be repeated several times (see Figure 8.1). Many nouns and verbs used here are synonyms or near-synonyms, or at least closely related, which makes for a thread of meaning running through the article, holding it together. Look back at the articles analysed in Chapter 7. In the article 'The great utility scandal', apart from the synonyms for 'boss' there is also the word group 'scandal', 'discredit', 'ridicule', 'mockery', 'greed', 'rotten', 'indefensible', 'wrong', 'incoherent', 'darken', 'outrageous', and so on. In the 'pickpocket' article we have 'nicking', 'thieves', 'steal', 'lifted', 'pinch', 'pickpocketing', 'dipping', etc.

Miscellaneous connectives

These express relationships with what has gone before, such as addition ('and', 'furthermore', 'moreover'); contrast ('but', 'however', 'nevertheless'), consequence ('so', 'therefore', 'the result that'); and example ('for example', 'for instance', 'to put this more clearly').

If writers, reading over what they have written, have to pause at such words or phrases as the ones given below and ask themselves the questions beside them, then their words have failed and their work lacks coherence. Remember that the reader is more likely to ask questions than they are, since his or her concentration will be less. Check your work for coherence in this way by putting yourself into the mind of the reader:

> these problems – what problems?
> less certain results – which results were more certain?
> on the other hand – as opposed to what?
> this leads us to – where have we been?

Does Britain need a 'boss' or a 'manager'?

A leader is not necessarily a manager -- the Duke of Wellington was a leader of battles. Lord Palmerston was a laid-back Whig statesman most of the time and a John Bull leader figure during the Crimean War: no one would ever have called them 'managers' in the modern sense. 'Haw, Haw!' Pam would have said.

Whatever the post may be called, organisations appointing a chief today should try to be clear whether they are looking for a leader or a manager, and the answer will depend on what kinds of problems they think they need to solve. In politics Sir Robert Walpole, Stanley Baldwin and Harold Wilson were the supreme party managers of their respective eras. A real leader like William Gladstone, will define goals, put heart into people, and motivate them to get moving. He usually makes people feel important, which is the secret of the love that the great leader wins. He differs from the 'boss' type, who is the bane of every organisation in the country, who wants other people to feel insignificant so that his own ego can fill the vacant space.

A manager, on the other hand -- and John Major is the most prominent and controversial current example -- is mainly concerned to keep things ticking over. He will aim to get on with the people around him, keep resources and commitments in line, take a look at shortages and sources of waste, and enable people to sleep soundly at night. He may not figure much in song and story, but his skills are always needed at a high level within the party, or army, or business - especially business. We may be able to do without leaders -- indeed it is arguable that we should learn to do so -- but civilised existence without managers is impossible to imagine.

Figure 8.1 Connections that make for coherence: an extract from a backgrounder piece (John Major had resigned to bring about a leadership election) by Michael Harrington in *The Sunday Telegraph* of 2 July 1995. Two separate networks have been shown: linked boxes of key terms ('leader' and synonyms); and balloons of pronouns and miscellaneous connectives

A linking word may be unclear because it is too far away from what it refers to, or because it refers to something in the writer's mind that has inadvertently not been written down. Figure 8.1 shows part of an article with linking words boxed. Some of the key connections are indicated by the network of lines.

Inevitable links

Some articles, because of the nature of the material and the writer's intentions, are so clearly structured, with the intro summarizing all the aspects to be covered, and the body taking them one by one, that the links have an inevitability about them. There is no harm in inevitability as long as it does not come across as dull.

Suppose you want to write about Colombia, South America. The intro can bring up the main misconceptions about the country: it is spelt with an 'o', and it is much bigger than generally thought this side of the Atlantic. It is also much older: there were Indian civilizations for thousands of years before the Spanish arrived. There are activities other than growing coffee and peddling cocaine and emeralds, problems other than landslides burying shanty towns on hillsides. It has a wealth of unused resources. . . .'

Subsequent paragraphs can take these aspects one at a time, linking with such key words as 'bigger', 'older', 'activities', 'problems', 'resources'. The dull-making repetition of such words as 'also' in this context would have to be avoided. The first sentences of the paragraphs might begin:

'One little-known fact about Colombia is that it is twice as big as. . . .'

'Another surprise for visitors is to discover that the country is older than they realized, in the sense that. . . .'

'Not only do visitors find Colombia older than they thought it was, but the activities of its people are much more varied. . . .'

A linking sentence like the last one, which repeats the key point of the previous paragraph and then adds the next key point, is a strong adhesive. Repeating 'visitors' may be overdoing it: it depends on how long the previous paragraph was.

Unobtrusive links

Links should be unobtrusive, and they are more likely to be so if they have suggested themselves in the course of writing, provided the writer knows what he/she wants to say and has a clear idea of the shape required. There are the occasional links – or transitions – that are little more than lubrication: the sort of marking-time phrase common in speeches to allow the listener thinking space. Examples are 'Having said that . . .', 'Whether these events were crucial or not ...' When you go through a first draft, you can slip one or two of these in, even if only to help the rhythm.

But don't overdo it. You may find you are too partial to them, and may have to remove some. Make sure that the longer linking phrases are not too elaborate for their purpose. 'But' needs to be handled with care. It is, I think, justified at the start of the previous paragraph. It is too often used, however, as an all purpose lubricator, to make a connection spiced with a little artificial tension where no real contrast is present; and it should not be followed by any of its synonyms – 'yet', 'however', 'nevertheless' – in the same sentence.

Beginning a paragraph by repeating the last word/phrase/sentence of the previous one can also provide a breather, while focus is being shifted to the next point. For example, a paragraph ends with '... freedom of information'. The next paragraph begins: 'Freedom of information may be crucial. But this has become something of a cult phrase ...'

Or, to avoid 'but': 'Freedom of information? This has become ...'

MESHING FROM DIFFERENT SOURCES

Where the information is urgent, rich in facts and from various sources, as it often is for a newspaper feature, then the linking matter may be fulfilling several functions at a time. Suppose the features editor of a newspaper wants a 'colour' piece on what the atmosphere is like in a town called Edenford after fifty people have died in a fire at a paint factory which broke out at 1 a.m. The newspaper's reporters have already obtained the main facts. It is now late morning. You are either a staff writer or a freelance living in a nearby town who has filed one or two similar stories for the paper in the past, including a fire at the same factory a year ago, when six people died. The factory's owners have not carried out all the safety measures demanded by the local authority at that time.

Staff or freelance, you talk to the local authority about the fire precautions, the fire department about the accident, and a factory spokesman. You arrange to visit the factory later. The town library and the town newspaper files give you background information about the town, and you still have your notes from last year. The local paper also has cuttings that follow up on the previous accident, with all the controversy that developed. At the police station and the town hall you get some addresses of relatives of the dead. You winkle out hints of who among these might be willing to talk to you to check how far you can go with quotes and comments without getting into legal trouble. You meet groups of people talking quietly on street corners – three old men on one, half a dozen school children on another – and you chat with them, making a few notes.

The pubs have opened – it is 11 o'clock – and there is a fight in one of them. Two men spill out into the street in the struggle, others trying to keep them apart.

You take more notes. One of the men has lost his brother, the other is a worker at the factory who had been standing up for the factory owners.

You talk to several relatives. The general mood is of anger. You talk to people in shops. People have varying ideas about what caused the fire, and about the sequence of events. You fit in the visit to the factory and talk to several executives and workers there. You meet a vicar.

You may start your article by plunging into the story of a family who had lost a son and a daughter in the fire. You have talked to the mother, Peggy. You intersperse her recollections of last night's events with some of your background material. You interpose 'then', meaning last night with 'now', meaning this morning, throughout the article, shifting back and forward (though not too indiscriminately) between people's immediate reactions to the events and their present feelings and thoughts.

Choosing the right tenses

Skilful use of tenses will link the events of a developing story. Peggy's general comments about the night's events might be given as past perfect tense (as below). Quoted, they are mainly in simple past tense – 'now' (meaning the time of the interview) things 'were' happening; 'today' (when the article is being read) feelings of anger 'are' growing in the community.

Here to illustrate, is an idea of how a couple of paragraphs of the imaginary article written in this way might go. My italics indicate words and phrases that both mesh and move the story on:

> Edenford today *is* a quiet, stunned town.
>
> Peggy *had wandered* up and down the street, shouting hysterically while sirens wailed. She had been taken home. *When the news was brought to her*, she had blamed God. *Later* she had blamed the Government, the factory owners, the local authority . . .
>
> *Now* she saw no point in blaming anybody. It wouldn't bring her children back.
>
> *Outside*, the streets *were growing quiet. Here*, in her sitting-room, Peggy's voice grew *stronger* as she told how the family *had moved* to this town from London five years ago.
>
> *Yes, they had been angry* about the previous fire. *In the days to come*, she *would be* even more angry with those responsible for this one. . . .

The meshing is helped by fixing on a particular situation – interviewing Peggy in her sitting-room – as the point of reference. All actions and feelings are related to that situation, and it is the tenses of the verbs, together with the adverbs that confirm the switches in time and place, which make the connections clear.

THE FUNCTIONS OF ANECDOTES

Today 'people journalism', or 'human interest', is in the ascendant. Editors faced with the news challenge of television dig deeper into the background and analyse the implications of the news, illuminating by reference to people. This is reflected in the number and variety of full-scale interviews and profiles, and in the frequency with which anecdotes (true stories) and quotes are used to illustrate points.

A common journalistic task is to talk to 'experts' on the subject being dealt with. Take mental illness. The academic experts (in psychiatry, for example) and people with the relevant inside knowledge and experience (mental health nurse, mentally ill patient) will be talked to. What they say will be shaped and interpreted in a manner appropriate to the readers aimed at.

Val Hennessy's article about the pickpocket in Chapter 7 contains many quoted anecdotes. Notice how they mesh into the main framework of the article by means of the author's linking bits of summary. Such anecdotes capture the reader's attention. This is real life, not abstract theorizing about social problems; it is genuine experience, not a journalist's reflections about someone's life.

Anecdotes can illustrate points vividly, or make them concrete in various ways. They can help clarify concepts that are not easy to define. They can move the reader emotionally, enhancing the lesson behind the story. Potent anecdotes are particularly useful at the start and ending of articles. They can add drama to a subject that might be short of it. A humorous anecdote, for example, by its immediate contact with the reader, can open a window into a subject, can cut straight through and reveal its essence.

To integrate anecdotes into the article, a 'once upon a time' link may be necessary. 'I remember the day ...' or 'there was an occasion when he ...' are typical, though some may fit in seamlessly.

There may need to be a bridge after the anecdote, to indicate its precise relevance to the subject: 'This explains why ...', for example, or 'That was only one of many occasions when. ...' But the more economical the grafting the better.

It goes without saying that anecdotes, however they are used, must be relevant, vivid, interesting, and thought-provoking.

WHEN TO QUOTE

I use the word 'quotes' to mean the exact words of someone interviewed, whether you did the interviewing or whether you had borrowed from another writer's interview as published; and also to mean any extract from published materials that are not enshrined in great literature or quotation books. If you did not obtain the quote in an interview, the sources should be acknowledged.

The word 'quotation' will be restricted to the famous literary or political ones that can be gathered from a reference book, or from the works of great writers, thinkers and statesmen of the past.

Quotes are used to give authority to a statement, or to indicate that it is worth readers' attention, because of the knowledge or experience of the person quoted. Quotes are also used to show that this is what the speaker believes, and that it is not necessarily what the author believes. To make that difference more explicit such phrases as 'it was her opinion that' or words like 'claims' may be employed. Where only one or two quotes are used in an article, they tend to stand out, and they must therefore be selected with particular care, to make sure they are effective.

In feature interviews and profiles the subject is quoted liberally in order to reveal the personality or character. The quotes must still be selected carefully, because much of what most people say, even in interviews, is fairly boring. Interesting quotes will come out of who the people are, what they do in life. Charm, quaintness or oddity rapidly wear thin on the printed page unless there is also some insight into an interesting character.

Is your quoting necessary?

Where mere facts are being relayed – 'the average salary in this company is £25,000' – they can be given in indirect speech. A quote should normally indicate something more than a mere fact.

Give the speaker's name early. If you take readers through a long quote, they may lose interest before they get to the end because they may be fighting against the desire to know *why* they should be interested. 'I was summoned to the manager's office,' said Andrew Cunningham, a young physics graduate who had been considered to have brilliant prospects when he started with the firm six months ago. 'He told me I was dismissed'.

That is one way of doing it. Otherwise, you can build up interest in the speaker before giving any of the quote. If, on re-reading, what you have written about the quoted person does not sound interesting enough, make it so. Looks after widowed mother? Photographs sharks in his spare time?

Accidentally killed his father while experimenting with a bow and arrow? has strange psychic powers, or believes he has? Such facts will get the reader interested.

Three or four paragraphs of uninterrupted quoting are usually excessive, unless they are short paragraphs and the quoted material is very good. Break it up by paraphrasing or summarizing.

When you want to indicate that you have a different view from the speaker, you can quote the word or words you distance yourself from or disagree with within a paraphrase or summary. For example, 'The manager had referred to Mr Cunningham's "personality defects" and "incompetence".' Leaving out the quote marks would imply that you agreed with the verdict, and you would get into trouble with Mr Cunningham, if not the law.

The need to interpret

You must make sure that you represent a speaker faithfully. People say things in anger, or with humour or irony, that they would express quite differently if they were writing for publication. People who are not used to being interviewed may have little idea of the impression their words will make when they appear in print. They may need to be warned, 'Do you really want me to print that?' On the other hand, when an interviewee inadvertently reveals the truth, which doesn't show him in a good light, and it is the truth you are after and you are asked, 'You are not going to print that, are you?', the answer has to be 'Yes'.

Things are said during an interview that need to be put into the whole context of the interview if they are to be interpreted correctly. Since only you, the interviewer, know all that the speaker has said, you must ask yourself whether what you have selected gives a fair representation. If Mr Cunningham makes one derogatory reference to the manager's character ('He was vindictive') and three others that are complimentary, you will be doing them both an injustice if all that you select is the derogatory one and if the clear implication is that this fairly sums up the manager's behaviour, because no compensatory statement is made.

Another occasion when the writer has to be interpreter is when the interviewee misuses the language. A malapropism may be used, for example, 'psychotherapy' instead of 'physiotherapy'; words not similar enough in meaning to the word intended, such as 'disinterested' for 'uninterested'; or a word that will ambiguous in the context such as 'trendy', where it is not clear whether the sense is complimentary or derogatory. Doubts about such matters should be cleared up, as far as possible, in the course of conversation. You don't, however, correct the kind of grammatical errors that reveal a distinctive way of speaking unless they would cause misunderstanding.

Incorporating the quotes

Once a speaker is established in the reader's mind, quotes can be inserted into different parts of the article without obvious introduction. Where you do need a saying verb, varying it once or twice can make effective joins: 'Mr Cunningham complained that the manager's attitude . . .' has a verb that neatly refers to what went before. But do not vary saying verbs for the sake of it: such a sequence as 'said . . . groaned . . . grinned . . . exclaimed . . . interjected . . . put in . . . gave out . . . would be an absurdity'.

The past tense of the saying verb is normal, especially if you have more than one speaker, each established in a different situation. The present tense may be used throughout as an historic present to provide immediacy, make the reader feel actually present in the situation while reading, provided it is consistently carried through. The present tense also indicates unchanging belief: 'When asked about the relationship between his private life and his business activities, Mr Cunningham says, "My private life is entirely my own affair".'

To quote or not to quote

Quotations from great writers' works should not be too well known, or they might appear as clichés. 'To be or not to be' will not do at all. 'Many a flower is born to blush unseen' and suchlike lines learnt in school that occasionally get up and go for a walk inside your head are also to be avoided. What you can do with famous lines is use them without quote marks – but sparingly, and not more than once in an article – so that your readers will pick up the allusion. Occasionally a neat twist is to change a word or two in the quotation: for example, substituting 'fears' for 'tears' in 'As one might say, thoughts that do lie too deep for fears'.

Is the allusion going to illuminate things, bring a smile to the readers' faces, move them? If not, leave it out. When you find such an allusion in your first draft, and it sounds pretentious, strike it out.

The quips that great wits come out with, often enshrined in an anecdote, can bring a shaft of light into an abstract discussion. For instance, on hearing that President Coolidge, a man of few words and even less action, was dead, writer and wit Dorothy Parker asked, 'How can they tell?' Here is one that makes a point about use of language: a critic reproached Winston Churchill, the wartime prime minister, for ending a sentence with a preposition. Churchill wrote him a note: 'This is the sort of English up with which I will not put'.

Quotes or quotations may be used, as suggested earlier in this chapter, at the head of an article as a subtitle or standfirst above the intro. Some page designs have them in bold panels or slotted into different parts of the page, to break up slabs of print, especially when there are no illustrations. Consult dictionaries of quotations if you like, but make sure what you use is relevant.

Jokes are another form of anecdote, but since a joke shouldn't need explaining, its integration into the article must be subtle. Many famous jokes come as quotes: those of Dorothy Parker, Oscar Wilde, Sir Winston Churchill and Groucho Marx being remembered, treasured and written down by others. As with famous quotations, they should be used with imagination – and in a context that does them justice.

ASSIGNMENTS

1 Study the following student's article and then rewrite it, using the suggestions below. It was aimed at women readers. Re-target it for a general magazine, talking to both men and women readers, or a national Sunday paper. Indicate target publication. Reduce to 1000 words.

- Do an outline of what is there, identify faults of structure and produce a new outline, with some links shown
- Update as necessary
- Provide a brief standfirst
- Make a more attention-grabbing intro and a stronger ending
- Avoid academic style and jargon and make it more readable
- Avoid changing the subject too often, especially within paragraphs. Take paragraph 7 in the original, for example: 'role reversal ... studies ... children ... couples ...'

House husbands: how well do they cope

1 It isn't easy to bring up children and run the home. Men have in the past underestimated the amount of work it involves and have been reluctant to help. But fathers of the 1990s are a different breed.

2 Since the 1950s, when it was recognized that problem children respond well to their fathers taking an active interest in them, fathers have increasingly become involved in the everyday care of their children, from birth onwards. The days

of Victorian patriarchs, rarely seen by their awe-struck children, are gone.

3 Today men are comfortable with the gentle side of their nature and many have realized their ability to nurture. A survey conducted by Bristol University showed that 9 per cent of fathers were the main carers for their babies.

4 But men taking on this role need as much support as possible. Until it becomes normal for men to be at home raising children they not only have to deal with the problems women have dealt with for centuries, but additional ones too, because they are men operating in a woman's world.

5 Many thousands of fathers have turned their lives upside-down in order to look after the children while their wives or partners continue working. For many families role-reversal is the way forward. Films such as *Mr Mum* and *Trading Places* reflect this growing trend.

6 There are many things to take into consideration when making childcare arrangements. Circumstances today mean more couples are choosing to reverse roles. These include increased unemployment, women's improved career prospects and earning power, better attitudes towards working mums, more egalitarian beliefs regarding childcare and the desire more fathers have to be involved in their children's lives.

7 Role reversal offers women a greater degree of flexibility and choice when looking after children and running the home. Children are not affected by the change, other than the benefit from improved relationships with their fathers. Yet many role-reversed couples return to traditional roles earlier than anticipated because of the difficulties fathers experience with their new position as house husband.

8 Difficulties stem from the attitudes of others, the way they perceive themselves as house husbands, the everyday demands of a new role and the change in their relationship with their partners.

9 Research shows that house husbands meet with disapproval from people around them because they are fulfilling an unconventional role. Although initially friends react positively to their situation, they find scepticism soon sets in, especially among relatives and male friends. One father said that his male friends didn't even consider childcare to be an activity, let alone work.

10   Generally excluded from the local groups women form, house husbands become isolated. They sense that some women feel threatened by them and are reluctant to include them in associated community activities. As Jes, a West Midland house husband explained, playgroups and school circles are closed to him. 'I tried taking my son Jack to playgroup but it was too embarrassing. I only went once. When I walked in the women stopped talking in groups and just stared at me'. In another case, a man was asked to leave his playgroup because husbands of the Indian women could not allow them to attend if there was a man there. Friendships between house husbands and house wives rarely develop as women prefer not to invite men into their homes. Consequently fathers lack support and company during the day. One father told me that he felt more lonely with a small child then he had ever felt on his own.

11   Fathers are not accepted as equals in the business of child rearing. They are referred to as 'good baby-sitters' and congratulated on the way they cope. While out with the children they are liable to be approached by women offering such advice as 'you need to keep him well wrapped up in this weather'. Men, apparently, are unable to cope. Men become sensitive to such criticism and feel they have to work twice as hard before they are accepted as good primary parents. It's time we took them seriously, granting them genuine recognition and, above all, treating them as equals.

12   A more serious, but thankfully less common, problem for house husbands is people who suspect them of being abductors. This experience seems to be more common among fathers who look unconventional and are in charge of very young babies.

13   Brian, a North Londoner, is a full-time parent to his eight-week-old daughter, Holly. He has dreadlocks, a full beard and casual clothing. He was once followed for four miles: 'I started home from the shops, a journey that involves two buses and a walk. A middle-aged woman was on the first bus and she kept looking at me and Holly. She got off the bus when I did and waited near me at the depot. She followed me onto the next bus and then when I got off near my road, she got off too. I walked to my house and she was still behind

me. She watched me go indoors and carried on walking.' He is convinced she thought Holly had been abducted. Men with children have been stopped by the police and asked to prove that they are the father. The children are asked, 'Is this your Daddy?'.

14   In our society men are brought up to behave in a masculine way, especially when socializing with other men. Schools, families, films and books educate them to expect to join the workforce and be breadwinners for their families. When they decide to swap roles with their partners they forgo much of this. In many cases this leads to them doubting their function in society and feeling their identity is under threat. They also feel more vulnerable as a result of having to expose the sensitive and caring side of their nature when with the children. In one study (Lewis and O'Brien) 40 per cent of fathers said their self-esteem was undermined by leaving paid employment and this was a major disadvantage of their new lifestyle. However, 42 per cent of fathers reported enhanced self-esteem and confidence, possibly a result of successfully fulfilling a new role.

15   House husbands are often shocked to discover how much work parenting involves. They need to adapt quickly to new tasks, unfamiliar emotions, demanding children and a heavy physical workload. Backbreaking buggies, designed at a height for women, and a lack of father and baby changing rooms serve only to exacerbate the situation. Town planners, marketing people and designers should recognize this growing section of society.

16   It is only to be expected that couples suffer relationship problems within the first few months of role reversal. Both parents suffer from stress as they adjust to the physical and emotional demands of new jobs. However, in some cases, these problems are not resolved and in fact, get worse. Deciding who is responsible for what can be a complicated business leading to uncertainty and arguments.

17   A common problem is that mothers are reluctant to hand over the responsibility for decision-making when it comes to the home and children. Some find it hard to trust their partners in this traditionally female domain. As a consequence, fathers resent the fact that they do not have the authority within the home that their wives would certainly have. They

are resentful because they don't have the same freedom to manage their new role as their partners do to manage their careers.

18 Richard, father of two living near Britain, said: 'The most difficult thing was my girlfriend's attitude. She was never fully comfortable with the role reversal. She seemed to think that her side of the arrangement meant becoming a "male chauvinist". She didn't value my role as a house husband as highly as her role as the main breadwinner and criticized the way I did things.'

19 Perhaps surprisingly, major problems occur in some families because the working woman does not necessarily support her partner. She may find it hard to accept him in a domestic role and therefore cannot sympathize with his worries and shortcomings. In addition, she may feel hurt if the children go to their fathers, rather than her, when in need of comfort. This, combined with being away from the children all day, can make her feel guilty. She may be resentful of the father's closeness with the children and is then unable to support him. Findings show that coping with the mother's emotional anxieties and exhaustion is a primary problem for house husbands.

20 Although these problems are many and complex, they are not insurmountable. Once problems are accepted, and in many cases resolved, men find they not only make good primary parents, but they enjoy it too. As Holly's Dad Brian explained: 'Being at home is great, mainly because I get on so well with Holly. Sometimes it can be a bit claustrophobic but we go out a lot. There's always something to do. I can't think of anything more important or rewarding than bringing up children.'

21 In order to maximize our position in the workforce we need all the available options open to us, therefore it is in our interests to make role reversal work. For many women it is in our interests to make role reversal work. For many women it is the only chance they have to pursue a career. Initially, we need to accept house husbands as our equals, as we want men to accept us as equals in the workplace. For continued success we must remain genuinely supportive. Until it becomes perfectly normal for a man to stay at home with the children house husbands are going to meet some, if not many, of the above problems.

22   Let's hope that employers, personnel officers, teachers, play-group leaders, designers, town planners, media image-makers, politicians and all the others who can change social policy and influence people's attitudes are willing to offer their support too in making it a more viable option. Swedish statutory changes encouraging men to spend time at home with their children have been very successful. More than a quarter of fathers now spend at least a year at home. Thus statutory changes can underpin cultural changes.

23   As Douglas Hurd, father of daughters 10 and 12, said when he was Employment Secretary: 'Men should play a bigger part at home, to encourage their wives to go out to work. This means a change in attitude – namely that bringing up children is a shared responsibility. It is not just the responsibility of the woman.'

24   The fact that men are ready and willing to take on the domestic duties really is a good opportunity so let's not waste it (1760 words approximately).

2 Write another two versions of your intro to the article, for other markets.

3 As for 2: write two other endings for those markets.

4 Find two articles at about 1500 words, one that you find very readable and the other hard going (though not difficult in the content). Highlight the links of each article and study them.

   ● How far was the hard going due to inadequate linking: what other causes were there?
   ● What were the qualities that made the other article so readable?

9 DIGGING DEEPER

Many successful feature writers in newspapers and magazines start off as reporters. They continue to regard reporting as the essential function of journalism: readers want facts before opinion. A trained reporter has the ability:

1 To identify and monitor information that has news value. It may be merely of public interest, but may also be, more importantly, in the public interest – of public concern.
2 To locate the most useful and reliable sources of the information; to establish contact with these sources; and to collect accurate information by observation/legwork, interviewing and research.
3 To select and interpret the data objectively, arrange it in a logical pattern, and communicate it accurately and effectively.

Writers of articles who did not start off as reporters must learn those skills. What the feature writer adds to these basic skills are greater gifts of self-expression, the ability to make deeper analysis based on facts, the ability to argue and persuade, and the ability to express opinions worth reading and considering. Opinions are rarely acceptable, in these information-hungry times, unless backed up by factual evidence collected in the ways described above. Some by-line columnists, aiming at experimental kinds of writing, fantasy, humour or satire, are exceptions; but even they need at least timeliness, and often use news items, if only as launching pads.

The reporter deals mainly with facts; feature writers base their articles on them. Facts are verifiable data. Reporters aim to be timely, newsworthy, accurate, objective, balanced, clear, interesting, brief and – because the paper cannot wait – fast. The last quality means that reporters fulfil the other aims as well as they can in the time available.

The 'monitoring' of information mentioned is often referred to as the reporters' 'watchdog' role. If this is taken further, requiring the digging out of hidden facts, facts that vested interests would prefer you not to know, it is called 'investigative reporting'; though there is no precise line between this and the straightforward variety.

NEWS VALUE DEFINED

'News' means new, not generally known. The public want to know about new facts/events if they are disruptive in some way, going against the normal pattern of events. That disruption, or change, may be beneficial – peace, progress or achievement. Or it may be harmful – conflict, failure, tragedy. Bad news tends to be more striking, more dramatic, tends to call out for action, and therefore tends to crowd the front pages of the news-papers. Reporters place greater news value on the extreme happenings: millions of pounds won or lost rather than thousands, many deaths rather than few. The event has more news value if it affects a head of state than you or me, or if it is the reverse of the usual happening – man bites dog.

There is broad agreement about news criteria, but much difference of opinion about priorities and choice of items. A thousand people killed in an earthquake in Santiago, Chile, would normally take precedence over 100 killed in a fire in Buenos Aires, but if the first group were all Chileans and the second contained twenty Britons, the second event would be considered more newsworthy by British newspapers.

The news value of a newspaper report is contained up front, in the first couple of paragraphs. Quite a different matter is the news content used in a newspaper feature or magazine article.

A newspaper feature may analyse and comment on news reported on another page in the same issue or in a recent issue, but it may simply be using the news as a topical peg. A remark made in passing by a politi-cian in a speech over the weekend may set off a think piece for Monday morning's paper. A military adventure somewhere may spark off a feature on new advances in weaponry. Features, as we have seen, might be pegged to anniversaries or other forms of seasonal newsworthiness.

Whatever the news value or news peg of an article, it is the viewpoint, treatment and style that will distinguish it from a straightforward report. Let us look at two very different articles to see how this enhancement of the reporting skills works in different ways.

A LEGWORK FEATURE IN A MAGAZINE

'Trudie barges through the Knightsbridge traffic in her big, black, borrowed bovver boots, braces lapping the paramilitary trousers, pale pink hedgehog hair, the outfit accessorized with one blue plastic bag and some good London dirt.'

So opens a *You* magazine article called 'You can't judge a woman by her cover'. The article continues in the urgent present tense. It was written by Joan Burnie, who accompanied model Trudie Joyce on two shopping expeditions to Harrods, two trips to the American Bar at the Savoy, and two trips to the night club Stringfellows. For each visit the model dressed in different clothes. The contrasting reactions of employees – doormen, sales assistants, waiters, barman, barmaid – and of the public made a revealing and amusing account, 'in the interests of sexual science and journalism'.

This article is of public interest because Sunday magazine readers enjoy 'lifestyle' pieces. It is, on the face of it, entirely legwork reporting and it is a good illustration of a subject where the most reliable source of information is the writer observing and experiencing events as they happen; next in reliability come other first-hand-sources – people participating in the event – whose reactions can be noted, or who can be interviewed while participating.

Is the choice of contacts, and the selection and interpretation of the facts in this article, convincing? Well, the thesis is imposed on the material rather than suggested by it. Colour pictures of the model in different clothes and situations reinforce the theme, together with suggestive captions. Readers may guess that various encounters which would have given a different impression from those that fit have been omitted. The style, too, is somewhat hyped-up, but one feels that readers will accept the general psychological truth about human nature that lies behind it all.

FEATURE WITH A WEALTH OF FACTS

By contrast, a *Guardian* article by Clare Dyer, 'Damaging Evidence' needs all the reporting skills mentioned including a fair amount of research. To deal with the obstacles encountered by parents in getting compensation for vaccine-damaged children, a study is made of the roles of the following organizations: the DHSS, the High Court, the vaccine damage tribunal (and the cases it had dealt with), the 1978 Royal Commission on Civil Liability and Compensation for Personal Injury (which produced the Pearson Report), the Edinburgh Court of Session, the Fife Health Board, the Government (its current attitude compared with earlier statements), the House of Lords, and a local health authority. Key interviews are those with two mothers of vaccine-damage children. The article illustrates well the point that a journalist is not so much a person who knows things as a person who knows how to find out things.

This article's new content is a story starting in 1979 when the two women apply for a payment under the Vaccine Damage Payments Act of that year. The story will not be overtaken by events because the article looks forward to tribunal hearings on days after its publication.

Here again the viewpoint, which is that the Government needs to do more to help vaccination victims and to solve the problem of lessening faith in the vaccination programme, is reinforced by the title. It is also assisted by some 'colour'. The first paragraph, for example: 'Thirteen-year-old Susan Loveday is hopelessly brain-damaged. She will never be able to look after herself. Her mother, Moira, insists she was a perfectly normal baby before the triple vaccination she had against whooping cough, tetanus and diphtheria'.

Eight-year-old Melissa, the other girl, in the words of her mother, 'actually passed out after her first and second injections, her eyes rolled and she went limp like a lettuce'. There is a touching picture of Melissa with her mother; but the strength of this feature article is not in colour (which is used simply to win over the reader) nor in the illustration but in its wealth of facts and figures, upon which is based the clear analysis and level-headed argument.

BUILDING UP YOUR CONTACTS BOOK

The best information for the above sort of article comes from the right contacts, and the best stories often from the least obvious one. The nose for good contacts is often of course the same nose that finds news.

Practice will make you increasingly adept at collecting good contacts, especially for the subjects you cover frequently. Note likely ones in the newspapers and periodicals you read, and from cuttings you take. Press officers of hotels and airlines, or big organizations such as the BBC and independent TV companies, and of film companies, suggest themselves. Trade magazines contain mentions of experts in many fields.

Get on the mailing list of organizations you are interested in so that you will get advance information about developments. From manufacturers you will be able to obtain handouts and free photographs if you write about new products.

Most organizations of any size have a press officer or PRO.

Press Gazette regularly list press officers, and this weekly trade paper for journalists produces a filofax-type contacts book that contains addresses and telephone numbers of editors, news agencies and TV and radio news editors and a year of forthcoming events. The publication also produces an electronic database (see below).

Official sources, as so many of the above are, may be generous with time and information, especially if they know your work and you have established good relationships. But, the truth being many-sided, you may need to talk to enemies as well as friends, consumers as well as producers.

You may be willing to pay for certain kinds of information. If you regularly write celebrity interviews, the services of the agency called Celebrity Service may be invaluable. For a fee you are provided every fortnight with news of the movements of film starts, opera singers, authors and suchlike, what they will be doing in London, Paris or New York, sometimes which hotel they will be at, which press agent has been hired for their particular activity in the city, with telephone number.

It may be worth your while to pay someone to do research tasks if it will save you time and money. You could pay, for example, a colleague in Glasgow to provide you with notes on the Scottish aspects of particular subjects, derived, say, from telephoning and legwork; otherwise you would have had to travel to Glasgow and spend a night or two there. Journalists in different cities make reciprocal arrangements. With some planning you can, as time goes by, build up a network of contacts like these.

A classified advert under 'Personal' or 'Information Wanted' may produce many contacts for a particular feature or series.

One contact leads to another. Before you leave a contact, ask 'Who else shall I talk to?' Write in your indexed book job titles of contacts, organization, address and telephone number as you come across them. Add a line summing up the person's usefulness: 'Knows history of company' it might be, or 'good on progress of Parliamentary bills'.

If you do a fair amount of research, your contacts book will include libraries, their specializations, their hours of business, the names of friendly librarians and where photocopiers are available 24 hours a day.

ELECTRONIC DATABASES

Press Gazette produces the *UKPG Contact Pro* disk (sponsored by Mercury Group), an electronic database for journalists, free for subscribers (sale price £29.50). This is a Microsoft Windows-compatible version of the Contact Pro program together with the database of 1400 contacts. It can easily be modified and extended. There are also versions for DOS and Apple-Mac.

It is not only in libraries that electronic databases are replacing certain kinds of reference books, printed bibliographies and catalogue cards; databases are also replacing such aids in journalists' homes. Freelance journalists working from home are turning to on-line databases, accessed by means of an IBM-compatible computer or Apple Mac linked to the telephone line by a modem. Access to the entry points to the various databases are provided by using a linking service such as Compulink Information Exchange (CIX) or Compuserve.

The possibilities are vast. Newsrooms access highly expensive database services, and have to make sure they are being used cost-effectively: researching in an unfocused way can waste time and money.

Journalists working at home, without having the benefit of expert researchers' advice at hand, need to work out carefully what equipment, software and access to databases they can afford. *Press Gazette* and *Writers' Monthly* keep readers up to date with the possibilities and pitfalls in electronic journalism, as does the Society of Authors' *The Author*, which now incorporates its quarterly supplement *Electronic Author.*

Many newspapers throughout the country now have in-house databases of their own editions and have stopped cutting to file.

British Broadcasting Corporation (BBC): The Library and Research Information Services contain 250,000 books, 22 million cuttings, research facilities, archives and databases. Many facilities and services are available outside staff.

British Library Automated Information Service (BLAISE): A computerized bibliographic service.

British Telecom Phone Base: An electronic form of the telephone book, allowing you to get numbers rapidly, and a quick way also of using Directory Enquiries. If you need this service for more than twenty calls a week, it is not expensive. Tel: 0800–919–199.

BT Information Business Services: Freepost PP205, Network House, Brindley Way, Hemel Hempstead, Herts, HP3 8BR. Tel: 0800–200–700.

Compulink Information Exchange (CIX): Suite 2, The Sanctuary. Oakhill Grove, Surbiton, Surrey KT6 6DU. Tel: 0181–390–8446. A way in to many and varied databases in the UK and abroad.

Compuserve, PO Box 676, Bristol BS99 1YN. Tel: 0800–289378. Access possible to well over 1000 databases. American based. Its *Executive News Service* accesses daily news stories from such agencies as Associated Press (AP), United Press International (UPI), the *Washington Post,* and Reuters Financial News Service.

Financial Times Profile: Provides access to all national broadsheets and to an increasing number of tabloids.

SpyBASE: Available from Micro Associates, PO Box 5369, Arlington, VA 22205, USA. It is compatible with IBM and Apple-Macintosh. An international database of intelligence matters.

World Press Centre (WPC): 3 Parolles Road, London N19 3RE. Tel: 0171–263–63331. Information gathered from organizations and governments throughout the world. Includes background information and profiles, and all information is constantly updated.

CHOICE OF SOURCES/CONTACTS

Participators in an event are your first-hand sources. These include your own observation and experience, and interviews or opinion surveys carried out at an event at the time. Second-hand sources include interviews with eye-witnesses and opinion surveys taken after the event when the recall may be less accurate (for questionnaires and surveys of professional standard, see books by Judith Bell and Hainville and Jowell, pages 294–5); official sources such as PROs and government departments and their publications/publicity material; experts' views, and what library research can provide in books, documents, articles and cuttings.

There are three essential criteria by which your sources must be judged, allowing for the restriction imposed by the time you have available. Are you sources *accessible*, are they the *best informed* and most reliable, and are they, where necessary, *multiple*?

- Are they accessible? There may not be time, for example, to try to dig certain documents out at the Public Records Office.
- Are they the best-informed? You may need both an eyewitness to the scandalous treatment of residents at an old people's home and the views of an expert on old age, thus using first-hand and second-hand sources to complement each other, shedding light on different aspects of your subject.
- Your witness may have given you a figure – say the number of old people who died of neglect in the past year. The expert you approach may have a different, correct figure and the evidence to prove it. Some eyewitnesses remember certain things; others remember other things.

Cross-checking for balance

Five facts you have discovered suggest that Mr A is alone responsible for some corrupt procedure. If you had more time, you might discover five more facts from other sources that show the blame should be shared between Mr A and Mr B; and, with even more time, you might discover that Mr C should share the blame, too. If Mr B and Mr C live in Paris, will the editor pay for travel/hotel/meals? The more sources you use, the more cross-checking of information you can do to verify facts, the more likely you are to arrive at a balanced and accurate picture.

If getting nearer the truth requires much more time and expense, and if telling the story so far risks libel, the editor might call a halt and pay you a 'kill fee' (normally half the agreed rate).

Since generally you are limited by time and space, choose witnesses, where you can, with a view to reliability, and check as much as possible with other witnesses. You can assess a contact's reliability from the replies to questions to which you know the answer. You know for certain, let us say, that your contact's firm has had to withdraw three products this year after being arraigned under the Trade Descriptions Act. But you ask, 'Sometimes, in your business, firms have trouble keeping in line with the Trade Descriptions Act. Has that ever happened to your firm?'

Selecting and interpreting the facts

Facts or case examples are worked into an article in order to develop the idea on which it is based, but what are the criteria for choosing them? In the article on Trudie referred to above, how many reactions of people were selected for use in the article, to show the striking differences in treatment given to the girl according to how she was dressed? Were they typical?

In *The Guardian* article on the vaccine-damaged children, do the two cases chosen as examples represent the average, or were they chosen to weight the evidence in favour of a verdict already seized on? Of course it has to be the latter. We have to concede that in the selection of facts the writer has to be trusted, but it must be done in such a way that the reader accepts that the belief being expressed is a sincere one, that facts are not being falsified, that a reasonable balance of evidence is supplied or implied.

The first article implies that civilized manners are only skin deep, and few readers will quarrel with that conclusion. The second article's conclusions are that the current Government had 'done nothing to ease the path to compensation for vaccine victims', and that increasing public awareness of the plight of vaccine-damaged children 'had done nothing to boost confidence in the vaccination programme'. The evidence given appears to support this view.

Reporting, in its gathering of facts, aims to get as near the truth about a situation as possible. Enough has been said about the need for multiple sources and on the restriction imposed by space and time. Notice what these restrictions amounted to in the two articles. It was not possible to take Trudie to twenty places in London to test a theory, nor to interview twenty mothers of vaccine-damaged children.

Some unreliable sources

Feature articles, especially in newspapers, often depend heavily on previous reports and articles in the press. Anyone who has spent an hour or two in a newspaper cuttings library will testify to the danger that lies in this dependence. Going back over the life of Elvis Presley, say, or the United Nations' use of force, you are struck by the way an error can be made in an issue of one paper and be repeated by the paper in subsequent articles, and by other papers, for months or years. Occasionally the matter may be put right, but by that time several other errors may have crept in.

The original error may be a printer's error. Notoriously, figures can anyway be manipulated to give misleading impressions. As a humorist said, 'Proper treatment will cure a cold in seven days, but left to itself a cold will hang on for a week'.

The traps are endless. There are unreliable sources whose judgement is clouded or whose memory is impaired. There are hoaxers who delight in ringing up newspapers to give them false stories. There are eyewitnesses who mistake what they see. The reporter's task is not easy.

If you are not sure of the truth of certain statements, you can attribute them in such a way that they are qualified. You can say 'Certain people believe that ...' or 'The impression has been gaining ground that ...' If you are seen to be taking care to distinguish opinion from fact, you will establish trust in your readers.

Acknowledging sources

In researching information make sure you are not breaking any copyright laws. Appendix 3 gives the Society of Authors' leaflet on the subject. Give sources for figures, especially official sources, to lend them authority. Acknowledge sources from which you have made heavy borrowings. Update facts and figures as necessary. Give dates of events rather than such vague terms as 'recently' – it may be some time before your article is published.

Integrate, evaluate and transmute the research information in your text so that it becomes an integral part of it. Whatever the sources, in the end put your mark on the piece as well as your name to it.

INTERVIEW SOURCES

A good interviewer is essentially a good listener. If you are interested in people, as well as in the subjects you are writing about, you are well on the way. If you are prepared to accept other points of view, then you will be able to frame questions that will elicit interesting answers. Tell people you want to 'talk' to them, not 'interview' them. Don't give off an aura of importance you may feel derives from the publication you represent.

A patronizing tone may either make your interlocutors say what they think you want them to say, or unleash a glassy-eyed raving fanatic who had been safely buried for years. Be calm and neutral and the response will come naturally. Not all people are willing to co-operate. Imagination and common sense will guide you in choosing likely candidates.. Try a smile, and be ready to apologize for your disturbing them.

Do not depend on switchboard operators to guide you verbally through the hierarchy of an organization. If you can use a name as a lever, it can help: 'Brian so-and-so suggested you might be able to tell me about. ...'

Telephone tactics

When approaching people by telephone, your voice should be polite but crisp. A little extra warmth can compensate for the lack of physical presence. Until you have the technology to see the person you're talking to, your words must be chosen well because you cannot modify them by your facial expression or change your style in response to the other's expression.

Except for high-ranking officials, first names are quickly adopted for contacts used regularly, especially among those in the media. But let the other person do this first. Some important people are more approachable than lesser ones. You might get straight through to them and hear them say, 'By all means let's do it now, I can give you ten minutes.'

Always try to make appointments by telephone rather than by letter (letters are sometimes ignored). You will then be told if a letter is expected, and may be given a hint on content.

If you have been commissioned to write the article by a well-known publication, this will be a strong selling point in obtaining an interview. If you are writing the article 'on spec', do not advertise the fact. There could be an advantage in the other person assuming it is a commission.

The method of interview will depend on your article. If you need to conduct several short interviews of perhaps a few sentences each, using the telephone will save time. If you have difficult questions that need considered answers by top experts or intellectuals, correspondence might be necessary. For key interviews, where you want colour and plenty of quotes, it will have to be face-to-face (developing these is covered in Chapter 13).

Keep in mind that interviewees have their motives, too. They may fear that a 'no comment' attribution will do them harm, and they will therefore be anxious to talk. Or they may be vain and hope that some publicity will help them up *their* ladder or help *their* business.

You may be asked to show your interviewee the typescript, however brief their contribution. Try to avoid this. Seeing their words in typescript makes some people feel they have been forthcoming, and they may want to change their remarks into bald platitudes. If the material is highly technical, however, or liable to be misunderstood, you could agree to submitting a manuscript on condition that changes are made only for reasons of accuracy. Sometimes reading it over the telephone, resulting perhaps in a few minor changes in emphasis, works well.

When the facts are withheld

PROs, information officers and press officers are a valued source of information for journalists, as this book will confirm frequently. But PROs start from different premises, and in any interviews with them, however short, journalists must may pay particular attention to what the PROs consider *they* are getting out of it. The quid pro quo nature of the encounter is tacitly accepted. Nevertheless there is no weighing machine for the reciprocal contributions. The PRO avoids giving information thought to be in any way compromising, the journalist tactfully avoids being used as a vehicle of publicity.

The PRO may give facts that put a product or service in a good light and omit several other facts that do not. Multiple check sources, as has been suggested, may be the answer to this ploy; but the reporter may be hamstrung by deadlines. Can more be got out of this interviewee? It may be also that the interviewee is one of the few who know the actual facts you want.

Bureaucratic stalling

You have embarked on a special feature on race relations in the area. You want, from a local careers service, figures to indicate whether or not black teenagers are victims of discrimination and are failing to get jobs. You write features regularly for a local weekly, the figures were promised a year ago and you have written several letters and made several telephone calls without avail. The local branch of the National Union of Teachers did a survey two months ago that suggested discrimination. The author of the survey, who is chairman of the union's working party on multi-racial education, has also failed to get any figures. So has the Council for Community Relations.

Various explanations are put forward by people in the service. The principal careers officer says the chief education officer is dealing with the matter. The chief education officer, you find, is 'not available for comment' but is working on it. Some days later you are told by the careers service that separate statistics on black school leavers are not kept , that 'a special report on black teenagers is being written', but that there is no deadline for it. When you manage to contact the chief education officer, however, you are told the department has not had time to extract the figures; you discover that the Council for Community Relations has been told that the chief education officer had not in fact approved the use of resources to collect the figures, and is about to persuade an education sub-committee that such resources should not be approved.

The officials, by withholding or not compiling the figures wanted, are in a powerful position. The pressure groups' scope for action is limited: they cannot plan a strategy to improve the situation until the figures allow them to see it clearly. The deadline is approaching for your article, and you have too much other work in hand to be able to commit yourself as wholeheartedly as you would like to this one; you have not got quite enough skill or experience perhaps to see how to counteract the stalling technique. As a strategy, you will probably decide to continue, with others, the slow struggle to erode the bureaucratic ramparts, but this will not get you the figures you want for your article.

Persuasive gambits

There are ways of persuading people who are reluctant to talk. You could try the tough way.

'Are you keeping back information that the law says I can have?'

'Do I have to tell my readers that you personally declined to give me this information?'

'Do you refuse to let taxpayers (or ratepayers) know what you're doing with their money?'

Such veiled threats are the last resort, however. When it comes to bureaucracies, such questions lose their bite anyway if you cannot determine where exactly accountability lies.

Asking for examples (as well as making your article more concrete) is a good way to jog memories. So also is, 'What happened then ... ?'

When interviewees come out with a revealing statement, perhaps inadvertently, and then clam up, thinking they have said too much, you can try being sympathetic. 'It's odd of course that they thought they could get away with that' might encourage expansion on prejudices against a particular group, or 'I'm very interested to hear that you say that, because I don't think many people have considered that side of the argument'.

'Why do you say that?' can unlock a few secrets. When you are told, 'I don't want to talk about it', the word 'Why?' can sometimes provoke an even more interesting answer than the one you originally wanted.

Interviewees may have brought evasion to the fine art of providing the information they have decided to give you irrespective of your question. They may even begin their responses with 'I'm glad you asked that question', and then almost completely ignore it. You then have to return them to the track. 'I'm afraid you haven't quite understood my question, I wanted to know . . .'. If greater firmness is required: 'You've not answered my question . . .'.

If an interviewee asks you to keep a statement 'off the record', ask if you can use the statement without attribution. Explain why you feel it is vital to your article and would not be a problem used in this way. If that doesn't work, you may be able to say that you can quote a colleague on the matter if necessary.

Fine judgement is required on these matters, though. Take the risk and print it if it is important, and you think publication is in the public interest. But if you think there is a legal danger, alert the office lawyer and let him/her decide.

ASSIGNMENT

Wind Farms – The Energy of the Future?
Wind Farms – Who Wants Them?
Wind Farms – A Foolhardy Policy?

Research and write a 1200-word article on wind farms for a targeted publication: local paper, national paper, consumer magazine. One of the above titles may suggest your point of view, but you may prefer to choose your own. The current economics of wind farms at your time of writing will determine your approach.

For wind farms	*Against wind farms*
Scottish Power	County Guardians
Manweb	Friends of the Lake District
National Windpower Ltd	Ramblers Association International

Wind Development UK
Centre for Alternative Technology

Conditional
Not in beauty spots: Friends of the Earth

Group work
Such assignments can be adapted for group work. Divide into FOR
and AGAINST teams. Each team could divide up research and
drafting work, with a spokesperson to present the team's case in
debate. The debate can then be open to the floor. Finally each
member of the group can write an article of 1200 words, without
any obligation to keep to the viewpoint of their team.

10 ILLUSTRATING THE ARTICLE

Illustration generally means photographs, but it can include drawings, old prints and engravings, sketches, various kinds of charts, maps, diagrams and graphs. As a freelance writer you have to decide when to offer illustrations with your articles, and whether it is worth while attempting to provide them yourself. Can you learn to produce them to the level of competence required? Should you hire the services of a professional photographer or illustrator? Should you do some picture research and deal with picture libraries and other sources? These are some of the decisions to be made.

This chapter examines these matters and will try to help you make the decisions. If you are already both a writer and photographer, you may want to move on to the next chapter.

You may, of course, find that those of your markets that do use illustrations, the newspapers and the weekly and monthly magazines among them, prefer to commission them from their own expert staff, draw on their regular freelance photographers and artists, or find what they need in their own picture libraries. Find out what their preferences are at article-proposal stage. Many magazines are picture-led: an article will be commissioned because some excellent pictures have been obtained.

You will find with some feature articles that you can get the illustrations you need free of charge from manufacturing or retailing companies, press offices and various institutions and agencies. But if your aim is to be versatile, or if you are compelled to be by the type of market you are selling in, you will be missing valuable opportunities at times if you are unable to provide pictures. There are many magazines for which good pictures will sell a competent article, and no pictures can mean so sale, even when the words are good. The combination of a well-written article with good photographs, either provided from picture research or by a writer-photographer who knows exactly what is needed to complement the words, is hard to match.

Take your own photographs, if your standards are good enough for the markets aimed at. If you are not good enough, and want to try, take lessons at night school, read a book or two and subscribe to a photography magazine, but submit your work only if you reach a reasonable standard. Your pictures must be both good and relevant. It may also, for your own purposes, be useful to take photographs of places and objects you are writing about so that you can refer to them for exact details.

SUBJECTS

There are a great number of subjects for which pictures are relevant, if not necessary: sports and recreations, all how-to subjects, oddities, people in pictures that tell a story, the arts, antiques, inn-signs, animals, travel articles, to name just a few.

Black and white prints should be glossy, borderless, not less than 7 in × 5 in and at least as big as they will be reproduced, since enlargement diminishes quality. 10 in × 8 in is the recommended size if quality is important. Colour pictures must be sent as transparencies: Kodachrome 64 is liked by many editors. Since there is no negative, and transparencies can get lost, you may want to keep duplicates.

Once you start using a camera regularly, ideas for articles will be suggested by the pictures you take as well as the other way round. Avoid taking pictures of cliché or over-familiar subjects – girls on beaches, Westminster Abbey, Sydney Harbour, all of which an editor can get cheaply in high quality prints from an agency – unless they incorporate something vital to your story. Your children lined up in front of the local museum is fine for the family album, but is not likely to have wider interest. People look more interesting caught off their guard. Animal pictures are a good bet, but are not easy: a zoom lens is an asset here.

WHICH MARKETS?

Some publications specialize in photographs. Writers' guides such as the *Writers' and Artists' Yearbook* say which (see Figure 2.1), but the information is sketchy, and you should supplement it by talking to editors and art editors.

Photography magazines are a useful example of the large how-to/hobby/ recreation market. There is a brisk demand by amateur photography magazines for how-to articles by writers who have become reasonably proficient photographers. In these markets you may be able to collect reproduction fees for photographs out of your stock, some of which may have already been used to illustrate articles for other kinds of magazines. They may now find a use as illustrations of different kinds of lighting, or different lenses or composition techniques. You may even be able to exploit your duds: pictures that show what happens when you stand too near, or commit some kind of photographic fault.

Another attraction of the photography magazine market is that the readership is constantly changing. New young readers latch on, with their latest cameras, while others move on, either to a magazine further upmarket or to a new hobby. You need to keep up to date with what is new in cameras, though the basic lessons remain the same: how to compose, how to use different lenses effectively, using flash, the various lighting tricks, choice of film for different purposes, choice of subjects that make for interesting photographs and those that do not.

A cautionary word here: it is best to query ideas for illustrated articles first to avoid expenses you may be unable to recoup. Generally it is better to let a publication choose from your black and white contact prints those it wants to print. It will then do the processing. If you are sending from a country where the developing is not of high quality, you may be asked to send a whole exposed roll of film for the publication to develop.

In studying the market for feature articles that take pictures, check on the kinds of articles; how much colour, how much black and white is used; what size of reproductions are used; what sort of caption material is needed. Note the general rules for composition – that subjects do not normally look out of the picture, that it should be simple rather than cluttered, that the eye should be drawn into the picture.

What are the functions of the illustrations in particular publications? Are they to help the reader follow instructions, do they supplement the text? How many are purely decorative, or to help in the page design? Ask the publication if it provides guidelines for contributors who want to send it photographs.

TAKING YOUR OWN PICTURES

If photography is new to you, start with a medium-priced camera, an inconspicuous, fairly lightweight, 35 mm single-lens reflex – which means you see through the lens that takes the picture. This will deliver thirty-six exposures and accommodate interchangeable lenses. Wide-angle and zoom lenses – useful for interviews – should be considered later, since they are expensive. Buy different lenses only as you need them, making sure that if you have two cameras, the lenses are interchangeable. Avoid the expense of much heavy equipment and sophisticated gadgetry, though a tripod is useful when using a slow shutter speed, or if you need plenty of 'mug shots'.

There are two schools of thought about automatic exposure and focusing. While they have the advantage of speed in instant shots, you will learn more about photography by doing your own adjustments. You will be able to experiment for different effects, taking several shots of the same subject, with different exposures ('bracketing') and comparing the results.

However, photographs wanted to complement a feature article should help to tell a story rather than depend on special effects.

It's a good idea for beginners to join a camera club. You can learn much from the advice you will get there, and it is a good place to pick up cheaply a second-hand camera. You will be able to use the dark-room too.

Art editors like to have a choice, so send them more than one version of a picture, including both horizontal and vertical. This will help in page design. Take a sufficient number of shots to offer a reasonable selection. Be careful with backgrounds. Fussy wallpaper or a sea of faces can distract attention from the subject. You may need to improve the lighting, if you are indoors and not using a flash, by opening curtains.

Give your photographs serial numbers.

WORKING WITH A PHOTOGRAPHER

You may prefer to work with a photographer. Your local camera club may be the place to find one. The *Writers' and Artists' Yearbook* gives photographic agencies. Or you could go through the classified advertisements in photography magazines, ask photographers' associations, or consult the *Publishers' Freelance Directory*.

You can arrange for article and photographs to be paid for separately or if the fee is for the package, work out a division with the photographer. For speculative projects, the photographer may ask for a fee whether the article sells or not.

PICTURE RESEARCH

Pictures can be obtained from many sources. As we have said, those glad of the publicity, such as the PR departments of companies, government departments, and trade associations will provide them free. Museums normally charge a reproduction fee, as do picture agencies. In the entertainment world artistes' and actors' agencies are glad to provide.

The procedure for getting and using pictures should be as follows:

1 Agree with your editor about any fees and whether they should be made by you or the editor.
2 Write to the picture source, or telephone if there is an urgent deadline. Explain the purpose, publications, dates, etc. Inspect the picture files if possible. Try to obtain 8 in × 10 in prints. Get copyright permission, with appropriate rights.
3 If given a choice, return all unwanted pictures immediately.
4 Credit the picture source.
5 Provide the editor with full caption details and any other useful information about the picture.
6 If a person is readily identifiable from a picture (most likely in a local paper or magazine), attach a permission note to it before submitting to an editor: better be safe than sued.

Two useful reference books are: *The Picture Researcher's Handbook: An International Guide to Picture Sources – and How to Use Them* by Hilary and Mary Evans (Saturday Ventures) and the *Directory of British Photographic Collections*, published by William Heinemann on behalf of The Royal Photographic Society. The *Writers' and Artists' Yearbook* has a brief but informative section on picture research. The British Association of Picture Libraries and Agencies in London (Tel: 0181–444–79130) will give advice.

GRAPHICS

The simplest kind of flow diagrams, charts or maps to illustrate articles require little artistic skill. Use a pen with a fine nib, black ink and drawing paper. Line drawings should be made at about twice the size they will be reproduced. Leave out lettering: indicate it on attached photocopy – the publication will get it set in type. If, like mine, your artistic skill is limited, find a talented friend or, if extra skills are needed, try the picture libraries or the *Publishers' Freelance Directory*. Figure 10.1 shows how computer graphics can come to your aid.

Don't drink or smoke
– what <u>do</u> you do?

The first research into the lives of today's news journalists shows we have pretensions to grandeur but embody the traditional characteristic of the trade, reports Naomi Marks.

So, we no longer smoke and drink like troopers, and we are more likely to hold an academic degree than an industry-recognised NCTJ certificate. Such are the results of the first in-depth study into the lives of British journalists today.

According to the research, fewer than three out of 10 male and fewer than two out of 10 female journalists smoke. And, although few are teetotal, six out of 10 describe themselves as only moderate but regular drinkers.

The survey finds that 49% of journalists hold a degree, but just 40% are NCTJ qualified.

Such news will undoubtedly stick like a salad sandwich in the throat of the unreconstructed hack, and cause him (and it is nearly always a him) to shed a tired and emotional tear or two over glorious careers begun as copyboys.

But the first thing to ask is how representative are these journalists, who agreed to tell all – from their voting patterns (just 6% intend to vote Conservative at the next election), to their sex lives (only one in 100 lives with a partner of the same sex).

The research, carried out by Anthony Delano, a former Fleet Street journalist and now senior research fellow at the London College of Printing's School of Media, and John Henningham, professor of journalism at the University of Queensland, was confined only to writing and production news journalists in national and regional newspapers, television and radio, wire services and news agencies. This was so

that data could be compared with similar research carried out in the USA and Australia.

Nevertheless, a whole swathe of journalists, many of these involved in news, has been left out. Those in the huge sector of magazine publishing – not to mention photographers and the growing number of freelances. (An NUJ survey published earlier this year showed that 23.5% of NUJ members classified themselves as full-time freelances.)

The second point about Delano and Henningham's research is: how surprising is it? This year has already seen the results of two surveys showing the changing nature of British journalism.

A Guild of Editors' report threw light on the "professionalisation" of what was once, proudly, treated as a trade or craft. It showed that 97.3% of newspaper trainees are white, nearly 70% describe themselves as middle-class, and one in five was educated at public school.

The NUJ survey came to the dramatic conclusion that "Lunchtime O-Booze is Dead", after results revealed that members were younger than ever and increasingly likely to be female.

However, the new research does highlight the equally important elements of our breed that have not changed.

Despite the increasing use of tape recorders, more than half (56%) of respondents remain dear to the belief that a journalist cannot be fully trained without shorthand.

Despite the growth in broadcasting and magazine publishing, the provincial press is still the important training ground it ever was: 44% began their careers on a regional weekly and 21% on a regional daily. A mere 6% started on a national daily and 10% in broadcasting. Only 3% started out in the trade press.

And, although journalists increasingly regard themselves as middle-class professionals (more than 60% think we deserve the same social status as solicitors and accountants, and more than 50% see parity with university lecturers and politicians), professional remuneration still eludes most of us.

Just 20% of journalists earn more than £35,000, with 16% earning £15,000–£20,000, and another 16% earning £20,000–£25,000.

As ever, journalists on the nationals earn the most, with a median salary of £37,500. Next come those with the BBC, wire services and agencies (with a median income of £32,500), and then those in independent broadcasting (£27,500). Regional journalists remain

at the bottom of the heap, on median earnings of £17,500.

Perhaps this is why a third of respondents say they supplement their income with freelancing, most of them for print outlets.

The research highlights the age-old disparity between the sexes. Women are particularly under-represented on daily newspapers, especially the tabloids. The highest proportion are in independent television and radio. News remains male-dominated, with only 25% of women journalists working in this area.

Sixty-six per cent of women believe it is harder for capable female journalists to get ahead in their careers, and 60% of women said that they had personal experience or knowledge of women being victims of prejudice in the newsroom. For men asked the same questions, the corresponding figures are 36% and 31%.

The median income for men is £32,500 – the figure for women is £10,000 less. Delano says the difference is partly explained by the fact that women journalists are younger. The median age for female journalists is 33, that for males, 38. Fewer than one in five female journalists are over 40, compared with 46% of male journalists).

Finally, the job itself – or at least the perception of it – has changed little. More than 90% of journalists single out curiosity as the one indispensable quality for aspiring newsmen and women. Ninety-eight per cent stress an urgency about delivering information to the public as important, with 88% putting a high value on scrutinising government claims. Nearly 50% feel that the provision of entertainment and relaxation is a very (47%) or fairly (44%) important part of their job.

When it comes to ethics, 86% feel it is justified to use official documents without authorisation, 73% have no problems with using hidden microphones or cameras, and 59% believe it is legitimate to claim to be someone other than a journalist to obtain information.

However, nearly half fear that media freedom is declining, with a similar proportion believing that standards in journalism have deteriorated within their own career span.

The picture drawn by Delano and Henningham is neither that of a radically changing profession, nor one stuck in a bygone age. There are no startling revelations and the research may be criticised for leaving out large groups of journalists.

But this is a first study of its kind. Comparison is difficult with little research having gone before.

And, as Delano points out: "You have to start somewhere."

● *The survey report is available, price £20, from the School of Media, LCPDT, 10 Black Hill, London EC1R 5EN.*

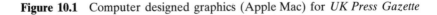

Figure 10.1   Computer designed graphics (Apple Mac) for *UK Press Gazette*

Figure 10.2 A line drawing projecting the two sides of a debate: *The European*

The publication you are contributing to may employ an artist who will do the whole drawing to your specifications or rough sketch. Where precision is necessary, the graphics must be done with great care – see the line drawings illustrating an article about building in Figure 19.3.

Line drawings of the artistic kind – cartoons, caricatures, and so on – aim at an immediate and powerful impact and must be done by experts. Figure 10.2 is a striking example.

CAPTIONS

There is a great variety of caption styles in newspapers and magazines. Some photo-stories rely on long captions to tell the facts. A long text, on the other hand, might be accompanied by one or two pictures that have only a few words of identification. Here are a few representative captions:

1 *Saul Bellow: story of a famous uncle.*
   Picture of Bellow with review of his latest novel (*Financial Times*).
2 *Broken wing of the sixth-form block that collapsed in the storm.*
   Picture with article about damage to an East Sussex school (*Times Educational Supplement*).
3 *Eyewitness accounts were given varying degrees of emphasis depending on which investigator recorded the evidence.*
   Picture of dead cattle with article about a lethal gas from Lake Nyas in Cameroon, that killed thousands of people and livestock (*New Scientist*).
4 *Cloistered gardens and Moorish architecture: The Hotel Babylon offers the ultimate in luxurious good taste – and a regime of salt-water baths and seaweed massages.*
   With article about the unusual services of this luxurious hotel in southern Spain (*Sunday Times Magazine*).
5 *Musicians here tend to think that once they've mastered the idiom they've arrived in the States. That's only the beginning.*
   Picture of the jazz musician club owner and collector of ceramics in his sitting room, with profile in the 'Room of My Own' series (*Observer Magazine*).
6 *Back to the drawing board ... Material supplied by UNESCO helps young schoolgirls in the Rwandan capital, Kigali, to learn about and heal the scars of the country's genocidal war. Across the border in Zaire, however, Hutu children in refugee camps are being given a different kind of lesson by teachers who deny the genocide ever took place.*
   A picture shows schoolgirls in Kigali at their slates (*The Guardian*). This article is discussed more fully in Chapter 16 and is illustrated in Figure 16.1.

The main functions

The above examples are chosen for their variety. Caption 1 identifies a mug shot. Captions 2, 3 and 4 indicate that the pictures illustrate effectively the main point of the article. Caption 5 repeats a significant quote. Caption 6 provides a taster and lead-in to the article.

In general, captions *add* something to the picture, often giving information that cannot be obtained from the picture. It must avoid stating the obvious. It is a bridge between the title and the article – part of the teamwork of the various presentational elements.

PREPARATION AND SUBMISSION

Put 'copyright' and your name, address and telephone number on the back of your own photographs. Either type the information on self-adhesive labels and stick them on, or get a rubber stamp made with the details. Photographs obtained from other sources should already be prepared in this way.

Captions may be stuck on your own photographs in the same way, or with a rubber solution. Sellotape may be used, but it can get in the way of marking up the picture. 'Marking up' means indicating by pencil lines on the back how the picture should be 'cropped' (what part of it is to be reproduced, and the measurements required of the reproduction given). Peel-off labels are useful for photographs not your own, or in case you may want to change the caption when you submit them to another market. Captions should also be numbered and written up on a separate sheet.

Use an envelope of a larger size than necessary, containing cardboard, to send the photographs with an article, inserting an adequate sized cardboard envelope for those that are to be returned to you. Alternatively use two pieces of cardboard, flat or corrugated, hinge them with Sellotape, insert the photographs, and secure with an elastic band. Use a strong envelope to send this in. Print on the outside envelope PHOTOGRAPHS: DO NOT BEND. Drawings should also be sent in stiff envelopes. Valuable material should be sent by registered post or recorded delivery.

Colour transparencies can be posted in the plastic storage wallets sold in photographic shops. List the transparencies on a separate sheet, with captions. Put a label on the outside with your name and address and the numbers of transparencies. Give every transparency your own serial number as with the B & Ws. These numbers can be used for your list, and can also go on the transparency on a peel-off label.

Store negatives in the thin plastic wallets available. For example, 35 mm negatives can be stored in strips of six with seven strips to a wallet. Give each strip a letter and each wallet a number to identity the negatives: 12d means strip d in wallet 12. Use ring-backed binders to contain the wallets and give them capital letters: A/12d.

When you have built up your own picture library, you may be able to obtain commissions for picture stories by sending off typed lists of themes covered by your files. Send a cv and a query letter with them indicating the field in which you are working.

ASSIGNMENTS

1 For any of the feature articles you have written as assignments
   so far: use a camera to provide *either* three B & Ws or colour
   transparencies, with captions. Provide a layout; *or* ransack old
   copies of magazines for three B & Ws or colour pictures, cut out
   and paste up in a layout, providing your own captions to suit
   your article.

2 Take three magazines and study the captions. Improve those you
   think need improving. Explain your rewordings.

11 DEVELOPING WRITING TECHNIQUES

'Literature is the art of writing something that will be read twice; journalism what will be grasped at once'. *Cyril Connolly*

This chapter concerns the machinery of language and how to use it, and the tools that go with it. The theme will be continued in the following chapter, which will move on from getting it right and clear to getting it individual, to finding your own style, your own tone of voice.

Whatever helpful prescriptions for good writing you find, your best lessons will be based on your own diagnosis: collection and analysis of good models, learning to identify your weaknesses, and then writing and rewriting within the time available until you are satisfied. A piece of writing comes alive for readers if their senses go into action, if they *see* what you are saying.

'Give not that which is holy unto the dogs, neither cast ye your pearls before swine, lest they trample them under their feet, and turn again and rend you' (*St Matthew*, VII, vi). The anecdotes of today's journalists are akin to Christ's parables, and if you need lessons in how to get a message moving, there are few better places to look at than the Bible in its authorized version.

Bad writing comes in two main sorts. One tends to be self-conscious, repetitive and rambling. It draws too much attention to itself because of its lack of clear content and aim, and too much to the writer because of the lack of rapport with readers. Like bad acting it leaves the audience bewildered, bored or embarrassed. The other common form of bad writing is under-playing. The writer is not interested enough, or stirred enough, or is careless, lacking in concentration. Such a writer may shake out any gold nuggets, along with the sand.

GOOD WRITING SUMMED UP

Assuming there is commitment to content and readers, here for the writer is a collection of specific principles collected from authorities as diverse as Aristotle, Schopenhauer, Somerset Maugham, Henry Fowler, Stephen Leacock, Sir Ernest Gowers, George Orwell and the American Rudolf Flesch (see Bibliography, page 411):

1   Choose the precise word.
2   Prefer the familiar word to the unfamiliar.
3   Use the concrete rather than the abstract.
4   Prefer a single word to a circumlocution, the simple to the complex.
5   Use a short word rather than a long one.
6   Use a Saxon word rather than a Roman one.
7   Use transitive verbs in the active voice where possible, avoiding the passive.
8   Put statements in a positive form rather than a negative.
9   Avoid unnecessary auxiliaries.
10   Use adjectives and adverbs sparingly: get the meaning into verbs and nouns.
11   Avoid 'empty' words – prepositions and conjunctions that clutter, especially the compounds ('for the purpose of' = 'for').
12   Cut out all superfluous words.

1 is crucial, and many of the other principles are ancillary to it. 2, 3, 5, 7 and 8 are intended to apply wherever possible. The abstract word, the long word, the Roman word, and the passive voice are sometimes the most appropriate. It is the richness of the English vocabulary from its different sources that gives us so much choice. The skill is in choosing precisely – 'freedom' or 'liberty', 'answerable' or 'responsible', 'lively' or 'animated' – in a particular context. The danger is in complacently feeling that any synonym or near-synonym will do.

Underlying the above principles of word choice are the aims of any effective piece of writing: precision, brevity, clarity, unity, coherence, proper emphasis (showing relative importance of points by proportion and order, and eschewing the irrelevant), and appropriateness (to content/ market/occasion). For journalism we must add the quality of being interesting.

Gowers in his classic *Plain Words* (Penguin Books) quotes many pieces of bad English to illustrate where things go wrong. Here is one that breaks most of the rules and seems devoid of any quality whatsoever: even worse, it says the opposite of what it intends:

In communicating these data to your organization after fullest consultation with all my colleagues also concerned, I would certainly be less than truthful if I were to say that this has occasioned the Ministry (and this section in particular) no little difficulty but that the delay is nevertheless regretted.

Gowers points out: The writer intended to say something very simple: 'I am sorry we could not send the information sooner, but we have found this a very difficult case', but actually ends up saying that the case was easy and he does not regret the delay.

Here follow some suggestions for how to avoid common ill-usages.

MAKING WORDS WORK

Precision takes time and thought, and we are often short of both.

Pairs of words that look like synonyms but are not can be a trap.

'Alternatives' is not the same as 'choices', nor do the following match up: 'chronic' and 'acute', 'comprise' and 'compose', 'uninterested' and 'disinterested'.

Unnecessary adjectives and adverbs are the first words to be blue-pencilled out by subeditors. 'The man is *very* big' may sound as if you are anxious the reader won't believe you when you say 'The man is big'. 'Lovely', 'fantastic', 'fabulous', 'trendy', and 'cool' are gush words, usefully chatty at times but almost meaningless. 'Trendier' adjectives such as 'destabilized', 'knee-jerk' (reaction), 'caring', 'supportive' can be short-lived, and writers trying hard to be up to the minute can be too obviously caught out if the words have become outdated by the time they have pinned them down.

Useful compression can be done by adjectives, and adverbs. The arts reviews of the weeklies, for example, have to pack a lot in. Consider how neatly the background information about character and situation is encapsulated by the adjectives in this paragraph from Philip French's review of the film *Sammy and Rosie Get Laid (The Observer)*:

> The eponymous anti-hero and anti-heroine are a cheerless, childless, thirtyish couple uneasily cohabiting a cluttered flat in Ladbroke Grove. An open marriage brings them no happiness, their portfolio of once fashionable left-wing views looks distinctly grubby. Sammy (Ayub Khan Din) is a London-born Pakistani accountant with a show-biz clientele and the weak good looks of a pre-war matinee idol like Gilbert Roland or John Gilbert. Rosie (Frances Barber) is a disillusioned English social worker whose circle of militant feminists and aggressive lesbians keeps her within the progressive fold.

Tabloid conciseness

The news stories of the tabloid press achieve pace by carefully attributed adjectives and adverbs that would otherwise need phrasal or clause explanations. In the *Daily Mirror* I find 'dramatic helicopter jailbreak', 'wrongly arrested', 'crippling health cuts', 'radical proposals', 'outraged fund officials'. Over-familiar they may be, but they are direct and to the point.

Adverbs are used excessively at the start of sentences to make them sound more thoughtful than they are: 'Predictably, the argument grew fiercer', for example. 'Sadly', 'inevitably', and 'hopefully' (meaning 'it is to be hoped that') are also given the job. Both quality national papers and the populars are culprits here.

Prepositions, everyone now knows, can be put at the end of sentences. But beware of pile-ups: 'Where did their father put the boat they were waved to out of from away?'

Conjunctions can be dangerous too. 'Unless', which lawyers use to bemuse everybody else, can lead to such conundrums as: 'Unless you don't disapprove of saying no, you won't refuse'. 'And' can be allowed to start sentences.

And even paragraphs. But not as often as 'but'.

But don't overdo it.

Stock words and phrases

'Ultimate consumer' is a funny way of saying you buy a cake to eat it. The words and phrases of jargon or clichés are used because they are ready-made, stocked on shelves in the mind, easy to take off and slot into whatever you're writing, especially if you are in a hurry and tired of thinking. There are all kinds. There are the pretentious ones, to be found mainly in the qualities – 'phenomenon', 'basically', 'inexorably', 'parameters'.

There are sinister euphemisms among them – attempts to prevent other people from worrying too much – such as 'pacification', 'population control', and so on. Apparently 'collateral counterforce damage of second strike capability' means 70 million dead.

A lie can be called 'an inoperative statement' (USA) or 'an economical use of truth' (Britain). More tongue-in-cheek, no doubt, an American journalist asked about a call-girl who slept with diplomats: 'Did she horizontalize her way to the information?' Are 'horizontalization' and 'horizontalizationize' on their way?

High-tech credentials used to be signalled by using such words as 'interface' and 'user-friendly'; but the applications have multiplied. They are now as likely to be referring to the insides of sandwiches and to vacuum cleaners as to computers.

Some American clichés have been worn to death. Does anybody 'out there' (as they say) know of the origin of 'all bright-eyed and bushy-tailed', and if so, can they explain what it means. Also, like Topsy, it just grew, and 'Cloud Nine'. But there are no prizes.

An occasional cliché has its place, like waving to someone as you turn the corner of the street. Giving them a twist can produce an amusing phrase, perhaps a good headline. For example, *Private Eye*, the satirical magazine, with notable contributions from Fritz Spiegl, deliberately worked the vogue-word 'situation', as in the phrases 'reaching a no-win situation' and 'recommended in adult education situations', towards a quicker death. But 'situation' is tenacious and seems to have survived such attempts, as have 'position', 'condition' and other 'ions'.

Such wordiness crops up in broadsheet papers and magazines. Tabloid newspapers have 'latest blast in a bitter war of words', 'amazing outburst', 'went overboard for the girl', 'a romantic weekend', 'put his oar in', 'curvy' or 'curvaceous' (as in 'the bubbly curvaceous leggy ex-model'), 'sizzling sheer stockings to make any girl feel a cracker', 'fellas faced with a bevy of beauties', 'dishy daredevil', 'hunky lover', 'causing a rumpus', and 'dawn swoop on the house'.

Occasionally humorous columnists have a go at jargon. But setting up as a judge brings its own hazards when words come in and out fast, and we all tend to overwork favourite words and phrases.

SENSE OUT OF SENTENCES

The trouble with the muscular modern sentence is that it can become muscle-bound. In avoidance of heavy subsidiary clauses, economic phrases can be overburdened and fail to connect: 'An avid theatregoer, she became one of the country's top biologists' is an example. The misplaced or 'dangling' participle is common: consider 'Unnerved by the commotion, it was a long time before he recovered' (read 'he took a long time ...') and 'Taking the baby into her arms, the bus was boarded with difficulty' ('she boarded').

Shifting the emphasis into the verbs so that the prose keeps moving is done in good modern journalism effectively. 'The rebels ran through the streets and overturned and burnt cars' is better than 'There was overturning and burning of cars in the streets that the rebels ran through'. The process is aided by using direct, simple verbs, but spoilt in some popular papers by the overuse of some, such as 'wed' and 'slay' (near-obsolete elsewhere), although such usages can be justified in headlines with their restricted letter counts.

Notice how the verbs in this story from *The Star* make for a clear, concise account:

> A hero was blasted to death when he tackled an armed robber yesterday.
>   The middle-aged partner in a mortgage brokers challenged the raider when he demanded cash. A scuffle broke out, a shot was fired and Christopher Nugent fell dying in a pool of his own blood.
>   Mr Nugent tackled the gunman in his offices in Mildenhall, Suffolk, after being alerted by a terrified assistant.
>   After the shooting the man raced from the offices and leapt into a waiting car which sped off.

Such action-packed prose works well if the story is short. The hunt for synonyms for, say, 'moving fast' – 'fled', 'whisk', 'swooped' – can become frenetic in longer pieces.

TV news bulletins, notably ITN's *News at Ten*, reflect the best kind of tabloid newspaper English:

> 'Somalia's lost generation. "A million walking skeletons," says the United Nations.'
>   'The toughest day of their lives. Are A levels now easier?'

Varying sentence structure

It is the shortest and simplest words that reach the heart (see Brian McArthur's *Penguin Book of Historic Speeches*, Penguin Books, 1995). The first version of John F. Kennedy's inaugural speech in 1961 read: 'We do not campaign stressing what our country is going to do for us as people. We stress what we can do for our country, all of us.' The final speech when the speech writers had finished with it, ran: 'And so, my fellow Americans, ask not what your country can do for you; ask what you can do for your country'. Note that half of the power of that comes from awareness of the audience and the occasion.

The healthy liking for short sentences, as with short words, can lead to monotony, of course, if care is not taken to vary the lengths, to put in occasional long ones, and to vary sentence structure. Consider this sequence, about food ideas to be found in a department store:

> 'There are some fine new biscuit moulds, which make a change from the usual ones. There are also more different kinds of cooking utensils than most stores have. As well as this, there is a cookery book with a difference, which concentrates on dishes for parties.'

The triteness caused by the repetition of words is compounded by the similarity of length and structure of the sentences. They are all loose sentences, which means they contain two clauses, the second being introduced by a conjunction or relative pronoun. The subject of each sentence is in exactly the same place, preceded by 'there is/are'.

Before sending off a feature article, examine its sentence structure. Is it almost always: subject, verb, the rest of the predicate? Try object, passive verb, agent occasionally. Begin with a preposition, or an adverb or a conjunction for a change. Put a result before a cause sometimes, saying 'This is what happens when. . . .'

Computers can now not only check your spelling and suggest synonyms when you seem to lack precision, but also consider the shape of your writing, and give you such advice as: '83 per cent of your sentences start with the subject. This compares with advice given by writing teachers that no more than 75 per cent should'. If you have access to such a machine, however, my advice would be to use it judiciously and not often. A text can get too much attention of the processing kind, as *Time Magazine* prose does, for example. A remark in *The New Yorker* once summed up its style as 'backward ran the sentences until reeled the mind'.

Tight, fast-moving prose needs linking that is flexible yet strong, linking that can provide breathers. It needs punctuation pauses that help to keep the reader relaxed. Key words providing a thread throughout are an essential technique (have another look at Figure 8.1). The ideas should be sufficiently spaced out with some other techniques of speech: the odd aside ('Good heavens', 'Well, well', 'If you like'), the odd repetition deliberately but sparingly used.

Weak warming-up openings to sentences should be avoided. 'I have often thought that among the many possible ways of losing weight' is better as 'You can lose weight . . .'

THE PARAGRAPH

A sentence has one main thought; a paragraph has one main topic, sometimes explicit in a topic sentence. The paragraph is an integral part of the article, a component of the theme, like one room of a house. It has to be fitted into the framework in such a way that the reader sees the plan, though not of course all the structural supports, any more than you will see all those of a house. It has to be linked, even if not obviously, with what went before and what comes after.

The paragraph should vary, like the sentence, in length and structure. Notice the great difference in the lengths of paragraphs in different publications.

The structure of a paragraph also depends on the kind of writing, whether descriptive, narrative, expository or argumentative.

There are two basic kinds of order – chronological/space order and logical order; and a special form of the latter, association, where the 'logic' is personal. Here the writer may make leaps across time and space impelled by memory, but in such a way that the reader can easily follow. Such 'flashback' techniques, common in films, are used in journalism as well as in fiction.

Within each of these patterns there are of course numerous variations. What imposes unity is the writer's viewpoint.

Notice how these basic structures underlie the paragraphs below, selected to illustrate the main kinds of writing.

DESCRIPTION

Here is an extract from Laurie Lee's *As I Walked Out One Midsummer Morning*:

> In the village square I came on a great studded door bearing the sign: 'Posada de Nuestra Senora'. I pushed the door open and entered a white-washed courtyard hanging with geraniums and crowded with mules and asses. There was bedlam in the courtyard – mules stamping, asses braying, chickens cackling and children fighting. A fat old crone, crouching by the fire in the corner, was stirring soup in a large black cauldron, and as she seemed to be in charge, I went up to her and made a sign for food. Without a word she lifted a ladleful of the soup and held it to my mouth. I tasted and choked: it was hot, strong and acrid with smoke and herbs. The old lady peered at me sharply through the fumes of the fire. She was bent, leather-skinned, bearded and fanged, and looked like a watchful moose.

The elements common to good description are all here. The reader is assailed through the senses. Nouns and verbs are as important as adjectives. The adjectives used are simple but exact and vivid words that bring the scene to life: no vagueness nor exaggeration. Clichés are out in such a context. Notice the pattern made by the shifting viewpoint as the author walks, from general (whitewashed courtyard) to particular detail (bearded and fanged woman).

There has to be charm about descriptive writing to win the reader over, since what interests one person about a scene might not interest another. There must be substantial powers of observation, but also strong (though not showy) personal vibrations in the way details are expressed. Ideally, readers will feel as interested in the writer as they are in the scene; they will feel that the writer is telling the truth about it, as he or she sees it. Thus readers are made to feel they are actually there. They will be able to come to some conclusion about the scene, or the object described.

The modern newspaper or magazine article likes description that is meaty with facts and pacy. Here is Tony Parsons in 'Slaves of Milan' (*Arena*, May/June 1988 and reprinted in *Dispatches from the Front Line of Popular Culture*, Virgin Books, 1995) inside the cathedral:

> In the cool shadows inside, among the massive white columns and the infinite stained glass windows, Milanesi businessmen in their lunch hour kneel before the Madonna and child, make the signs of the cross and clasp their hands in prayer. One of them – wrapped up against February in a deep camel hair coat, squat and heavy bearded, like a company man Martin Scorsese – catches my eye. He looks like the archetypal hard nosed, go-getting Milano corporate cowboy. The sight of him – with his head bowed, his lips muttering in supplication, not worried if he gets the knees of his million lire suit messed up – is strangely moving. After long minutes lost in prayer he eventually rises and checks his watch. Five past two. Time to get back to the office.

NARRATION

This extract is taken from Peter Benchley's *Jaws*:

> A hundred yards offshore, the fish sensed a change in the sea's rhythm. It did not see the woman, nor yet did it smell her. Running within the length of its body were a series of thin canals, filled with mucus and dotted with nerve endings, and these nerves detected vibrations and signalled the brain. The fish turned towards shore. . . .
>
> The vibrations were stronger now, and the fish recognized prey. The sweeps of its tail quickened, thrusting the giant body with a speed that agitated the tiny phosphorescent animals in the water and caused them to glow, casting a mantle of sparks over the fish. . . .
>
> The fish smelled her now, and the vibrations – erratic and sharp – signalled distress. The fish began to circle close to the surface, its dorsal fin broke water, and its tail, threshing back and forth, cut the glossy surface with a hiss. A series of tremors shook its body. . . .
>
> . . . The fish, with the woman's body in its mouth, smashed down the water with a thunderous splash, spewing foam and blood and phosphorescence in a gaudy shower.

The most important element here is suspense: narrative writing must be constantly making you ask 'What happened next?' There is often a fair amount of description mingled in, so that you see the happenings clearly and become interested in the protagonists. Normally this description is skilfully interwoven so as not to slow the narrative down. The story must have continual interest and authority if it is to sweep readers along. If readers feel something has been missed out, or that the order is wrong, the spell is broken, and the attention will wander.

I think this piece meets the main criteria. In particular, the facts about sharks have been well researched and there is just enough physiological detail to give authority and add effectiveness. Notice how the verbs carry a descriptive function so that the narrative doesn't lose pace.

The order here is straightforwardly chronological, the description being used to heighten the drama.

A *Sunday Telegraph* account by James Brightgold of a New Age holiday camp in Somerset packs in the scenes and incidents, even in the middle, background/commentary part. At first there is a definite flavour of 'controlled insanity' that needs a vivid event. It arrives in a late-night tarot card reading in Reginald's van:

> ... Suddenly, sounding terrifying in the still of the night, someone outside began screaming. It had just turned 4 a.m.
>
> 'What's happening to me! Please God, help me! I'm lost! Lost! Lost!' And then hilariously, 'Reel me in, Alison Duckworth!!'
>
> The man outside continued screaming for about half an hour. Then, with a roar, one of the camp vans was started and the psychic casualty was thrown in and taken to hospital. Shortly after, a woman began yelling about witches on the camp site.
>
> It was just another night at the Oak Dragon 'Astrology, Myth and Magic' camp near Shepton Mallet. ...

EXPOSITION (HOW-TO)

Here *The Good Housekeeping Step-by-Step Cook Book* (Book Club Associates) gives the recipe for 'Roquefort Lamb Chops':

100 g (4 oz) Roquefort cheese
5 ml (1 level tsp) salt
5 ml (1 tsp) Worcester sauce
Pinch pepper
8 Loin lamb chops, cut about 6.5 cm (2.5 in) thick
298 g (10.5 oz) can condensed consommé

1 With a fork, stir and mash the cheese in a small bowl, with the salt, Worcestershire sauce and pepper until well mixed.
2 Trim the chops, leaving only a thin layer of fat. Place the chops on a rack in the grill pan. Grill for 8–10 minutes on each side.
3 Hold each chop with tongs and spread the Roquefort mixture evenly over the outer edge of the chops, over the fat, or over one flat side. Arrange the chops in a shallow flameproof dish, pour over the undiluted consommé and grill for a further 2–3 minutes or until the cheese has melted and is bubbling and the sauce is hot.

Authority is needed for exposition: every word should indicate that you know your subject, that you have studied it thoroughly, or have plenty of experience. The explanation and analysis must be clear: you aim at objectivity. The picture must be complete, for if there is an important detail you are not sure about and leave out, the reader will sense there is a gap.

Such a straightforward how-to piece as cooking a chop makes these requirements obvious. It is not as easy to get it right as it looks. It is easy to forget to say what you do with a particular ingredient, and working out the best order for the instructions requires thought if the result is to be achieved.

There is little attempt to be elegant, every attempt to be comprehensive and clear. It was not necessary to repeat the word 'chops' so many times, but it does not matter. The reader is interested in precision, not 'style'.

EXPOSITION (NARRATION-STYLE)

The following extract comes from Tony Barber, 'Serbs, Croats and Muslims: who hates who and why?', *The Independent on Sunday,* 9 August 1992:

> The Serbs are Orthodox Christians whose religion was crucial in keeping alive their national identity during almost four centuries of Ottoman Turkish occupation. Of the nations that formed Yugoslavia in 1918, the Serbs were alone in having liberated themselves from foreign rule and set up an independent state in the 19th century.
>
> The Croats spent centuries under the Austro-Hungarian empire and their Catholicism and Central European outlook were equally important in shaping their identity. They resented the fact that the first Yugoslav state, which lasted from 1918–1941, was to a great extent Serbia writ large, with a Serbian king and army and a Serb-dominated political system.

A great deal of article writing is exposition: explaining. The facts that are daily divulged in the news pages are put into order, their significance determined, forecasts made, perhaps problems anticipated and solutions suggested. Expository journalism of this sort is contemporary history – history as it is happening. Much of a foreign correspondent's work is putting into perspective the events of the country reported from, making sure at the same time that everything that needs explaining – customs, ethnic balance, the governing system – is explained clearly when necessary.

EXPOSITION (SCIENCE/TECHNOLOGY)

Here is an extract from 'Danger Down-play', *The New Internationalist,* December 1987 (but still relevant in 1996). The article commented on the lessons to be learnt from the breakdown of the Chernobyl nuclear power station in the Soviet Union:

> The future of the nuclear power industry lies in the balance. One more major accident, especially in Europe, will prevent any more power plants being built. The incentive, therefore, for the industry to conceal, deny or play down incidents has never been greater. That must have helped prompt Ecoropa – a British environmental action group – to produce their latest concise and well-written pamphlet on nuclear power.
>
> Here are some of the key points: What is the main problem with nuclear reactors? They provide heat which, via steam-driven turbines, produces electricity. Reactors are extremely complex, each having, for example, over 30,000 valves; and they are inherently dangerous. They require elaborate safety systems which all depend on perfect engineering and/or infallible operators.

In an increasingly scientific and technological age there is a great need for specialist journalists who can interpret current developments. They may write for a variety of markets, carefully assessing the level of knowledge of each readership. They often have to 'translate' the jargon of experts who may have fewer communication skills.

The reader may need to be told where further information is available. In the Chernobyl article the technique of anticipating readers' questions and then answering them is used effectively. What happened at Chernobyl? Could Chernobyl happen elsewhere? So what is the problem with radiation? Why is nuclear waste dangerous? It's a particularly useful technique when the subject matter is complex.

Teaching or lecturing is a good training for expository writing. There are some differences, however, that have to be kept in mind. The lecturer who turns to writing may work from well organized notes but tend to ramble and be repetitive in performance. This can work well with a live audience, if the key points are made to stand out so that they are easily noted (perhaps even provided as lecture notes). Repetition is necessary because the audience cannot go back, as they can in a book. A piece of writing, on the other hand, is linear: it must advance strongly. The occasional cross-reference is usually all that is necessary to remind the leader of related points.

Teachers and lecturers can become dogmatic and pompous as well as wordy, especially if they are used to captive audiences. They must remember that a pupil may need courage to walk out of a class, but a reader needs no courage to close a magazine or book or throw it across the room.

Live audiences provide a writer with useful experiences of putting thoughts together, of experimenting with different kinds of explanation, of practice in ordering and simplifying ideas. The simple, direct language used in speech, trimmed of the repetition mentioned, is the right basis for expository writing.

The essential qualities of good expository writing are comprehensiveness, logical order, and clarity. Among techniques to achieve these are the following:

Analysis

In the approach to a subject analysis is a useful tool in arriving at clarity and logical order. Break the subject down, divide and subdivide; decide in which order the subject may best be understood by the reader; then produce your checklist or outline.

This will help in ensuring comprehensiveness in an expository piece. To give an example, think of all the electrical jobs around the house that could go dangerously wrong if the instructions in a how-to article were left incomplete.

Definition

An article about the effects of divorce on children would need to make it clear exactly what the difference is between care and custody. Such distinctions are made by defining the terms. Whether or not misconceptions might be in question, key terms used in a subject, especially technical ones, need to be defined to make sure writer and reader are on the same wavelength.

Some definitions are established in law. What exactly is meant in legal terms by a 'homeless' person? Some terms may need more than one kind of definition: mental illness, for instance, may need to be defined both legally and medically.

Analogy, illustration, example and anecdote

These amount to the same thing in the end. They turn abstract into concrete and, by bringing people and significant detail on to the scene, make the reader *see* what is in your mind. For instance, the complexity of a nuclear reactor is more clearly established when the example of one with more than 30,000 valves is given, and an African country's starvation problem is defined further by reference to 5 million peasants and, say, 950,000 tonnes of food.

ARGUMENT

Argument – unless it is entirely abstract – builds on description and exposition. To be effective, the writer must make clear to the reader what the premises are and what the terms used mean. The following extract from 'The realistic price of human life', by Robin McKie, in *The Observer* is a good example of this technique:

> A car driver is 18 times more likely to die in a crash than a train passenger. Yet public alarm which follows rare rail disasters has resulted in continual safety improvements to trains. These cost money and force up rail fares, causing more people to travel on roads – where they are far more likely to die.
> This paradox is the result of popular misunderstandings about the daily hazards we face. Alarming examples of these are to be published later this year in a report by Britain's most respected scientific body, the Royal Society.
> The report highlights massive sums spent to reduce only slight dangers while serious hazards are ignored. For instance, building regulations – introduced after the Ronan Point gas explosion killed several council tenants – have cost an estimated £20 million for each life saved.
> 'Catastrophic accidents, killing or injuring many people as the result of one event, have little influence on the level of individual risk but have a disproportionate effect on the response of society,' it states.
> Other misconceptions about risks include popular fears which rate cancers as being twice as frequent as heart diseases, although the reverse is true. Similarly murders are believed to be as common as strokes. In fact the latter are 10 times more likely to occur.
> It would be wrong to blame only public ignorance, say the report's authors, a team of medical researchers, statisticians, economists, and scientists led by Sir Frederick Warner, a consultant engineer. 'There is also a public mistrust of "experts" which is not without justifying evidence,' they say.

Added to the expository techniques, argument, as indicated here, can call for extra thinking power: the ability to analyse the more complex problems, to weigh up evidence, to come to conclusions.

Reason in control

When political arguments are emotionally charged, care must be taken to back up statements with figures. This Anne Applebaum does in her article 'Do We Need People Like Michael Howard?' (*The Spectator*, 22 May 1995.

> There is no evidence that illegal immigrants are 'stealing' jobs from natives; there is no evidence that they are 'stealing' from the state. There is no

evidence even that they are a demographic burden: when emigrants and immigrants are compared. Britain actually suffered a loss in 1992, the last year for which statistics are available, of 11 million people.

The ending sums up the criticism that the article has made of the Government's policy, while first putting in the balance what is reasonable in it:

> There is in fact a set of legitimate political arguments both for favouring some kinds of people over others and for holding down the numbers of immigrants: when too many people of a very different culture appear at the same time in the same place, it usually upsets the natives. Cities with large immigrant populations – Miami and Los Angeles – tend to be violent; countries with large immigrant populations generally experience a racist backlash. And every country has the absolute right to decide who may live there, based on any principle it likes.
>
> But that needn't mean that people who do come here should be constantly under popular or political attack. Some of them really have suffered terrible things, even if the Home Office doesn't believe it; others are happily employed by the British, even if the Home Office doesn't approve. If the Government really must manipulate tales about benefit fraud and invent stories about crocodiles to get rid of immigrants, it might at least do them a favour of doing so quietly.

Emotion is often needed first in an article that aims to persuade – to get past readers' indifference, change attitude or mood, make receptive. It is worth repeating, though, that reason must be in control. Emotion can lead a writer to produce non-sequiturs, to beg the question, to weight the language inequably, to produce red herrings, to indulge in prejudices and witch-hunts. As a matter of technique, *harnessing* (let's not say *exploiting*) emotions can be done by irony or other form of subtle suggestion. Think of such classic examples as Mark Antony's funeral speech in *Julius Caesar*.

ESSAYS, THINK PIECES AND POLEMICS

The political weeklies offer homes for essays that delve into history or cultural forays, which journalists tend to call think pieces, but the Op Ed (opposite editorial or leader) spaces in national papers also accommodate them. They will almost certainly be pegged to the news. The *Daily Mail*, for example, takes off into a polemic from a call made by Government adviser Dr Nicholas Tate for our national identity to be put on the school curriculum. Here are some of the main points of 'Why we lost our pride in being British' by Andrew Roberts:

PROPER NOUNS: if they have adjectives, use them. Thus a Californian (not California) judge, the Pakistani (not Pakistan) government, the Texan (not Texas) press.

PROTAGONIST means the chief actor or combatant. If you are referring to several people, they cannot all be protagonists.

PROTEST. Objectors protest that a decision is unfair, or they protest at or against it. Employers have protested against the examination boards' decision to take no account of spelling in A-level marking systems is right; The NUT protested the penalisation of children from ethnic minorities for writing poor English is wrong.

PRY: use prise, unless you mean peer.

PUNCTUATION

APOSTROPHES. Use the normal possessive ending 's after singular words or names that end in s: boss's, caucus's, Delors's, St James's, Jones's. Use it after plurals that do not end in s: children's, Frenchmen's, media's.

Use the ending s' on plurals that end in s - Danes', bosses', Joneses' - including plural names that take a singular verb, eg, Reuters', Barclays', Stewarts & Lloyds', Salomon Brothers'.

Although singular in other respects, the United States, the United Nations, the Philippines, etc, have a plural possessive apostrophe: eg, What will the United States' next move be?

People's = of (the) people.

Peoples' = of peoples.

Try to avoid using Lloyd's (the insurance market) as a possessive; it poses an insoluble problem.

BRACKETS. If a whole sentence is within brackets, put the full stop inside.

Square brackets should be used for interpolations in direct quotations: "Let them [the poor] eat cake." To use ordinary curved brackets implies that the words inside them were part of the original text from which you are quoting.

COLONS. Use a colon "to deliver the goods that have been invoiced in the preceding words" (Fowler). They brought presents: gold, frankincense and oil at $35 a barrel.

Use a colon before a whole quoted sentence, but not before a quotation that begins mid-sentence. She said: "It will never work." He retorted that it had "always worked before".

Figure 11.1   A page from *The Economist Style Guide*

- After 50 years drift, British pride has to be put on the curriculum.
- Egalitarianism has denigrated achievement.
- Public schools (quality) derided, comprehensive schools (failures) regarded as best educational system.
- Tax system has encouraged laziness.
- The empire has been dismantled and we are relying on the EU.
- Liberals and left-wingers are the culprits.
- Ordinary Britons are not embarrassed to feel pride in Britain.
- 'Ties of blood and sentiment' prevail abroad; here liberals teach the stripping of national identity.
- Conservatives know that this loss leads to schizophrenia and loneliness.

Such an argument aims at passionate consciousness-raising rather than cool reasoning. It is well structured: it raises the problem, it answers the question and explains the causes, it provides the solution (stop the rot). But it moves forward rhythmically, a passionate lament rather than a logical argument. The theme is repeated, like an incantation, in words that link up resonantly: 'British', 'Britain', 'Britons', 'self-respect', 'boasts', 'hope', 'opportunity', 'superiority', 'patriotism', 'worthy', 'ties of blood and sentiment', 'stirring'. . . .

HOUSE STYLE

Here it is convenient to deal with 'house style', which means the particular forms and usages preferred by different publications. You can follow these by studying the publication. You find out which spelling is preferred when there are alternatives, which form of date is used, the form for military ranks, etc. If you contribute to a publication regularly, you may be able to obtain its 'style sheet' or 'style book', or the most important dictates may be incorporated in its writer's guidelines. *The Economist Style Guide* is excellent, starting off with general principles along the lines of those at the beginning of this chapter, and then continuing like a glossary. A page of the former is reproduced here (Figure 11.1), and that of *The Times* is also recommended. Of the books on English usage, apart from Gowers's, most useful are Fowler's *Modern English Usage* (OUP), Strunk and White's *Elements of Style* (Macmillan), a brilliantly concise guide; and for forms, *Hart's Rules for Compositors and Readers at the University Press, Oxford,* and *The Oxford Dictionary for Writers and Editors,* both OUP.

ASSIGNMENTS

1 Rewrite the extract from *The Observer* (page 198), imagining the Royal Society report was written yesterday, to make a *Sun* leader. Study some *Sun* leaders first.

2 Describe someone practising a sport, explaining the technique and assessing the skill (golf, swimming, hang-gliding ... not a team game), in 300 words, for a student magazine.

3 Watch a group of people playing/enjoying themselves (children in a playground, a mixed group in a pub ...) and write as amusing/interesting account of it as you can: 400 words, to be passed to a colleague to read and sub down to 200 words.

4 Watch a skilled person doing a job (carpenter ... decorator ... gardener ...) and write for the relevant trade/hobby magazine a 400-word piece. Include a quote or two from the person and relate the personality to the job in a readable way.

5 Write a 1000-word article for an appropriate market with the title 'Have we lost our pride in being British?', updating as necessary the subject-matter of the article 'Why we lost our pride in being British', discussed on pages 199 and 201. Come to your own conclusions on the subject.

12 THE QUESTION OF STYLE

We begin with Henry Mayhew:

Then as the streets grow blue with the coming light, and the church spires and chimney tops stand out against the sky with a sharpness of outline that is seen only in London before its millions of fires cover the town with their pall of smoke – then come sauntering forth the unwashed poor, some with greasy wallets on their back, to hunt over each dirt heap, and eke out life by seeking refuse bones or stray rags and pieces of old iron (*The Unknown Mayhew*. Selections from the *Morning Chronicle, 1849–50*, Penguin Books, 1984).

The second extract comes from V. S. Pritchett:

We arrived at Camberwell Green in a street off Coldharbour Lane in which the smell of vinegar from a pickle factory hung low, a street of little houses, like Great Uncle Arthur's in York, and little shops that sent out such a reek of paraffin and packages that one's nostrils itched, we settled into one of our most original residences. It was, to our excitement, a flat. People lived above us. We could hear them trampling on the floor, children raced up and down until the ceiling shook. We all got measles. A strange smell that had puzzled my parents soon showed its cause. Dry rot. We woke up one morning to find our bed was at a slope. The foot of the bed had gone through the floor. Father was equal to this, of course. He 'got hold of the landlord' and said 'Confound you. For two pins I'd knock you down' (*A Cab at the Door*, Penguin Books, 1970. First published by Chatto & Windus, 1968).

The third extract is by Diana Vreeland:

One night I was invited to a Condé Nast party. Everybody who was invited to a Condé Nast party stood for something. He was the man who created the kind of social world that was then called Café Society: a carefully chosen *melange* – no such thing as an overcrowded room, mind you – mingling people who up to that time would never have been seen at the same social gathering. Condé picked his guests for their talent, whatever it was – literature, the theatre, *big* business. Sharp, chic society. Why was I asked? I was young, well dressed and could dance (D.V., Weidenfeld & Nicholson, 1987. From an extract published in *Vogue*, July 1987).

Consider these three extracts in terms of writing techniques: their make-up can be readily described. The first piece builds up slowly, subordinate clauses of similar length on top of each other, carefully stitching the detail together, creating atmosphere, and suspense. The clauses reflect the calming rhythm of evening, and the scene is remembered in tranquillity. A sentence of this length (82 words) is rare today.

Pritchett has the modern, staccato rhythm of 120 years later. Even the first, long, sentence shoves in the detail, in phrases of varying length, so that there is tumbling surprise and excitement, reflecting the experience of moving house, making you savour each moment as it comes. The effect is heightened by bending the rules – no 'and' after 'itched', then many short sentences together. The first sentence is longish (60 words) but the short ones that follow correct the balance.

The third extract, by an ex-editor of the American *Vogue,* is more colloquial, but just as consciously crafted – just the right number of chatty asides ('mind you', 'Why was I asked?') and high-society French words.

BEHIND THE TECHNIQUES

No rules of grammar are broken in these extracts, the techniques are effective, and the results please the audiences aimed at. Yet there is more to style than observing writing techniques. Read the passages again, trying to imagine the persons who wrote them. No one else, you feel, could have written them exactly in those ways. There is magic at work, mystery behind it all.

You can watch a magician doing tricks for hours, yet fail to see how they are done. Even when you do see how, that is no guarantee that you will be able to reproduce the tricks. You need to get inside the magician, to understand the individuality and professional commitment behind the technique, to believe in the magic.

These writers are not consciously trying to project themselves: they are too interested in what they have to say. It is this commitment to the content, their feelings about it and the way their energies are concentrated on the expression of it, that make up their style.

Journalists' commitment to content and to their readers and their acceptance of the constraints of limited space and time mean they are not as likely as other kinds of writers to parade their egos in a pursuit of 'style'. They know in their bones that the essence of a 'good style' is to make it as easy for readers as possible, and it is a matter of making their writing natural and readable.

The two passages that follow, with their very different aims and functions, have these qualities, I think. The writers did the hard work. The readers they were aimed at found the pieces not only easy to read but readable.

> What's this? Three big beer-drinking blokes and they're going to fight it out with this shy little girl?
>
> By the 'eck! This looks like a rum do up in Ramsbottom, Lancs.
>
> I mean look at them. The size of them. They're as solid as coal sheds with – well. No-one's saying, beer bellies. No one's saying that lads, OK? But they're none of them slender.
>
> And look at her, sitting there shy as a fawn. Thirteen years old and a mere slip of a thing.
>
> Good job the coming encounter is not one of these see-you-outside variety but a match in the Bolton Table Tennis League.
>
> In see-you-outside, young Andrea Holt would be at a distinct disadvantage.
>
> In table tennis, the odds are more evenly balanced.
>
> She is the best player in Britain for her age in this sport ... (From 'A Little Smasher' by Michael McCarthy, *Daily Mirror*).

> The interplay between our responses and our general moral beliefs is in some ways similar to that between observations and theories in science. A scientific theory can be modified or refuted by the experimental falsification of a reproduction derived from it. But when a theory is well established, there is great reluctance to accept that it has been falsified and a tendency to explain away the supposedly falsifying observation as unreliable. There are no formulated general rules of scientific method that tell us how much weight to give a theory and how much weight to give to an observation apparently incompatible with it. In extreme cases, what is rational is fairly clear. When a theory has little supporting evidence, the disconfirming of one of its main predictions by a few reputable experimenters will normally undermine it. On the other hand, very firmly established theories are not rejected because of daily failures to confirm their predictions in school laboratories (Jonathan Glover, *Causing Death and Saving Lives*, Penguin Books).

Among the lessons these pieces teach us are:

1 For a simple story about people the tabloid market gets as near as possible to the way it would be told in a pub, or cafe or over a garden fence. But reduce the verbiage by about 90 per cent. Notice how the who, what, where, when of the story are neatly slotted in, in a way that you do not notice. But you would have noticed if they weren't.

2 If your subject needs a paragraph that is profound and abstract, if bringing people into it and making it vivid and concrete would result in absurdity, then just say what you have to say as simply as possible.

With a pencil, circle the connectives in Glover's piece and make a new network of lines, as was shown in Figure 8.1 (page 147). Notice that the sentences are fairly short, that key words ('theory', 'predictions', 'weight', 'observation') are repeated to make those threads that aid comprehension, that the whole paragraph develops a readily acceptable analogy. This analogy gives the paragraph a balance and provides a complementary balance in various sentences. Apart from the key terms, most of the other words are simple. Those that are not particularly simple are precise: 'modified', 'refuted', 'incompatible', 'disconfirming'. This is the language of a textbook or learned journal but it is just as skilfully attuned to its market.

A tone of voice

Style is attitude, and tone of voice; it is attack; it is varying rhythms. A 'good style' for a journalist (though journalists rarely use the phrase) means having an ear for what will read well to the particular readers aimed at. Read the Bible, Jane Austen, and the best contemporary writers so that you unconsciously pick up good rhythms. You have to make subtle gradations in style as you move from one market to another, and yet remain yourself. You veer from the chatty to the analytical, from the concrete to the abstract, within articles and from one article to the other. Notice how the buttonholing tone of the opening of the table-tennis piece is gradually being modified paragraph by paragraph, yet without it being lost altogether. In fact it emerges just as strongly at the end.

People listen to what you're saying and understand what you mean because they are held by the tone of your voice as well as because the words interest them. It is hardly possible, for example, to listen or to learn anything from a lecturer who has a toneless voice. The listeners are already expected by a lecturer to do a great deal of work: sorting out what the words mean, restructuring the sentences in their minds, relating the meaning of each sentence to the meanings of the sentences that went before, preparing the mind for what comes next. A lecturer cannot expect them to work at all this without wooing them, drawing them on, making it all sound interesting. This is what the style of an article means, too, and why a writer's 'tone of voice' is just as important as a speaker's.

Your style of writing is as individual to you as the quality and tones of your voice. It is part of your originality. But just as you don't normally *cultivate* a tone of voice just to be 'different', or sound other than what you are, so should you let your writing style develop unconsciously, naturally. Your style reflects genuine feeling; if you strive deliberately after effects, what is being expressed is shallow – its motivelessness, its lack of substance are obvious. Your style grows with you, and you are reflected in it. Style has to start from inside. Smile if you feel like smiling, but don't wear a forced one because you feel it is expected.

Your style, you will find, is integral to your point of view, and grows naturally out of it. It is the quality in writing that makes people feel at ease in your company, makes them feel you are interested in *them*, and makes them want to listen attentively to you.

IMPROVING YOUR STYLE

There are ways of consciously making the most of the style that is natural to you, of making it more effective, without falsifying it. Do a lot of listening – especially to people who greatly enjoy talking and know how to talk, how to hold people's attention. Notice how they get their audiences' attention, how their interest in their audiences comes out; and note their timing, their pacing, their rhythm, how they draw the audience on. Study the way stand-up comedians operate.

Read as much as you can in very different styles, clip and paste models, make notes. Particularly note what was described under writing techniques as variety of sentence structure and what must, under style, be called maintaining interest and attention.

Writing must be lively, alive. There must be surprises, both in what you say and how you say it. There must be some of the tension there is in life. Do not overdo the polishing; do not iron everything out into blandness. An individual has edges.

If the reader is to be surprised sometimes, you have to be surprised yourself by what you write (the truth, of course, being just as surprising as fiction). As I suggested in an earlier chapter, allow the unconscious to spill out occasionally; you can edit out the irrelevancies afterwards.

Figuratively speaking

More consciously, you can turn to figurative language to create some of your surprises and felicities. Typical of newspaper journalism are the kinds of metaphor that make for compression. Syllepis, for example, can be effective: applying a word to two others in different senses, as in 'wearing a bright red cardigan and an impudent smile'.

But figurative language must be fresh. You can turn to satire and learn from such masters as Voltaire and Swift (who suggested various ways children could be cooked in Ireland as part of the solution to poverty there). You can get both structural and style ideas from the great names of literature.

Writers consciously developing their styles, however, should not be seen to be doing it. 'Against the orange glow of the setting sun the towers of the Bexham Green Estate were sharply etched ...' So begins a newspaper article about glue-sniffing children on an estate in a Midland town. It is an attempt to build up atmosphere. But 'sharply etched' – haven't you heard that before somewhere? Didn't you put that in a school essay more than once?

Style is constantly asking yourself, 'What are the most compelling things about what I have to say?' and then saying them in *your* way.

ASSIGNMENT

Rewrite the intro to any article you've written recently in the style of:

1 *Daily Mirror.*
2 *Daily Express.*
3 *Daily Telegraph.*
4 *Woman's Own.*
5 *Loaded.*
6 *GQ.*
7 *Cosmopolitan.*
8 *The Spectator.*

13 PROFILES AND INTERVIEW FEATURES

Skill in interviewing, as Chapter 9 demonstrates, is an essential part of the information-gathering process. In this chapter we look at the more ambitious task of basing an article on a face-to-face interview and building a whole article round an interview or group of interviews.

The terms 'interview' and 'profile' are applied interchangeably to an article about one interviewee; 'profile' is also used for the more rounded portrait derived from various sources.

CHOICE OF INTERVIEWEES

The interviewee for your feature may be a celebrity or an 'ordinary' person who has experienced something extraordinary, or who represents an idea or theme; or he or she may be an expert of some kind – a psychiatrist, say, or a mountaineer – presenting an expert view. Whether for news-papers, or magazines, you are often going to interview a person who has just become news for some reason, or is just about to be. The actor has just received an award or made a come-back, or is about to open in a play in the West End; the author is about to have a book published; the politician has just joined the Cabinet; the local councillor is a leading figure in a housing controversy.

If you specialize in interviews, you will know that you have to keep ahead of the news so that you can get in first with proposals to editors who will want to time the publication of the interview to be as topical as possible. This anticipation can be difficult for a writer starting out, but it gets easier, especially if you concentrate on a particular field. You will watch for news of the activities of likely people in newspapers and other media sources, get information regularly from agents, press offices, TV producers. You may subscribe to *Celebrity Bulletin.*

If you are interested in authors, you can have the publishers' advance catalogues sent to you; if in acting or in showbiz generally, you will have contacts in Equity, the actors' union, and the technical unions, who will keep you in touch. One interview tends to lead to another, and the contacts book can fill up rapidly as your activities grow. Some magazines run series of interviews with celebrities under the same rubric – 'A Life in the Day of . . .', 'At Home with. . . .'. 'Roots', 'Man of the Week', 'A Room of My Own', etc.

As a freelance writer setting out in this field, start with minor celebrities. Big names tend to give interviews to big names. When you have impressed a few agents and editors, you will find the bigger names willing to talk to you.

In fact you may prefer to avoid celebrities altogether and develop your own ideas about who makes an interesting interview. Celebrities can be boring as subjects, especially if they have been interviewed many times. Of course it is often the boring interviewers, asking the same question over and over again, who are to blame for this. In the fields that you cover, the obvious treatment for many ideas will be through a feature interview or profile. Oddities, eccentric or offbeat characters, are a fruitful field. Watch for them if you do a lot of newspaper clipping; you can follow up news items about bakers who are also black belts in judo, bank clerks who become steeplejacks on Saturdays.

For the local paper there will be mileage to be got out of the head teacher retiring after fifty years, businessmen planning factories, idiosyncratic councillors, the local girl who has a part in a soap opera, or the policeman who has won the MBE.

THE APPROACH

Approaching people for information requires confidence. The reporter gets used to barging into places, extracting a couple of juicy quotes and barging out again. Feature writers tend to be more sensitive souls. In addition, demanding an hour of an important person's time for a full-length feature needs extra confidence.

Some people will appreciate the publicity you will be giving them. Others less used to, or less dependent on, the press may be more nervous than you are, and some will be anxious that you do not misrepresent them – particularly if they have not been treated well by the press in the past. Be prepared to be rebuffed.

In setting up some interviews you will need persistence. Fairly important people tend to be protected by agents and secretaries. Try to find out what is likely to be the best way to ask: by letter or by telephone. If you are a beginner, a short letter is probably best. You may then be asked to telephone for an appointment, and the whole operation may be made smoother.

Elusive celebrities

Or it may not. You might telephone over and over again, and still be a victim of a scenario like the following. The film actor Dustin Hoffman is at the Dorchester hotel in London for three days before going to Paris to work on a film. You are asked by a magazine to get an interview. You telephone his London agent. 'I'll ring you back' is the answer. You get a sympathetic response from a secretary in Mr Hoffmann's suite (I'll ring you back') and from the press officer at the Dorchester. You ring the hotel several times, you ring the agent several times. 'Mr Hoffmann is very busy but he's going to try to fit you in,' they say. Suddenly on your tenth telephone call you discover Mr Hoffmann has just left for Paris.

In one of the Sunday papers you find an interview with Dustin Hoffmann. You ring up a friendly hall porter at the Dorchester. He tells you that the Sunday paper journalist spent several hours in the lounge, cocktail bar, and restaurant, continually monitored Mr Hoffmann's movements, and had a fair number of the hotel staff helping him. You have been stitched up.

Some interviews do demand extra initiative. Albert Einstein was difficult to pin down. He was staying once at a small-town hotel in the United States. Big-name foreign correspondents crowded the lobby waiting in vain for a word or two. A local reporter put on some dungarees, marched into Einstein's room and said he was sorting out the telephones.

He had a long chat with Einstein as he tinkered away. It was a scoop. Here are some tips:

1 Obtain a commission first, if you can, or at least a 'We'll-have-a look-at-it'. Then you can say, 'I've been asked to write an article on . . . for . . .'.
2 If there have been other interviews recently with the person, indicate that your interview will be something different.
3 Try to avoid spelling out too precisely what you have in mind if there's a chance it may not sound appealing.
4 Try to get agents or secretaries on your side. It helps.
5 If you are asked to leave a message, try to make it something that will arouse the subject's curiosity.
6 Try to obtain the person's home telephone number. A call there rather than at a place of business often works.

Do not meet a pop star or actor immediately after performance. Over mid-afternoon coffee is best, preferably in the subject's home or at a hotel.

This applies to all showbiz people and others who keep late hours. Avoid trying to talk on film sets and at TV studios. You may spend hours hanging around, and there will be much noise and interruption. Restaurants are also noisy places when you listen to that interview you taped over lunch.

PREPARING THE GROUND

Read cuttings of previous interviews with your subject. Read up on their books, plays or films, political activities, private life, etc.

You should be sufficiently knowledgeable about the person to inspire confidence. Show that you have informed yourself about the person's business and interests. You will impress if you indicate that you have picked up errors or misleading statements about the person or organization. That means you will have done a fair amount of cross-checking through different sources, and it can provide a good talking-point to start with. Perhaps this is the interview to put the record straight, your contact might be thinking.

Most important of all, your research will make your questions interesting and relevant, and help you to assess the quality of the answers.

PREPARING THE QUESTIONS

Your questions should be aimed at obtaining explanation, opinion and interpretation, rather than mere facts. You should either know the facts or have access to them – facts such as how long a company chairman has been in the job, and what last year's statement of accounts showed profits to be.

Even for a brief interview, questions should be carefully prepared to make the best possible use of the time. Your state of preparation should be revealed by your not asking what you should know already. Your purpose is not primarily to fill up the gaps in your own knowledge, but to find out what your readers would want to know, things which the person is most fitted to tell you. Your preparation will also help you to judge if the answers are comprehensible to your average reader. You cannot communicate to your readers anything that you have not fully understood yourself, so you may want to have alternative forms of difficult questions ready to get satisfactory answers. Be ready to rephrase questions on the spot to make sure you get at the point.

Questions should, on the whole, be specific. 'Do you enjoy being a solicitor?' is not a good question. It is too vague. What good to you is the answer 'sometimes'? 'Which of the jobs you have to do as a solicitor do you enjoy most?' is better, perhaps followed by 'Which do you dislike most?' Such discussion will gradually reveal the person's attitude to the job.

Avoid questions that take you into a cul-de-sac. 'What would have happened if you'd killed him?' Answer: 'He'd be dead.' (Well, what kind of answer did you want?)

Dig for concrete and vivid answers. 'Mr Smith, I am told, always treated his backward pupils well. He knew how to boost their confidence during class discussion. Could you give me an example of that?' This hunt for anecdotes and examples is especially necessary with abstract subjects.

The wording of questions may have to be adapted to your interviewee. It can speed matters up if you can use advertising jargon when talking to an account executive. If there is an age gap, you may have to do an occasional translation. The word 'trendy', for example, tends to have favourable connotations up to a certain age, then derogatory ones.

Questions for children need careful phrasing. They do not respond well to abstract questions such as 'Do you enjoy the weekend?' Try the more specific 'What do you like doing best at weekends? Swimming? Playing football?' Up to a certain age they will not be sure what 'recreation' means. On the other hand, they may know a lot more about certain aspects of life than you did at their age.

On the whole, keep questions short. If some lead-up or putting-into-context is required, try to get it into the conversation naturally, pause, then put the question. 'I was interested to read that you. ... Is that a fair account of your attitude ... ?'

Open-ended questions

Ask open-ended questions, that is, questions that cannot be answered by yes or no. Instead of 'Do you agree with the new Education Bill?' try 'What is your view of the criticism that the Bill is likely to be divisive?' That should get a discussion going easily.

Avoid too many 'leading' questions, those that prompt the answer you want, whether the prompting is in the words, the phrasing or the tone of voice. 'You've had a lot of arguments with the players this season, haven't you?' might provoke an angry as well as non-committal response. Find another way to approach the subject.

Arrange your questions in an order you think will make a good conversation and elicit good answers. It will probably be different from the order in which you will write up the answers. For example, you will site the awkward ones judiciously – immediately after a particularly welcome question might be a good place, or near the end.

Your list of prepared questions must be used as a guide, not too rigidly. You need to produce the lubrication of conversational gambits as you get to know the person and can judge how best to put the questions. Be prepared to vary your approach in the light of the answers you get.

Your interviewees might embark on subjects or supply information you did not anticipate. If these are interesting and relevant, be prepared to adapt your plan as necessary, perhaps cutting out a few of your less interesting questions. But do not be deflected from what you believe important to your theme. The danger with young and inexperienced interviewers is that the control of the proceedings will be too easily taken over by the interviewee, and that they will be given what the interviewee wants to give them.

Something like this:

Question: Do you agree that bad language and violent behaviour when criticizing your children are not the best kind of model to present your children with?

Answer: I agree that children should be encouraged at every step of the way. I constantly give my children encouragement. . . .

Question: Have you now decided that you are not going to use bad language in the presence of your children?

Answer: Have I now decided to take particular care to say 'We'll done' when they do the right thing? Yes, I have. . . .

It is useful to jot down some of the answers, even if you are using a tape-recorder. It helps at the editing stage.

THE DEBATING STYLE

If you are doing an important set-piece interview with a controversial public figure, careful research notes jotted down with your questions help the dialogue. Such interviews can seem like public debates in which the readers expect the interviewer to participate.

Ivan Rowan accepted such a challenge in an interview with Conservative MP Enoch Powell, published in the *Sunday Telegraph* (19 January 1986) which covered key events of Mr Powell's career. Rowan incorporated longish pieces of background (including revealing quotes he had gathered in 1967 when he had discussed Mr Powell with twenty senior Conservative politicians), in an article which was a combination of profile and on-the-spot interview.

Rowan referred to a speech Mr Powell made in 1968, attacking immigration policy and warning of 'the River Tiber overflowing with much blood' and suggested that it had affected Mr Powell's career and that he regretted it. Notice the lead-up of the first question in my extract, and the polite but firm probing that follows. Mr Powell's answers are given in italics.

You have been quoted as saying that if you had realized it would get you thrown out of the Shadow Cabinet, you would have re-worked the speech. You have also said a politician's business is to persuade. Would you have been more persuasive – and stayed on the Opposition front bench – if you had instead said that you condemned racial violence, that you wanted a stiff jail sentence for any white youth who beat up a black –

Or vice versa –

– but that Britain lacked the resources to deal adequately with all the causes of racial tension?

I don't think anything said, however said, would have affected the subsequent course of events.

It affected your career.

How could a career which enabled me to go along with the conventional and obligatory connivance at what was happening and has happened in Britain – how could that be, in the sense in which I think we are using the term, persuasive?

That speech cost you the support of Edward Heath?

Might we examine that for a moment? It made me in the view of Edward Heath a liability of which he would be wise to disembarrass himself.

You say you are a man without regrets – don't you regret leaving Wolverhampton in 1974, when as things turned out you and not Margaret Thatcher might have got the leadership, and you, and not she, might have sent the battle fleet to the Falklands?

I hope the second is true on the hypothesis described, but the first I do not believe to be correct in any hypothesis. My guess is that the Conservative Party is too shrewd to choose a person like myself as its leader. I am too interested in politics.

That is a disqualification for a Tory leader?

Perhaps we must analyse my use of the word 'interested' I can be committed to improbable objectives, or objectives which are not early and easily attainable. It would be too simple to say I have a taste for lost causes, I have a taste for long causes. . . .

Notice that although the questions are rigorous, they do not impose the interviewer's point of view. Rather they try to discover what Enoch Powell is like, and what many readers will want to know about it. The interviewer is seen as a link and interpreter between interviewee and public.

QUESTIONING FORMULAS AND TECHNIQUES

The following formulas can help:

1 The specific question: try to get on the person's wavelength and hit on their enthusiasms. If you have done your research, you will be able to use the jargon of the profession or trade your interviewee belongs to get under his/her skin.
2 The general question: notice in the extract above how Rowan's questions are general enough not to reflect his own views. Enoch Powell is thus allowed to feel that he has considerable influence on the direction of the conversation. At the same time, Rowan maintains control by probing further on certain key details that emerge from Powell's replies.
3 Questions to get over a lull in the conversation: 'Could you describe your typical day?'
4 Questions setting off the imagination.
   'If you weren't you, who would you like to be?'
   'Which age would you have liked to live in, if given a choice?'
   'If your house were flooded, what are the first things you would try to save?'

Techniques for tough questions

The late film actor Humphrey Bogart produced a neat apothegm about interviewing: 'The best technique is to make tiny pricks in the subject's ego and let him expel hot air slowly'.

The celebrity interview fails if it is full of sycophantic gush. Yet there are many ways of extracting fascinating, damning confessions without raising your voice or losing your sympathetic expression. In *The Craft of Interviewing* (Writer's Digest Books) John Brady quotes Allen Barton's classic guide for what he called the 'Did you kill your wife?' formula for asking such questions:

Casual approach: 'Did you happen to kill your wife?'

Everybody approach: 'Many people have been guilty of killing their wives. Do you happen to have killed yours?'

Other people approach: (a) 'Do you know any people who have murdered their wives? (b) How about yourself?'

The Kinsey technique – with an air of assuming that everyone has done everything: 'Did you kill your wife?'

Other techniques for tough questions are:

1 Attributing the toughness to others rather than yourself. 'There are people who say that . . .' 'Some people would say that . . .' 'Perhaps they misunderstand your motives, but some people thought killing your wife/husband was going too far. . . .'
2 Softening up with praise. 'The publicity you have received on this new venture has been very favourable so far, hasn't it? . . . Except for. . . .'
3 Separating questions that if put together would impede a completely frank answer. Separate, for instance, 'Are the regulations in your company about what can be claimed as expenses quite strict?' from 'I suppose you'd feel freer to pursue those activities if your company could stretch the rules on expenses a little. . . .'

If a question appears too painful to answer, you might be able to return to it later, rephrasing it so that it sounds different. If a relative has died recently, and the person would like to talk about it but is finding it difficult, you might try switching off the tape-recorder, or leaving the room for a few minutes while the tape is running. Some people find it easier to talk to a tape recorder without being inhibited by the thought that they might break down talking to others.

A possible last question: 'Is there anything you would like to add to what you have said?' It could provide useful thoughts. But even if you haven't got an answer to a crucial question by the end of the interview, all may not be lost. You stop your tape-recorder, close your notebook and you both relax. On the way to the door, or the lift, you refer to the question again, in different words, and this time you may get a good, relaxed answer.

For difficult interviewees

The way you actually phrase your questions will depend on what sort of animal you've got in your cage. Busy and important people are often friendlier and more co-operative than hustlers on the way up, while a hint of criticism or reference to unfavourable publicity in the past can upset some celebrities. Frank Sinatra has spat on journalists, and his extraordinary singing talent has been matched over the many years by creative use of invective against the press. Some celebrities with big egos, especially when bolstered by many years of wealth and fame, delight in making the interviewer look small by insults and outrageous behaviour.

Some interviewees refuse to answer any question to do with their private lives. Others have been so drunk and so badly behaved that the article has become the record of a confrontation. A drunken London restaurateur declared he was the greatest in the world and shortly afterwards vomited over the lunch table. It made an arresting start to the article. Such encounters can of course produce interesting pieces, even if they are far from what was intended.

The most difficult interviewees, generally, are those who have not a great deal to say. This may be because they are reluctant to reveal themselves, because of the thought of their statements being made public and giving an unimpressive image of themselves, or because they are reduced to silence by the interview situation.

Sympathetic, not sycophantic

A mainly sympathetic attitude mingled with a little, strategically timed ruffling of the feathers should succeed in getting some interesting answers. Stephen Repello works this way to effect with Denzel Washington in *Arena* (July/August 1995). He starts off:

> 'I thought we were here to talk about movies and stuff', says Denzel Washington, shooting me a lightning look. 'What you're talking about, that's ... *private.*' Well, now. I'd been apprised that Washington can be testy, but surely not over such an innocuous question. It's not that I haven't come prepared with a slew of potential feather-rufflers. Such as how Washington, a married man and father, feels about being cited by *People* magazine as one of Hollywood's more unfaithful stars. Such as whether he quit or was fired by Michelle Pfeiffer, his intended co-star of 1982's *Love Field*. Such as whether he is trying for a Harrison Ford-style career on the back of his nuke submarine thriller *Crimson Tide*. Such as why one of Hollywood's best-looking men has made a fuss about not wanting to appear nude when, in fact, he already has. But all that is to come later.

After he has got on to his subject's wavelength and established good rapport, in other words.

Some interviewees, even with sizeable egos, prefer a little confrontation – in other words a real conversation – even though they may be momentarily taken aback when they read the published article. Here is Lynn Barber, in the *Sunday Express Magazine* of 27 October 1985, interviewing Jimmy Boyle, who was sentenced to life imprisonment for murder in 1967. He was released in 1982, had become an author and was running a rehabilitation centre for drug addicts in Edinburgh.

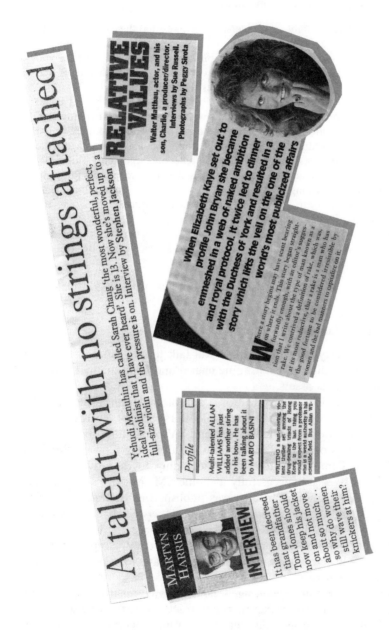

A talent with no strings attached

Yehudi Menuhin has called Sarah Chang 'the most wonderful, perfect, ideal violinist that I have ever heard'. She is 13. Now she's moved up to a full-size violin and the pressure is on. Interview by Stephen Jackson

RELATIVE VALUES

Walter Matthau, actor, and his son, Charlie, a producer/director. Interviews by Sue Russell. Photographs by Peggy Sirota

When Elizabeth Kaye set out to profile John Bryan she became enmeshed in a web of naked ambition and royal protocol. It twice led to dinner with the Duchess of York and resulted in a story which lifts the veil on the one of the world's most publicized affairs

Where a story begins may have scant bearing on where it ends. This story began forwardly enough, with an editor's suggestion that I write about the type of man known as a rake. We contrived a definition of rake, which was, at its most reductive, that a rake is a man who has the good fortune to be considered irresistible by women and the bad manners to capitalize on it.

Profile

Multi-talented ALLAN WILLIAMS has just added another string to his bow. He has been talking about it to MARIO BASINI

WRITING a fast-moving, violent thriller set among the drug-dealing triads of Hong Kong is the last thing you would expect from a professor who is a world authority in his scientific field. But Allan Wil-

MARTYN HARRIS

INTERVIEW

It has been decreed that grandfather Tom Jones should now keep his jacket on and not move about so much . . . so why do women still wave their knickers at him?

Figure 13.1 Interview features and profiles: a great variety of formats

Ms Barber worries that 'the Jimmy Boyle of the present is *so* respectable, so assured, so word-perfect in the lingo of social concern, it is hard to believe he is the same man. . . .'

> All this sweetness and light and universal forgiveness has the effect of making me feel more acid and I ask if he has ever read Tom Wolfe's book *Radical Chic.* He hasn't, so I explain: 'It's about the sort of trendy scene where you have terrorists and murderers going to cocktail parties with judges and celebrities, and being treated as celebrities themselves.'
>
> He takes a deep breath before replying: 'Look, let me tell you, I could move into London tomorrow but I don't want to get into that trendy shit. There's all these middle-class trendies and academics who think they've got the answer to everything, and meanwhile they just leave people on the scrapheap while they stand around having intellectual arguments. But really the only people who can find the solution is the scrapheap, and I'm right in the thick of it, working at street level. Yes, I have acquired middle-class tastes, but my roots are still in the Gorbals and I wouldn't be doing the work I'm doing if they weren't.'
>
> A good answer, though any pretence of friendliness between us has now hit the dust. 'Why are journalists so cynical?' he keeps asking. 'Because it's our job to be cynical,' I keep telling him.

She would not have elicited that 'good answer' without a little aggro.

Encouraging revelations

It is not easy to explain why a person will talk to one journalist and not another, but the ability to listen, some charm and good manners but also firmness, are obvious assets.

Such a combination Nancy Mitford, author and journalist, has. She was strongly critical of the Famous Writers School correspondence course when she interviewed columnist and TV personality, Bennet Cerf, Chairman of the Board of Random House Publishing Corporation, one of the 'Fifteen Famous Writers' who, according to the advertisements, 'will teach you to write successfully at home'. Ms Mitford's article, 'Let us now Appraise Famous Writers', was published in *Atlantic*, July 1970, and later collected in *The Making of a Muckraker* (Michael Joseph).

Mr Cerf, who said he went up to the school once or twice a year to talk to the staff, admitted (according to the interview): 'No person of any sophistication whose book we'd publish would have to take a mail order course to learn to write'.

The way Ms Mitford encouraged her interviewees to reveal themselves is illustrated in this extract from her article. Note the way she participates, and the way she uses her reactions to link together the interview quotes:

While Mr Cerf is by no means uncritical of some aspects of mail order selling, he philosophically accepts them as inevitable in the cold-blooded world of big business – so different, one gathers, from his own cultural world of letters. 'I think mail order sell has several built-in deficiencies,' he said. 'The crux of it is a very hard sales pitch, an appeal to the gullible. Of course, once somebody has signed a contract with Famous Writers he can't get out of it, but that's true with every business in the country.' Noticing that I was writing this down, he said in alarm, 'For God's sake, don't quote me on that "gullible" business – you'll have all the mail order houses in the country down on my neck!' 'Then would you like to paraphrase it?' I asked, suddenly getting very firm. 'Well – you could say in general I don't like the hard sell, yet it's the basis of all American business.' 'Sorry, I don't call that a para-phrase, I shall have to use both of them,' I said in a positively governessy tone of voice. 'Anyway, why do you lend your name to this hard-sell propo-sition?' Bennet Cerf (with his melting grin): 'Frankly, if you must know, I'm an awful ham – I love to see my name in the papers!'

The participation on the writer's part can be managed in various ways at the writing-up stage. Here is Jane Wheatley, subtly indicating that her subject, the newscaster Pamela Armstrong, is over-serious (in *You* magazine):

She said she'd like to talk about women in television. She said it had long ago ceased to be legitimate for the press to treat female newscasters as a novelty. 'If Fleet Street continues to do that then it is marginalizing their work. It is trivializing the efforts of these women and then they are not viewed to be in the mainstream of the work process.' Whew! She leaned over. 'Have you got that down? It's very important.'

NOTEBOOK OR TAPE-RECORDER?

A short interview is often best done with a notebook, especially if you use shorthand. It is less of an encumbrance than a machine.

When you use quotes it is safest to use the actual words said and you must be completely faithful to the intention. When you don't use quote marks, make sure your summaries or paraphrases are quite comprehen-sible, that they don't need for full understanding statements that you have weeded out.

If you have a good memory, you may prefer to manage even set-piece interviews with a notebook. Here is interview specialist Hunter Davies on his craft, in *The Independent* of 20 April 1994 (see also his *Hunting People*, Mainstream Publishing, 1994 for a selection of his thirty years of interviews with the famous). He first saturates himself in information (always wise):

I don't have a written list of questions. Only in my mind. It's topics, rather than questions, I want to bring up, things that have puzzled me, or theories I want to try out on them. I have read every major interview with them beforehand, checked in *Who's Who* or other reference books.

The big advantage of a notebook, as opposed to tape, is that I am editing as I go along. I jot down only the good stuff, the flavour, people's speech mannerisms. If they come out with something particularly outrageous, I might not write it down, not at that moment, but simply nod and look sympathetic. I wait for them to tell me something truly banal, about how they love children, always help old people across the road, at which stage I write down the previous outrageous remark. I jot down details of their clothes, their face, the setting, conversations with other people, any interruptions, especially interruptions. All interviewers are dying for the unexpected, to give us colour, show the subject in a different light.

For a set-piece interview, however, the advantages of a tape-recorder are many. A tape is an insurance if you are not sure whether you will have time to write up the interview immediately. Use a notebook as well, to make notes about the appearance of the interviewee, etc. as Davies does.

Write down all names and figures clearly. They may not be clear on tape. Ask for names to be spelt. Go back over any figures you are doubtful about. Ask 'Did you say fifteen thousand or fifty thousand?' Also make any arrangements about photographs and future contact as necessary. A telephone check call later may produce a few extra comments on quotes if you find the transcript thin in some areas.

Editors often feel easier if there is a tape in case there are any complaints from the interviewee about misrepresentation, or even threats of libel. People can be astonished when they see their casually bestowed words in cold print. 'Did I really say that?'.

Interviewees' reactions vary: some welcome the tape recorder because they feel they are less likely to be misrepresented, others clam up. Do not insist. If you are doing a fairly long interview on tape knowing you will be jettisoning material, practise selectivity as you go, using the tape indicator number to help you locate bits later.

EDITING THE TRANSCRIPT

One disadvantage of tape is that you may be inclined to let the interview go on too long, feeling that you can easily edit the transcript – but transcription can take three times as long as the interview. When you have taped a long, relaxed conversation, you might wish you hadn't, when faced with the task of transcribing it. I have already suggested how you can make this easier by using the numbers on the machine indicator for selected playback. Even so, for a major interview it can be useful to have a complete or near-complete transcript to edit from. In such cases it is worth photocopying your transcript before taking scissors and paste to the original.

Paste up the sections on A4 sheets, in the order in which you want to use them, leaving plenty of space between each for your linking material. Be prepared, in the light of the answers, to modify any draft outline you had in mind.

However well controlled an interview is, talk is more rambling and repetitive than printed material. This is something that is more conspicuous to the eye than to the ear. So squeeze out most of the water. Not quite all, otherwise you will have unlikely sounding subjects expressing themselves in a succession of gnomic utterances. Leave in the odd mannerisms – 'you know', 'indeed it is', 'not me, matey', whatever they are – for reality's sake. This is important when you are doing a piece that is presented as one long quote, in a series such as 'A Day in the Life of . . .'

Be careful, in your reductions, not to misrepresent. Summarize the bigger chunks you want to remove in a few sentences if they are needed for context. Space out quoted pieces, indirect speech pieces, background pieces in a satisfactory pattern.

You can alter quotes discreetly to fit the framework better. You may have asked: 'Do you think your team will get into the First Division next year?' Answer: 'Yes'. But you may want to combine the 'Yes' with the answer at the start of the next paragraph. So you make it: 'I think the team will get into the First Division next year because. . . .' Check on the telephone or send your subject a typescript if you think there may be any danger of misrepresentation in the editing.

Vocal patterns might need some attention. Indicate a person's accent at the start if it is interesting or distinctive, but do not produce slabs of incomprehensible dialect. Do the same with grammar where it is distinctive or unusual, then translate into an English that won't sound patronizing.

THE AIM OF PROFILES

A profile from various sources preferably but not necessarily includes an interview with the subject. A reclusive subject may be profiled in an 'in-search-of' like a detective story, making use of cuttings and other sources – crediting direct quotes. A profile should not be based on information gathered too readily from agents and other publicists. Achieve balance by talking to friends and enemies, relatives, acquaintances, colleagues, ex-colleagues. Look for unfavourable accounts of the subject in cuttings. Look for what makes the person tick, or if you prefer the expression, what drives the person. Examine whether the image you discover differs from the conventional public image of the person. At the same time, don't over-load with too many different angles.

Profiles may be based almost entirely on cuttings. An example is a 3000-word profile of Elizabeth Taylor in *Woman's Own* in 1985 by Donald Zec, pegged on the film star's emergence from the Betty Ford clinic after treat-ment for drugs and alcohol dependence. Zec is able to enliven it by memories of a relationship going back over many years:

> I remember early on in our sometimes friendly, sometimes abrasive rela-tion, finding myself alone with her in the back seat of a Rolls, in Rome. Embalmed in the limo's exotic upholstery, with Elizabeth Taylor looking as seductive as (to quote Burton) 'an erotic dream', I had the uncanny feeling that she was nestling all around me. The euphoria ended abruptly as she murmured, 'You know you're a shit, Donald dear'.
>
> This unsolicited testimonial, I was to learn, stemmed from some taunt of mine printed a couple of years earlier about her role in *Cleopatra*. Something like – '57 varieties of cleavage scarcely adds up to a performance. . . .' For some reason she never forgot it.

WRITING IT UP

Comparing interview features on the same celebrity in several publica-tions (which you will do to prepare your own) will teach you much about different markets and the different approaches and format they want for these features.

Deciding on how to start needs some thought. Try to get the following into the piece very early: a strong quote, a topical peg, the setting where the conversation took place, the appearance of the subject, perhaps a distinctive mannerism. Above all, get across to the reader the reasons why this person is worth listening to.

Susan Crosland does most of these things, if not more, in the first two paragraphs of an interview with Shimon Peres, then Prime Minister of Israel, in *The Sunday Times* (19 January 1986):

> When we meet in the prime minister's office in Jerusalem, the bags beneath his eyes are no more pronounced than usual. This wiry man is as spruce as if he's just begun the day. In fact he's had no sleep. From 6 p.m. yesterday to 7 this morning he's kept ten inner cabinet ministers locked together until the five right-wing ones agree, after six months' blocking, to Peres's deal for warmer relations with Egypt.

Patient, ready to compromise for an end, when at last the deed must be done, Shimon Peres – 'this biological miracle' – relentlessly uses sheer stamina to wear his opponents down. Born in Poland in 1923, raised in what was then the village of Tel Aviv, director general of defence at 29, a technocrat, Peres is a self-taught intellectual who loves words, paradoxes.

Next, pull out a particularly significant quote or comment for the end. Ms Crosland brings out a tough question, phrasing it tactfully as 'Some of your international friends feel Israel is too ready to flatten any Palestinian if you can't get hold of the villain himself'. Mr Peres says the raid on PLO centres was done 'in a very careful way. ... And if we do nothing, other international friends are disappointed. Some of them wanted us to go to war against Libya. We have to make our own judgement. And our judgement', he adds, 'is not void of moral consideration'.

In the course of a skilfully orchestrated conversation, where there is good rapport, people say some of the more interesting and illuminating things in unguarded moments. Make good use of them. Also look for contradictions. Therein trouble lies, however. You can't print two contradictory statements, even if they are very clearly on the tape.

Linking together the body of an interview can have its special difficulties because of the various kinds of juggling, including switches between past and present, between direct and indirect speech, slotted in background material, and commentary. Examine how this is handled in the pickpocket interview in Chapter 7.

Avoid, in putting the piece together, being left with too many aspects and too little development and integration. You will find it difficult to link the interview together in a convincing way, and will be in danger of producing non-sequiturs heralded by such weak or cliché phrases as: 'It's no surprise that ...', 'Looking back ...', 'Actually ...' or 'For the record. ...'

Try to find a pattern in the quotes that will allow you to stitch them together into an interesting story.

Unusual formats

The format of interviews varies greatly, as can be seen from the examples I have used. Read several issues of each publication aimed at and analyse how they seem to like it done, and how much variation of approach might be possible.

You may want to try a really novel structure. Suppose you interviewed a City worker who likes to dress up and talk like John Wayne when he gets home for dinner. The whole piece might be written as if it were John Wayne talking. An interview with columnist Bernard Levin was written in one sentence, to reflect Levin's taste for extra-long sentences, except for the last sentence, which read: 'By the way, Bernard Levin writes lots of short sentences too'.

ASSIGNMENTS

1 Get someone (tutor or fellow student?) to read to you a published interview of 1200 to 1500 words. Make notes, as if you had been the interviewer. Make sure you include the main facts, names and figures. Write it up in half the length of the original. Compare your version with the original to see what important things were missed.

2 Do the research and write up a 2000-word 'scissor-and-paste' profile. Then do outlines for three 800-word profiles of the same celebrity for separate markets, focusing on a separate aspect for each market.

3 Write up one of the profiles outlined in 2.

4 *Group*: If a talk by a feature writer on the skills of interviewing can be arranged, follow it up with a Q and A session. The members of the group then produce an 800-word feature on the event aimed at a journalism students' magazine.

5 *Group*: A large group can divide into fours for this one. In each small group, an interviewer and interviewee are chosen. The interviewee chooses a subject to be questioned about. The other members make notes of skills of both interviewer and interviewee (body language, persuasive manner, articulateness, etc.).

14 WRITING A COLUMN

The following quotes come from well known columnists:

> My advice to anyone wanting to be a newspaper or magazine columnist is: lead a rich life, have strong opinions, read a great deal, and have children, as they keep you in touch with educational problems ... pop music, and the youth culture generally (Mary Kenny, in a letter to the author).

> I don't set out to achieve anything in particular, except to entertain. Perhaps what I am good at is looking at people's ideals and worrying at them. I'm meant to be controversial; it has become a burden. I never say things on purpose to wind people up, but my value to editors depends on the hate-mail they get (Julie Burchill, being interviewed).

> The only times I've regretted a column is when I haven't written it – because I thought I'd regret it. It's a highly self-critical, self-analysing process where you spend 90 per cent of the time deciding what to write, justifying writing it, and then the remaining 10 per cent doing it. And for that reason, perhaps, because I know what I'm doing, no, I've never been sued. If ever I were, it would be on purpose (Keith Waterhouse, in a letter to the author).

> The one problem I never have is choosing something to write about. I don't think a general column can be done for long unless you *are* interested in a wide range of matters (Bernard Levin, in a letter to the author).

A new writer will not find it easy to take possession of a column; a regular space is unlikely to be offered to a new contributor to the pages of a newspaper or magazine in any case. But editors are always on the look-out for fresh talent and different voices.

Among newcomers into journalism, specialists may get the opportunity to develop the kind of confident, individual tone of voice that becomes punditry. Other feature writers with pulling power may be given their heads and go the same way: notably arts reviewers and commentators on political/social questions. It is this personal approach that is the concern of this chapter.

My main and first concern is with what are called 'personal' columns. They have the widest scope and require the greatest variety of techniques. The numerous possibilities in specialized columns are also indicated.

Editors like columns. They provide the security of all features: at least those spaces will be filled. Since a good deal of news in newspapers tend to be bad news, columns that can provide a welcome dose of humour, or a light touch, or a spot of controversy, to make the world's burdens easier to bear are highly valued. Personal columns can bring depth and perspective to the consideration of events. They can provoke thought, move to action, inspire, uplift, to a greater degree than other kinds of article. Star columnists can sell papers, – even those dealing in such specialized areas as personal advice, fashion, shopping, sports, recreations and seasonal topics.

HOW TO BECOME A COLUMNIST

Most freelances like the idea of producing a column, but not all find the task congenial. It requires much discipline and often much ingenuity: finding something new to write about regularly because you have a space to fill can become burdensome. You can run out of steam.

Columnists are therefore usually knowledgeable or opinionated. There will be a self-motivated engine in them somewhere, fuelled by the curiosity to dig out information, and by the passion to interpret and communicate it.

They are often extrovert people who have a lot to say about anything, though people who have a lot to say about anything don't necessarily make good columnists. What sounds like a deep sense of moral outrage when you hear it at a dinner party ('How can a woman leave her baby on a *doorstep*') can look naive in print. Imaginative sympathy is an important quality in columns surveying the world at large – the capacity to understand different kinds of people.

Even if you have a good idea for a column that you think a publication would like, you will need to produce at least half-a-dozen samples with indications of how you would continue for many weeks/months after that. Maintaining continuity is particularly important for the personal column: you may have six brilliant weekly columns in you, but have you any more?

Personal columns may be so wide in scope or distinctive in style that the writer's name is a sufficient label, or they may be accompanied by such vague clues as 'Bernard Waterhouse's Week' or 'As I See It', or 'My Word', or 'The Way It Was' (local history). But a title, even one kept at the back of the mind, can usefully define the purpose. If you can think up a good new title which expresses what you have in mind, this could be a selling point.

If you are staff, writer or subeditor, you will be living and breathing the world of the paper or magazine: replacing your duties or adding to them by writing a column (assuming there's room for one or the current incumbent is very poorly) may well be part of your career strategy. If you are freelance, before coming up with ideas, you must market-study more keenly than you've done before. Decide on a likely target publication or two. Study back issues closely – months of a daily paper, a year or two of a monthly magazine. List both the staff writers and those who are obviously freelances who have their regular space, whether its material is specialist, semi-specialist ('country matters' or 'video games' that you don't know much about but which you're interested in and could research), or personal opinion on affairs in general.

Find the gaps

List the topics covered by these writers in the period under review. Discover the gaps that you could fill as a freelance, and that your market study tells you would appeal to the editor(s). Then make your approach, with a few samples and a brief account of your background, including any experience that qualifies you to write on the topics or along the lines proposed. If the gap is video games, find out about them, work out how you could keep that subject going, and start with that. You're not likely to get a regular column immediately, but once established as an occasional feature writer, it will be easier to cross the bridge.

Extra personal qualities are required too. To keep up a good standard indefinitely needs self-discipline. You are exposing yourself to the public gaze in a way that the straightforward feature is not, and must therefore like any performer (actor, musician) be prepared to suffer criticism.

Local paper columns

There is always something local to comment on:

> If you've had cause to pass by the Internevis old folk's home recently you've probably noticed the lovely cherry blossom trees which are blooming there at the moment. I'm told that the family planted them in memory of a patient back in the days when the Belford Hospital was on that site. What a nice way to be remembered (Maria Kerr in *The Oban Times*).

You may not be allowed to be as relaxed as that. If a cheery chat is wanted, note that such themes as visits to the dentists ('Our dentist isn't just a wizard on the high speed drill, he wants to have a meaningful relationship with his patients') can soon wear thin.

Conversely, even if your brief is to stick closely to local politics and council meetings, and other serious matters there will be ways of perpetuating a personal touch.

Roger Bing, for example, in his *Croydon Advertiser* column, has an eye for any item of news that can be pegged to a local connection. He writes in one issue that the coming Sunday will see the start of a TV series on *The Great Commanders* with Nelson:

> Did you know that one of the country's great historical figures was, like all right-thinking people, a keen cricket watcher? Lord Nelson, who very nearly made the name Horatio trendy, but not quite, lived at Merton Place, and when time and sea battles permitted, he particularly liked to go along to watch play at Mitcham Cricket Green. And yes, Lady Hamilton used to accompany him.

The title 'Trivial Pursuit' allows Des Clarke in the *Kentish Times* to encompass all kinds of subject matter:

> We journalists live in constant terror of making the sort of slips which earn us a place in 'Private Eye' or 'Punch'.
>
> Pity the poor sub-editors who spawned these headlines: 'Three Men Held in Cigarette Case,' 'Leak in Council Chamber,' 'June Babies Flood Hospital' and 'Magistrates to Act on Nude Shows'.

THE INDIVIDUAL VOICE

What editors value above all in the personal column is an individual voice. They like letters to flood in from readers, reacting strongly to the columnist's view – for or against. The best of these letters keep their correspondence columns lively. Some editors value the columnist who draws bagfuls of hate letters.

This does not mean that editors want venomous, eccentric or whimsical outpourings for their own sake. The basic qualities in which a good column is rooted remain those of all journalism: good, accurate reporting. To this has to be added a thoughtful, forthright, or lively commentary, preferably a combination of all three. The letters it brings in help to keep the columnists well stocked with fresh ideas.

If you feel strongly about certain issues, by all means be as provocative as the publication will accept. It is not uncommon for a star columnist to have political leanings at odds with the publication being written for, or for a columnist to be upmarket or downmarket of a publication. This perversity can be quite calculated: it can blur any impression of appealing to too narrow a sector. But to fake passions, political or other, is courting disaster. You can be found out.

Personal columns generally have a formula, or a special format, in a publication, a familiar shape on the page that triggers off the right mood of expectancy in the readers. Readers encountering a personal column as they leaf through a publication tend to be flagged down. What has the pundit to say today? The column must therefore start well or the whole thing will fall flat on its face.

Too many 'Is'

Too many '*Is*' are irritating, especially when the culprits have run out of anything worth saying on current events and mores; whimsical chatter about the little domestic upheavals around them can be groan-making. *Private Eye* did an 'I' count in the personal columns and those chosen for their regular parodies tended to have high 'I' counts among other failings. Of course, whoever takes on a personal column, particularly in the national papers, may have to be prepared to make more enemies than they bargain for (even if they provocatively bargain for many).

Local papers and certain kinds of undemanding magazines can be a likelier home for whimsy, but surely a magazine aimed at the retired is also aimed at retirement if it continues to give room to such pieces as the one that began:

> I am no Adrian Mole, but he, with another 50 years behind him, might well turn out to be just like me. Now 64½ I still search my face for pimples past and principles present (or is it the other way round?) and, having taken early retirement and being on a small pension, also have difficulties with my pocket money.

Be effectively vivid or angry and the 'Is won't stick out so much, as Cassandra's didn't. He (Sir William Connor) was the star columnist of the *Daily Mirror* who for many years voiced the frustrations of ordinary people about bureaucratic inefficiency, the waste of taxpayers' money, and other ills that we are all heir to:

> An extraordinarily large part of my life is spent holding a black plastic object that stretches from my mouth to my ear.
> I talk, shout and whisper down it for hundreds of hours a year.
> Much of the time when I do this I am in a small red room that is usually filthy, always uncomfortable and frequently ill-lit.
> This constricted house of pain is called a telephone kiosk.

Quoting endings out of context is rarely revealing, but a good column on one subject is all of a piece – there should be an inevitability about the way it finishes, as there is with a good essay. The trick of echoing the 'lead', discussed in Chapter 8, can be effective in the essay-type approach of the columnist. Try to avoid ending, desperately: 'Oh well, you can always escape into the nearest pub'.

Where there are several items, it may follow the pattern of a good meal. But don't just bring out the ginger biscuits at the end and hope for the best – each dish must be carefully prepared.

CONTENT AND TOPICALITY

The typical personal column is about the world around the writer. At one extreme it might be about large political issues, or personalities and what they are up to; at the other it might be about why your spouse always rushes to answer the telephone as if it might be news of a pools win. You do not have to be aggressively provocative to keep interest alive: if you regularly produce a thoughtful piece, you will get reactions from your readers from which you might work up themes for future columns. This is what Neal Ascherson does (among other things) in his column in *The Independent on Sunday*. Here is an extract from *The Observer* column he wrote before he moved:

> A reader from Penarth writes to inquire why I don't shoot myself. He says that I am worse than Michael Ryan at Hungerford [the maniac who killed several people in his village with a shotgun], because I use words as bullets against 'the White Race'. From the other extreme of politics, a Bromley reader calls me a paid warmonger for recalling the rapes of German women by Soviet soldiers in 1945. This is what happens when one writes about a word 'culture'. Between Penarth and Bromley, a number of you were more friendly and appreciative. But for some, the impulse to reach for the revolver at the mention of 'culture' evidently remains strong. This is important, because the guiding thread I have tried to run through all these columns is an approach which is not 'cultured' or 'cultivated' but cultural. And those letters make a good opportunity to examine the whole relationship between columns, readers and newspapers.

Reflective columns almost always need topicality. You must be careful to be up to date with any current story at the moment your column is submitted. In magazine columns that limitation has to be indicated subtly, and the topical piece written in such a way that events occurring in the gap before publication will not make the references absurd. If you want to write a paragraph about heart transplant operations, you should not have missed a major TV documentary on the subject shown the evening before your column was due. You must be careful to explain any references to events that your readers might have forgotten or have missed for one reason or another – as I have done for Michael Ryan in the quote from Ascherson's column, quoted above.

Keeping it fresh

Whatever the content, the discussion must be kept fresh. Readers are not interested in your generalized reflections on marriage, Women's Lib, the rise or fall of the Yuppies. They want new angles or a different treatment of known facts, a newsy name or two, a confrontation, a controversy that can be aired with forcefulness and wit.

Yoke together apparently alien or dissimilar ideas, to make new patterns, fresh insights. Avoid over-airing subject matter or looking too closely too often near to home. When a column starts following its author and family round the home, collecting the crumbs of domestic conversation or reactions to TV programmes, it is time the author was put out to grass.

Personal columnists also have to beware of being overtaken by their image and of their prejudices becoming too predictable. A probing mind should be well exposed to people and events. It is fatal for columnists to bury their noses in their own cuttings.

ARGUMENTATIVE STYLES

Readers are prepared, in personal columns, for arguments that are idiosyncratic and less balanced than a feature article would allow. The line is not easy to draw. A light touch, with humour or irony, is usually a better weapon than indignation: moral outrage too often looks sanctimonious in print. Some columns, particularly in popular nationals, make a point of being outrageous, but the columnist's role-playing, and relentless saloon-bar style, can remove most of the bite. An example is John Smith ('Man of the People') in his 'Straight Talk' column in *The People*. Here he is (16 August 1992) objecting to the way a professional burglar with a total of twenty years in jail for 230 break-ins was cleared of a burglary charge at the Old Bailey, when the jury knew nothing of his criminal record:

> Under existing laws they weren't allowed to hear about his dishonest past, in case it influenced their verdict.
>
> Explaining the need for such protection, Judge Michael Coombe commented: 'Maybe sometimes we go too far'.
>
> Damned right we do, M'lud. I can't help wondering why the man in the dock always seems to get a better deal than anyone in court.
>
> Innocent rape victims are forced to parade the most intimate details of

Figure 14.1 Columns make familiar shapes on the page

their sex lives while their attackers smirk their disdain, confident that even if they have a record of rape it won't be introduced in evidence.

Old ladies who have been mugged are accused of being confused or making the whole thing up while sniggering thugs are presented as decent, upright citizens.

No, I don't suggest that anyone who appears in court with a criminal record should automatically be assumed guilty.

But surely, in the interests of justice, it would help if the jury knew whether they were dealing with first offenders or dyed-in-the-wool villains.

Newspaper columnists in particular feed off each other, of course. Paul Johnson in *The Spectator* reproached Lynn Barber of *The Independent on Sunday*, and Mick Brown of the *Daily Telegraph* for coming to interview him without having read any of his books. 'Once again, the tired old stuff came out of the clippings machine. I got the impression he would have been more at home interviewing, say, a pop-singer.'

More often the columnists are 'obliged to comment upon the same small round of facts, all picking away at the same heap to find something original to say about John Major or Bosnia or Bienvenida Buck, or, whatever is the particular flavour of the week' (Robert Harris doing a guest turn in the *Spectator* diary of 9 April 1994).

To avoid being called a vulture, carve out your niche.

Mary Kenny's Week in the *Sunday Telegraph* (16 October 1985) deals with socio-cultural questions. She doesn't want to live to be 90:

'Unwanted grannies' will replace 'unwanted babies' with people arguing that the elderly aren't really people – they no longer enjoy consciousness and besides they are too expensive to maintain. Foreign grannies will be shipped over here to be 'euthanased', since the Latin countries will probably be behind in euthanasia legislation.

There is a charming Christian notion that it is a friendly thing to die naturally after your given life-span on earth: you are making room for someone else, playing your part in the cycle of nature. Euthanasia as such is wrong, but our safety first attitude to life is also silly and the California idea that in future we can all have spare parts so as to prolong our lives to 120 or 130 is wickedly selfish.

She gets away with this 'Madonna of the Moral Majority' stance, as journalist Yvonne Roberts called it, because she regularly and thoughtfully pursues these themes and avoids shouting.

How to be provocative

A fault with many personal columns in British publications is that they are inhibited, middle-class, cosy, whimsical deliberations about nothing very much; or sycophantic gossip about 'celebrities' and 'superstars' – a sad fault when a personal column can have a licence to shock in varying degrees. So a young iconoclast who can write (if editors are looking properly) has a chance to break into this field. Such a writer is Julie Burchill, described as 'youth-culture analyst and spirited interpreter of the passing scene', whose work has appeared in the magazine *The Face, New Society* and *The Mail on Sunday*. Here is the part of one of her pieces for that newspaper:

> Was I the only person to drop my genuine Our Lady of Lourdes cigarette lighter in awe when the Papal Tiger gave that amazing lecture to Hollywood on the danger of creating images that 'weak, defenceless, old and unattractive' people could never live up to? Apart from the fact that it's very rude to talk this way about Terry Wogan, it was terminally rich coming from a man who leads a church full of priests – celibate of course – who know enough to advise their flocks on every problem of family life and whose ideal woman is a mother who is also a virgin. The truth is that the idea of being born in original sin has mixed up and maimed more people than a million soap operas ever could.
>
> Not only are half the tarts in London convent-educated, but a large number of the drunks, dossers and assorted human flotsam lying around the streets speak with an Irish accent.

Well, you may not agree with it, but it probably makes you think, or smile, or perhaps both.

Polemics on class

Such vituperation in wide sweeps makes for refreshing if not inspiring reading. The point is to shock. The danger for the writer is of typecasting (see Burchill on 'the burden' quoted at the head of this chapter). Tony Parsons probably doesn't feel the burden because his scope is wide and he keeps moving. In *Arena*, under the heading 'The Tattooed Jungle' (reprinted in *Dispatches from the Front Line of Popular Culture*, Virgin Books, 1995) he takes on the working class:

> They love their country – eat shit, you Argie sheep-shaggers – but they don't care enough about the street they live on to bother binning their rubbish. My skip overfloweth ... In fact everything about these rich serfs in their Velcro-welded and boulder-rubbed denim is a throwback to the bad old days, the days when being born on the wrong side of the tracks meant you would always be a dumb prole.
>
> They are the real class traitors, betrayers of the men who fought the Second World War, those men who fought for Churchill but voted for Clement Attlee. But in the tattooed jungle they have no sense of history. The true unruly children of Thatcherism, they know their place and wallow in their peasanthood.

The middle class, of course, don't escape. They are 'The Polenta Jungle' of another of his columns for *Arena* (also in the book):

> ... With their scrimping and saving, their timid infidelities, their emphasis on life lived as part of a couple, their endless round of dinner parties and their complaints about house prices, the middle class wine and dine their way through life.

Since there is 'precious little to admire about either the working class or the upper class', however, and although 'there are many things to despise about the middle class', they believe in self-improvement, and 'you have to admire that'.

Attacking with facts

A cool observer of recent British decline used figures rather than insults. Glenn Frankel, about to leave Britain after three years here for the *Washington Post*, was given a column in the *Sunday Telegraph* to comment on Britain's decline. Frankel blamed mainly 'the ways in which the schools reflected and maintained the class system of social classification that plagues this country':

> The cold fact is that after thirteen years of Tory rule, the majority of British students still leave school at sixteen, as John Major did in 1959, while in the United States, Canada and Japan more than 85 per cent remain. Less than 20 per cent of British students attend post-high-school degree or training programmes – compared with 60 per cent on the United States.
>
> Less than 50 per cent of Britain's workforce is classified as skilled, compared with nearly 85 per cent in Germany and 75 per cent in France. That is one major reason why, despite a slight closing of the gap during the 1980s, worker productivity in Britain remains 22 to 30 per cent below its chief European competitors.
>
> George Walden, the Conservative MP and former Minister for Higher Education, who is no stranger to these columns, argues that the class system remains a basic problem. 'By and large the entire education system is designed to perpetuate class – it provides a leg-up for the children of the people who run the country', says Walden, himself a product of the state system who now spends more than £20,000 a year to send his own three children to private schools.

Veteran iconoclasts

Of another generation are Auberon Waugh (the *Telegraphs*, *The Spectator* and *The Oldie*) and Keith Waterhouse (*Daily Mail*). On Scout organizers in Reading cancelling Bob-a-Job week on the grounds that the boys might be mugged or sexually assaulted, Waugh thought that, 'despite all the encouragement given to sexual perversion by Left-wing councils ... I simply do not believe that Boy Scouts are assaulted any more frequently than they always have been'.

Don't expect spontaneous sympathy from Waugh if you are young or working class, or even worse, both. Nor if you are unthinkingly against Europe. Commenting on an NOP survey showing that 49 per cent of Britons do not feel European at all', he said:

> Perhaps our best hope is to convert the rest of Europe to our idle habits, but we won't be able to influence it in any direction if we keep up our sullen opposition. Nobody likes change, and change which comes with new regulations and various foreign languages attached to it is particularly to be avoided, but Europe represents our only hope of retaining our major national characteristics, let alone our buildings and our countryside. Without it, we face a future of American rubbish and American filth, poor, resentful and self-pitying, with a leadership which sees its function as repeating the silliest opinions of the stupidest and most timid people in the land (*The Daily Telegraph*).

Keith Waterhouse can be brilliantly concise. He shoots from the hip at whatever party or group deserves a reprimand; it gets a rocket or a raised eyebrow, whichever is going to be most effective. In March 1986, after a severe winter, his column, appearing then in the *Daily Mirror*, drew attention to the plight of the old:

> Head for head, more old people died from the cold in Britain last month than in any other European country. How's that for a record? ... When a country is built on coal and oozing in oil, it takes an organizing genius to allow 1200 people to freeze to death in a single winter.
> That genius exists in abundance in the centrally-heated corridors of power.

From 1992 he has appeared in the *Daily Mail*. 24 April 1995 found him claiming that 'plenty of greybeards like myself who were taught in classes of 40 or 50 got a better education than today's unmanageable classes of 30'. He thought 'not class size but class quality is what the teacher should be concerned about'. The main item ridicules the government ploy to introduce identity cards, allowing time for public airing of views:

> Ah, consultation! That's when the council sends round a questionnaire asking: 'When we tear up the cobbles in the market square, would you prefer them to be replaced by paving stones or herringbone bricks?' What size would you like your ID card? Any colour preference? As well as your name, address, place of work, National Insurance number, driving licence details and credit card numbers, is there any other little piece of information you would like stored on it? Blood group perhaps? Next of kin?

FANTASY AND SATIRE

Among the greatest of columnists have been those who have taken off into fantasy while working within journalism and its purposes and keeping to its restrictions of length and deadline. Below are a few samples, although there's space only to give a taste of their quality.

J. B. Morton wrote the best known of fantasy columns as Beachcomber for *The Daily Express* for over 40 years from 1924. The law in operation provided some of the funniest moments. The first day of the case of Miss Ruby Staggage v. Broxholm Hydraulic Laundries and Others caused Mr Justice Cocklecarrot much trouble, with laborious talk of multiple cozenage, ultra vires, *sine die*, 'tutamen being implicit, with or without barratry, responderia and plonth' ... wivenage, etc.

On the second day:

Cocklecarrot asked Mr Honey-Gander, counsel for the defendants, what the twelve red-bearded dwarfs could possibly have to do with the Broxholm Hydraulic Laundries, and how they came into the case. Mr Honey-Gander made the sensational reply, 'M'lud, I understand that these gentlemen have a controlling interest in these laundries. In fact, they *are* Broxholm Hydraulic Laundries.'

Cocklecarrot: Then why do they call themselves 'Others'?

Mr Honey-Gander: I believe, m'lud, that there are others connected with the laundries.

Cocklecarrot: Red-bearded dwarfs, too, I will wager.

Mr Honey-Gander: So I understand m'lud.

Cocklecarrot: How many?

Mr Honey-Gander: Forty-one, m'lud.

Cocklecarrot: Merciful heavens! Call Mrs Staggage.

Mr Honey-Gander: Your name is Elvira Staggage?

Miss Staggage: No, sir. It is Amy Clowte.

Mr Honey-Gander: I see. You own a rocking-horse factory?

Miss Staggage: No, sir. I act for the real owners.

Mr Honey-Gander: And who are they?

Miss Staggage: A number of red-bearded dwarfs, sir. I see them over there.

(From J. B. Morton, *The Best of Beachcomber*. Selected and introduced by Michael Frayn, Mandarin Paperbacks, 1991 (first published by William Heinemann Ltd, 1963.)

The case is complicated by the fact that the dwarfs are both hydraulic launderers and rocking-horse manufacturers, and so are both plaintiffs and defendants. . . .

Outrageous puns and anecdotes that start in recognizable Irish life and take off in a balloon before you've had time to think of arguing are the hallmarks of the comic genius of Brian O'Nolan, who was 'Myles na Gopaleen' above his famed *Irish Times* column (1929–66), and Flann O'Brien for some cult novels. Recurring characters include The Brother, who has an answer to everything and pours scorn on the constant inadequacies of the professions, and the Plain People of Ireland, who interrupt Myles's flights of fancy with stone-wall clichés. Early samples of the column are collected in *The Best of Myles*, Pan Books, 1977. The above-mentioned delights need more space to do them justice than is available here. Here is a brief extract from the *Catechism of Cliché*:

> In what can no man tell the future has for us?
> Store.
> With what do certain belligerents make their military dispositions?
> Typical Teutonic thoroughness.
> In what matter do wishful thinkers image that the war will be over this year?
> Fondly.
> Take the word 'relegate'. To what may a person be relegated?
> That obscurity from which he should never have been permitted to emerge?
> What may one do with a guess, provided one is permitted?
> Hazard.
> And what is comment?
> Superfluous.

A section under the (strictly Gaelic) heading 'Sir Myles na Gopaleen' sounds like a forerunner of *Private Eye*. Note the intrusion of the editor in the piece below, and also the similarity of this to 'Pseud's Corner' – from the real-life quotes in that magazine:

> Myles himself, the brilliant young journalist, will be out of town for 14 days. No letters will be forwarded. An indefatigable first-nighter, he is keenly interested in the theatre and has written several plays. Life he regards as a dialectic that evolves from aesthetic and extra-human impulses, many of them indubitably Marxian in manifestation. The greatest moment of his life (which occurred in 1924) was when he made the discovery that life is in reality an art form. Each person, he believes, is engaged on a life-long opus of grandiose expressionism, modulating and mutating the Ego according to subconscious aesthetic patterns. The world, in fact, is a vast art gallery, wherein even the curators themselves are exhibitors and exhibitionists. The horse, however, is the supreme artistic symbol –
>
> *The Editor:* We can't have much more of this, space must also be found for my stuff.
>
> *Myself:* All right, never hesitate to say so. I can turn off the tap at will.

Fantasy columns are not commonly perpetuated at length today. *Private Eye* uses them to satirical effect. The regular column 'The Secret Diary of John Major, aged 47¾' gave us the low-down on the new shape of the Conservative Party following Major's re-election as leader:

> I was just puzzling over the main headline in the Telegraph, 'HEZZA RINGS YEZZA', when the new Party Chairman Mr Mawhinney came through my office. 'Don't touch those papers, John,' he shouted in his funny Irish voice, 'I've put them out for Mr Heseltine. He wants to look at them before the Cabinet meeting he's called.' 'Oh,' I said, 'is there a Cabinet meeting?' 'Not for you, John,' he said, 'You're officially on holiday.' He then put a card into the sliding doors, and they opened. I was about to follow him when the doors shut again, and the red light went on saying 'Wait'. There is something very odd going on there, which I don't completely understand.

Michael Frayn, veteran *Guardian* columnist-become-playwright, produced an imaginative one-off onslaught on the cliché in that paper (9 November 1994). He has visited the Old Tropes Home:

> The Matron who showed me round spoke very reassuringly. 'I understand where you're coming from,' she said. 'So let me just bring you up to speed. We're very definitely state of the art here, and I don't need to tell you which art that is – it's the art of living. And if you're up at the sharp end then you've got to get your act together and show your street cred. That having been said, what gets up my nose is that people can't get their heads round this. I mean, what are we talking? . . .'
> I said it sounded to me like some dialect of English.
> 'We're talking serious money,' he said, 'We're talking megabucks. Because what are we looking at here?'
> So far as I could see it seemed to be the ancient flagpole outside the window, up which things were run to see if anyone saluted them.

Frayn found it no problem keeping this up for 1500 words and more.

THE PLACE OF CREDIBILITY

It might seem that almost anything goes in a personal column – exaggeration, eccentricity, fictionalizing, fantasizing – but the line should be drawn before misrepresentation of the facts. The truth is more than the sum of the facts, and journalists dispensing opinions who have not got the time to collect as many facts as they would like are tempted sometimes to stretch what they perceive as the truth to cover the inadequacy of the facts.

This is dangerous on two main counts. First, for credibility's sake. A writer won the Pulitzer Prize for a *Washington Post* story some years ago about a child drug-addict on the streets of New York. It was a brilliant story, brilliantly written. But the Pulitzer Prize is for non-fiction: the girl didn't exist. The writer was ridiculed, and the paper was ridiculed; both suffered a considerable loss of credibility. The writer lost her job. The writer who can use fictional techniques to achieve an end is highly valued, but in journalism the lines should not be deliberately blurred.

The second danger (in assuming you are a visionary plugged into the truth by a more direct line than most other people) is that you will tend to develop a cavalier attitude to facts. Your reporting will get sloppy; you will lose credibility with yourself, however much you may be unconsciously disguising the process with burgeoning powers of imagination, wit and writing skills.

Caricatures to be recognized

It is not always a straightforward question of course. The contents of satirical magazines – columns such as Waugh's and Burchill's – that depend on outrageousness and caricature for their effects, seem on the face of it to have no regard at all for the principle outlined. But the point of a caricature is that it departs from the reality in order to heighten it: the exaggeration is not to be taken at face value, and there is not a deliberate attempt to betray the facts or mislead the reader.

This debate will continue, because who can draw the line between intention and effect, fact and fiction, truth and belief with absolute certainty? If asked to extract from this discussion a guiding rule for the tyro columnist, I would say: continue to make it as clear as you can where your facts end and your opinions begin. When your columns are sought for your opinions, always indicate where the factual basis lies. The context and style should make it clear when you are employing fiction as a tool, as in the *Private Eye* extract on page 241.

As for the violence that opinion-formers can do to reputations, fear of libel is generally a sufficient check. Make sure such allegations are in the public interest, 'fair comment' and without malice; and if you feel you may be risking libel action, obtain legal advice, for the law is complex. See Tom Crone's *Law and the Media* (Focal Press) and for ethical principles in general, the NUJ Code of Professional Conduct (Appendix 3) and the Press Complaints Commission's Code of Practice for the Press (Appendix 4).

ANTHOLOGIES

The better known personal columnists are sometimes persuaded to anthologize their columns in books, but they tend to disappoint in book form, despite being enjoyed when they were written. Journalism has the unmistakable whiff of ephemerality about it, however carefully the embalming is done. Among those that have transferred successfully, I think, are the columns in some of *The Guardian Bedside Books,* columns of the essay type such as Alice Thomas Ellis's collection of *Spectator* pieces, *More Home Life* (Duckworth) and *Cassandra at his Finest and Funniest* (Daily Mirror/Hamlyn).

SPECIALIST COLUMNS

The specialist by-line column – the kind written by a lawyer, doctor, or an expert in educational or social problems, or even an 'agony aunt' – can cover a wide range of subjects in its field in an equally wide range of newspapers and magazines in all kinds of formats from bits-and-pieces to essay-style. The more technical are dealt with in Chapter 19.

Go, by all means, for a subject that has not been tried before but make sure it has potential for continuity. You will be in trouble with a new sport or hobby if the fashion rapidly fades. If you cannot find a valid new subject within your specialism at least look for new angles: finance for schoolchildren, sex for the retired, recreations for the overweight. *The Oldie* magazine has had two fruitful column formulae based on celebrities: 'I once met ...', and 'Still with us ...'. Think of various ways of adapting those formulae to your specialism without making it obvious that you have pinched them from *The Oldie.*

Above all, use constant legwork and research to ensure you are not rehashing old themes. Before you launch a column, work out how much legwork and research, including in libraries, you will need to do to keep on top of a subject. Keep in mind that a columnist in a particular field needs to be enough of an expert to assess reliably the value to readers of information obtained from printed sources, new products, interviews, etc. Whereas the one-off article can be written from the layman's stance, a regular specialist column is expected to be definitive; the readers will depend on the information and advice given.

Give an aim to your column: is it mainly to give advice or to entertain or to provoke to action? Is it to be one-essay form, a three- or four-item menu, a catalogue of information (as, for example, a consumers' guide to cameras or computers), an interview feature, a question-and-answer format answering queries from readers as in an 'agony' column, or is it basically a how-to column?

Whatever the formula, your sample material must be able to convince a potential editor that you can keep it going indefinitely if need be.

ASSIGNMENTS

1 Write a 100-word opening to personal columns built around two of the following topics, updating as necessary, either developing an argument from them or merely using them as triggers to other thoughts. Aim them at national newspapers:

   ● A court awarded two British women £3,000 for 'trauma' after being pestered by waiters in a Tunisian hotel. The Association of British Travel Agents, however, say that some women consider a lack of sexual harassment as cause of complaint (*The Independent*).

   ● An America tycoon offered his estranged wife £3 million to 'sit down with him and smile' at a party. Timber magnate Joe Hardy ... made the offer to ensure the success of 'Lord Hardy's Feast'. Each year he flies 100 Warwickshire residents on Concorde to Pennsylvania to commemorate his buying of the title of Lord of Henley-in-Arden for £85,000 in 1990 (*Daily Mail*).

   The above pieces were quoted in the *Sunday Telegraph's* 'Spirits of the Age' corner (August 1995).

   ● Violence on TV does not trigger real-life crime, according to David Gauntlet of the Institute of Communication Studies of Leeds University (August 1995).

   ● An accident victim won more than £250,000 from British Rail, following a five-year battle, after her legs were severed by a moving train at Wandsworth Common, London.

2 Select any news story from a national paper and write a 1200-word argument round it for a general interest magazine. Choose an inside-page home news story rather than the major ongoing political one. Do the necessary market study of the target publication first, and allow for any updating of the material. Give some space to the opposite side of the argument.

3 Find a personal column overloaded with 'Is'. Rewrite it, removing all the 'Is'. Write a short paragraph explaining how the removal affects the piece. Choose two 'Is' to replace and explain your choice.

15 THE REVIEWER

'The critics – you shouldn't even ignore them.' Sam Goldwyn, film mogul.

'Critics are like horse-flies. They prevent the horse from ploughing.' Anton Chekhov.

'The best judge of a feast is the guest, not the cook.' Aristotle.

'A good reviewer combines the knowledge of the scholar with the judgement and cogency of the critic and the readability of the journalist.' Philip Larkin, 'Foreword', *Required Writing* (Faber & Faber, 1983).

The creators and the critics work from different premises. Goldwyn, the tycoon, could afford to rubbish film reviewers (in inimitable style). Chekhov was thinking mainly of bad theatre reviewers, who couldn't appreciate his new approach to playwriting. In the critics' camp, Aristotle had philosophical and political concerns. Philip Larkin's is a good definition for broadsheet reviewing.

As with the byline column, whether personal or specialist, reviewing is unlikely to be the first task a new writer will expect to be doing. Yet it is an obvious specialization for those interested in the arts, and there are successful freelance journalists, and reviewers, who did begin this way. A good deal of the arts coverage on local newspapers and small magazines comes from part-time specialists with the writing skills and the background experience needed. In fact, at all levels in the media, book, theatre and music reviewing is dominated by outside contributors. Some of those who write for the quality dailies and Sundays have built up formidable reputations in their fields.

The terms 'criticism' and 'reviewing' refer to telling about, explaining, interpreting and evaluating books of all kinds, plays in the theatre, films, TV and radio programmes, concerts, art exhibitions and other cultural events. 'Criticism' is used mostly to refer to the academic kind of commentary to be found in books and literary journals; 'reviewing' suggests workaday journalism in newspapers and magazines, and I shall stick to this term.

Because of the different premises, it's difficult to pin down what is fair and unfair comment. On the whole each side is aware of this and refrains from joining battle, but occasionally war does break out in letter columns and TV studios. Libel considerations mean in effect that the reviewer's comments should not directly threaten the ability of practitioners to earn their living, and must be written without malice. (An actress won damages when a reviewer said her bottom was too big.)

The main faults of reviewers, about which practitioners justifiably complain, can be listed. There is the tendency to use the piece under review, if considered bad, to exhibit the reviewer's arsenal of vituperation or epigrammatic wit ('Okulov played Chopin last night, and Chopin lost'), rather than to analyse what went wrong.

Reviewers are also guilty, at times, of using the work under consideration as merely a launching pad for their views on the world; of insufficient study of the work and its background/context; of lacking the taste or imagination to appreciate its insights; of criticizing a work for not being something it didn't set out to be.

Reviewers are not so often accused of sycophancy, but they can be guilty of this, too. Once you go over the top, there's nowhere to go but down. Ending a piece on the film *Out of Africa,* a reviewer says: '... finally, it is the commitment to perfection in every aspect of the film – the acting, the period, the settings, the photography and the people – that makes this such a sparkling film'. This rings false because of the inadequate final adjective.

THE REVIEWER'S TASKS

First reviewers have to decide where their readers are at, whether or not they could have read, seen, heard (etc.) the work. The following tasks need to be modified accordingly:

1 To say what kind of work is being reviewed, and what it is about.
2 To give an informed judgement as to whether it is worth the readers' time and money (not usually applicable to last night's TV assessments).
3 To back up with evidence (as has been emphasized in the context of article writing), and persuasive language based on knowledge and experience.

4 To act as a bridge between practitioners in the arts and the audience. This is the reviewer's interpretative role. The reviewer must be sensitive and perceptive enough to recognize the merits of new or difficult-seeming work.
5 To help, while trying to be readable and entertaining, to set standards, moral and aesthetic, in the arts.

Reviewers need to have the courage of their convictions to do their job. Producers and directors have their 'tame critics'. Hospitality is doled out at TV previews; authors get little notes from their publishers saying, 'Do you know any reviewers among your friends?' Theatre reviewers have to avoid too close friendships with actors and actresses in case they are tempted to be partial.

Reporting

Reporting is at the heart of all reviewing, and the disciplines of reporting are reflected in the kinds of questions being answered:

What is it called?
What is it about?
What is it like?
Who wrote it (directed it, plays the leading part . . .)?
When does the action take place?
Where is it showing/Where can you buy it?
Why was it written/painted/made?
How much is it?

Assessing

Added to these are questions of opinion and assessment:

What are its merits/defects?
Is it worth the time and money?
Did I like it?
Will you like it?
What sort of people will like it?
Is it interesting/moving/entertaining?
How does it compare with other works by this practitioner?
How does it compare with contemporaries' work?
How far does the practitioner succeed in achieving what he or she set
    out to do?

For some of the more probing of these questions, there will not be room or inclination in the popular markets, and the emphasis will be on how entertaining the work is.

In all kinds of reviewing, skill at compression is essential, to summarize what a work is about, and to weave the complex tapestry of facts and assessments that is required. Upmarket, the review takes on some of the characteristics of an essay, veering between the academic, analytical kind and the more consciously literary kind, but constantly reflecting in style the work it is responding to, as it moves around it. Common to all reviewing is the need to report the main facts about the book or film or whatever early in the review, so that there is a clear context in which all assessments can be immediately grasped by the reader.

The road to reviewing

The differences in the ways popular and quality markets deal with the arts are striking. Prospective reviewers must therefore study markets with particular care, collect cuttings and analyse them, and decide in which markets they would feel most comfortable. Even within the main categories of market, editors' expectations can vary considerably.

Reviewing jobs for national papers may be out of reach, but new writers should study the reviews in such markets carefully for techniques. Currently (to generalize) the *Telegraphs, Daily* and *Sunday*, look for strong reporting as the basis for reviews. *The Guardian* hopes for exceptional writing skill in the reviewer (as in other feature writers), while *The Sunday Times* wants to make the arts more accessible. The broadsheets will justify any caustic reviewing on the ground that readers prefer to measure their own assessments against a strongly opinionated writer than against unfocused blandness or showing off. Note, however, that approaches change with new arts editors, and check the above remarks with your own findings.

Covering showbiz

The tabloids put the emphasis on lively, entertaining reading, and in several (*The Sun, News of the World,* and *The People*, for instance) arts coverage blurs into showbiz gossip. Many provincial papers (again, a good place to start) cover much amateur work, which requires a different approach, as will be described. Another good place to start is in low-circulation little magazines: arts editors watch them, along with university magazines, for new reviewing talent.

There are several magazines devoted to the arts that should be studied. Numerous consumer magazines, weeklies and monthlies give space to reviews, and then there are the free sheets and free magazines to consider.

It will help you to obtain work in reviewing if you have already had other kinds of writing published in the market aimed at. Perceptive letters to arts editors discussing published reviews could be tried. Samples of reviews already published (if any) should be enclosed. Otherwise, write some to send.

Once you are an established reviewer, make contact with press officers, PROs, production departments, etc. and get on mailing lists for publicity material.

BOOK REVIEWING

To approach book reviewing from the middle ground, Graham Lord, who ran a very readable books column in the *Sunday Express* for many years, told me:

> My policy is that I should cover the most important and interesting book for a middlebrow readership, write a feature that can be understood and enjoyed even by the non-literary layman, say what the book is about, give some extracts from it, and say whether I liked it and why. Anything else is an ego-trip by the reviewer, which is why the 'heavy' book pages are so dull. Too often they review books nobody wants to read and give acres of space to books they end up saying are no good.

Book reviewing is rarely interesting or valuable unless backed up by knowledge of the subject (non-fiction), or wide reading among authors of novels and short stories, and not only among current output (fiction). Peripheral reading is advisable in preparation for the review: for example, other works by the same author and similar works by contemporaries for the sake of comparison. In more amateur publications, and in those aimed at a young audience, a less sophisticated approach may be acceptable, the reviewer being seen as a typical member of an audience eager to learn.

If you have knowledge or wide reading, background research will come easily. Publishers' handouts or the blurbs on the dust jacket will start you off: they may give you a brief biography of the author and some account of previous books. This information can be expanded by reference to *Who's Who*, books of criticism, published reviews and the author's works, articles about the author, interviews with the author, and so on.

It is important to place the novel in the context of the author's body of work. Is it the first, second or thirtieth novel? The reader will want to know whether there is a great deal of promise (first) whether the first's promise is likely to be fulfilled (second), whether this novel is a typical product or whether the author is taking a new direction (thirtieth).

Note-taking method

In making notes, as you read, insert your own reactions in square brackets. Note the likely effect of passages on readers. This will help in interpreting the author to your readers. Note also page numbers of passages you might want to quote.

The progress from notes to writing the review varies. Some reviewers prefer to write while their impressions are fresh, others sleep on it. Some prefer to write without being hamstrung by concern for details, and then to check against notes and fill in afterwards. Others build up the review patiently, with constant references to an outline, into which are slotted the various points and quotes of the notes.

Certainly, where possible, the review should be put away for a day or two, then polished up and the facts rechecked.

Non-fiction

Before reviewing a non-fiction book, be sure you know, or have access to, up-to-date sources that cover the same ground, so you can check the author's work against experts. Do not rely on memory when making points or referring to facts or figures. It is important to recognize wrong figures, wrong dates, errors of fact, misprints, and so on. Readers are relying on your advice.

Lack of attention to accuracy is a serious fault in a non-fiction book. It erodes confidence in the accuracy of other statements in the work and casts doubt on the author's authority. Similarly the reviewer's authority is in danger if errors go unspotted.

Here is an example of a reviewer (Peter Kellner in the *New Statesman*), who has done the necessary research, and is doing the necessary hatchet job on a book, riddled with errors, which purports to reveal the underlying amateurism in some of Britain's elite groups:

> Harold Macmillan became Prime Minister in 1957, not 1956. David Steel entered Parliament in 1965, not 1964. When George Woodcock stepped down as TUC general secretary in 1969, he was succeeded by Vic Feather, not Len Murray. In the 1979 general elections the Scottish Nationalists did not fall 'from fourteen seats to four' – they fell from eleven seats to two. 'The two-year premiership of James Callaghan' in fact lasted for three years and one month. Today, Labour constituencies do not 'insist on reselecting their members every two years' – they do so once in each Parliament.

The error-detector should distinguish between author's and printer's errors and may need to fault the publisher's proofreading.

The intro of a typical non-fiction review might include a summing-up of what the book is about, the theme underlying the content, the book's merits/defects, and the author's general attitude to the subject.

Summarizing the content of a non-fiction book is normally done in the present tense – partly because a book's contents are felt to be permanent (the text is always there) and partly because there would otherwise be too many bewildering changes of tense. Actions before the time-scale of the chief events of the book are in present perfect or past tenses.

Fiction

References should generally be made in novels or short stories to the following elements: story/plot, theme, setting, period, narrative technique, characters, style (language). Discussing these elements in a rigidly analytical way, however, would produce a mechanical piece of writing, and you might still fail to answer the questions uppermost in the mind of the reader of the review, namely:

What is it about?
Would I like it?
What is it like?
Is it worth buying?

The budding reviewer might concentrate too much on the story, and neglect the theme, the significance of the story, the meaning of it all. Running through the main details of the story does not by itself give any idea whether the author tells it in an interesting way or not, whether the attention is held, whether it is better or worse than other books of its kind, whether it has merit.

If you get the main story/plot across early in the review, readers will have references to enable them to see the significance of your points.

Answering the question 'What is it like?' includes indicating what genre of book it is: literary, detective novel, thriller, adventure story, spy story, romance (romantic novel), historical novel, and so on. Comparing and contrasting it with other books by the writer and similar books by other writers will be useful to fiction readers. Analysing the interplay of the various elements listed above will also help to show the sort of book it is.

The following brief review from *The New Yorker* illustrates this point and is an example of a structure that would adapt well to any length of review:

Beyond the Mountain, by William Dieter (Athenaeum). A wide melodrama set in South Park in the Rocky Mountains, near Denver, around 1920. Mr Dieter writes in a manner reminiscent of Faulkner, but the story he tells recalls O'Neill or John Webster or the 'Oedipus Rex' of Sophocles. Brook Hartman returns to his family's ranch from a spree in Denver to find his father missing and presumed dead after a presumed fall from a mountain top. The cast that Mr Dieter confronts us with includes Brook's mother, a woman who has always treated him with contempt; his favourite uncle, Caleb, a one-armed veteran of the Great War; a young woman, the wife of a clergyman, come from Kansas to visit his mother, an ancient Basque retainer; and a couple of hired hands. Everything is dark and savage here. The characters, though nicely realized, move as if on a stage, as if well aware that they are involved in heavy drama – in a period drama – as indeed they are.

Significant elements

A few attempts to define the significant elements more closely for readers will be welcome here. In a particular novel, decide which elements deserve most attention, and which order would be best.

- The *story* is what happens, the *plot*, is the structure of what happens with the causality indicated.
- The *setting* – the place, the ambience, the atmosphere – needs special attention when it's unusual: for example, if a little known, exotic place, or an imaginary planet in a science fiction work. You should make it clear what is, as far as you can gather, the book's *period* or periods. Is it about today, or twenty years ago, or a century ago? In reviewing a historical novel, you should pay the same attention to background facts as you would to the facts in a non-fiction book; certain kinds of error can destroy the illusion.
- The *theme*, or message behind the story, may have to be carefully distinguished from the story itself.
- There may be a *moral*, borne out by the working of the story. It is naive to find fault with immorality being described in a story or novel if the intention is honourable and the theme morally sound. Keep in mind that your readers may not share your religious/moral convictions.
- *Narrative technique* sometimes needs careful scrutiny, and may need special comment. How does the author use time? Is the sequence clear or confusing? Are flashbacks and other techniques effective?
- *Characters* may be larger than life: caricatures, as in Dickens; or true-to-life, as in George Eliot or Jane Austen; or symbolic, representing ideas, as to some extent in Henry James and D. H. Lawrence.

Discussing the characterization in a novel is a minefield: the task tests your knowledge of life and your imaginative sympathy. Consider this attempt to attribute the triumph of an Iris Murdoch novel to her success with characterization:

> This book is a triumph for Iris Murdoch, I feel, because she creates characters which are ultimately believable, despite their weird actions. But this slightly discordant action allows Ms Murdoch to contrast the real with the imaginary.
> Her characters are neither wholly good nor wholly bad (except perhaps Crimond, whose dark excesses permeate everyone). And this is perhaps a strength. There are no stereotypes. One character works for the Foreign Office in Whitehall but not for him the perfect matching private life: his wife Jean leaves him twice for the same person.

No indication of what the characters are like is given, so that phrases such as 'ultimately believable' have little meaning. The 'weird actions' seem to refer to a series of events which culminate in a woman leaving her husband, having an illegitimate pregnancy and dying. But why 'weird'? Aren't such events happening all the time? 'This slightly discordant action' apparently refers to the same events. But it is unclear what the sentence means. The repetition of 'this' and 'perhaps' adds to the ambiguity. It seems to be a review written in a hurry, with insufficient thought given to what the novel is all about or to the novelist's choice of words.

● A novel's *style* may be so straightforward as to be hardly noticeable: this may be a case of art concealing art, or it may simply be that an unobtrusive style is more effective for what the author wants to do. The style might, on the other hand, be nearly the whole point, as in James Joyce: his universe is in his language. Styles can be tortuous, laborious, flat, or full of fireworks, but you can hardly consider them separately from content and aim.

Quoting the evidence

As far as possible your assessment of a novel or story should be backed by evidence, which may mean quotation. Carefully selected extracts may give a good idea of what a book, and a style, is like. You must, however, match quotations effectively with your discussion, and they may require interpretation and comment. They must not be used merely to fill up space, with such remarks as 'This passage shows how good his/her description (or characterization, or dialogue . . .) is'. Quotations must be used sparingly because of the limitations of space.

The late Angela Carter, in a review of Peter Carey's *Oscar and Lucinda* in *The Guardian*, related the author's theme to his style, quoted and commented judiciously, and pushed the novel's story forward in this extract:

The novel deals with sin, guilt, obsession, compulsion, the nature of religious belief and the destructive innocence of God's elect but nothing rumples the bright precision of the writing and the observation behind it. This precision gives the writing its profoundly unsettling quality. For example, 'A fox terrier was placed in the ring. The fox terrier was called Tiny. It wore a woman's bracelet for a collar. It took the rats one by one, picked them up like fruit from a bowl, broke them while the clock ticked and the men roared so loud you could not hear your companion speak to you'.

To bet on the results of this small massacre is the most degrading thing the Rev. Oscar Hopkins can imagine. He will do so, of course, soon after, and on a Sunday, too. 'Because it was a Sabbath and there was no other betting to be had.'

THE THEATRE

Most books are produced by a single person. The performing arts are produced by complex teamwork and the reviewer needs to give attention to the distinct roles and contributions of the members of the team and to interpret and assess the result.

What were the *originators* (screenwriters, composers, etc.) trying to say, do?

Were they well served by their *directors* (conductors, etc.) and interpreter/catalysts (actors, musicians)?

What should be said about the *audience's* reception?

Plays have elements in common with novels: plot, theme, setting, period, characters and language. There are, however, other elements to be considered: for example, set design, clothes, lighting, music (sometimes), special effects, and, most important, the acting and direction (which add up to the interpretation). The play reviewer is concerned with how well or badly all these combine *in a particular performance* of the play in the theatre, not primarily with how marvellous or otherwise the text is.

Amateur or professional?

Assessment of the production, including lighting, sets, etc., direction, and acting must be based on whether the play is being done by professionals or amateurs. If members of a well established theatre company, amateurs may be near-professional in their abilities, and it should be made clear at what level they are being judged. Other amateur groups may have various activities, of which theatre is only one. Their main purpose may be to enjoy themselves, and the audience may be mainly their relatives – factors that would obviously need to be mentioned in assessing the benefits.

Some of the greatest plays written have been given performances that have been called 'disasters' or 'flops' by reviewers. This is usually because the actors have not worked together as a team to bring out the meaning of the play. These two faults were present in a noted production of Shakespeare's *Macbeth* given at the Old Vic Theatre in London in 1981. The great tragic scenes provoked laughter from the audience because the actor playing Macbeth 'went over the top'.

Macbeth is notoriously difficult to do, partly because it is not easy to represent effectively, to an audience used to the realistic effects of cinema and TV, such aspects of the supernatural as witches on a Scottish moor, visions of daggers and ghosts. This is part of the challenge to the director.

Reviewer as juggler

The reviewer needs to assess the play as a whole, juggling, as the discussion proceeds, with the text, the acting, and the direction/production. A play being the product of teamwork, it is difficult sometimes to measure the contribution of the director, but the reviewer should try to indicate somewhere what the director's interpretation of the play is, and how effective the guidance given to the actors is, and the evidence for such comments deduced.

In the following paragraphs from the start of Irving Wardle's review of George Bernard Shaw's *Misalliance* for *The Times* (10 October 1986), he manages to say a great deal about the director's role, in a few words. Notice the masterly compression throughout: background, director's role, success, plot, characters, theme, setting, characters interwoven with theme:

> Never a great favourite, either when it first appeared in 1910 or during the Shaw revival of the 1960s *Misalliance* arrives at the Barbican because somebody believes in it. That person is evidently its director John Caird: and by the end of Wednesday night's glorious performance, that should go for the audience as well.
>
> The title seems to apply to an Edwardian engagement. Lacking any other suitor, Hypatia Tarleton, sole daughter of a prosperous underwear manufacturer, has settled for marriage with the son of a colonial governor: one Bentley Summerhays, a weedy but obstreperous youth given to lying flat on the floor and howling when anybody thwarts his slightest whim. As the piece develops, though, and the company talk their way through an endless summer afternoon overlooking the unvisited beauties of the Surrey landscape, the title spreads out to absorb a whole network of family relationships.
>
> There is Hypatia yawning through her father's literary exhortations, and her self-satisfied brother claiming to be the real brains behind the under-

wear sales. Lord Summerhays arrives, wearily disclaiming all responsibility for the unspeakable Bentley. Later an armed intruder arises from a portable Turkish bath and stuns old Tartleton with the celebrated line 'I am the only son of Lucinda Titmuss', as a prelude to avenging himself on her seducer: another son trying to strike the father dead.

In a later paragraph Wardle discusses the acting, but notice how the discussion is linked to the rest of the review, and how it is illuminated by physical detail relating to the action:

> As the direct embodiment of the Shavian Life Force, she is an idealized figure daunting to any actress: and Jane Lapotaire, got up in a lumpy flying suit, does not look the part for all her consciously athletic pirouettes. She does excel, though when engaged on resolute business (disarming the intruder or hauling Bentley off to the gym), and delivers her ringing denunciations with well-studied Polish vowels. Otherwise the company take superb advantage of a set of characters who display Shaw's power wholly to discredit the character, alter the circumstances and then redeem the victim.

Acting as interpretation

When discussing acting, reviewers should try in this way to relate the actors' performance to the intention of the playwright, to the meaning of the play as a whole.

Indicate the kind of role the actor has to play, not merely the name of the character, and comment on the actor's interpretation. For example, 'John Trelawney plays the part of David Ryan, a corrupt bank manager' is not usually enough (unless it's a very small part). How does Trelawney play the part? Is this the best way to play it? Has the director misled the actor by a wrong interpretation of the play as a whole? Make a clear distinction for the reader between the actors and the characters they are playing.

The acting may depend on display of emotions rather than any physical action. If so, John Peters (*Sunday Times*) shows the way: 'Tyzack plays Lotte with a sense of self-deprecating, ramrod integrity, her sad, proud façade cracking with pain: a marvellous example of how much you can say through restraint'.

Make the content of a new play clear before any discussion of it. Here is Michael Coveney in *The Observer Review* (28 May 1995) on Ronald Harwood's *Taking Sides* at Chichester:

> ... Harwood has compiled a stern tribunal drama – Sartre's *Altona* meets Hochhuth's *The Representative* – in which the Nazi 'credentials' of the conductor Wilhelm Furtwängler are examined by a philistine American officer during the 1946 denazification proceedings in Berlin.

Note that those allusions to other playwrights give the substance concisely, but they must be readily picked up by readers. Do you think they were in this case?

For a 'revival' – that is, a new production of a well-known old play or 'classic', such as Shakespeare, Chekhov or Ibsen – less attention may be given to content. However, a reminder of what even a well-known classic is about is necessary for most markets.

The reviewer should identify the *kind* of play: tragedy, comedy, straight play, farce, musical, etc. Points should be backed up by examples: the review must not merely say a play is 'boring', but explain why; nor that it is 'funny' without giving some evidence.

Being fair to plays

Book reviewers can reread passages if they are not sure about the fairness of their first drafts. A play reviewer does not usually see a play more than once before reviewing. On the national dailies there may be only one hour in which to write the review and catch a midnight deadline. At this speed, calm, considered judgement is not easy, though with experience the reviewer learns to cope.

When reviewing a very early public performance of a new play it is difficult to be completely fair because the play may improve considerably in a week or so (the reviewer may want to point this out). Some productions are 'tried out' in the provinces so that improvements can be made before they reach London or New York. The first performances ('previews') are cheaper and reviewers are not normally invited to these.

Reviewers should interpret a particular audience's reactions to a play in terms of the likely reactions of the market being written for. For example: 'Not a lot to *think* about, perhaps, but a good time was had by almost everybody', or 'I found it heavy going, but I noticed that the high-brow critics were chuckling knowledgeably'.

FILMS

If reviewing regularly, obtain publicity material from film distributors. This normally gives full cast details, potted biographies of actors, details of the production, etc. It is given out at previews. Reviewers of feature films and TV plays should have some knowledge of the technology and of the production techniques used inside and outside the studio. They should keep in mind the effects of the different technical requirements: the fact that a film is not divided (by curtain drops or otherwise) into acts and scenes as a play is; that it is a montage of many short scenes, skilfully edited to produce a 'flow' with appropriately varied pace. It is the challenges posed by the limitations of the medium that stimulate the artists' imagination.

Reviewers needn't show expert knowledge in these matters, however, unless they are writing for very knowledgeable audiences – for example, readers of the British Film Institute's magazine *Sight and Sound*:

> The camera keeps in close-up as much as it dares, to get the most from the performances, to heighten tension, and to suggest a larger-than-life interplay of emotions. The backgrounds are painstakingly done, with the Dresden set-piece an expectedly impressive wasteland of rubble and smoke, casually littered with desultory human figures. The Tralfamadore interior is glaringly lit, in keeping with the alien view of garish human living standards, and the special effects aren't too implausible.

Whereas bad plays come across as pretentious and can rarely be saved from disaster, even by the most skilful acting, bad or run-of-the-mill films can be enjoyable. There's so much to look at, and often you don't have to take it seriously. The reviewer for a popular or middlebrow market should respond to such films by reporting the story and significant images in an entertaining way, with appropriately light-hearted, even when critical, comment.

Rose Lloyd manages all that in a review of *The Lost Boys* (*South London Press*). She begins:

> What's got long hair, an ear-ring, a ghetto blaster, and fangs?
>   Well, it's something out of *The Lost Boys*, which mixes a vampire movie, and creates a whole new breed of monster – Teenychoppers.
>   The vampire tradition, now a bit long in the tooth, gets some much needed mouth-to-mouth resuscitation, when moved to pretty seaside town Santa Carla, populated almost entirely, it seems, by creatures of the night.

Despite the chatty tone of voice, the opening firmly places the film in its genre and tells us what it's all about.

There are a 'bunch of motorbike-riding, cave-dwelling, bloodsucking, heavy metal bats, who hang around the fairground savaging anyone who dares stick their neck out'. A vampire killer, who hangs out in a shop selling Batman comics, says, 'We have been aware of some very serious vampire activity in the town. We are almost certain that ghouls and werewolves occupy top positions at the town hall'. Ms Lloyd's comment here is 'Well, could you resist a film with lines like that?' and at the end sums up by calling it 'A likeable and entertaining variant on *I was a Teenage Werewolf*'.

Looking for the images

Film tends to be more of a director's medium than a writer's. It is normally what is done with the images that matters rather than what is done with the words.

The film of Tolstoy's *Anna Karenina* opens with Anna descending from a train at Moscow station while steam belches from the engine. She meets an army officer and you know that they immediately have fallen in love and guess that it will bring tragedy. The steam eddies around them as they try to see each other clearly. There are other omens. The clank-clank of an iron rod on the railway points has been heard. Anna, leaving the station, learns that the old man with the iron rod has just been killed by a train backing into him. At various crucial moments in the film the image of the old man, representing Death, returns. Anna finally throws herself under a train on the same station, while the same clanking of the points is heard.

The film reviewer notices the use and effectiveness of omens, and the symbolic resonance of such images as water (in lakes, rivers and seas), mirrors, storms, sunrises, sunsets, lightning splitting trees, fairgrounds, city tower blocks, institutions such as prisons, hospitals and monasteries with long corridors, doors opening, doors closing, etc.

Recurring images and sounds and the use of symbolism are necessary aids to the memory in films. The viewer can't be expected to keep turning back to refresh the memory even when it is on video.

The film cannot have the psychological subtlety of the play or the novel, so the reviewer shouldn't look for it. With the words of play or novel, contradictory ideas can be presented in the balance, one after the other. The film heightens the drama but simplifies the issues. A contrasting or contradictory image will drive out of the viewer's mind the image that preceded it, so directors generally aim for a repetition of an image, or for a series of images having the same import, for maximum impact. Such images can be powerful, sometimes hypnotic, and can stay in the viewer's memory for a long time.

The reviewer should be alert to the special responsibility of the film maker that goes with this power:

Is the film maker being responsible in the way he or she manipulates viewers' feelings and thoughts?
Is the writer's emphasis (if known) being shifted?
Are the writer's intentions being frustrated, the message being traduced?

Awareness of the medium

The strength of the film medium is in the way realism is rapidly established. In a flash we are in Rome or in a London park or inside a castle. A large country house with a Rolls-Royce outside means a very rich man inside. A ragged man jostled in a teeming city slum means a very poor man. Against this success with broad effects, however, is the limitation that it is not so easy to get inside a character's head.

Characters in many films tend to be stereotyped, as goodies and baddies, and it is up to the reviewer to indicate where this is done meretriciously or with blatant propaganda. David McGillivray is unhappy about such stereotypes in a review of the film *The Delta Force* in *Films and Filming*, about Arab terrorists hijacking a plane taking Americans from Rome to New York:

> Held hostage aboard a Boeing 707 en route for New York is a fine array of mid-air drama clichés – a spunky Jewish momma (Shelley Winters), a priest and two nuns, a pregnant woman and a man with a heart condition – and every last drop of sentimentality is wrung from the scene in which men with Jewish names are separated from the rest of the passengers.
>
> Later, when the Jewish men are transferred to a dungeon in Lebanon, the women and children are released, and everybody else remains on the plane, it is hard to know with whom to identify. The rescue, with Norris, as the head of the SAS-style Delta Force zapping terrorists with rocket launchers attached to his motorcycle, is standard hokum bound to delight the star's fans.

Reviewers must be constantly aware of the medium that are discussing; with the challenges imposed by that medium. For instance, film cannot easily establish different points of view, as a novel can. It tends to be the godlike camera's point of view. But you have to notice the ingenious ways in which the point of view of a particular character is communicated – by means of a flashback, say, and a voice-over of the character.

Film reviews compared

To help you decide on which markets you should aim at for reviewing (you can do the same for profiles and other slots), cut and file different publications' treatments of the same product/person, etc. Compare, for example, the following extracts (both second paragraphs) from two reviews of the film *Six Degrees of Separation*.

From *Loaded* (July 1995), by Mick Bunnage:

> Transferred from stage to screen, *Six Degrees* is a comedy of manners, sharper than a paper cut across the thumb and based on the true story of a young street kid who passes himself off as Sidney Poitier's son and blags

his way into the highest echelons of Manhattan's super rich art world for no reason other than to prove that he can. It's a laugh a minute once you get past the first 15. Donald Sutherland and Stockard Channing play the pomped up art duffers who come to realize that they don't know their assholes from their Picassos when a complete stranger named Paul (Will Smith) lumbers into their plush penthouse pad nursing a (self-inflicted) knife wound and touting a line in steaming bullshit so credible you could almost slide a shovel under it and spread it on your roses. He delivers a brilliant apparently spontaneous diatribe on *Catcher in the Rye*, which so beguiles the stuffy aesthetes they instantly offer to feed, clothe and house him for the rest of his life. Nice one.

From *Empire* (July 1995), by Kim Newman:

Playwright John Guare turned this freak news item into a Broadway hit, which was a stage triumph for Stockard Channing in the role of the society matron shaken by this encounter with the bizarre. Fred Schepsi then turned his screenplay into a film which has been sitting on a shelf for nearly two years. And despite some fuzzy thinking in the third act, when it gets hard to see what is on Guare's mind, the result is a thoroughly engaging and pointed movie. Channing, who justifiably earned herself an Oscar nomination *last* year, is excellent as the precise, fussy, yearning wife of Donald Sutherland's stuffy but oddly childish art dealer, and Smith intriguing as the smooth-talking stranger.

Both markets have a grading system: *Loaded* gives the film 9 out of 10; *Empire* gives it **** – very good (***** being unmissable, *** good, ** fair, and * tragic).

TELEVISION

Drama

My comments on feature films apply to a large extent to TV plays. The distinction between the two in fact is being blurred: many films are now made with finance invested on condition that they will have plenty of TV as well as cinema outlets. Nevertheless there can be important differences in the way film makers look at the two media and, therefore, in the reviewing of the two products.

First, the cinema has a large audience in one place, the TV audience is in small groups. This tends to make TV 'domestic' (especially as it's usually seen in a smallish room on a smallish screen), and domestic drama tends to work better than, say, epic westerns. Second, whereas features films are on average 1½ to 2 hours long, TV drama is of various lengths – though mostly shorter than films – and the reviewer must learn

Figure 15.1 Reviewers – working 'from different premises'

to judge it accordingly. Third, one-off TV plays are increasingly rare, and a special kind of critique has been developed for series and serials: to discuss, for example, the way characters who may go on for years have to be firmly established in early episodes and to discuss the so-called 'natural' style of acting demanded by some and the more melodramatic style demanded by others.

Putting-down wittily

A local paper TV reviewer discusses *Sins*, a vehicle for the soap opera star Joan Collins, saying among other things:

> Joan covered her bets and worked on the premise that the best way to look young is to surround yourself with old people. For this reason, Gene Kelly was wheeled on to play the mature romantic lead and Joan heaved her bosom non-stop in a brave attempt to convey great passion.

The rest of the 650-word review was in similar vein, a mix of comments on Collins's personal life and her acting performance. The reviewer's aim was to be witty, but put-downs of overblown material cannot afford to be overblown themselves. If it was not worth watching, it was hardly worth so much space.

It is noticeable that the pairs of alliterated adjectives tend to pile up when the reviewer is trying to be readable about the unwatchable. When *EastEnders* was going through a rocky stretch, a popular Sunday commented:

> Dirty Den is becoming bald and boring, while ex-wife Angie has lapsed into a ludicrously pathetic parody of genuine London . . .
>
> The saga of sluttish Mary and her tug-of-apathy child, the gruesome gay love affair, the health hazard of a café, deranged Dot Cotton and her foul family . . . all have ground to an enormous full stop in entertainment terms.

TV documentaries

The TV documentary may be compared to the well-researched feature article or the non-fiction book in reduced form. The need to spot inaccuracies and false reasoning is as important, and my relevant remarks on non-fiction reviewing are equally applicable to documentaries.

Keeping the medium in mind, however, it is distortion of emphasis that the reviewer will be looking for rather than errors of fact. As mentioned above, the film maker can manipulate viewers' feelings and thoughts by careful selection of images. Is this selection too one-sided in a particular programme, so that the final picture/argument is unfairly presented? This is the kind of question that must be asked.

TV documentary makers use a wide range of research material, and the reviewer's job is to indicate how well or badly this is used, and how it all contributes to the total effect. Interviews inside and outside the studio, photographs, drawings, paintings, maps, charts, old newsreels, current newsreels, reconstructions by actors of real-life incidents – these are among the devices used. Sometimes documentary makers overdo the general 'make-it-visual' principle; too many coloured figures may be moved about on too many coloured maps to express the simplest of facts or processes.

A wealth of different kinds of sources can confuse the viewer unless identity and significance are made clear. Yet labelling everything precisely and using subtitles can be heavy.

Reviewing a documentary generally means putting the programme into context.

Is it part of a series? (Obvious enough.)

- What knowledge did the viewer need to bring to it? How clear was the background to a viewer who may not have known much about it?
- Was the programme's treatment of the argument fair? As balanced as it should have been?
- How did it compare with similar earlier documentaries that readers may have seen? (Keeping in mind of course that they may not have seen either.)

Documentaries are often accompanied by offers made on screen after the programme and also in the listing magazines to send information. This may be in the form of a free factsheet (send SAE), or you may have to send a cheque for something more elaborate. If there's time before reviewing, such back-up information is well worth having: it is often laced with reliable figures, quotes from experts, a brief bibliography, etc., that don't get aired in the programme.

If such offers are not made, and you want to know more about the background to any programme, try the station's Press Office or the office of the programme's producer. If you review regularly and are on the necessary mailing lists, you may be able to get all such information free of charge and in advance of the broadcast.

Because TV is a medium, the way its products are approached by reviewers can vary considerably. Here is Christopher Dunkley in the *Financial Times* (24 July 1995), deliberating on the genre of the programme, after previewing:

> The [Summer Dance] season begins next Saturday with *Martha Graham: The Dancer Revealed*, a biography of the great Americana choreographer which is a documentary rather than a performance programme. Naturally

it contains numerous examples of Graham's art, both as choreographer and dancer, but this is quite definitely the story of a life, and a most extraordinary life.

Having continued giving performances well into her seventies, it seems that Graham hit the bottle when it looked as though she would be unable to continue. . . .

The personal TV column

Then at 79, she 'came off the booze, created twenty new ballets, and thirty major revivals, and lived to be 97. It is an astonishing and inspiring story.'

In other markets TV columnists give unity to the juggling act that is TV reviewing by knitting together assignments as another kind of personal column by the performer/pundit/humorist/reviewer. Such columns have their detractors among people who think TV should be taken more seriously; some think the job should be divided up among specialists in drama, sitcoms, current affairs and so on. But perhaps the pot-pourri approach better suits the nature of the medium, people's patterns of viewing, and the expectations of the readers.

While a daily paper reviewer might deal with just one item (a documentary or a one-off play), reviewers for a weekly paper or magazine, notably the weekly reviews, can take more time (and usually space) to analyse trends and make comparisons.

Whatever approach is preferred by the publication a lively mind that appreciates the good things in TV and writing that has wit and readability are essential for a TV reviewer.

Nancy Banks-Smith is inimitably quirky in *The Guardian* (24 April 1995):

> If I thought Mary Goldring was a wicked old thing (she doesn't look like a wicked old thing, she looks like a headmistress with a particularly unsatisfactory fourth former caught in her headlights) I would say she was pulling my leg.
>
> Trawling through the tourist industry for *The Goldring Audit*, she found among other shortcomings – her defection of the New Ambassadors Hotel in Bloomsbury will be spoken of wherever two chambermaids are gathered together – that after August 6, the Changing of the Guard only happens every other day. It seems we are short of soldiers.
>
> 'Can the Ministry of Defence provide the extra 37 soldiers needed to change the guard every day, or can't it?' she whipcracked. 'And if not, what's wrong with actors?'
>
> Well, look, how long have you got? . . .

Downmarket, the humour is not of a more earthy kind. Charlie Catchpole managed to give plenty of space to the *News of the World*'s traditional concerns on his TV page (5 December 1993), yet had a refreshingly no-holds-barred way of dealing with underachieving material. 'Story went from bot to worse' heads a piece on *A Woman's Guide to Adultery*. The first scene showed a man's bare bottom 'moving aimlessly':

> We never discovered who it belonged to . . . the guy got the bum's rush as soon as Rose realized he was married . . .
>
> Rose's resolve was tested when she enrolled in a photographic course run by Paul (Sean Bean).
>
> Married (you guessed!) Paul wanted to get Rose into a dark room and see what developed.
>
> 'Love doesn't care what goes on around it,' he said.
>
> 'People are always trying to tidy love, to tie it down, to tame it with vows and promises. But it doesn't work. Love's not like that.'
>
> Love obviously turns your brain to custard and makes you spout this sort of cringe-making twaddle. . . .
>
> *Unadulterated drivel.*

MUSIC

There are special difficulties in reviewing performances or records of music and in reviewing art exhibitions. The reviewer has first to interpret in words what is non-verbal. There may be some aspects that will help the translation, the associated verbal content of opera, for example, and representational painting. But the essence of these forms will not be captured through these associations alone.

The artists (composers, painters, sculptors) and interpreters (conductors, players of musical instruments) can be contemptuous of efforts to translate their visions/performances into words when they do not by nature belong there. At the same time the reviewer still has to produce a readable article that can be enjoyed by readers who did not go to the concert, or art exhibition.

Complex or 'difficult' modern music or art has a well defined small minority audience, which can be assumed to be well informed: the reviewer's approach here can be highly technical and intellectual. A review of a Gilbert and Sullivan operetta by the local amateur operatic society, on the other hand, can include something of the plot, can refer to the performances from the leading singers, and may concentrate on the fun had by all. The inadequate phrasing of the baker's wife's coloraturas in the leading female role is unlikely to be dwelt upon.

While the market for music takes in many demands, the reviewer's task of translation remains. Writing about rock and pop requires knowledge, a lively style, and a vocabulary as special as any other sort of music. You know what 'rap/hip hop's aggressively mechanistic attitude' means or you would not be reading about it. Here is a brief review from *Time Out* that suggests the style:

> Ladbroke Grove's club champions celebrate their first number one with another gout of live fire in Charing Cross Road. The current show highlights the slicker, poppier Lover's Rock side of their oeuvre but retains much of the power and splendour of their great days and is Loud. A useful double bill headed up by the fierce (sometimes a trifle melodramatic) rock social realism of Deacon Blue, whose finely-produced debut album on CBS suggested that here was an outfit preparing for the long haul. Fairground Attraction's light, airy pop won them the dubious distinction of being a TO Pop Pick for 1988.

Mojo, devoted to music, can spread out a bit, with fine writing in places and psychological insights. Consider the intro and ending of Tina Jackson's review of Vic Chesnutt/Tindersticks at the London Forum (July 1995):

> The place we're stopping at is where broken hearts and broken bodies come out of the shade and exorcise their demons in public. Tonight we're wrapped in a comfort blanket of music for people who never had beauty to hide behind or protect them from knowing that their dreams were going to get broken anyhow.
>
> . . .
>
> A Night in, Tiny Tears, the wonderful single No More Affairs, all blend into a lurching dance for the doomed. My Sister, sounding like Pulp on downers, has the bleakest, blackest wit you ever heard. They finish with a song called For Those Not So Beautiful. The audience howls. And a shy, wolfish, pleased expression flickers across Staple's [the singer's] face.

Attentive at the opera

Reviewing opera requires attention to all the usual elements of theatrical production, including set, design, costumes and machinery as well as matters of acoustics and use of amplification – and acting as well as the singing and the conducting. Tom Sutcliffe, also in *Time Out*, was disappointed by the English National Opera's *Magic Flute* at the Coliseum Theatre in London, but notice how he judiciously balances praise with blame:

> Casting and singing are generally more resolute than beautiful. Nan Christie's Queen of Night (shorn of her second definite article) was loud, mostly accurate and well applauded.
>
> Helen Field's Pamina was edgier than usual and rather frigid until her final rescue by the Three Boys, a musical high-spot. Her grieving aria had fetching tones but lacked legato line.

Ivan Fischer's conducting, at best urbane, plodded. Textures were dense. There was little evidence of a good ear placing instrumental colours or achieving choral coherence. Mozart conducting needs transparency and alertness as well as Fischer's uninspired but self-satisfied fullness.

Reviewing discs of classical music needs comparisons with other artists' efforts, with reference to any unusual tempos, as in this extract from a *Gramophone* review of Imogen Cooper's playing of Schubert's Piano Sonata in A minor:

Again, in the A minor Sonata she takes her time. Certainly her spacious conception of the opening movement allows her to orchestrate it to the full, with a splendidly wide and rich dynamic range. But here I sometimes wondered if there was sufficient underlying tension to sustain a tempo rather slower than we often hear – as, for instance, on the old Decca LP recordings by Lupu and Ashkenazy, both of whom also offer a more urgent finale.

The middle ground

The middle ground of musical taste is probably the most difficult to write about, and you see some of the strain in this review of a recent transfer to compact disc of three of Rodgers and Hammerstein's most popular scores (also from *Gramophone*):

Oklahoma! is an incomparable score combining poetry and humour in equal measure, whilst in *Carousel* Rodgers and Hammerstein rose to still greater heights of lyricism and drama. The King's songs in *The King and I* don't reach that level of inspiration, though Anna's 'Getting to Know You' and 'Hello young Lovers' are a delight, and their dance floor encounter, the swirling polka 'Shall we Dance?', is a further high spot. From the vocal point of view this recording is the least satisfactory, with Deborah Kerr and Marni Nixon, her 'ghost' voice, more than ever overparted on CD. There's some crude singing, too, from the young lovers. However, where this recording offers an undeniable thrill is in the playing of the 20th Century-Fox studio Orchestra under their conductor Alfred Newman, who also conducts *Carousel.*

ART

Reviewing art exhibitions requires assured descriptive powers. If you are to describe the old masters, it helps if you have humanity and sensitivity, and can relate them to today. Richard Cork, in *The Listener,* discusses Goya's blind beggar, *El Tio Paquette*, among the paintings of the Baron Thyssen exhibition at the Royal Academy:

Painted with a freedom strangely prophetic of Francis Bacon, the sightless singer opens his mouth in a grotesque, gap-toothed smile. Nothing distracts from a face caught in the spot-light of Goya's scrutiny – affirming the resilience of a man who stubbornly refuses to be defeated by adversity.

Tim Roberts has a lively down-to-earth manner with the lives and works. For *Tonight* (a London freesheet) of 22 February 1995 he covered the Willem de Kooning Paintings exhibition at the Tate Gallery:

> The Tate show opens with some pretty dreadful work. But from about the mid-Forties, de Kooning starts to evolve from bogus Cubism into a flowing, equivocal, Miro-esque style: floating amorphous blobs, variously derived from dislocated body parts (*Fire Island*) or jagged, deconstructed heavily worked Cityscapes (*Excavation*).
>
> This period saw the first in his series of Woman paintings. *Woman 1948*, de Kooning's first effort, is quite funny. The cheesy grin, splay-legged pose, melon tits, and flailing octopus limbs set the general format for dozens of paintings to follow.
>
> These culminated in the terrifying *Woman 1* from 1950–52. The figure is demonic, squatting, eyes like black saucers, teeth bared in a hideous rictus, breasts slung like sacks of flour.

Courage of convictions

So volatile is the world of art that art reviewers need to have more courage of their convictions than other reviewers. The versatile A. A. Gill does a hatchet job on the Impressionists in *The Sunday Times*. An exhibition at London's Hayward Gallery aimed to point up their political, revolutionary aspects by hanging them in alternate rooms alongside landscape paintings in the 19th-century studio tradition – 'state-sanctioned, state-purchased art':

> ... You walk round the exhibition and look at all that bloody sunlight and all those succulent little dabs of paint and think, if this is political, then Picasso was gay. ... The pictures in the exhibition that arrest attention, that make you stop and look, are all from the official Salon rooms, not necessarily because they are better but because they are unfamiliar and assertive. On the other hand, the rooms of impressionists look like wallflowers, pictures without a thought in their pretty little painted heads. It is time we questioned the pre-eminence of impressionists in the canon of art. ...

As for the minefield of contemporary conceptual art – of which Damien Hirst's pickled sheep in a glass case is a well-known example – reviewers know they're walking through it on a tight-rope. It's hard to avoid being pretentiously abstract about it, in the attempt to steer clear of snap judgements. Kevin Jackson lapses at one point in his attempt to guide readers of *Arena* of Summer 1995 through it; 'There's a lot of stuff about biology ... some of it nagging at feelings about the Cartesian split between body and mind.' But the rest is straightforwardly informative – it's left to you whether you keep a straight face. First he sums up what has been on show in the past year or two:

> ... there were Helen Chadwick's *Piss Flowers* – incongruously elegant 3D records of her own urinations in the snow – and her work in molten chocolate, rather faecal to some eyes. (Incidentally, chocolate is big – another young artist, Anya Gallaccio, has covered the gallery walls of Karsten Schubert with it.) There was Gavin Turk's waxwork self-portrait as Sid Vicious, now on show at the Saatchi gallery, and Mark Wallinger's *A Real Work of Art* (1993), consisting of the purchase, training and racing of a thoroughbred racehorse.

We feel some sympathy when Jackson turns to David Lee, the editor of *Art Review* for an assessment: 'The vast majority of conceptual work is a load of nonsense; there's nothing to it at all. There are no known, or accepted criteria by which it can be understood, let alone judged, and the result is that a lot of well-informed people justifiably think that it's rubbish. And when the artists try to justify what they're doing in terms of some philosophy, they just spout platitudes.'

THE LANGUAGE OF COMPRESSION

There is an unusual burden of compression on the language of reviewing, and it is worth drawing together some of the scattered remarks about it made in this chapter, and putting the point in sharper focus.

Reviewing has to be extremely informative, often about dissimilar elements simultaneously. The compression involved in this can make for heavy reading. This can be lightened by the occasional 'by-the-way' aside to give the reader a breather, the use of colloquial phrases to create an easy rhythm, and the odd cliché to put familiar ground under the reader's feet. The trick is to use sufficient of these devices to serve the reviewer's purpose.

A few samples of phrases that should be avoided at all costs are: 'a top-notch cast', 'played in fine style', 'a voice perfectly suited to. ...,' '.... a totally believable character', 'the cast worked hard and well' (it sounds quite painful), 'with such an excellent and distinguished cast, it is only a pity they did not have better material to work with' (your mother or your son was in it?), 'a manic performance' (good or bad?).

Avoid also too many pairs of adjectives when summing up performances: 'witty and effective', 'conniving and cruel', 'warm and moving', 'bouncy and bedraggled' – particularly, as we have seen, alliterative pairs: they usually come together thoughtlessly. *Three* assessing adjectives may suggest that you have given a definite verdict.

The chatty aside must be skilfully slotted in – not just breezily plonked down, as in: 'So no prizes for guessing how the film ends – just go prepared with a boxful of tissues and run-proof mascara (for those who wear it!)'.

Here are a few examples of openings and endings of theatre reviews, which provide examples of how compression can be relieved and the writing illuminated by the odd colloquial touch:

1 Edinburgh's devotion to the work of C P Taylor is not, so far, doing him many favours. Written in 1967 and hitherto unperformed, *The Ballachulish Beat* at the Corn Exchange turns out to be a raucous, semi-coherent fable about the exploitation of a Glasgow pop group, by both the hard left and the commercial right. The problem is that this kind of broad-based political pantomime now looks hopelessly dated.

   . . .

   It is put across by the Edinburgh-based Fifth Estate, in Allan Sharpe's production, with a certain comic-strip energy that makes up in volume what it lacks in subtlety. (Michael Billington, *The Guardian*, 21 August 1992.)

2 Guns were not only banging away on the grouse moors on the Glorious Twelfth. Chichester's exuberant new staging of *She Stoops to Conquer,* which opened that evening, has shooting, birds falling dead from above, birds exploding in clouds of feathers, a splendidly docile dog and an equally docile ferret. It also has a marvellously robust play, ideal for Chichester, whose audience responded with wave upon wave of laughter and rounds of applause after several strong exit lines.

   . . .

   An excess of stage business during several scenes sometimes suggests that Wood does not always trust his play or players to keep the audience amused; but he is wrong. One brilliant scene follows another, and you are taken unawares by the lines. How about this one: 'I vow, since inoculating began, there's no such thing as a plain woman.' Goldsmith rules. (Alistair Macaulay, *Financial Times*, 14 August 1992.)

3 *Richard III*, RSC, The Other Place. Sam Mendes' novel production may have been given an East European chassis – Doc Martens, trench coats, ominous shadow lighting and a two-floor backdrop of wooden doors – but it generates a compelling atmosphere of *film noir*. Simon

Russell Beale's Richard clomps into Edward IV's court as if he'd just unpeeled himself from a Goya painting: gloved, mis-shaped arm, heavy limp, and crew-cut head sticking tortoise-like out of a stooped, hunch-backed body. All he lacks is a glass eye.

. . .

It's a mesmerizing performance by Simon Russell Beale. With well-worked battle scenes and several telling amounts of ultra-violence to boot – notably Clarence's demise (Simon Dormandy) and the wonder-fully perverse image of Richard burying his walking stick into the parcel containing Hastings' head – Mendes' production is full of entertain-ment value. (James Christopher, *Time Out*, 19/26 August 1992.)

4   The subtitle to Oliver Goldsmith's comedy, *She Stoops to Conquer* is *The Mistakes of a Night*. Let me stoop to concur. There are plenty of *those* in the revival at the Chichester Festival.

. . .

Denis Quilley is splendidly outraged as the country squire whose daughter's suitor mistakes his house for an inn, and I liked Susannah Harker and Iain Glen as the young lovers. But the vital class-based comedy that Goldsmith put into the squire's uncultured second wife and her spiritedly asinine son wholly eludes Jean Boht and Jonathon Morris. (Kenneth Hurren, *The Mail on Sunday*, 16 August 1992.)

5 As familial bequests go, the syphilis passed on to Oswald Alving in Ibsen's *Ghosts* is plain sailing compared to the complex web of finan-cial chicanery handed down to Edward Voysey in Harley Granville Barker's *The Voysey Inheritance*.

. . .

What you get here are some attractive individual performances: booming out his fatuous certainties, Peter Blythe is very amusing as the bone-headed, blimpish brother and Gillian Martell as the deaf Mrs Voysey, is even funnier, giving the character a faintly barmy serenity, not at all put out, it seems, at being cut off. And what you get, too, in an albeit muffled form, is one of the most intelligent plays in the language. (Paul Taylor, *The Independent*, 20 August 1992.)

6   In the first half of Alan Frank's new play *The Mother Tongue* we appear to be firmly in sit-com land. Harrier is a modern woman with a growing family, a husband away producing a documentary in central America, a studiously untidy home in south London and a snooty mother come to stay for an indefinite period. It is a world of stock

characters, from the middle class teenage son with his carefully nurtured working class accent to the mis-matched harridans of Harriet's women's group.

. . .

Some of the script lines and events are too obvious and some of the emotional baggage needs discarding. Director Richard Cottrell needs much tighter control of the second act which, on the evidence of opening night last Monday, stood in too splendid isolation from the first. (Darryl McCarthy, *Kentish Times*, 6 August 1992.)

7 Theatre was one of the first arts to feel the chill of reaction, but one of the first to reflect a change of mood after the fall of the Berlin Wall. Now, the temptation to prefer today's suburban values to yesteryear's utopian aspirations seems hard even for erstwhile radicals to resist. Militant ways of seeing the struggles of the past crumble into less taxing visions, and laughing at Lefty becomes an easy way of avoiding painful memories. For this reason, April de Angelis' new play *Hush* (at the Royal Court Theatre) has delighted some critics with its images of disillusioned radicals.

. . .

Not confusion, but optimism, would surely have been a better way to celebrate the end of the cold war. We are liberated, for example, from the my-enemy's-enemy-is-my-friend syndrome, which in 1975 gave us *Fanshen*, David Hare's romanticized Red China. Other writers have hit tougher targets than middle-class leftists: Trevor Griffiths' *The Gulf Between Us*; Harold Pinter's *Party Time*, or even John Lahr's updated version of *The Manchurian Candidate* have all attacked the new world order. But for de Angelis, today's problems are drowned in yesterday's recriminations. For her, the 1970s ended not with a bang but with a *Hush*. (Aleks Sierz, *New Statesman and Society*, 21 August 1992.)

Notice the skilful summary of 1, the enthusiasm of 2, the qualities of the production in 3, the taut ending of 4, the yoking of actor to character in 5, the swiftly indicated world of 6 and the way the political theme is put into context in 7. Compare 2 and 4, on the same production.

ASSIGNMENTS

1 Review an important TV documentary as for a named national broadsheet daily and compare it with any review of the same programme published in that daily or any other national broadsheet, daily or Sunday. Don't read any reviews of it beforehand.

2 Review a newly released film without looking at any reviews of it first. Study other film reviews in a magazine, decide what length they would want, and aim your review at that publication. Then compare with the review that actually appears in the magazine.

3 Write as above, about a play at the theatre. Aim at a local paper that you know has covered it or will cover it.

4 Write a review column as for a broadsheet Sunday paper, choosing books, TV, film or theatre. Produce three linked items. If book reviews are chosen, use three novels or three non-fiction books published in the past year, borrowing from friends or from your local library. Try to compare with published reviews of the same.

16 THE FEATURES DEPARTMENT

This book addresses journalists at large, whether staff, freelance or a bit of both. So far there has been a concentration on the individual efforts demanded by the researching and writing. This chapter focuses on how features and special reports (the distinction is in places blurred, especially in the big national Sundays) are produced in-house. A great deal of feature writing is originated, editor-led, and closely monitored in-house as it develops. Important things here are the editorial conferences and face-to-face chats with section editors and colleagues that staff writers need.

Such close monitoring is essential on newspapers where the breaking news is constantly overtaking what is being written, so inside newspapers is where we shall be most of this chapter. Much of this account of the feature department's role and operations will translate readily into magazine terms, though magazine requirements will demand special attention here and there.

THE IN-HOUSE SET-UP

First we analyse that context, under the headings:

- Development of ideas.
- Deployment of staff.
- Use of resources.
- Commissioning and briefing.

Development of ideas

Apart from seasonal subjects and follow-ups to the news, ideas are suggested by the various publications and press releases received, and by the reporters' and feature writers' contacts books.

Chapter 3 showed how freelances adapt an idea to suit different publications. Newspapers and magazines similarly adapt and update stories from *other publications* for themselves. The raider has to go one better and at its most intense – in the national dailies – it becomes a battle. If an early edition of a national has a scoop another may frantically change its front page with a 'spoiler' (capping the original). Both are likely to flag their stories 'Exclusive'. On 10 October 1995 there was the absurdity of several national papers having 'exclusives' on the defection to the Labour Party on the eve of the Conservative Party conference of Tory MP Alan Howarth.

The *UK Press Gazette* of 16 October 1995 had a profile of Fiona McIntosh, newly appointed editor of *Company*, by Naomi Marks containing a revealing example of how to 'spoil'. As a regular writer for the *Daily Mirror*, Ms McIntosh was sent to Australia to interview a Sydney couple at the centre of a BBC TV 12-part documentary series, *Sylvania Waters*. In Sydney she discovered that *The Sun* had arranged to fly them to London. She bought a camera, joined the same flight, talked to them, took her pictures and did her spoiler.

Press releases may yield a feature rather than a news story. A local paper receives one from a novelty musical act called The Three Charlies which involves clowns combining playing instruments, juggling, and contortions. The release mentions that the act is based on a famous music hall act at the turn of the century. A feature writer is sent to check cuttings. Not only are there articles on the original troupe appearing at the now defunct theatre in the area, but the local library has posters that can be reproduced.

At the local council meeting the reporter hears the water company representative, asked about the recent water shortages, say that there is no problem. In the *reporter's contacts book*, however, is a water engineer who has been helpful with leads in the past. He says that there are leakages and that more money needs to be spent on maintenance. The reporter is asked by the editor to check cuttings and do an investigative piece. It is agreed that the engineer will be described as 'a reliable source'.

Ideas are *both originated and developed* in editorial meetings: preliminary meetings of section editors with their writers will often precede the main editorial conferences of newspapers at which the editor checks on progress of news and feature projects with section editors. Everyone will have read the morning papers. Ideas will be expressed about how to follow up, better, or scoop the stories rival publications contain, as well as ideas about how to move forward the projects that originated in-house and that they hope their rivals haven't got wind of. Decisions will be made about whether a story is better treated as straight news or, with more space and analysis, on news review or 'Focus' pages, or whether it is general feature material. A project may begin in one camp and end up in another.

A features editor on a national paper will watch current news stories and discuss with writers and the news editors likely follow-ups before reporting to the editor at the main conference.

Deployment of staff

The 'features department' is a loosely defined, constantly changing group of writers organized day by day or week by week to meet current requirements.

Staff specialists (politics, health, education, etc.) are likely to work on both reports and features, and a particular project may be hard to define precisely as either. A specialist regularly working for either department may often be seconded for work in the other.

Flexibility is the name of the game: a writer working on an in-depth article on, say, security in supermarkets for the news review pages may be required to reduce it (or deliver it to be reduced) to a straightforward news report for the front news section. The editor has decided that the former section's mix was lacking a 'thrilling' or 'dramatic read' element, and that this has been found in a story that has just broken, containing revelations in a US murder trial involving a famous film actor.

The arts review pages of a national Sunday might be considered a less volatile environment. On *The Sunday Times*, at least when edited by Andrew Neil, it wasn't necessarily so. In one case Marina Vaisey had produced the review section's main article on Renoir and Van Gogh pictures being sold for £100 million to an unknown buyer. At 2.45 p.m. on a Friday the buyer was revealed as Tyoei Saito, a Japanese businessman. It was decided to spike Vaisey's piece and build the news element up on the news pages. Meanwhile Vaisey had to fill the hole so she produced at home an article on the sculptor Phillip King, filing at 7 p.m. Pictures were biked from the gallery where the works were being shown. (Recounted in Brian MacArthur, *Deadline Sunday: A Life in the Week of The Sunday Times*, Hodder & Stoughton, 1991.)

A staff specialist's efforts may be aborted altogether, even after much time and expense when, for example, what looks to be a wonderful scoop fails to stand up. An apparently sound preventive measure against cancer has been found, but then a key expert riddles the thesis with holes. A local council corruption scandal has all the evidence it seems to need, but if there isn't an 'absolute rubbish' quote from somewhere just to keep the story out of the libel court it is decided that it's too risky to run.

Use of resources

The features editor controls *an agreed budget*, but must justify high spending. Examples are given below of how extraordinarily high fees have been paid for serializations, which nevertheless proved well justified by the resulting increase in sales.

An extensive list of *freelance support* is kept up-to-date, so that experts and general feature writers outside can be contacted immediately in an emergency.

Each publication's *library resources* will vary greatly, and will be organized in different ways, depending on market, edition areas, traditional concerns, etc. Hard copy (yellowing cuttings) and electronic files of cuttings are available in most newspaper offices, from both their own stable and from those of other publications. Examples of databases were given on pages 165–7 and the electronic picture desk is discussed on page 369. See also David Spark, *A Journalist's Guide to Sources* (Focal Press, 1996).

Commissioning and briefing

Like any editor, features editors must study the market closely and be keenly aware of a publication's needs. They must be able to respond rapidly to changes in needs and to successful moves by competitors. On newspapers, such responses are most likely to mean commissioning staff writers or freelances whose work is well known. The young outsider must develop strategies for breaking in.

Commissioning involves choosing the right person for the right job, not as easy as it sounds. Choosing the 'safe pair of hands' is the tendency when the pressure is on, but can lead to a predictable set of feature pages. The trick is to know when the safe is also the best, and when you need an unusual combination to lift an article out of the ordinary: when to send, for example, a fat, middle-aged, chain-smoking humorist who knows nothing about sport rather than a sports buff to interview a quirky and egotistic star athlete.

Features editors must commission and give follow-up briefings clearly or there will need to be much rewriting, by themselves or their subeditors, or by the authors. A news-pegged article on a national newspaper has to be as near right as possible first time; there may not be time for any rewriting and promising material may have to be spiked. Commissioning policy will be influenced by special requirements of different subjects, traditional ways of treating them, and on the relationship developed between editor and writer – how they succeed in getting on to the same wavelength. One writer may need to know how the feature is likely to be projected on the page, an idea of the likely headline, some precise questions that should be asked of interviewees; another is spurred on rather by being given a clear idea of how the typical reader will feel after reading the article, or in what way their attitude to the subject is expected to be changed.

The processing of a newspaper staff writer's article may have to be done in a day or two, or in an afternoon. The space requirement may change, pictures may be found that the writer didn't anticipate, breaking news may require some rewriting at the last moment: section editors and sub-editors may have to work on it in the middle of the night. Freelances (and staff writers on magazines) are more likely to be given the time and the extra briefing to make the changes themselves, or at least to be consulted. On the other hand, staff writers are more likely, provided there are none of the above emergencies, to get it right first time. They can instinctively anticipate exactly what the paper wants.

What all *commissioned writers* have to understand is that editors, despite the insight described above, will often not know exactly what they want *until they see what they don't want*. An editor and a writer must work effectively as a team. They strengthen their teamwork in informal chat, some via computer, as well as in the formal conferences and group meetings, and this is where staff writers have a built-in-advantage over freelances, who may have to make judicious use of telephone conversation and faxes to compensate. In the end an article is a finely judged compromise – having to satisfy editor, readers, writer, lawyer and to varying degrees proprietors.

THE DEPARTMENT OUTPUT

Many of the following subject areas have been discussed in previous chapters. Here they will be considered in their in-house context, where there is something to be said that has not already been said.

The labels are of course not definitive:

- Backgrounders and situationers.
- Follow-ups and spin-offs.
- Interpretations.
- Leaders and other opinion pieces.
- Investigations.
- Show business and ghosting.

- Serializations.
- Women and family matters.
- Reader involvement.
- Miscellaneous.

BACKGROUNDERS AND SITUATIONERS

Backgrounders are news-pegged features that analyse events, identifying causes, unravelling implications, predicting consequences. Situationers are more general background features mopping up an area of interest – for example, investment opportunities in the third world, job opportunities in the EU.

Colour, facts and sidebars

A common combination for the backgrounder close to the news is the colour of a delayed-action intro, followed by straight facts or quotes. Sidebars, complementary articles, may go alongside them or on another page. They may contain an aspect that needs further discussion, or may add further colour, statistics or details that would have cluttered up the main article.

An article 'Er ... why grunting fails the job test' by John Salmon and Alastair Law in the *Sunday Express* has this combination:

> The telephone rings at a leading employment agency trying to help Britain's biggest companies recruit the cream of the summer's new graduates.
> Agency representative: 'Good morning, sir, how can I help you?'
> Caller: 'Er, I'm a graduate. I'm, er, after the job.'
> No name is given, no civil introduction proffered. Not even the slightest hint of the post the so-far anonymous graduate might be seeking.

It is five sentence-paragraphs further on before we get to the news peg, which is Education and Employment Secretary Gillian Shephard's labelling the lack of language skills in graduates as 'communication by a grunt'. Seven paragraphs further on we learn that Mrs Shephard is launching a Government campaign to boost communication skills, with students graded on those skills at the heart of it.

A news feature of this kind depends on a selection of facts rather than laboured argument. It's assumed that few readers will disagree. There are interviews with Dr Bernard Lamb, national committee member of the Queen's English Society (TV is the main culprit), Professor Roland Meighan, Special Professor of Education (the rigidity of the National Curriculum), Colin Graham, chief executive of the graduates' Yellowbrick recruitment agency (employers are 'unimpressed' by lack of skills), Rory Cockburn, executive secretary of the Association of Graduate Recruiters (failure of universities). For 900 words odd that is a Wagnerian chorus of experts.

Mr Cockburn is allowed to end with the point of view:

> Rory Cockburn, the association's executive secretary, said: 'More youngsters are going on to universities after A-levels, but they are not being properly prepared for the work-place.
>
> 'Universities may be good at educating the mind, but they are clearly failing to educate graduates in the importance of being able to communicate in good, clear English. "That's what employers want".'

The sidebar, 'How children are stifled by the TV screen', takes this communication failure further with quotes from the acting head teacher of a primary school.

Giving two sides of the question

Editor-led debates originate in a newspaper's conferences. A strong line on an issue (if not exactly a campaign) may, it is felt, be best served by setting it against the opposing philosophy. For example, '*The European* discovers a centre which puts youngsters on the right track in a country planning US-style "boot camps" for wrongdoers'. This full-width strap-line above two articles by Charles Garside (1000 words) and Sandra Smith (600 words) of 21–27 September 1995, makes it clear that the views expressed are the paper's own.

Garside's article, 'Forging a Career', explains how disadvantaged and difficult youngsters at the Camelia Botnar Foundation in Cowfold, West Sussex, are given practical training and taught the social skills to look after themselves when they leave at 21. On the other side of a big picture showing trainees in the forge, Sandra Smith's article 'Tough time for young offenders', starts in straight news style: 'Britain this week confirmed its tough line on juvenile crime by unveiling controversial plans for a harsh new prison regime for young offenders . . .'. These include 'a 16-hour day of drill, physical exercise and kit inspection'. Thereafter its facts – for example, Britain locks up more juveniles than any other country in western Europe – add up to implied criticism of Britain's treatment of them.

'Wrap-rounds' and wider perspectives

Even more closely monitored in-house have to be the 'wrap-rounds' on, say, the most recent developments in Northern Ireland, put together from various sources (for example, news agencies, foreign correspondents, press

14 | FOCUS/WORLD CLASS   The Guardian Saturday September 9 1995

As pupils begin to drift back to school, Guardian writers look at those who find the best years of their lives blighted by social, political and religious strife

Back to the drawing board . . . Material supplied by Unesco helps young schoolgirls in the Rwandan capital, Kigali, to learn about and heal the scars of the country's genocidal war. Across the border in Zaire, however, Hutu children in refugee camps are being given a different kind of lesson by teachers who deny the genocide took place

Rwanda's new lessons in hatred

Children are an easy target for the latest weapon of ethnic intolerance – history, writes **Chris McGreal** in Goma, Zaire

Teachers lament a divided society

James Meek in Moscow

'Little Katya in my class has got all the signs of TB on her face, and she'll get it if nothing changes for the better'

Bavaria rises in religious revolt

Katrina von Waldersee in Bonn

Figure 16.1 Variations on a theme: a *Guardian* page presents wider perspectives to a topic releases from government departments, cuttings libraries, databases, and so on).

From theme with variations to variations on a theme: a foreign editor's briefing is clearly behind the content and presentation of a *Guardian* page that takes one topic through different countries in three articles (see Figure 16.1). Beside a picture of young Hutu schoolgirls at their slates in the Rwandan capital Kigali, deep across seven columns, that heads the page, is a standfirst to the package in bold, thick type:

As pupils begin to drift back to school, *Guardian* writers look at those who find the best years of their lives blighted by social, political and religious strife.

Like many foreign reports, these features tend towards colour, plenty of quoting, and with background information and history unobtrusively slotted in. The articles are: 'Rwanda's new lessons in hatred', by Chris McGreal in Goma, Zaire; 'Teachers lament a divided society' by James Meek in Moscow; and 'Bavaria rises in religious revolt' by Katerina von Waldersee in Bonn. This is a thought-provoking combination for a paper that takes care to keep its armies of teachers reading.

The caption to the picture was discussed on pages 181–2 as an example of how a caption can provide a taster and lead-in to an article. As well as the linking up role, note how much information is packed into it:

Back to the drawing board ... Material supplied by UNESCO helps young schoolgirls in the Rwandan capital, Kigali, to learn about and heal the scars of the country's genocidal war. Across the border in Zaire, however, Hutu children in refugee camps are being given a different kind of lesson by teachers who deny the genocide took place.

The first article tells how the orphans in the camps are being given a distorted version of recent history by teachers who 'were among the most heavily implicated in the slaughter of Tutsis'.

The second looks at the plight of badly paid Russian teachers in the context of growing divisions between rich and poor in Russia, through the experience of Yelena, a secondary school teacher for twenty-nine years.

Article number three tells of the religious maelstrom awaiting children returning to school in staunchly Roman Catholic Bavaria, over a German court ruling that the display of the crucifix in classrooms (prescribed by Bavarian law) was a violation of religious freedom. The result was a growing confrontation between parents and teachers.

Each article is given depth and resonance by association with the others. The introduction to the package and the presentation contribute to the overall effect.

Situationers and their roles

Feature writers will work on situationers in their slack periods and keep them in hand until events call out for them. If you tell your editor you've worked out how things are on the whole between doctors and the National Health Service at the moment and the response is 'so what?' or 'who cares?' you guess it's not the opportune moment. Situationers have various roles. They can be a standby resource to fill an early edition slot, to show the flag to certain areas of readership, to contribute to a special readership or even to pull in adverts in banking, the manufacturing industries, etc.

To show how a situationer works, let's look at how an article in the Weekend *Financial Times* of 2–3 December 1995, 'Revenge of the bean-counters' by Andrew Adonis, about the cutbacks in the civil service and the low morale of the traditionalists, pegs the ongoing process of management 'rationalization' in Whitehall to several recent events and lifts it out of 'so what?' territory.

The following key events and activities are sprinkled throughout the analysis:

1 Chancellor Kenneth Clarke 'this week' noted recent efficiency gains and said a further 12 per cent reduction of running costs was expected over the next three years.
2 The executive agencies have worked to improve efficiency since their establishment in the late 1980s.
3 The head of the senior civil servants' union objects that 'no proper analysis has been undertaken of the proportion of operational budgets actually required for running costs'.
4 Civil servants have been annoyed by emphasis by ministers on the superior virtues of the private sector. Examples of 'can do' managers replacing long-standing mandarins.
5 The privatization of some agencies, including the Recruitment and Assessment Services has been another cause for controversy.
6 Nevertheless a recent speech by Sir Robin Butler, head of the home Civil Service, pointed out that reforms have been going on since the late 1960s, and that agreement about what the Civil Service stood for has been maintained.

The article could have been pegged immediately to Clarke's speech but leading in with the latest Bond film lifts its readability:

> *Goldeneye*, the new James Bond film, will be lapped up by civil servants smarting from the latest cuts announced in the Budget. 'M', the head of M16, is portrayed by Dame Judi Dench as the apostle of the new breed of Whitehall accountant managers.

The 'evil queen of members', as she is known to her staff, refuses to send 007 on missions because of the cost and danger. She is forced to relent, whereupon Bond saves London from an imminent rocket attack and the fraud of the century. Presumably he was rewarded with a performance-related bonus.

No such salvation awaits thousands of more humdrum officials whose career prospects are threatened by the ongoing process of Whitehall rational-ization. Even Sir Robin Butler, the head of the home Civil Service, acknowledged earlier this month that the pressures on Whitehall are creating a 'feeling of insecurity' as Britain's officialdom is forced to reshape itself 'faster than perhaps we have ever had to before'.

Mr Kenneth Clarke, the chancellor, turned up the pressure. . . .

A situationer must generally end in upbeat mode. There must be hope for the future. Note how the last sentence rounds it all off:

He [Sir Robin Butler] stressed the degree of continuity despite all the changes. 'There remains widespread agreement on the value of maintaining a civil service based on the key principles of political impartiality, account-ability through ministers to parliament, objectivity, integrity and recruitment and promotion by merit'.

He might have added that however low morale may have sunk, there were 7000 applicants last year for Whitehall's 115 fast-stream vacancies for young graduates. As for budding 007s, M16 refuses to disclose the demand for its places.

The piece is dramatized by a line drawing by Ingram Pinn of Judi Dench's M cutting a little civil service figure in half with a large pair of scissors, with several more little figures waiting in the in-tray. Running costs of Whitehall departments are illustrated by a computer graphic.

FOLLOW-UPS AND SPIN-OFFS

Reporters on local papers turn into feature writers when they develop straightforward news reports into news features. For example, a reporter is covering a landslide into the sea. Cracks have appeared in houses near a cliff edge. The district council says the house will now have settled, and that it is planned to shore up the bank with some boulders to prevent further erosion. End of news story. But the editor tells the reporter that ten years ago the same reassurances were given to people living in an isolated house near a cliff edge some miles farther down the coast. Their house collapsed in the middle of the night, and they were lucky to escape with their lives. A sea wall was eventually built.

'Investigate it,' the editor says. 'It may be that the sea wall will have to be extended. Get as much as possible from the cuttings, then go back to the surveyors on the council.'

The reporter might discover from cuttings sources that might be contacted not only to update on the topic but to extend it and develop a more ambitious backgrounder: the Department of the Environment, the Professor of Geology at the nearest university, the local secretary of the Farmers' Union, perhaps. The editor is persuaded to allow more time. A feature has been born.

A sudden spate of foxes killing chickens, burglaries on an inner-city housing estate, road accidents on a dangerous corner, the selling of gifted players by the local football team though its performance is deteriorating, and the sudden increase of customers for local swimming baths are other stories that might similarly suggest background features on a local paper. Some might be worth rewriting after widening the research as spin-offs, for national publications.

Combinations with sidebars

An interesting combination of news features appeared in *The Independent* on Wednesday 13 September 1995. The news pages had 'Town shocked by a priest's revelations' by Louis Jury and Alan Murdoch. This had large pictures of the town of Dungarvan in County Waterford, Southern Ireland, and of Father Michael Kennedy, who at the previous Sunday's Mass at his Roman Catholic church had claimed that an HIV-infected woman had slept with some eighty men 'in revenge on society'. At a meeting with health officials on the Tuesday Father Kennedy repeated his claim.

The article, though it talks of Aids experts casting doubts, and quotes Dr James Walsh, formerly Ireland's national Aids coordinator as saying 'possible but unlikely', goes on to treat the priest's account respectfully. A sidebar, however, 'Experts try to explain risks', by Louis Jury, quotes an expert (unnamed) on the biological reasons for believing that the scale of infection envisaged by the priest is unlikely.

In Section Two of the paper, 'Myth of the Aids avenger' by Mary Braid and Ian Mackinnon, follows up the doubts into ethical territory. It repeats the main facts and the experts' conclusions but concentrates on whether a female Aids avenger could, like the Angel of Death, be knowingly infecting men, as one or two notorious male HIV sufferers in the USA knowingly infected women. More experts are wheeled on, and the consensus is that the monstrous Aids avenger is a myth, reflecting the priest's fantasies, and fears and the constant need society feels to apportion blame for the disease.

INTERPRETATIONS

Great care has to be taken when important legislation, government policies, or economic developments have to be explained. How far, for example, will some new legislation affect the readership? How far will the effects have to be analysed in terms of age groups, income levels or other factors? What kind of statistical information will the readership be familiar with? How complex can any graphics afford to be?

Figures 16.2 and 16.3 show how different markets tackle such questions. Richard Grant's 'The hole in the budget', in *The Mail on Sunday*, anticipates the 1995 Budget. The artwork shows the Chancellor's red box opened, one side Income and the other Expenditure, with wads of banknotes labelled to show amounts for different items. Bill Jamieson's 'Pension Time Bomb' in *The Sunday Telegraph* is illustrated by computer graphics with various charts comparing pension costs, ageing populations, unemployment figures, etc., in various European countries.

Popular markets like seen-at-a-glance tables. The revenue produced by possible tax changes are a boxed list in *The Mail on Sunday* as follows:

Change standard rate of income tax by 1p	£1600 million
Change personal allowance by £100	£430 million
Change VAT rate by 1%	£2540 million
Beer up 1p a pint	£105 million
Wine up 5p a bottle	£35 million
Spirits up 25p a bottle	£30 million
Cigarettes up 5p a packet	£185 million
Petrol up 1p a litre	£335 million
Vehicle excise duty up £5	£130 million

The intro runs:

The proposed Budget tax give-aways of £3 billion to £7 billion, being suggested by various Tory pundits, seem enormous.

But contrasted to Government spending plans – last year they reached £301.2 billion – these amounts are small.

Instead the figure that economists believe gives Chancellor Kenneth Clarke little room for manoeuvre on Budget day is the amount the Government has to pay each year just to service its total debt.

Says Maurice Fitzpatrick of accountants Chantrey Vellacott: 'It is something neither the Government nor the Opposition talk about much, because there is little they can really do.'

Itemized in Treasury documents as the Public Sector Debt Interest, it is the Government's equivalent of an overdraft. And just as the interest on an overdraft increases in line with an increase in debt, so the Government's annual interest bill has soared.

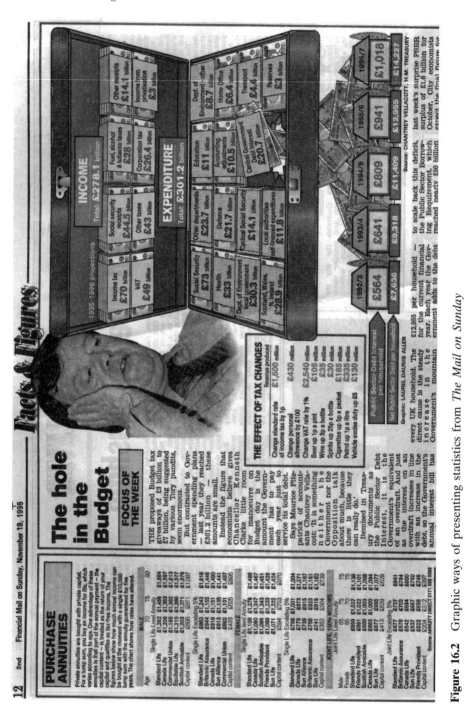

Figure 16.2   Graphic ways of presenting statistics from *The Mail on Sunday*

Figure 16.3 Graphic ways of presenting statistics from *The Sunday Telegraph*

Compare the simplicity of that (and the way economic terms are explained) with a couple of paragraphs a third of the way through the much longer *Sunday Telegraph* piece, which points out that Maastricht failed to show a smooth path to a stable currency because pensions were overlooked:

> The state pension schemes in Europe pay benefits out of current contributions. Thus an increase in the share of the elderly threatens to impose even higher levels of tax on future working populations unless the system is restructured or benefits reduced. Without drastic action, Europe's largest economies face the prospect of tax on pay having to double if benefits are kept at current levels.
>
> Alongside the growth in the numbers of old people is a shrinking of the base of working adults to pay taxes. Across the largest European economies the ratio of people aged 15 to 64 supporting those aged 65 and over will halve in the opening half of the new century. Push taxes higher? That would only accelerate the fearful economics of decline.

LEADERS AND OTHER OPINION PIECES

Care is taken in editorial conferences and informal discussions to discuss the leader or magazine editorial in the context of the next issue, to organize the way a publication thinks and expresses its thoughts, to make sure it is projecting its identity clearly.

The way opinion pieces are developed in-house varies greatly from publication to publication. Pieces are rejected or rewritten because 'it's not *The Times*', or 'it's not *Horses and Hounds*', or 'it's not the *New Statesman*'. This sense of a publication's identity doesn't rule out articles provocatively contrary to the usual line. We have seen examples of name columnists with regular think piece slots – a Simon Jenkins column for *The Times* in Chapter 7, and some freer-wheeling pundits in Chapter 14 – so this section will concentrate on the contribution of the leader to in-house thinking. Ideally it is the clearest expression of the publication's identity, its moral stance and its heart and soul.

Identity

The leader is the publication talking in its own voice. It reveals the publication's attitude to the world, and its aspirations. Identity, of course, includes the identity of its readers as well as of its writers and editor. The publication leads from behind as well as from the front. Even when it leads from the front the way a publication thinks has to take into account the way its readers think. The leader of a serious publication may reflect the way it estimates its readers think at their most moral. It has to aim at taking its readers with it: that is its democratic mandate.

Moral stance

Ideally, special pleading, whether from the world of politics or business, is out and basic moral values are in. When the leader contains vacuous moralizing on foreign affairs or fringe matters while corruption and injustice are ignored, you can guess that the shadow of proprietorial or other special interest has loomed over editorial policy-making, or that for one reason or another the vitality of the organ is ebbing away.

Heart and soul

The leader's or leaders' energy flows into the body of the paper and the energy of the body flows back into it.

The editorial context

Consider these three attributes at work in a leader from *The Daily Telegraph* and its surroundings.

The national papers of 13 September 1995 had the story of research scientists forecasting pig hearts for humans in five years. *The Daily Telegraph* gave it the front page lead under the headline 'Pig heart swap for human patients'. The intro runs:

> British patients will be the first in the world to be offered transplants using hearts and kidneys from genetically altered pigs. Cambridge scientists said yesterday that they had succeeded in transplanting transgenic pigs' hearts into monkeys, bringing new hope to thousands of patients. The breakthrough is regarded as the biggest advance in transplants since the introduction of the drug that suppresses organ rejection ten years ago.
>
> Hearts and kidney transplants using the pigs' organs will be offered for the first time to chronically ill patients next spring if research continues as expected, the Cambridge team said ...

... and the ending:

> The British development is not likely to raise ethical problems, since pig insulin is used for diabetes and pig heart valves in heart repair surgery. However, the farming of large numbers of animals for human medical use raises another issue.
>
> Michael Thick, a surgeon of Freeman Hospital Trust, said at the British Association meeting in Newcastle that the demand for hearts was 200 per million people per year, but only 10 per million a year were supplied in Britain.

Transgenic kidneys would be more important than hearts, Mr Thick added, reducing the cost of keeping patients on dialysis.

Cross-references were made to: 'Designer pigs: Page 4. Editorial Comment: Page 20'.

On page 4 was a quarter-page article with pictures, 'The men who designed a new pig', about Imutran, the research-based biotechnology company. Here we learn exactly what a 'transgenic' pig means – 'an animal implanted at the embryo stage with a human gene which would succeed in tricking the human body into seeing pig cells as human and not rejecting them'. A sidebar charts ninety years of experimentation with transplants.

What did the *Daily Telegraph* second leader say about it (the first was on 'Brussels and jobs')? How do you think it anticipated the objections of animal rights' campaigners? Cover up the next three paragraphs, and jot down a few notes on what you think the paper said.

Then compare with the following – the first two paragraphs of the second leader and the last:

The advocates of animal rights have been adopting increasing militant tactics, and relentlessly advancing the frontiers of their demands, in recent years. Henceforward, however, they will face a much greater test of pro-animalist principle, with yesterday's news that vital organs from pigs and other species may soon be suitable for transplant into humans. A shortage of suitably matching human organs is already severely impeding the transplant industry.

So human lives will be saved by this latest breakthrough, and reputations and fortunes made.

Animal rights militants will undoubtedly oppose the rearing of animals for 'harvesting' for transplant purposes. They will regard this as a further example of unjustifiable exploitation of animals. Yet we continue to assert the critical principle that human beings and animals do not possess equivalent worth in Christian, or even-post Christian society.

. . .

Testing using monkeys have already achieved survival times stretching into weeks rather than days; and the experiments have been conducted within the legal guidelines on animal welfare. At first many of us will feel instinctively uncomfortable about the notion of transplanting an animal's organs to those of a human. But if, in consequence, human sufferers who would otherwise die prematurely, and especially children, can be given a chance of life, then it seems entirely right to grasp it.

(From 'Survival before sentiment', *The Daily Telegraph*, 13 September 1995. Passages reproduced with permission of The Telegraph plc.)

Special treatments

Editors will provide the forum when special treatment is needed. Have another look at Figure 10.2 (page 181), which projected the two sides of the big European debate for the UK, in *The European*. *New Statesman & Society* also put side by side the two sides of this debate, more robustly. The nationalist argument goes first this time (Europe is 'a chimera with the real side-effects of damaging monetary rules for its weakest partners'), the pro-Europe argument imagining that 2035 Britain, having turned its back on the EU, is 'losing industry and brewing angst'.

INVESTIGATIONS

Investigations are often carried out by a team of writers. They may include reporters, feature writers and research assistants, supervised by an editor. Investigations – which may be called 'Special Report' or something similar – is a useful label, although all journalism is investigative to some degree. It is a label that serves to distinguish from the general run articles that are:

● Based on some original research.
● Prepared by getting information that people wanted to keep secret.
● Engaged with matters of public concern.

Often information has to be obtained from organizations or individuals who would prefer it not to be made public. Finding a reliable source who is prepared to talk is crucial. Injured party? A dismissed employee? A vigilante for a cause? Negotiations may require an editor's cheque book.

The importance of a subject to the public is the more debatable area. The sex lives of people in the news is considered by some commentators on the press to be given far too much importance; others will justify the attention given to them by referring to such concepts as 'role models for the young'. Whatever the subject-matter, the investigative skills required are often high. For the purpose of this section we shall confine ourselves to stories that have more obvious social and political ramifications.

Chapter 9 dealt with the research and writing skills required by investigative writers on their own. Particularly useful accounts of research sources for the more investigative feature are David Northmore, *The Freedom of Information Handbook* (Bloomsbury, 1990), Hennessy and Hodgson, *Journalism Workbook* (Focal Press, 1995 – Chapter 10 on Resources), and David Spark's *A Journalist's Guide to Sources* (Focal Press, 1996).

Investigative sources

Examples were given of *Sunday Times* Insight pieces on the prescription of dangerous drugs and the causes of aircraft accidents. Other more recent examples in this newspaper are the Ku Klux Klan aiming to find British far-right Parliamentary candidates, MPs who accepted £1000 to ask a parliamentary question, and the Barings Bank collapse.

The Observer has given us an account of junior doctors working dangerously long hours, and revelations by defectors from Iraq that Saddam planned secret atomic bomb tests and a second Kuwait invasion.

Reluctance to tell

David Northmore points out that the more in-depth projects are becoming scarcer:

> Few journalists working for the national media have the opportunity to engage in investigative journalism. There are two main reasons given for this: the development of 'infotainment' journalism and the perceived cost of allocating journalists and other resources to undertake in-depth research and reporting.
>
> (Quoted in Richard Keeble, *The Newspapers Handbook*, Routledge, 1994, Chapter 13.)

Time and costs

There is also the danger of being prosecuted for contempt and incurring legal costs. At the time of writing the *News of the World* was being threatened by the Attorney General over a Triad gang warfare story published in August 1995, and a *Sunday Times* 'Insight' feature on athletes and steroids published in October 1995 (reported to have taken four months and to have cost around £100,000) was the subject of a writ.

The accessibility of an increasing volume of information on newspapers' databases can have disadvantages. Staff writers have to acquire new skills in coping with the flood and when they are daunted, and when time and money are limited, they might be encouraged by editors to strike out for shallower rather than deeper waters.

Using fictitious names

When the focus is on the crime rather than the criminal, as it is with drug addiction, legal problems can be avoided by changing people's names. 'The Cocaine Epidemic', in the London *Evening Standard*, by Mark Honigsbaum and Marina Baker (additional reporting by Kate Bernard) tells how ordinary middle-class Londoners get the cocaine habit, what it does to them and the risks they run. The four interviewees are pictured in colour drawings, and there is a photo of a queue outside an anonymous nightclub in London's West End. There is a sidebar by a psychiatrist,

Dr Mike Farrell, and a graph (Metropolitan Police Forensic Laboratory) showing figures for crack cocaine seizures.

Exposing injustice

The hedonism of the glossy magazines has been tempered by some hard-hitting exposés in recent years. *Marie Claire* has a good record. The July 1995 issue contains 'Worked to Death', a 2800 word account by Abigail Haworth on conditions in factories for young women producing clothing, household goods and electronic products in Export Processing Zones in the Philippines, Taiwan and Sri Lanka. The zones attract foreign investors: they are free of tax and red tape, and cheap labour is abundant – the women swarm in from poverty-stricken rural areas, sending home money on which their families depend.

It is a shocking story. The workers endure such humiliations as virginity tests, two fifteen-minute breaks in a sixteen-hour day, two-minute limit on visits to the toilet, with an average wage of £2.50 a day. A woman who led a strike for a 15p pay rise was found murdered the following day. Multinational investors are criticized for their silence.

Magazine articles like to end on a positive note and this article is no exception. Nike, Reebok and Levi Strauss, we are told, are American companies that exact basic standards; and Marks & Spencer is reported to have successfully campaigned against using child labour for its products. One sees punches pulled, though, when important advertisers come into such stories.

SHOW BUSINESS AND GHOSTING

The requirements of family and young readerships account for the time devoted by the popular tabloids, the middle-of-the-road dailies, local papers and popular magazines to telly watching, programme notes, showbiz gossip, celebrity chat, records and the whole pop sub-culture. No features editor in this market can afford to neglect such things.

Both staff and freelance contributors in this area must be avid monitors of the press and other media news of major and minor celebs, so that they can come up with feature ideas. If features are to be pegged to a new book, film or TV programme, the average six-week gap between idea and final product must be kept in mind.

The *Sunday Mirror* keeps in touch with the actors in soaps and series. An interview with the black *Casualty* actor Patrick Robinson centres round his decision to leave the hospital drama after his request for a black lover rather than a white was refused. The story continues with some interesting criticism by Robinson on the way racist issues are tackled in the series, and his arguments over some of the scripts he was given. Such pieces recognize the important cultural role played nowadays by popular television.

Another interview with *EastEnder* actress Patsy Palmer makes do with a seasonal peg: how will this single mum spend Christmas Eve with her three-year-old Charley, and on Christmas Day with her mother and other members of her family?

Christmas of course provides the context, or the excuse, for acres of information of this kind. *Yes! The People Magazine* regularly explores this territory. The ingenuity lies in finding new angles. Your best and worst presents? Disasters in the kitchen?

There's a tendency to use celebrity by-lines to boost circulation. Sports celebrities and TV presenters or performers, for example, may be valued for the inside knowledge and gossip they can purvey. Some celebrities have a natural gift for journalism, others don't. Even novelists, film directors and other creative people may not be able to order and tailor what they have to say to the precise requirements of the market, whether upmarket or downmarket.

That's where ghosting comes in: producing features in collaboration with a journalist. It's an interesting and rewarding task for the journalist if the frustrations can be endured. The celebrity may be paid a good deal more than the journalist, may be hard to pin down and may do a great deal less work. The resulting feature or series is not always credited with 'as told to', 'talking to' or whatever. Journalists should insist on recognition in the byline.

Features ghosting may lead to books: helping to produce the autobiography of the celebrity, commonly with a credit such as 'as told to' and 50 per cent of the royalties. It can be a lucrative but again a frustrating job. The subject may want to tone down or withdraw revelations, at proof stage or before, for fear of legal problems or because of vanity or objections from relatives or others involved in the story. The disputes, common in any literary collaboration, can be compounded with two kinds of artist on different wavelengths.

It is nevertheless an area of journalism which has its own marketable skills for writers who find they are good at it, and specialist ghost-writers are not often short of work. There are some specialist freelances who do little else and make a good living from it.

SERIALIZATIONS

Serialization of a well-hyped book just before publication can boost circulation. The serializations of William Manchester's *Death of a President*

(John F. Kennedy) in 1967, Richard Burton's biography in 1987 and Kitty Kelly's unofficial biography of Nancy Reagan in 1991 notably added sales for *The Sunday Times*.

Serializations can be expensive and it's not always easy to be sure the money will be well spent. Although *The Sunday Times* has benefited from them, there were burnt fingers when the Hitler Diaries turned out to be a hoax. Raising sales to peaks anyway won't necessarily maintain the plateau of sales aimed at.

Negotiations can be tricky. Andrew Neil, *Sunday Times* editor, negotiated buying traitor George Blake's memoirs. Should the paper be associated with a traitor? Would Blake get the money? Would it be worth reading? The deal went through on condition that Phillip Knightley, ex-ST journalist, specialist writer on espionage, did the interviews; he was not likely to be misled about the value of the product.

A book is usually gutted for serialization by a staff writer or subeditor, extracts being chosen, needless to say, that will particularly appeal to the publication's readers. When *The News of the World* bought the Shah of Persia's memoirs, it was for the sake of one chapter where he dealt with his relations with Princess Soraya. The then deputy features editor Freddie Hodgson spent a week at the Persian Embassy arguing the paper's case.

The gutting process may be, as above, to select a particular topic, or to select several topics, perhaps making a series, following the threads through the text. Bridging links may be inserted in italics and extra anecdotes, quotes or interesting details can be boxed off: magazines in particular like to do this.

Fiction editors usually have a more complicated task when it comes to serialization. A novel is organic, not easy to truncate without showing the wound, so the aim is normally to treat the work as a whole, carefully removing sub-plots, with some rearrangement of the material so that it is easy to follow in instalments. That rearrangement may provide some kind of cliffhanger at the end of each instalment. The bridging summaries must be done in such a way that nothing essential to the plot is left out.

WOMEN AND FAMILY MATTERS

Women's pages in popular markets, like showbiz and entertainment pages, tend to encompass the interests of the family in general. Pages once labelled Women are now labelled Family (though at weekends you will see both taglines), taking account of the increasingly integrated concerns of the individual members of the family at home, the increasing contribution made by fathers to housework, shopping, etc. In fact the labelling of areas – Fashion, Style, Women, Female, Family, Parents, etc.

– is overdone: there is confusing overlapping within one paper, never mind the confusion of different connotations in different papers. Fashion, health and beauty, and family matters will be convenient areas to consider here, without worrying too much what the tagline says.

Fashion without clichés

It is hard to steer clear of clichés, both in terms of language and of topics, when writing about fashion. Harriet Quick had a stab at doing so in *The Guardian* (an illustrated centre spread in the tabloid section, called Style) when the new autumn/winter 1995 fashions hit the shops. Three women – of different ages and living in different cities – were given the task of buying cheap and looking chic. After familiar remarks about the difficulty of doing so – fashion shopping is 'a game of stealth and cunning' – the scene is set: each was given £100, a time span of one day in which to spend it and the task of finding an outfit which had to comprise at least three pieces.

Subjects of such case studies must come out as individuals – must not be processed to sound the same – and must be people the readers can identify with. Here are samples of what they said:

> Journalist and writer (46) in London: 'I prefer to wear a tailored jacket and jeans than a suit and shirt which can look restricting and ageing.'

> Trainee clinical psychologist (27) in Glasgow: 'After the first few shops I was disillusioned. The sizing is so erratic. I am a 14, but a 16 skirt might be too tight on the hips and loose round the waist ... In Miss Selfridge the assistant came up to me and said, "I do not think you will find anything in here". She didn't mean it maliciously but it was so rude and unnecessary.'

> Jade Wieland, student (16), in Newcastle: 'I like to stick to my own style. A lot of my friends wear jeans and sweatshirts and they laugh at me. But my mum usually comes shopping with me. She's very good at telling me if I look daft.'

Health and beauty topics get into what's right and what's wrong with lifestyles – with case study (as above) and diary formats effectively used in popular markets to give clear and concise pictures of the lifestyles under scrutiny. *Today's* Woman's Editor combined these formats in a feature on stress, an aspect currently receiving much press attention: we get typical days-in-the-life of (1) a housewife with four children, (2) a single career girl and (3) a separated working mum with two children. The diaries were analysed to judge how well the subjects coped with stress by leading Harley Street specialists Dr Malcolm Carruthers. His verdicts were not, perhaps, predictable: (1) Type B personality (easy-going), 2 out of 10; (2) Type A (go-getting), 5 out of 10; and (3) Type A, 8 out of 10.

Here is part of the working mum's diary:

Danielle Gale, 35, training manager for fashion house Nicole Farhi, separated with two sons, Joseph, 8 and Alexander, 5.

5.15 a.m.: Joseph wakes me wanting me to read a story. Alexander joins in.
7 a.m.: Alarm goes off and I've got an hour to get all three of us up, washed, dressed and breakfasted. Make coffee, which I never drink. Wash my hair and put a load of washing on.
8 a.m.: Nanny Siri arrives to take over.
8.15 a.m.: Travel to work by tube. Have a cup of coffee . . . and enjoy my first cigarette of the day.
8.55 a.m.: Arrive at work, much of the day is spent working on training programmes and assisting customers.
12–12.30 p.m.: Lunch is grabbed – sandwich, a coffee and a cigarette.
5.45 p.m.: Leave work, picking up the company profile-and-bible because I'll be working on a script for a meeting at some point tonight. . . .

Two boxes at the bottom of the spread contain Stress Symptoms and Stress Tips.

There may be more to come. A note at the bottom of column one of the article invites readers who have 'found a way to tackle stress' to write to *Woman Today*.

Among the formulas for family matters is interviewing two members to get two sides of the family story: husband and wife, father and son, brother and sister, etc. Under the tagline Relationships, Angela Brooks of the *Daily Mail* talked to Susanna York, actress, and son Orlando, Oxford student, pegged to the opening of a play *Look Back in Anger* at the Firehouse, Oxford on 16 January 1996, which she directed and he played in.

READER INVOLVEMENT

Readers can contribute to features pages in various ways. Letters to the editor, and letters addressed to agony aunts and other kinds of experts are encouraged. Among straightforward pieces encouraged from time to time are reactions to controversial arguments published, and personal experiences related to such pieces or to such problems as stress (see above), or to past events whose anniversary is being celebrated.

Contributions to the Letters to the Editor page or pages are carefully selected to reflect a range of readers' interests as the days or weeks or months go by, and by skilful subbing avoid repetition and make good use of the space. A hot topic, nevertheless, might be highlighted for several issues. It is well known which topics will provoke plenty of reaction: articles for example that criticise or misunderstand some aspect of the work of doctors, teachers and dentists are likely in most markets to release a passionate flood of objections from those professions. Personal columnists can, as has been noted, start a debate going in the letters pages that can stimulate further columns (as can the letters they receive personally).

Readers are sometimes invited to respond to controversial pieces, providing useful feedback on such subjects as drugs in sport, or euthanasia. *The People* engineered a debate on this subject in this way:

> Last week *The People* told the heartbreaking story of tragic dad Nigel Nelson whose brain-damaged baby daughter Naomi died after he increased her dose of pain-killing drugs. We asked you to tell us whether intolerable suffering justifies mercy killing. Your verdict was an overwhelming Yes, and our post-bag contained some of the most moving letters we have ever received. Here is a selection . . .

Children are encouraged to send letters, jokes, drawings and news items to the Children's Page, and the elderly to contribute personal experiences related to past events whose anniversary is being celebrated.

VJ Day brought memories of how family members suffered as POWs under the Japanese. On the more positive 'local hero' note the *Croydon Advertiser* wanted to know if you had fought or sparred with Frank Bruno in the days when he trained at the start of his career in a boys' club in Croydon.

Advice columns

Letters addressed to agony aunts and other kinds of experts fill pages. An interesting example of an advice feature is run by Tom Paley, specializing in personal finances/investment opportunities in *The European*. One of his columns answered the query:

> I am an American living in Ireland. About two weeks ago I answered a newspaper advertisement offering for sale legal titles of nobility. I thought it might be too good to be true. I wrote off, and I received details, plus a price list. Are these titles legal? The details say that a noble title can be a priceless asset in business, but can you advise me before I part with all my money?

It was discovered by the tireless Mr Paley that the president of the company offering the title, styled Professor of the Popular University of Torre Annunziata in Italy, was professor of a university that didn't exist, and that the sale of such titles had been forbidden since 1991.

Advice columns are generally backed up by secretarial staff to help with the personal replies, and to send out leaflets or lists of addresses where further advice may be obtained.

Readers' contributions are sometimes obtained by surveys. A *Daily Express* readers' survey, on which a feature 'New Man: Is he real or just a myth?' was based, asked 547 men aged 22 to 50, 'What is important to you?' and got the following percentage answers:

Wife: 41%
Health: 20%
Children: 18%
Job: 10%
Friends: 3%
Sport: 2%
Hobbies and pastimes: 5%
Don't know: 5%

MISCELLANEOUS

Other areas worth some attention here are personal profiles, service columns, consumer round-ups and supplements.

Personal profiles

Personal profiles of celebrities are often done in-house. They are easier to arrange when the writer is a well-established staffer, and they may have to be done quickly, since they are usually closely pegged to the news. When the news broke, for example, that Rowan Atkinson had won three out of five major Montreux TV prizes with the comedy series *Mr Bean*, *The Sunday Times* decided on the Thursday to front the Arts section with a major profile of Atkinson together with Gerald Scarfe's caricature. Similarly, local heroes have to be written up fast on local papers to back up news of achievement.

Service columns

Apart from the more obviously reader-led columns already mentioned, there are numerous service columns that may or may not solicit readers' contributions, with secretarial back-up to deal with them. Money pages advise on investment, mortgages, and so on. Health, medicine and the law are among the subjects handled by specialists. Other service columns cover such subjects as gardening, DIY, cooking, motoring, travel, chess, children's pages and horoscopes, travel, video games, word processors and home computers.

Increasing doubts about where to get the best possible professional advice are reflected in an interesting dichotomy: people turning on the one hand to expert guidance on where to get it; and on the other hand to astrologers with their horoscopes (many of the same people clearly interested in both). A feature in *The Mail on Sunday*, 'Taming the Professionals' by Jody Brettkelly was a well-structured example of the former. She introduces a series of case studies that identify the appropriate advice service in a no-nonsense manner:

> As someone who qualified as a barrister and solicitor, I am cynical about professionals. After all, some of my best friends are lawyers and accountants, and I know how many lectures they skipped at college . . . The amiable here-to-help bank manager is disappearing . . . widespread mis-selling of pensions has tarnished the image of independent financial advisers. . . . We are also suspicious that professionals are just grinding their own axes. . . .

By meeting her readers' fears and suspicions first she gets on their wavelength, before showing what to do, where to go, and who to phone.

Consumer round-ups

Consumer round-ups are a kind of service column, advising on the use of facilities (hotels, leisure centres, etc.), and on how to get value for money when buying goods. Round-ups don't win journalism awards, but they delight editors and readers when done well, and are obvious ad-getters. Seasonal opportunities, such as schools reopening, mean that a great deal of planning of advertising and editorial can be done in advance.

Ingenuity (or imaginative use of a quotations book) is needed to create a lively start to a tight package of information. Here's *The European* with a prelude to a rundown of hotel management training schools:

> Bernard Shaw the Irish playwright, said: 'The great advantage of a hotel is that it's a refuge from home life.' Anton Chekhov, in *The Kiss*, was also less than flattering about home hospitality when he observed that 'people are far more sincere and good-humoured at speeding their parting guests than on meeting them.' Good hoteliers, though, manage both.

The trick with such seasonal round-ups is to find some fresh way of getting into them each time without it sounding contrived.

Supplements

Some of the subject areas mentioned above have special supplements devoted to them on a regular basis: business, gardening, motoring, and travel for example. The Sunday papers in particular have found them a profitable business. The mother of (most) supplements in the UK was the first colour supplement to a newspaper – that of *The Sunday Times* in 1962, which brought its circulation up by 127,000 copies in three months to 1.1 million. The other Sundays followed: there was a thirst for colour and the different, more surprising, long range and offbeat articles that add up to the special mix of a consumer magazine and that are outside the remit of newspapers. Advertisers were inspired to greater creativity. More recently the colour supplements have spawned the special supplements, partworks, and extra newspaper sections, again with *The Sunday Times* leading the way.

ASSIGNMENTS

1   It is hard to ring the changes in a seasonal story that has to be told year after year. The following extract is the intro to a local paper report in August on both state and independent schools in the area. Adapt it to the schools in your area for your local paper. Make use of adverts, prospectuses, local paper reports, your own or others' experiences. The local library and the local paper's cuttings library may be useful sources of information if they are easily accessible. Make your intro twice the length, but grab the readers' interest and summarize the information that would follow in detail.

> How do you find a school for your child? Where should you begin? Parents too often feel defeated by the decisions involved in this important aspect of a child's life, but it's quite simple really.
>
> You should begin at the beginning of course, but you should always have the end in view.
>
> You should always be thinking about your child's education as a whole, not simply the present stage of it, or even the next one.
>
> For the little ones, there's the nursery school, usually starting at two-and-a-half or three years of age.
>
> More and more these days parents regard a nursery school education as the foundation for all that comes afterwards, and therefore very important indeed.

2   After some research into the breeding of animals for human medical use (including growing a human ear out of a furless rat), write an 800-word think piece, giving space to some of the animal

rights' campaigners' objections, coming to your own conclusions, and target it appropriately. Try to time it with a peg to a news story.

3   Write a 700 word article on your local magistrates' court after two or three visits and an interview with one of the magistrates. Read up on the functions of the court in Tom Crone, *Law and the Media*, Focal Press, 3rd edition, 1995 and Chapter 8, Reporting the Courts, in *Practical Newspaper Reporting* (Harris and Spark, Focal Press, 2nd edition, 1993).

4   After doing the necessary legwork and study of catalogues, and interviewing one or two journalists who use tape recorders, write a consumer roundup piece on tape-recorder for a students' journalism magazine.

5   Write a 400-word humorous item for a personal column on the subject of stress for a national broadsheet daily.

17 EXPANDING YOUR MARKETS

You can usefully add to your markets by going through the writers 'guides' lists. Don't neglect the back pages of *Willing's Press Guide*, the classified index of journals and magazines. It points the way to particular markets for subjects covered in this chapter and others, and it also includes some Commonwealth publications and publications that welcome cartoons.

FILLERS, ANECDOTES AND JOKES

Keeping a file called 'Oddities' enables you to explore the more offbeat markets for 'snippet journalism': that cutting about the 4-year-old girl who cannot eat or drink anything but human milk (twenty pints of this needed daily) or the one about the Jekyll-and-Hyde Presbyterian minister who mutilated corpses in his chapel in the middle of the night, might do. Inject a new idea into the paragraph – a reflection or a punch-line of some kind.

Figure 17.1 shows the sort of guidance to this market provided by *Freelance Market News*.

Reader's Digest pays £150 for a previously unpublished true anecdote showing the lighter side of life for 'Life's Like That', 'Studied Wit' (real-life college humour) and 'Humour in Uniform' (life in the armed or civilian forces). Jokes accepted for 'Laughter, the Best Medicine' earn £100 and other short items £50 (1996 fees). Write to Excerpts, Reader's Digest, Berkeley Square House, Berkeley Square, London W1X 6AB. There are markets in the UK, particularly in local papers and popular magazines, for this sort of contribution. But payment will be modest.

You may be able occasionally to work up anecdotes about the famous. Rudyard Kipling, in the early 1900s, received a letter from a man, enclosing £5 and saying 'I've heard that you get £5 a word, send me a word'. Kipling

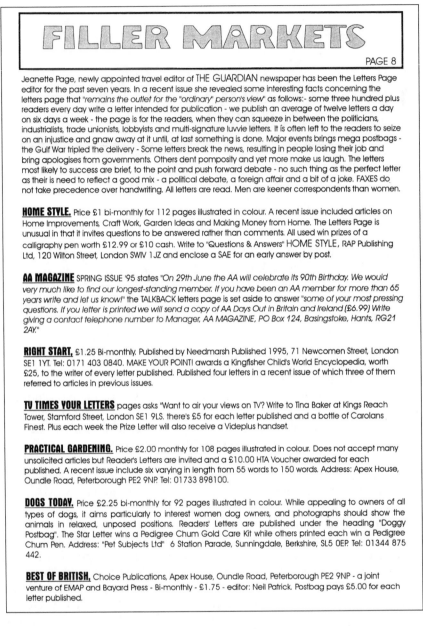

FILLER MARKETS

PAGE 8

Jeanette Page, newly appointed travel editor of THE GUARDIAN newspaper has been the Letters Page editor for the past seven years. In a recent issue she revealed some interesting facts concerning the letters page that *"remains the outlet for the "ordinary" person's view"* as follows:- some three hundred plus readers every day write a letter intended for publication - we publish an average of twelve letters a day on six days a week - the page is for the readers, when they can squeeze in between the politicians, industrialists, trade unionists, lobbyists and multi-signature luvvie letters. It is often left to the readers to seize on an injustice and gnaw away at it until, at last something is done. Major events brings mega postbags - the Gulf War tripled the delivery - Some letters break the news, resulting in people losing their job and bring apologises from governments. Others dent pomposity and yet more make us laugh. The letters most likely to success are brief, to the point and push forward debate - no such thing as the perfect letter as their is need to reflect a good mix - a political debate, a foreign affair and a bit of a joke. FAXES do not take precedence over handwriting. All letters are read. Men are keener correspondents than women.

HOME STYLE. Price £1 bi-monthly for 112 pages illustrated in colour. A recent issue included articles on Home Improvements, Craft Work, Garden Ideas and Making Money from Home. The Letters Page is unusual in that it invites questions to be answered rather than comments. All used win prizes of a calligraphy pen worth £12.99 or £10 cash. Write to "Questions & Answers" HOME STYLE, RAP Publishing Ltd, 120 Wilton Street, London SW1V 1JZ and enclose a SAE for an early answer by post.

AA MAGAZINE SPRING ISSUE '95 states *"On 29th June the AA will celebrate its 90th Birthday. We would very much like to find our longest-standing member. If you have been an AA member for more than 65 years write and let us know!"* the TALKBACK letters page is set aside to answer *"some of your most pressing questions. If you letter is printed we will send a copy of AA Days Out in Britain and Ireland (£6.99) Write giving a contact telephone number to Manager, AA MAGAZINE, PO Box 124, Basingstoke, Hants, RG21 2AY."*

RIGHT START, £1.25 Bi-monthly. Published by Needmarsh Published 1995, 71 Newcomen Street, London SE1 1YT. Tel: 0171 403 0840. MAKE YOUR POINT! awards a Kingfisher Child's World Encyclopedia, worth £25, to the writer of every letter published. Published four letters in a recent issue of which three of them referred to articles in previous issues.

TV TIMES YOUR LETTERS pages asks "Want to air your views on TV? Write to Tina Baker at Kings Reach Tower, Stamford Street, London SE1 9LS. there's £5 for each letter published and a bottle of Carolans Finest. Plus each week the Prize Letter will also receive a Videplus handset.

PRACTICAL GARDENING. Price £2.00 monthly for 108 pages illustrated in colour. Does not accept many unsolicited articles but Reader's Letters are invited and a £10.00 HTA Voucher awarded for each published. A recent issue include six varying in length from 55 words to 150 words. Address: Apex House, Oundle Road, Peterborough PE2 9NP. Tel: 01733 898100.

DOGS TODAY. Price £2.25 bi-monthly for 92 pages illustrated in colour. While appealing to owners of all types of dogs, it aims particularly to interest women dog owners, and photographs should show the animals in relaxed, unposed positions. Readers' Letters are published under the heading "Doggy Postbag". The Star Letter wins a Pedigree Chum Gold Care Kit while others printed each win a Pedigree Chum Pen. Address: "Pet Subjects Ltd" 6 Station Parade, Sunningdale, Berkshire, SL5 0EP. Tel: 01344 875 442.

BEST OF BRITISH, Choice Publications, Apex House, Oundle Road, Peterborough PE2 9NP - a joint venture of EMAP and Bayard Press - Bi-monthly - £1.75 - editor: Neil Patrick. Postbag pays £5.00 for each letter published.

Figure 17.1   *Freelance Market News*: Filler markets

sent it; 'Thanks'. Some weeks later Kipling received a cheque for £100 from the man with a letter saying that he had sold the story of the one-word reply to a magazine for £200, and was enclosing Kipling's half.

Anecdotes are best sent in batches of four or five, each on a separate sheet. As with letters, do not expect a reply. Check carefully that they are used and paid for.

Cuttings can provide the basis of useful anecdotes. Keep a file for them. Others can come from your daily routine, your children's remarks, chance encounters, but they must have a point, there must be a build-up to some kind of punch-line, and they must be concise if they are going to have impact.

Greetings cards are big business, and there are writers who make a fair-sized income producing the jokes and sketches. Your cards have to sell in vast quantities. When you thumb through cards in a shop, you might wonder if the writers are competing to produce the most inane or most sentimental. There are gaps in the market here for something better, though the work is not as easy as it looks.

It is not necessary to have drawing talents. You can sell the idea with the words alone; greetings card companies use staff and freelance artists to illustrate gag lines. It is usually best, however, to ask a company for guidelines and requirements before sending samples. You will be given such advice as avoid the words 'nice' and 'sweet', or verses can be rhymed or unrhymed. You may be given a recommended number of lines, and guidance on associating words with a picture or design.

GOSSIP

People attempting to look anonymous slide into a Soho pub to pass on small brown envelopes to one of the staff of the satirical magazine *Private Eye*. Apparently they are paid well for the paragraph or two of revelations they deliver.

There is a thriving freelance market in gossip paragraphs. Writers who have inside knowledge of celebrities' activities telephone the 'diary' columns of newspapers and magazines to dictate paragraphs for the day's or the week's gossip column. Such columns are normally associated with a star name but much of the material comes from outside contributors and is rewritten in house. The veteran contributor to these pages of course knows how to adapt material to the styles of the different publications served. The same news items may thus be adapted and used in a number of publications. Magazines and local papers, though paying less than the national dailies, are a particularly fruitful market for gossip material.

WRITING FOR BUSINESS ORGANIZATIONS

This field is not easy to get into, but once you have established yourself as a reliable writer on business matters, regular, well paid, long-term work can provide a solid base for a freelance career. Demands for writing help from financial institutions, law and accountancy firms, in particular, have increaed in the past few years.

Some business organizations already have in-house staff to do various kinds of promotional writing, and staff members may have titles to do with PR, press, publications, marketing. Some of them may be ex-journalists. Their work can range from press handouts to instructional pamphlets. The usefulness of outside help for such writing tasks depend upon the company organization, and the individual freelance might have to provide convincing evidence of potential use to the company.

When offering such writing services, find out first the name and job title of the most appropriate person to talk to. The titles vary greatly, from promotions or publicity director, sales promotion manager to marketing director and advertising manager. *Campaign, Marketing Week* and similar magazines give copious news about publicity people in this field.

Having been given a briefing from the appropriate publicity executive, be sure to talk directly to their clients as well as company people when preparing material. Fees can be negotiated on an ad hoc basis or as a regular retainer.

How to compete for the work

The publicity departments of companies are often approached by consultancies and advertising agencies, offering publicity writing services. Show why, as a freelance, you think you could do this work better. Indicate in your letter, having done some research into the company and its clients, that you know what kinds of writing and publicity the company needs. Enclose samples of these kinds of writing.

Once you become knowledgeable about a particular business or industry, organize your workload as suggested in Chapter 6. Suppose you build up expertise in the hotels and catering business. You might have such long-term projects as books, both general interest (*The World's Most Unusual Hotels*), with ideas for spin-off articles; and specialized (*New Ideas in Hotel Organization*).

Shorter-term projects might include brief career guides for publishers' series on catering and hotels, and perhaps educational texts on related subjects such as diets, home economics, etc. You might write brochures on hotels for tourist agencies or the texts for tourist boards' publications.

At all stages there could be specialist spin-off articles, and perhaps even a regular column somewhere.

Manuals and technical publications

Manufacturers need fairly complex technical catalogues, manuals and brochures, to explain to customers how their products work. A freelance writer with some knowledge of the subject may be the person to write them. The information will almost certainly be collected by engineers and technicians who may lack altogether the communication skills to put over the benefits of the products to those in the customer company who will assess them. The instructional manuals that are provided are proof of this. The writer addressing experts must have well-honed expository powers: clarity without over-simplification must be the aim. Above all, texts need to be 'customer-friendly'.

When it comes to training publications or instructional material for consumers, technicians may be too close to the subject to appreciate clearly what the layman's or novice's needs are. Too much insight or knowledge in the customer tends to be assumed. Home-computer manuals have been notable offenders. Writers who have first to make efforts to understand all the instructions themselves will readily anticipate the consumer's problems and be better able to provide comprehensible texts than the expert who takes his/her knowledge for granted.

Chapters 18 and 19 have more to say on writing for business organizations.

CRASHING THE AGE BARRIERS

Writing for children is a special skill that doesn't come to everyone. You should in the first place be plugged in to your early life, so that you have imaginative sympathy to draw upon. Care must be taken with the vocabulary levels appropriate for different ages. Every sentence needs to be examined to make sure wrong assumptions are not being made about the reader's understanding.

Allowing the age barrier to show is the most conspicuous fault. You must enter the world of your readers rather than address it from a distance. You must not assume you are more knowledgeable or wiser than younger readers; you have had more time to become dafter. Wisdom will out, if it is there.

Conversely, if you are writing for an older age-group, do not assume that they spend most of their time sitting in armchairs soaking in nostalgia and not hearing the telephone.

OVERSEAS MARKETS

Try to get specimen copies of overseas publications before writing for them. Publishing companies in the US are reliable, and will send copies in exchange for International Reply Coupons or international money orders.

Failing this, study any writers' guide entry, for example, *Writer's Market* or *Ulrich's Periodicals Directory* before querying. To save time and expense, you may want to suggest several articles at the same time: a questionnaire-format letter could be used. The editor will be able to tick off the ideas that appeal.

You may prefer to use some overseas markets for articles already published under a First British Rights Only agreement. Since about three-quarters of the world's magazines are in English, there is vast scope overseas.

If the article you are sending abroad has already been published in the UK, make any necessary alterations and retype. If sending to the US, use American spelling. Change any cultural references that might perplex: illustrate a point by referring to a baseball game rather than a football match, for example.

Freelance Market News has produced for some years regular overseas information (see Figure 17.2). Recent issues have given guidance on the requirements of publications in all parts of the world. Complementary to the well-known guides, the *FMN* also keeps you up-to-date on how to approach editors, save on postage, and use agents for foreign sales, foreign rates and similar matters.

SYNDICATION

Syndication means the simultaneous publishing of an article in a number of publications. You can do it on your own: offer the same article to newspapers all over the country, specifying release time and date, and indicating no overlap in circulation areas. There are generally some readjustments necessary for different markets, fees for each sale tend to be low, and you have to take into account the extra photocopying. The opportunities at home are the provincial papers, and the freesheets (where supplying features supporting the advertising is a good bet).

On the other hand, re-slanting an article for different markets, as already described, though, is usually a better alternative in the UK. A market like the US, with few nationally circulated newspapers, tends to be more amenable to domestic syndication.

PAGE 9

THE BLADE MAGAZINE, 700E State S. Iola, WS 54990-0001, USA. Published eight times a year. Editor: Steven Shackleford, who says: "give us something new and unusual on knives." Articles on the making, collecting and history of knives, and personalities who used them. The slant is positive they do not use material in which knives are shown as negative weapons. Length 500-800 words. Rates start at $250.

FRIENDS, 30400 Van Dyke, Warren, Michigan 48093, USA. This is a controlled-circulation magazine which goes to about one million people monthly. The editorial scope of this publication for Chevorolet owners - is broad with an emphasis on people and activities. Appropriate subjects would include profiles on chevorolet-owner celebrities, travel stories on unique destinations, features on sports, outdoor action, entertainment and the American family. Story lengths range from 600 to 1200 words and payment starts at US$300. When applicable, good colour trans should accompany the text. First-time contributors, however, are strongly urged to query first with brief proposals, accompanied by clips of previously published articles.

THE HIGHLANDER, Box 397, Barrington, IL 60011, USA. This can be a good market for the UK based writer on account of its subject matter: Scottish history, heritage, clans, families and personalities. Its coverage runs from about 1300 to 1900 and it should be emphasised that the travel aspects of articles is more or less secondary to the prime interest of Scottish history. Ideal length around 2,500 words and factual accuracy naturally is a must. FNAR are purchased and payment is negotiable with the editor.

DENVER POST, 1560 Broadway, Denver, Co 80202, USa. This newspaper offers good opportunities for the freelancer especially in its travel section with well over 100 mss bought annually. The Travel Editor prefers articles of about 1000 to 1200 words with sidebars of about 300 words and the angle ideally should be on an old, well known travel destination. Seasonal pieces should be submitted between 3 to 6 months in advance. Uses colour and pays US$25 per photo taken by the author while articles get from US$100 upwards depending on the length and quality of the story. It also considers press releases for the "Travel Notes" column, as well as short news items.

SINGLES ALTERNATIVE, 206 New London, Turnpike, Glastonbury, CT06033, USA. The singles scene in the US is big and this is reflected by a host of magazines given over to singles. This US magazine is best approached with a query in the first instance.

BIRD WATCHER'S DIGEST, PO Box 10, Marietta, Ohio 45750, USa. Edited by William H. Thompson III, the magazine aims at an audience ranging from the backyard bird watcher to the very knowledgeable field ornithologist. Article word length runs from 700-3000 words. The editor recently noted: "We are especially interested in fresh, engaging accounts of closely observed bird behaviour and displays and of bird watching experiences and expeditions." The bi-monthly magazine at $3.50 pays from $50 per article on publication, with fees for colour photographs. They do take pieces from outside the USA; these are usually "travel pieces" for their "Far Afield" section.

NEW ZEALAND GARDNER, PO Box 11 Waikanae, Wellington, NZ. The Editor Julian Matthews, invites submissions on gardening and related topics. It is a glossy monthly and all articles have of colour illustrations. The articles are around 1,200 words. The magazine is generally concerned with gardening in New Zealand, but the February '95 issue had articles on back care for gardeners, a guide to overseas garden tours and an interview with a Chelsea Flower Show Judge.

Figure 17.2   *Freelance Market News*: Overseas markets

A syndication agency is worth considering: rewriting and photocopying will be covered in the average 50 per cent agency fee. If you can keep a regular feature going until it becomes eagerly anticipated in many different areas, you may be catching sight of substantial rewards. See the syndication agencies and news and press agencies listed in the *Writers' and Artists' Yearbook* and make a few enquiries. But they are not likely to be interested in taking you on until you are already established, even if only locally, and can offer a package rather than just the occasional article.

The subject and the practice are somewhat controversial. The National Union of Journalists, for example, is concerned when its members are crowded out of publications in which 'moonlighters' (non-staff) and non-members of the union are being syndicated, especially when their articles are being bought too cheaply.

On a small scale you can handle some multiple submissions abroad on your own account. If you are ambitious enough to want to follow such prodigiously successful columnists as the American Art Buchwald, whose humorous pieces are syndicated round the world, then you will need a syndication agency. Have you a brilliant idea for a personal column? Can you convince a syndication service of a lasting international quality? If so, you may be taken on board.

Themes for international syndication must be of wide interest. An agency recently stated that a story should have the elements of God, sex and action; and must be of interest to New York (and therefore to the US), to Finland (if they have heard of it, all Europe will be interested), and to India (then Asia as a whole should want it).

ASSIGNMENTS

1 Look through several issues of *Reader's Digest*, studying the anecdote fillers mentioned on page 305. Then produce a filler for each heading.
2 Adapt for overseas markets any three of the article proposals you have produced while working through this book. (One paragraph of 100 words for each.) Study the writers' guides and issues of the target publications if you can obtain them. Write one article based on what seems to be the most promising proposal.

18 OPENINGS IN ADVERTISING AND PUBLICITY

Journalists and prospective journalists often find themselves attracted to the world of advertising and public relations (PR). The writing for both has much in common, and cannot always be sharply separated in a particular publicity campaign, but there are distinguishing features.

Advertising, according to the British Institution of Practitioners in Advertising 'presents the most persuasive possible selling message to the right prospects for the product or service at the lowest possible cost'. Less kindly, Stephen Leacock said it was 'the science of arresting the human intelligence long enough to get money from it'. It includes adverts placed in newspapers and magazines, sales letters, leaflets, 'fliers' (one-sheet 'mail-shots'), posters and brochures, and also the various forms of broadcasting advertising.

Advertising material also includes that hybrid called advertorial writing. Although this is PR-orientated on the whole, it is hardly distinguishable in appearance from editorial writing in a paper or magazine, but uses paid-for space and is often labelled 'advertising'. Whether the copy is produced in-house within the newspaper or is commissioned from an advertising/PR agency, it is subject to legal and ethical restrictions that come with normal editorial responsibility, and usually has some editorial supervision.

Public relations comprises informing and educating, rather than selling. The practice, as defined by the British Institute of Public Relations, is 'the deliberate, planned and sustained effort to establish and maintain mutual understanding between an organization and its public'.

A PR operation does of course use advertising and other means to achieve specific objectives, and the results of a PR campaign can be measured by marketing research techniques. After all, PR is 'selling' an image as part of the process of selling products and services. PR writing aims, with information and education, to create a favourable environment or market to sell in. A brochure or a newspaper advert, when it does this, is called 'corporate' or 'prestige' advertising, and the function is a PR one rather than an advertising one. There is no ambiguity, however, about the PR credentials of news (press) releases, feature articles and the writing for house journals. They are subject to editors' control, and if they do not match up to the journalistic standards of the publications they are sent to, they will not get published.

SCOPE FOR JOURNALISTS

Publicity writing of the sort just outlined merits a chapter in this book for two reasons. First, many journalists move into this field. They may have reached a stage in their careers on newspapers and magazines when further promotion is proving difficult, or they may find that PR pays better. They have amassed experience and contacts that will be useful in publicity work.

They may have spent hours rewriting clumsy press releases and may believe they could be particularly effective at the production end. Of course, they may find that they have a lot to learn about the new work. There are many different publics/readerships to identify, varied clients and groups to please, perhaps including more than one executive in each of the companies, consultancies and agencies worked for; and there are various compromises to be made. Each piece needs much discussion and thought, and can be very different from the previous one. Journalists will not take readily to this discussion perhaps: they are used to writing rather than talking about writing. Commercial and promotional writing is a constant test of a writer's ability to handle ideas as well as of a writer's versatility.

The second reason for giving publicity writing a fair amount of space in this book is that freelance writers may find attractive openings for occasional, or even regular work. They should find no difficulty writing feature articles straightforwardly giving information about a company and its products. Other demands will be less familiar, and they will have to adapt. If they can write effective advertisements of all kinds, including sales letters and leaflets, their work will be increasingly appreciated by companies, and a smaller company, or one starting up, may find it more economical to hire a freelance writer or two than to use an advertising agency or PR consultancy.

Travel writers obtain commissions to write brochures for travel agents, and writers for trade magazines obtain commissions to do copy-writing aimed at those markets. Both staff and freelance vacancies are advertised in the magazines listed under Advertising and Public Relations (page 414 –15). Freelances find it worth their while to place their own adverts in them.

Freelances can look for the publicity work described in this chapter by offering their writing services to companies directly, or to advertising agencies, or to PR consultancies. The publicity manager of a company should be approached initially – *Advertiser's Annual* or *British Rate and Data* (BRAD) *Advertiser and Agency List* give names. Articles in the advertising and marketing publications will suggest which companies might respond. Alternatively, freelances may advertise their services in such magazines as *Press Gazette, Campaign* and *Marketing Week*.

Working through agencies and consultancies has its advantages. They find the work for you. There are also disadvantages. You have lost some independence, you are further removed from the client, and you have to depend on the agency briefing you well. Contracts might be for each task completed or on a retainer basis.

Whatever their situation, publicity writers need to pay sharp attention to the nature of the audience. Journalists writing articles are used to having a definite age group/social class/professional group in their sights. Publicity writers often have to sharpen the focus, even to think of an actual person who would represent the target audience: the 19-year-old daughter of a next-door neighbour if a young women's perfume is being promoted, or favourite uncles if insurance policies for those about to retire are the subject.

Surveys are often used to identify a market, and its ways of thinking, before the writing is thought about. The social grades scale of readership provided by JICNARS may be studied so that the extract segment at which to pitch the message can be determined. Publicity writing aimed at a trade journal, for example, will contain exactly the amount of technical jargon appropriate for that particular audience.

The writer may be asked to write several versions of a press release – about a motor car, for example – for different markets: middle-age up-market, yuppies, technical, woman's, downmarket, and so on. Different media may be used for one campaign – peak-hour TV to get the main message to as many people as possible, followed by adverts in the quality papers and popular dailies perhaps, and selected magazines, to highlight the attractions for those particular markets.

ADVERTISING COPYWRITING

An advertising agency invited to apply to a client for a commission presents, after some research, a 'strategy'. This identifies the audience aimed at, media that will provide access to that audience (target publications, etc.), general approach, expenses (for example, any survey that will be needed), and an estimate of fees. It is the ultimate form of the journalist's query letter, and it ensures that agency and client are on the same wavelength.

Copywriting means providing the words for advertising, whatever form it takes, but it is most readily identified with the most traditional form – display adverts in newspapers and magazines. The aim of these adverts is not as easy to identify, nor is their effect as easy to assess, as may appear. 'Image' comes into the reckoning strongly. The influence of the words on any action in this field has to be measured. How many products did the advert sell? Even where the direct effect of the advert is obvious – for example, when coupons are filled up and sent in for more information or samples, or when one version of a recruitment advert produces many applications for a job, and another version produces few. There are so many imponderables that discussion about the whys and wherefores can be prolonged.

What an advert *must* do is clear enough: it must grab the reader's attention, arouse desire (or stimulate interest in the proposition), sustain interest, provoke to action (fill up a coupon or buy something), or make the reader remember the name. To do these things, in a small place usually because space is expensive, the advert must use words skilfully and with great economy. Clearly this is good practice for any writer.

Slogans for compression

Great economy encourages tricks, puns and various unusual ways of compressing, especially in slogan-headlines, as well as the alliteration, rhyming, catchphrases, reference to song titles and so on, common in newspaper and magazine headlines. For a poster, the slogan with a picture is enough. Here is a mixed batch of old and new ones: 'Mars are marvellous', 'We'll Keep You in the Picture' (DER Television), 'We'll Take More Care of You' (British Airways), 'In the Inch War Ryvita Helps You to Win', 'Out of the Flying Plane into the Foyer' (transport for airline passengers), 'Don't be Vague, Ask for Haig', 'It's good to talk' (BT).

Slogans are effective in many places other than headlines: posters and radio/TV jingles, for example. At their best they can perform many tasks all at once – they can get the message across economically, endure in the memory (sometimes with the brand name), quickly associate the product with friendliness/humour, and so on.

Slogans have their disadvantage, of course. They have to fit the times, and by their 'trendy' nature tend to become dated quickly. After a while they might bore, like a too-often-repeated joke. Competitors might exploit the idea with more effect, so the aim is to find an idea that cannot readily be adapted by a competitor. 'Who made the going great?' (Pan Am) was

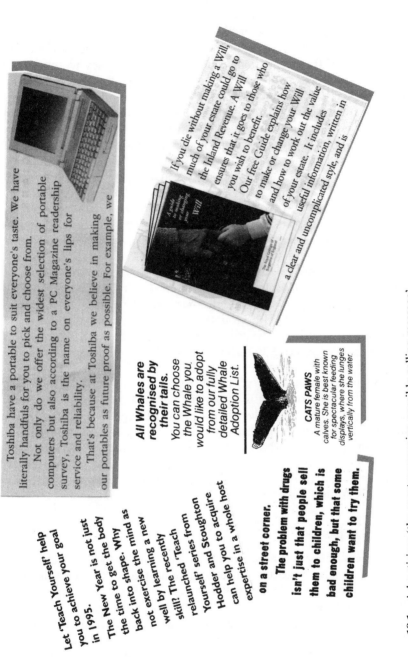

Figure 18.1 Advertising: 'the most persuasive possible selling message'

Toshiba have a portable to suit everyone's taste. We have literally handfuls for you to pick and choose from.

Not only do we offer the widest selection of portable computers but also according to a PC Magazine readership survey, Toshiba is the name on everyone's lips for service and reliability.

That's because at Toshiba we believe in making our portables as future proof as possible. For example, we

If you die without making a Will, much of your estate could go to the Inland Revenue. A Will ensures that it goes to those who you wish to benefit. A Will Our free Guide explains how to make or change your Will and how to work out the value of your estate. It includes useful information, written in a clear and uncomplicated style, and is

A guide to making or changing your Will

All Whales are recognised by their tails.

You can choose the Whale you would like to adopt from our fully detailed Whale Adoption List.

CATS PAWS
A mature female with calves. She is best known for spectacular feeding displays, where she lunges vertically from the water.

Let 'Teach Yourself' help you to achieve your goal in 1995.

The New Year is not just the time to get the body back into shape. Why not exercise a new skill? The recently relaunched 'Teach Yourself' series from Hodder and Stoughton can help you to acquire expertise in a whole host

on a street corner.

The problem with drugs isn't just that people sell them to children, which is bad enough, but that some children want to try them.

followed by the 'Who made the Boeing great?' of the British Overseas Airways Corporation, as British Airways then was.

A witty slogan can stick in the mind, but the budding copywriter has to recognize that there is a lot more to the job than being clever with words. One of the occupational hazards is the tendency to seize on the latest techniques of competitors and try to adapt to them the message being worked on. It is like the middle-aged trying to look like teenagers. Such adverts may draw attention to themselves rather than to the product, and may have more artifice than life. There is a tendency for PR and advertising agencies to operate in a hothouse atmosphere in which stereotyped images flourish about what makes a good advert, in which they give each other awards, and in which they can lose touch with the outside world.

Thus an advert that looks good, sounds good and reads well may fail to get good results. The message may be obscured by the technique, or it may lack force for the target audience. The old concept of 'unique selling proposition' is still valid. A message should be reduced as far as possible, so the prescription goes, to the one concept or idea that will persuade the consumer to buy it. Feature writers new to the business are, of course, well used to finding the 'controlling idea' for a piece of work (see pages 8 and 134). Around this, the unique selling points (USPs) are made, in a satisfactory order. The reader is to be left in no doubt that the product/service is different from or better in some way than competitors' products.

Another approach to a good advert is via an 'image'. This means showing that the product satisfies psychological needs. The reader's unconscious is played on. An advert for central heating says, 'Come in from the cold'. Some adverts play on the reader's fears of being left behind in the rat-race, whereas others promise increased sexual powers or opportunities. The most blatant ones, associating scantily dressed women with a product, annoy many women and bring complaints to the Advertising Standards Authority.

Developing the ideas

The process of composition, from knowledge about the product, through selection of subject matter to be communicated, to proposition/idea or image, has close parallels with the process of developing ideas for articles, described in Chapter 4. A slogan or a catchphrase for an advert which neatly encapsulates the idea for copywriter may come early in his endeavours, just as a title may come quickly to feature writers. But the research to identify the audience, and subject research, can be more extensive for an advert of 200 words than for an article of 2000.

Copywriters do legwork where appropriate. They may visit factories, for example, to see electronic typewriters, perfumes, clothes, or wine if those are the products they are writing about. They talk to manufacturers, to journalists who assess them in trade papers, to people who use them. They study their agencies' 'guard books' of clients' accounts, which contain all the adverts done for the client so far, and also the adverts of the clients' main competitors.

A useful approach to deciding on content is to try out the five W questions used by reporters, but with slightly different kinds of questions. Who is involved? What is it? Where will it be most useful? When is the best time to use it? Why and how is it used? Why should this product be bought rather than competing products?

What sort of subjects attract attention, and then keep a reader interested? Arthur Christiansen, a renowned *Daily Express* editor, said there were three subjects for a mass circulation newspaper: sex, money and sport. To these, advertisers have added: animals, babies, cars, disasters, entertainment, fashion, war and weddings. They are all useful triggers, but must be exploited freshly.

Techniques and language

As well as cliché subjects, there are cliché words that have their uses as a kind of shorthand. There is no point in avoiding 'bargain' if it means ten words instead of one.

Clichés more recently coined or emotive words handled like clichés are called 'buzz' words: they are signals, immediately recognizable, setting up predictable reactions. They include 'new', 'now', 'free', 'introducing', 'announcing', 'secret', 'magic', 'mother', 'unique', 'economy', 'breakthrough', 'guarantee'. Action words should be short, for example, 'phone', 'send', 'take', 'buy', 'ask'.

Adverts often work by being ironic, or by sending themselves up: using clichés can work as part of this style. Similarly the normal rules of grammar and spelling can be broken to good effect: 'Beans Meanz Heinz', 'bright 'n' breezy'. Copywriters are as anxious to economize with words, take short cuts to the emotions and stir the imagination as poets are, and there are various techniques common to both. Yoking two kinds of ideas together in a collision, as poets do, was the technique of an advert for a weekly review: '*New Statesman*. Things you would not find in a month of Sundays'.

If there are several selling points to make within the one main message, subheadings might be used. Their use can be suggested by the design, or they can determine the design.

Most advertising includes a PR element: the good name is indistinguishable from the product. In corporate or prestige advertising, 'advocacy' as it is called in the USA, the PR purpose is most noticeable. A good example of how corporate advertising can directly affect product sales is the way increased brand sales rapidly followed for Guinness during Saatchi's PR campaign to help make the successful bid for Bells'. One of the most famous slogans, 'Guinness is Good for you', from the 1960s was revived. The privatization activity (British Telecom, British Gas) and take-over activity of 1987, and increased interest in the stock market, encouraged a flood of corporate advertising.

Typography and layout

Typography and layout are important in the newspaper/magazine advert, and this is a convenient place to mention them. In an advertising agency the copywriter will normally work very closely with a visualizer from the art department, and they will share ideas about illustration, design and words. A freelance writer who does some copywriting may join up with one or two others as a team to share different kinds of expertise. The 'situations vacant' columns of the advertising and marketing weeklies can provide meeting places for such work.

Some journalists, particularly those who have worked in the editorial departments of magazines, will know the basis of good advertising layout. These are appeal, immediate comprehensibility (so that target readers recognize they are being addressed), a focal point, a logicality of design (making the eye move easily from one point to the next), originality of some kind, and unity. A writer's feeling for good design can help the choice of words and sentences from the beginning.

Assessing an advert

To assess an advert you have written, you should ask the following questions:

1 Does it follow the strategy agreed with the client?
2 Is it boring, or too predictable, lacking life? Sometimes there is a good idea buried in the middle of an advert, as there is in many an article. It may be possible to pull it out and give it emphasis: perhaps by building a new title/opening on it.
3 Is it, as they say, an ad out of Adland? Does it have that air of contrivance that comes from prolonged reverence for the techniques of past successes or from being dazzled by competitors' latest wheezes? Does it have too much consideration for the kinds of quality that win ad awards but do not necessarily prove more effective in selling or getting the message across?

4 Does it grab the attention of the audience it is aimed at, or is it merely catching everyone's superficial attention by some kind of cleverness?
5 Have you made it memorable? Does the name of the advertiser stick in the mind? Which adverts in publications, and radio/TV, have stuck in your mind over the past day or two, and why?
6 Have you made the promises of the advert clear? Have you associated the promise clearly, if not too obviously, with the motivations appealed to – whether noble, such as love of others, or shameful, such as lechery/pride?
7 Is there simplicity/directness/unity in the advert even when there are a number of selling points?
8 Will it fall foul of the Advertising Standards Authority?

DIRECT MAIL

Various forms of literature are sent by direct mail, sales letters, 'fliers' and brochures being the most common. These may be sent to people or companies by name when there is an exact notion of prospective customers. Sometimes prospective customers have been discovered by an advert with a reply coupon. Addresses are gathered from various sources – the yellow pages of the telephone directory, for example, or from agencies selling mailing lists. Other mail shots are associated with other parts of a campaign. Adverts may be aimed at wholesalers in the trade press, for example, while mail shots are aimed at retailers.

A newspaper may send sales letters to estate agents pointing out that it has a property page every Thursday, and that agents find advertising on that page fruitful.

A mail shot may include any combination of the following: sales letter, flier, leaflet, brochure, newsletter, price list, and the annual report and accounts. Many of these materials, of course, will have a purely PR function.

Letters that talk

A sales letter obviously has to be quietly and unobtrusively forceful, though less dramatic than an advert, with a more intimate tone of voice. Gimmicks and jokes are rare, and since there is no help from display, the words may have to work hard. The letter must be just as sure as the advert in its aim to move the reader from attention to action.

The pompous, stereotyped sales letter has almost disappeared, but such excrescences as 'your esteemed order' and 'we beg to remain' are still seen. So are passive expressions such as 'it is regrettable that' and vague phrases such as 'with regard to' (about), 'one of a number of such cases', and 'will you be good enough to inform us' (for please let us know). In the publicity world letters are sometimes written to newspaper editors suggesting ideas for competitions that will boost products (with prizes) for readers, or ideas for articles. Letters are sent to TV producers suggesting how products can be incorporated into programmes. The matter may have been discussed on the telephone with the addressee, which will already have broken the ice; if not, it is useful to find out a little about the person and his job before writing. The aim should be to make the tone of the letter intimately one-to-one, confidential without being conspicuously chummy.

Fliers are usually somewhere between the confidential tones of sales letters and the generalizing of adverts. They can get some help from typography and design, and a little gimmickry is not out of place. It is important to get the audience clearly in focus. Writing fliers for a travel company selling package holidays to coach operators throughout the country, I found I constantly had to check on whether I had the audience clearly in my sights. I was selling to the coach operators, not to their customers. What the operators needed to know was whether the holiday described had something different, something that would appeal to a fair number of people in their localities, whether it was competitive with similar holidays, and so on. The moment the piece drifted into typical holiday romanticizing was likely to be the moment when the coach operator would switch off.

In travel writing of all kinds it is difficult to avoid clichés: the promotional kind is particularly vulnerable. Doing some extra research into the holiday/country to get some specific details in can help. Occasionally clichés can be exploited by sending them up; I tried this in a piece about Norway called 'The Norwegian Experience':

> This holiday is something special. Thrilling doesn't quite describe it. Exalting sounds too posh, exciting too ordinary. Norway is all of these things, and more. It's crazy, it's inspiring, it's mind-bending. It's a unique experience, and the visitor must expect to be transformed by it.

This was helped by being balanced by the fairly specific, though restrained, description that followed:

> The mountains are steep, jagged and mysterious. The fjords are deep, glassy blue-green in the clear, bright air. They reflect the high, rocky walls that shut them in, the green valleys and forests, the snow-peaked mountains and the sky.

The coach operators in different parts of the country knew their prospective clients much better than I did, and what those operators of course did was some rewriting or reshaping of the holiday descriptions to produce their own handouts, making them appeal to the particular aspirations of the local people. Whether the intermediary between the writer's message and the eventual recipient is a businessman aiming at customers or, as with news releases, an editor aiming at readers, writers have to keep both the intermediary and the final audience continuously in their sights.

Brochures

Brochures may vary in size from six to sixty-four pages or more. There are product, service, consumer, and business-to-business brochures. They present a fair amount of information, often complex, in such a way that it is readily intelligible.

It is usually better for writer and designer to work together, for the designer can be severely hamstrung by having to work with completed copy. Recipients of a brochure often want to skim through it first to find the information most relevant, which will be easy if design considerations have influenced the writing. If headings, subheadings and other typographical devices, graphics and illustrations all serve to throw the most important information into relief, the brochure will probably be filed away as a reference source. This quality is particularly valuable in business-to-business brochures, or others where there is much complex information that needs to be kept.

The features of a product must be expressed as benefits to the readers. For example, if business performance is improved by a product, this should be pointed up, and shown clearly to be related to the particular feature of the product. Don't just state the feature and then say vaguely that 'of course' (or words to similar effect) the feature produces that improved performance. Similarly such productivity benefits as a reduction in operating costs and more technical reliability should be demonstrated. When clearly there are several selling points to make about a product, or about a company for that matter, it is advisable to make a checklist first and have it looked at by the person in charge (or colleagues, or client) to make sure the plan is comprehensive.

Brochures, leaflets and similar material should be immediately appealing, designed so that the main points can be taken in at a glance. The reader should be able to decide very quickly whether it is worth reading straight away or worth keeping to be studied at leisure later. The missive may be 'junk mail' shoved through the letter box or information about some new product which has just been demonstrated at its launch in a department store. Design, including the use of illustrations and captions, headings, subheadings, and 'bullet points', is obviously of great importance. Care must be taken to match the technical level to the reader aimed at, to ensure consistency in the terms used, and to follow the house style throughout.

Brochures that advertise services can cause controversy, notably misleading holiday brochures. The Consumers' Association would no doubt like services to be treated in the same way as goods under the Trade Descriptions Act, but the difficulty is obvious. Holiday brochures, for example, have undoubtedly improved under pressure in recent years, and customers have become more sophisticated in their interpretation of the brochurespeak of travel agencies (not to mention estate agents). 'Bustling' suggests to them overcrowded, 'lively night life' an all-night disco in your hotel, 'wonderful opportunities to explore the activities of the area' probably indicates twice-weekly coach trips to a boot polish factory and a quaint village.

PUBLICITY AS JOURNALISM

Publicity writing aims to get past editors into the editorial pages of newspapers and magazines and must be regarded as journalism. Press releases, specially written PR-orientated feature articles, and the content of house journals, might be promoting a company or its products or services, but the writing considerations vary little, in essentials, from their equivalents in straightforward journalism. The writers must behave as journalists, and the work must fulfil the requirements of journalism.

This condition prevails, whatever the provenance or degree of editorial control. When the space is not paid for, as it is not for press releases, the promoter has no control over what is published. Press releases, when not rejected, are often drastically cut and rewritten for newspaper use. In practice feature articles, although using space not paid for, will not be tampered with, but must follow the agreement made with the editor on length and treatment, and style. So must advertorials, even though using paid-for space. The content of house journals, in contrast, is controlled by the companies producing them, although they are bound by the same legal restrictions as newspapers.

PRESS RELEASES

There are various kinds of press releases. A hard news release means one that contains news value for a newspaper or general magazine. It might, to give an example, be about the launch of a new kind of lawnmower that will cause the considerable expansion of the manufacturing company in an area, with more jobs in centres of production. Though the purpose of the release might be to promote the product, the news value must come first and must be projected. The release will be shaped to highlight employment gains in the particular areas when sent to local editors. For a trade magazine, on the other hand, the innovatory factors of the new machine may become the main news value. And so on.

Whenever a release is sent, the aim should almost be to make it publishable as written. That means an attention-grabbing title, an intro which projects the news and explains why it is news, a body which maintains interest, with the news theme predominant, and no tailing off.

A completely new kind of breakfast food – a concoction of bacon, sausage, tomato, mushroom and corn, for example, in the form of a pancake mixture to which you simply add water and heat for a few minutes in a pan – might make the national press: the return of the traditional breakfast with no more calories than a plate of muesli might be the angle if the country is diet-crazy. Such releases will find a readier welcome, however, from the cookery pages of regional papers and the consumer magazines.

After an important event in a company's life, there might be a continuing story of developments to tell: longer background releases might be prepared, from which editors are invited to select material. Technical accounts of chemical plants and microelectronics may need considerable skill if they are to be turned into hard-news releases for newspapers.

Other releases might present summaries of speeches/documents/survey reports, or be extended picture captions. Then there are brief news items such as those that appear in the *Financial Times* or the trade magazines of the PR and advertising industries, such as *Campaign* and *PR Week*.

Contacts, with telephone numbers, should be given at the end of releases: they will include the writer and key sources of information. Editors often want to follow up a story suggested by part of a release, even if they don't want to use the material as it is.

Getting past editors

Writers of news releases must put their PR faculties to sleep and turn into journalists if they are to win editors over. Eight out of ten releases go straight into the wastepaper basket. The copytaster or the news editor is very busy and has a lot of them to choose from.

The main faults in those rejected are the following. There is a lack of news value, or the news value that there is lies buried somewhere in the middle. It should be in the first paragraph, and many releases are not read past the first paragraph. There may not be time for rewriting or reshaping. There is often no sign of attention to the specific market in releases: general interest for national markets and the appropriate local interest for regional must hit the editor between the eyes. A great number of releases sent out sound too much like adverts: plug, plug, plug. Many are too long.

Notice the tired phrases (my italics) in this paragraph of a news release for newspapers, no doubt both national and regional in aim:

ANOTHER SUCCESSFUL MOVE

The National Homelink Service, launched by the National Association of Estate Agents two years ago, *has proved a resounding success* with *the number* of offices throughout the UK and Channel Islands *now amounting to* over 600. A new link has recently been formed with an American Real Estate Company, which has joined Homelink *and therefore extends the service* across the Atlantic. *A valuable addition* which *enhances the links already in operation* in Europe through members in the UK.

This is the service congratulating itself. The words do not seem to be aimed at anybody in particular. What is *important* about the *new* link? Who will benefit from the service? How does it work? The second paragraph begins to tell us, but again in weary language.

Homelink *was designed to make* house hunting easier, and *the number of enquiries received* show that this free referral service is *of considerable benefit* to anyone moving to another area. . . .

A brighter start (while trying to avoid too blatant a plug), would be something like:

HOUSE HUNTERS' NETWORK

House movers can now link into a national network of over 600 offices to get speedy contacts, and the referral service is free.

The release, however, does give all the facts required, and ends with the necessary contacts:

For further information please contact:

Assistant Secretary   Office:_____
                             Home:_____
Chairman of the Homelink   Office:_____
                             Home:_____

It is not advisable for companies or local authorities (frequent offenders) to cover up negative news with positive. A regional health authority produced a news release in which there was a lot more than met the eye. Headed 'Health Authority Takes Speedy Action to Further Improve Hygiene Standards', it opened:

—— Authority today endorsed action designed to further improve its good record on food hygiene. The lessons learned from the food poisoning outbreak led the Government to remove Crown Immunity in relation to hospital kitchens at the beginning of this year.

—— Authority has moved swiftly to draw up an immediate programme for training the two thousand or more staff it employs who may handle food, and to enhance its cleaning, maintenance and redecoration programmes to meet the new requirements.

The rest of the release referred to the chairman of the authority emphasizing its 'good record' on food hygiene matters, and listing its various services, including the production of some 3000 meals a day for patients and staff.

What the release did not say (but which was dug out by a suspicious news editor) was that the authority itself had been responsible for some food poisoning.

Adapting to different markets

To consider content in more detail, let's take a fictitious example. A new building company has been established to exploit a central heating system using solar energy. The system is about to be launched with demonstrations in newly built model houses in large towns throughout the country. The system uses plastics and other materials that are cheaper than traditional building materials. Labour costs for building the average three-bedroom house will be greatly reduced. A revolution is expected in the industries producing the system and those producing the materials, and in the house-building industry generally.

For a national paper the news peg selected is likely to be the prospect of a revolution in the house-building industry, together with possibly a great improvement in employment figures. The regional papers will latch on to the launch with demonstration arranged in the newly built model house in the nearest of the towns selected. Trade magazines devoted to solar energy and plastics will expect the more technical information that will interest their readers.

In adapting a news release to such different markets, aim for each piece to be publishable as it stands. That means careful market research before sending them out. The above example of a story could be adapted several times over for different markets by changing only the first paragraph. Contacts listed at the end of the releases in case the editor might want to follow up the story could include government departments, local housing departments, manufacturers and suppliers of solar and plastics products.

Having decided where the news value lies, expressed it in a compact title or headline if possible, got it into the first paragraph, or the second if the intro is interesting enough, the writer should build the facts about the product/service into a news story in a natural way.

The story must be of intrinsic interest to the general reader of the publication. The facts should be strong enough evidence of the merits of the product to speak for themselves. Too many emotive adjectives such as 'lovely', 'fabulous', 'excellent', 'world-beating', 'unique', and 'revolutionary' are out of place and a put-off to editors.

Writers of releases must think hard about what people really need or want to know, before filling themselves with enthusiasm for what they have to sell, whether it is mobile cassette libraries or a new kind of nicotine remover. If readers will not be readily convinced that they need a service or a product, whatever is said about them must be said with some subtlety. A news peg may have to be manufactured (picture of celebrity using nicotine remover). The facts about a product will normally include the name of the organization discussed, its main establishments (or its various locations, regional papers obviously being interested in those nearby), why the product is important and to whom, a description of the product, and the advantages (particularly noting whether it is cheaper/easier to use than competitors' products).

Trade releases

This has brought us to the sort of questions that a trade release, rather than a hard news release, might find room for. They are the following. Who will benefit particularly? Exactly how will they benefit? What questions are particular groups of readers likely to ask about the product? A council employee will be looking for different qualities in a lawnmower, more staying power, for example, than the owner of a small garden, whose main interest may be in extra-close mowing.

Trade releases aim to persuade retailers to stock the product. They are being sold a market rather than merely a product. Retailers want to know if a product will sell quickly, if it will fit marketing plans. Apart from the questions about the product and the target audience given above, retailers will be asking what discounts there are, the sales potential and whether there is any research evidence pointing to this. They will also want to know whether the selling pattern is likely to be seasonal, occasional, or regular throughout the year. How will the product be promoted? Is there any advertising or press information available? Will there be demonstrations and/or special offers? A launch by a celebrity or two might provide the main news value of a trade release, or part of it. What may be uppermost in the retailer's mind is what special trade deals are available.

Too much specific detail *might* help rivals in the field to fight back. Therefore some information – about media campaigns planned, for example – might be put in general terms.

Many trade releases succeed in listing the necessary facts and benefits, but fail to inspire with an idea. The news value might be brought out by putting the product, with some imagination, into the context of current social trends. A solution for polishing metal antiques, for example, could be associated with rapidly growing home-ownership rates and house pride.

To repeat, the news story ready for printing has the essential facts in the first paragraph or two. If the news value is directly associated with the product, and putting the product into the first few sentences would sound too much like blatant advertising (a 'plug'), the product's name can be delayed for some sentences. Freesheets, which are paid for by the advertisers, are more tolerant about plugging in releases.

As far as possible, the pyramid news story shape should be used, even for trade magazines. Pieces can then easily be cut towards the end as other stories crowd in, demanding space, though a well-turned last paragraph is useful in this sort of writing.

To prevent copy reading like an advert, concentrate closely on the *facts* that are evidence of the merits being projected, and on the explanations required. Qualities should be shown in action, not overlaid with vague words of praise.

House styles differ greatly. Study them carefully when analysing publications for indications of level and tastes of readership.

Where how-to activities come into a news release, they are generally best expressed by employing the passive, or perhaps 'the user', so that they can be adapted editorially to different groups of readers. If the release has been adapted for the cookery page of a woman's magazine, to say 'you' might be acceptable, whereas it might not be appropriate in another publication.

FEATURE ARTICLES AND ADVERTORIALS

Promotion of the more complex products/services that need much explanation, or have many ramifications or applications, may require feature article format and length. This can vary from about 500 to 3000 words: the market aimed at must be studied carefully to determine an appropriate length. Specialist staff or freelance journalists are usually asked to write articles by companies or their publicity consultants after discussion with selected features editors. PR consultants may have staff, often ex-journalists, who concentrate on features, or various members of staff might produce features from time to time, according to the requirements of clients. PROs might find working to length a problem if they are accustomed to producing news releases and shorter pieces. They might find it useful to break the subject down into smaller units – subject headings – and then establish an average length for each aspect. The earlier chapters of this book, on the planning and procedure for writing a feature article, explain this, but here I'd like to highlight those points that I think PROs will find particularly helpful.

Planning and coherence

The feature article is not usually pyramid-shaped. Since it is invariably planned in advance, it is not assumed that it will be cut, so important points may come at the end. The content and order is decided on by making a checklist of points to be covered, and ensuring it is comprehensive.

Planning a feature article of some complexity may require developing the checklist into a more elaborate schematic outline of the type described in Chapter 3. A simple checklist of points, however, in a reasonable order may be enough to produce a satisfactory first draft. A final shaping, with some reordering of paragraphs, etc., may be done more easily on the draft. A typical formula for feature articles written for publicity is the case history: intro/problem/search for solution discovery of new product/process or service established/results/future.

A formula for a more popular market might be:

This product/service affects you.
The problems/achievements.
How they will make you suffer/benefit you.
What you probably think about it.
What you can do about it.

Readers of a publicity feature are looking for particular information. Who are they, and what are they looking for? A promise should be made to satisfy them early in the article, their interest should be maintained throughout, and the promise must be fulfilled.

Linking the main points, to produce a coherent pattern and a unified whole, is neglected by writers used to writing at shorter lengths. The reader's path should be made easy, though in an unobtrusive way. Paragraphs should have only one topic, and there should usually be a topic sentence round which the others are built. Categories/aspects can be summarized in an early paragraph, for example, then details can follow in subsequent paragraphs. Such linking may be done in obvious (for example, first, second, third ...) or in not so obvious ways.

There may be room in an article for more expansive writing or speculation, but needless to say there is no more room for verbosity than there is anywhere else.

Articles for technical magazines, professional journals, and similar markets may be heavily informative, using technical vocabulary unknown to the layman. Thorough care is needed to ensure complete accuracy and clarity. The news value must be extracted with care and presented interestingly.

General-interest articles must woo the readers: their interest cannot be assumed. Like journalists, and more so, publicity writers must avoid being more concerned with what they want to say than with working out what the reader will want to know.

Bringing people in

The writer must also explain to the readers *why* they should be interested. It is not easy to keep the reader interested when writing at length. It is helpful to talk about people and objects rather than about states and processes and abstractions. People are brought into stories so that readers can identify, sympathize, and picture what is going on. Anecdotes, quotations and other devices do this. Emotion and humour can be used, but there must be a foundation of fact, whether the article is for newspaper or magazine. Anger about such crimes as pollution is justifiable, as long as convincing evidence is given.

Both an article and a news release should be built round an idea, which can often be expressed in the title. The idea will provide the thread running through the piece, on which facts and points can find their place and be given significance.

Regional interest must be built in if possible when writing pieces for regional papers. For example, local people employed by a new company, local amenities and resources of particular value to the company, possible transformation of a region by the stimulus of new jobs – can all be brought in.

There must be a journalistic accent on information, entertainment and persuasion. Such a piece must not read like an advertisement.

Advertorials must be considered as feature articles. To repeat: a client's advertising or PR agency has contracted to buy space for them in publications at special rates. The article should be headed, 'Advertiser's Announcement' or simply 'Advertisement'. The advertiser's name and the specific product will be mentioned by brand name, and the retailers' names and addresses may be printed, sometimes in a box. But in all other respects, an advertorial, as with any other successful writing in this field, is not written as advertising but as an interesting, readable piece of journalism on the subject for which publicity is being sought.

Advertorials are often written by PR executives, because they are familiar with the advertiser's concerns, but the job is also done by journalists. Because the space is paid for by the advertiser, a good deal of control over content is given to the PR consultancy, but it should be remembered that final responsibility for everything that goes into a newspaper other than actual adverts rests with the editor. Careful study of the market, its readership and house style is as necessary as with the ordinary feature to make the advertorial a successful piece of journalism. House journals usually offer more control to the provider of the material.

WRITING TECHNIQUES SUMMARIZED

Descriptive writing

Avoid too many adjectives and adverbs. More burden of meaning should be given to nouns and verbs. Description means making the reader see, hear, smell, taste, touch. . . . Specific, concrete words should be used rather than abstractions.

Narrative writing

Putting the meaning into the *verbs* will help to keep the story moving. Saying *what happened* is essential; but initial thoughts/plans/problems, how it began and how it progressed, may not be.

Expository writing

Avoid over-long sentences. Planning is particularly necessary when explaining something. A preparatory checklist is essential, to make sure no point or fact has been neglected.

What kind of order is required – chronological or logical? Who are the readers? How readily will they understand? How technical can you be? What, exactly, is being explained? Do the readers have to understand how to carry out the process themselves, or merely understand, roughly, how a machine works . . . ?

Avoid a confusing mixture of pronouns: 'one', 'he', 'you', etc. Consider using the passive or 'they' to get out of a difficulty. Punctuation is important. A comma in the wrong place can completely change the meaning.

Argument/persuasion

In news releases and persuasive articles the facts must be marshalled clearly to support the proposition. There is a tendency to 'knock' the opposition simplistically in some news releases, but it is better to talk generally about the dangers or difficulties that have been surmounted in a new product or service, and concentrate on its positive virtues. In most writing aiming at persuasion it is useful to anticipate objections/criticisms before going on to the virtues. State improvements realistically; the facts will convince if they are good enough. Superlatives seldom convince.

ASSIGNMENTS

Improve the following press release in 400 words, targeted at national broadsheet Sunday papers.

11 AUGUST 19--
CHARLES COLVIN NEWS

Ski Hols, now part of Charles Colvin Leisure plc, has launched its 1997–98 programme offering departure airports nationwide, 4 new resorts and big savings on regional coach departures.

This new exciting brochure marks Ski Hols' tenth successful season of providing excellent skiing holidays for all grades of skiers, by putting into practice a wealth of experience and knowledge of clients' needs gathered over these 10 years.

NEW THIS SEASON

o Two more departure airports – Luton and Bristol, are now included in the programme, giving holidaymakers a choice of 9 airports nationwide.

o Two new resorts have been introduced – the Austrian village of Ellmau and the first class resorts of Les Menuires in the Trois Vallées region of France. This brings the number of resorts to 21 in four countries with travel by air from £—, coach from £— and self-drive from £—.

o Also new to the brochure this year are Twin-Centre holidays which enable skiers to enjoy two resorts in a two week holiday at no extra cost.

SAVING MONEY SCHEMES

o The famous Ski Hols' Snowcoaches are available from 25 departure points and new this season, no supplements whatsoever on regional departures which means substantial savings. Holidaymakers wanting to relax, save time and money can take advantage of Ski Hols' coach out/jet back or jet out/coach back arrangements in the low seasons.

o Due to the over increasing popularity of the Learn-to-Ski weeks, Ski Hols has expanded the programme and holidaymakers can now choose from Kolsass-Weer, and new this season, Itter or Kirchdorf in Austria. Special prices for these weeks start at £— and are fully inclusive of travel, lift pass, instruction, accommodation and equipment hire.

o Another money-saving innovation from Ski Hols is roomsharing. A member of a mixed group or someone travelling alone who does not have anyone to share a room with, can avoid paying single room supplements by taking the 'Share and Save' option. This option means that holidaymakers will be allocated a twin room to share with someone else of the same sex, saving up to £— per person a week. In Kolsass, up to £— per person a week can be saved by taking advantage of Ski Hols' Room-Mates plan. This plan allows groups of friends or holidaymakers of the same sex to share a 3 or 4 bedded room at reduced cost.

o Ski Hols' group discounts are bigger than ever this year and apply all through the season. A party of ten travelling together at the same time to the same resort qualify for one free place by jet and one and a half free places by coach.

THE SNOW GUARANTEE

Once again, clients will be guaranteed no price surcharges and the snow guarantees continue to operate. The snow guarantee means that if unusual weather conditions cause the closure of lifts and pistes, skiers will be transported free of charge to open ski areas or another resort, or receive a £— refund for every day spent unable to ski.

WEEKEND BREAKS

For the busy enthusiast or those who simply want a break for a few days, there are fabulous ski weekends in France and Austria. The Snowcoach departs on Friday morning, travels through the night and arrives in the resort in time for 2 full days skiing before departing for the UK on the Sunday evening. Prices start at £—.

WIENER-EISENSCHLAG – EXCLUSIVE TO SKI HOLS

This unique resort offers the perfect combination of a friendly atmosphere, good skiing, lively apres ski and is just right for families too. Ski Hols' exclusive hotel contracts mean that the traditional village way of life has been maintained and is Ski Hols' most recommended resort.

FUN FOR ALL THE FAMILY

Ski Hols still offer the free Mini Club at Bad Freiberg for children aged 3 to 12. The Mini Club keeps the children amused during the day with an assortment of pastimes while the parents are out skiing. Many resorts have kindergarten and nursery facilities and, of course, there are Ski Hols' fantastic family discounts. On certain dates children can even go free.

The Ski Hols; 19— is currently available from all ABTA Travel agents.

19 WRITING AS A SPECIALIST

Much has been said about the advantages to self-employed writers of specializing in particular subjects. This chapter aims to approach specialized writing from the other end. How do trained, professional people, who have something worth communicating to the wider world, produce saleable and readable articles, should the urge and opportunity arise? Non-specialist journalists who want to develop a specialism or two will, I think, find the advice on techniques here equally useful and may even be inspired to new subject matter.

Non-journalist specialists may take up writing as part of their work, or as an extra activity. They may be motivated by the desire to communicate knowledge to others, to improve their career prospects, to add to their income, to study a subject more deeply – or they may be preparing for a shift into a freelance writing career.

These are some of the questions this chapter will answer:

- How can article ideas be extracted from specialist knowledge?
- What are the markets for and purposes of specialist writing?
- How do market requirements differ from those for non-specialist writing?
- What forms of writing are in demand from specialist writers?
- How does specialized technical content affect the structure of articles?
- How should academic research and fact-checking techniques be modified for journalistic purposes? Are the necessary reference books and databases going to be readily available?

But first, make two lists, side by side:

1 The sort of articles you believe you could write.
2 The gaps you perceive in the markets. You should spend more time studying all possible markets.

OPPORTUNITIES GALORE

The pace of change accelerates constantly. People find it hard to manage the flood of information reaching their own patch of expertise. They need experts in their field or in associated fields who can guide them in the selection of relevant information and its application – experts who can communicate, who can write the right sort of articles.

Compared with the journalist writing a service column, the professional person has the telling advantage of being on top of the subject. Familiarity with how new information is being applied reduces the research time for an article. Opportunities for such experts can arise in reporting, book reviewing and feature writing (including regular columns) in news-papers and general magazines as well as in specialist journals. Such experts can also perform a useful role writing, for example, reports, booklets, manuals, technical brochures, for government departments, associations, business organizations and publicity firms.

At one time the slowness of top professionals to recognize the need to communicate was compounded by the slowness of editors in seeking out their services. This has changed. The growing popularity of a wide range of specialist periodicals has pointed the way, and there is an increased demand for the services of 'outside' specialists in general magazines and newspapers.

A survey of examples

A recent brief survey showed a doctor talking in a South London paper about the anniversary of a typhoid outbreak, a doctor's casebook article in the *Sunday Express*, an article on snobbery by an Oxford don in *The Mail on Sunday*, an article on genetic drugs in *The Guardian*, two psychiatrists writing on 'sex and politics' in *The Sunday Times* and, also in *The Observer*, a London university professor writing on the reform of the universities. In other papers and magazines were articles by all kinds of professional people, on subjects as widely separated as computer guidance systems in care, genetic engineering in plants, glue sniffing among the young, child abuse, bottling wine, share buying, running a guest house, basic flying and the problems of building inspec-tors.

Medicine probably tops the list for scope. Specialists writing in this field may be doctors or ex-doctors, biologists, nurses, dietists, experts in para-medical subjects, dentists, vets, pathologists and psychiatrists among many others. Also in demand are engineers, builders, economists, accountants, research scientists, generals, architects, carpenters, gardeners, sociologists and horse breeders. And the list goes on.

The writing skills needed for general interest publications, however, don't come easily, particularly for specialists well advanced in their careers, whose writing experience has been limited to addressing highly specialized audiences or reporting to learned journals.

Finding up-to-date ideas

Information and opinions to fill specialist articles will come from interviews with colleagues and from being up-to-date on the latest technical and academic work in a given field. You, as a specialist, will need to be aware of the main reference books for your subject. Some will be on your shelves, many others will be available at a good reference library.

The British Library's *Research in British Universities, Polytechnics and Colleges*, in several volumes, gives details of research projects being undertaken in the UK, together with the names of experts in specialist subjects. The various *Abstracts* (*Horticultural, Psychological,* etc.) summarize the most significant of recent academic texts. You should also have access to the directories listing members of your profession or trade, with details of their work, such as *The Medical Directory*.

There are numerous ways a writer can exploit reference books for article ideas, some of which have been mentioned in earlier chapters. Some ways are not obvious. PR consultancies dealing with specialist areas (see *The Hollis Press and Public Relations Annual*) will provide you with masses of information from which you will be able to extract good material, depending on your subject. So will the publicity departments of business organizations.

A MARKETING STRATEGY

You should subscribe to specialist journals, depending on your subject; the research results or latest developments reported in them can form the core of articles for newspapers and magazines. A rule-of-thumb principle for finding information or a story in one kind of publication and adapting for another is to go more than one level up market or down. For example, medical specialists can more easily use the research results reported in a specialist journal such as *The Lancet*, for an article in *Woman's Own* or their local paper than for such professional magazines as *GP, Pulse, Doctor* or *Modern Medicine*. For the middle-range professional magazines are already well aware of the contents of the specialist journals.

Conversely, the same medical specialists will find interestingly angled stories in popular markets that they will know how to develop by a little research. A story about an elderly person surviving laser surgery will send them through the specialized geriatric journals for detailed coverage of the subject. They may obtain material to rework in several ways – for a technical publication, one of the health magazines, or for magazines for the elderly or those who care for them.

Querying the specialist market

Specialist publications have a clearly defined editorial policy for a clearly defined audience. The specialist pages of newspapers and general interest publications should also be market-studied with extra care. Here are some do's and don'ts:

- *Show that you have market-studied* the target publication.
- *Angle your proposal* so that it is right for the target readership.
- *Find the gaps* in your chosen market.
- *Indicate ability and qualifications* either in your query letter or by enclosing cv and samples of published work, if wanted. (But note below *Campaign's* feeling on this.)
- *Don't propose ideas which have recently been covered.*
- *Don't invade the territory* of well-established correspondents in the proposed subject, unless there's a gap or a neglected aspect.

Once a commission has been obtained, a specialist publication tends to set up a dialogue with the writer on content and angle as the work progresses, and may even be liberal with research ideas, sources and materials.

Commissioning at *Campaign*

I talked to several commissioning editors of specialist magazines for the purposes of this chapter and feel that one or two examples of the way *Campaign*, the weekly magazine serving the advertising and related industries takes up ideas and develops them together with writers would be particularly useful.

Says Caroline Marshall, Features Editor of *Campaign*, 'I like a brief letter initially – two or three paragraphs – because we know exactly the kind of thing we want. We like to develop the idea with the writer. I'm not too interested in cvs or cuttings, but in background experience very much so. I like people who've recently had a career change. They have interesting new angles. It's amazing the number of people who write queries without studying the magazine – every editor says that. I usually phone to reject ideas.

'When I was new to the job a lot of briefing went on, to the writer and back and forth internally, until I got used to them and they got used to me.'

Figure 19.1 shows examples of an initial brief to a freelance setting out the terms of the commission, with some specific suggestions for angle, interviewees and illustrations; and Figure 19.2 a follow-up brief to a writer nearing deadline.

MOVING THROUGH AGE GROUPS

When writing for different markets, keep in mind not only the level of difficulty required but the age range of the readership. Among target publications will be those for the elderly, perhaps, and also those for the young. Remember that the elderly can be well off and fond of reminiscing about the past and that the young are mostly not, and don't – just one example of the subtle shifts of attitude needed as you move from market to market.

If you're getting wrinkly and well off yourself, and have risen in the world somewhat, you may be inclined to talk about £50 bottles of port, and how it is rather *de rigueur* always to pass it from right to left. In fact many if not most of your wincing readers may know that you can buy a fine vintage port for £15, and that most regular port drinkers are increasingly discerning 25 to 44-year-olds who don't care which way it comes round.

SAMPLES OF MARKETS

Specialist writing has to adapt to a wide range of literacy in the given subject, from the popular national or local newspaper to the highly technical trade/professional journal.

Both specialist writers and journalist specialists need to keep up to date with their subject. Readers want complete accuracy and authority and once an editor finds you lacking in these you're not likely to be asked again. That means usually plenty of reading: the journals, the magazines, the most important books, the accounts of the latest research in the *Abstracts* and the appropriate volume of the British Library's *Research in British Universities, Polytechnics and Colleges* (RBUPC for short). You will also need to develop good contacts: experts in various fields (names obtainable from directories). Freelances launching into a specialism should take a crash course in the subject to provide themselves with a good foundation.

Fax to: M. B.
From: C. M., *Campaign*   **Ref:**   Trademarks Act
Word rate: £200/1000 words   **Publishing date:** 11 November 1994
Pages: Spread   **Copy deadline:** 21 October 1994
Headline: TRADEMARKS: WILL ADVERTISERS BE CAUGHT IN THE ACT?

Content: On 31 October, UK Trademark law will undergo its most important change for 50 years. You should explain the background, which is that brand owners have been urging the government to outlaw copycat products and own brand lookalikes for some time.

The main thrust of the piece should be about the implications for knocking copy and comparison-based ad: while providing brands with the protections they appear to lack, and minimizing disinformation, the Bill will also be restricting creative freedom.

You should also talk briefly about possible privacy legislation at the Department of National Heritage. When, and why? Which ads will be affected?

You should get views from clients (including a retailer), creative directors, the IPA, ISBA and the ASA (legal rights may depend in practice on the ASA's adjudications). Try Ted Blake, director of marketing and communications at the Patent Office for the government point of view. Leagas Shafron launched a compaign for the Patent Office in preparation for the new law in February this year.

Length: 1500 words running copy, plus 150 word box summarizing the key points of the legislation.

Visuals: Can you find examples of the five types of infringement from recent national ad campaigns, and explain, in a couple of sentences for each why they would be banned under the new Bill. For example, Delta's current ad knocking BA which uses the 'World's favourite airline' line and picture of Concorde with its nose growing. Would this be unlawful under the new Bill?

That's about it. Please give me a call and we can discuss the best way of getting the Textline search for you. Perhaps I could send it by bike?

Speak soon,
C. M.

Figure 19.1   Initial briefing to a freelance, setting out terms of the commission

To:	B.D.
From:	C.M.
Re:	World ads feature

Some late thoughts from A.C. which could be useful for your feature?

'The global creative role doesn't have any credibility. I can't imagine a single creative head thinking that he reports to a global creative person. Management thinks a global role is a step up the career ladder for a creative director, but it means nothing. The global creative role has authority but no power. You never get to touch the ads until it is too late. It's purely a ceremonial role from the agency point of view.'

Ogilvie and Mather operates without a global creative head, but with worldwide creative directors on each piece of global business. A.C. suggests this is the only way to raise standards.

A.C. is on 0171-123-4567. He probably won't go on the record but suggests we try J.S. for a similar point of view.

Figure 19.2   Features editor developing an idea with staff writer

Media

There's increasing scope for the technically endowed and practised to write about technological advance in the media, including the pros and cons of the Internet for journalism trade papers and computer magazines.

Press Gazette and other journalists' magazines cover news and features on the perennial concerns of the media; questions of law and morality, the current conditions of employment, the business, etc., as do the media pages of the broadsheets. More philosophical are the essays of the *Journalism Review*, edited by Geoffrey Goodman.

Social problems

The frenetic reactions of the media, even of some quality broadsheets, to social problems make particularly welcome the calm analysis and considered arguments of weekly reviews or monthly journals of whatever political persuasion.

In the years since the murder on 17 February 1993 of three-year-old James Bulger in Liverpool by two ten-year-olds there has been much media reference to the case in the context of advocating tough punishment to combat evil. *Red Pepper*, the monthly founded by the Socialist Movement, provides (June 1995) two examples of expert, clear and persuasive writing on the neglected side of the story. First, Colin Chalmers, former editor of *Scottish Child*, described as working with a counselling and information service for young people in Brighton, writes on the social problems and abuse which turned the boys into killers ('Little Horrors').

Second, Angela Phillips, a prolific freelance writer and author of *The Trouble with Boys* (Pandora, 1993), contributes 'Boys Will Be Men', an edited version of an essay that first appeared in *Families, Children and Crime* (published by the Institute for Public Policy Research). She describes the 'culture of violence that creates dangerous delinquents'.

Medical

An article on health or medicine may include explicit or implicit advice, so keep in mind that even a minor error or ambiguity could kill. Doctors receive free magazines and a variety of publicity material from the pharmaceutical and other companies that advertise in the magazines. Non-doctors who write on medical matters can get on the mailing lists.

Apart from studying these subjects thoroughly, non-doctors should know where the experts can be found for important checking. Medical professionals are busy and will not be willing to be interviewed unless there's a firm commission to support your request.

Talking of the medical fields: readers of such articles cannot fail to have met the name of Dr James Le Fanu, which crops up everywhere. Here he is in action, in three rather different markets:

> Argument centres on how Queen Victoria acquired the haemophiliac gene which she passed down to her various offspring. It could have been a spontaneous mutation, a random garbling of the microscopic part of the DNA that coded for the production of Factor VIII, which is essential for the clotting of the blood.
>
> (From a review in *The Financial Times* of *Queen Victoria's Gene*, by D M Potts and W T M Potts, published by Alan Sutton.)

> Dr Thomas Friberg of the University of Pittsburgh has reported six cases of 'sudden visual loss associated with sexual activity'. Thus, 'a 39-year-old man describes sudden blurring of vision while his partner was performing 'a variant of heterosexual intercourse on him'. Clinical examination showed evidence of haemorrhage from a burst blood vessel in the retina at the back of the eye.
>
> (From 'Blind spot when it comes to sex', *Sunday Telegraph*.)

> In the 22 years from 1969 to 1991, concentration of all the major air pollutants – sulphur dioxide, ozone, particulate and oxides of nitrogen –

declined by 50 per cent in the city of Philadelphia, while during the same period mortality rates from asthma increased markedly. Even more intriguing is a study of the prevalence of asthma in Britain, which shows that it is more common on the non-polluted island of Skye in the western Highlands of Scotland than in urban Cardiff.

(From a column called 'What's up, Doc?' in *GQ*.)

Other items under his name deal with subcutaneous artificial penile modules, taking ribbed condoms a step further in the Far East ('the venerable beads'), and 'Foot fault', about fungal infections under toenails.

Dr Vernon Coleman, author of numerous self-help books, becomes lively and down-to-earth for his column in *The People*. He is advising a caravan couple suffering from the bad behaviour of children in the next caravan whose parents excuse them by saying they are hyperactive and cannot be controlled:

> Bollocks. The chances are that if you could stick the little bastards up to their necks in a vat full of warm sewage for 10 hours they'd soon learn some manners. Most of the children diagnosed as suffering from 'hyperactivity' are no more hyperactive than they are rabid.

The best way to annoy people in caravans, says the doctor, is to throw bread on to the roof. The seagulls dancing on the metal roof 'will quickly drive your neighbour potty' and they will then go home. . . .

Science, computers, arts and sports

Where two or more of these come together, there is a rich harvest of ideas to be gathered, with news developments coming fast. Take, as just a quick indication, the Science page of *The Daily Telegraph*, where science editor Roger Highfield provides articles on digital dancing and the use of motion-capture technology in sport:

'Cyberman makes his dance debut' is based on a visit to the Georgia Tech Centre for Arts in Atlanta. Here was a showcase of the Dance Technology Project, fusing computer technology and dance, pioneered by the Centre. A ballerina danced with 'a replay of a computer-generated man projected on a large screen. The cyberman danced to the edge of the screen, then his real-life brother appeared from behind to join the ballerina in an erotic dance.

'Telling you how to make a splash' tells us that 'the sport of an aspiring athlete may one day be selected by computer, according to body size, shape and range of movements, thanks to the emerging use of computers to capture and analyse every nuance of a movement. . . .' There will be medical spin-offs: movement and gait after an operation will be analysed.

In the long term, the technology will allow sports scientists to deduce the optimum body shape for given sports, regulatory bodies to test the difficulty of set routines, and golfers to develop an ideal swing. . . .

Trade press opportunities

The more technical part of the trade press, aimed at managers, engineers and technicians, provides many opportunities for people following these careers to become writers.

The products of such trade publishing houses as Morgan Grampian, United Trade Press, Reed Business Publishing, and Haymarket should be studied by specialists to see where they might contribute. The scope for spin-offs and recycling material is plentiful in this field, because there are often several magazines covering the same aspect of an industry that are not necessarily competitive, and different magazines for each sector of readership.

In building there are separate magazines for architects, surveyors, draughtsmen, construction engineers, managers, suppliers and buyers.

An important area for specialists is regularly testing new products for the trade magazines or doing it occasionally in a regular newspaper or general magazine column. A horticulturist will discuss new weedkillers or lawnmowers, a doctor various kinds of home diagnostic equipment or first aid kits, a carpenter new kinds of wax polishes. Contributors to a writers' magazine can discuss merits of new word processors or advise on computer magazine markets for writers who use computers but are not experts. A similar opportunity is reviewing the important books in your field as they are published.

APPROACH TO CONTENT

There are vast differences in the needs of particular markets, as the above has indicated. In readers of trade and technical publications, for instance, readers' interest in the subject for its own sake can be assumed. For the more popular markets, the thrust of a piece will need to account for how information might impinge more practically on the lives of the readers.

In spite of these differences the following approach to content should underlie any piece of specialist journalism. It should:

1 **Inform the reader using the most up-to-date facts available, like any other kind of journalism**. First, decide what level of information/ explanation you are aiming at. Where your subject is a science or a

technology, the level can be measured fairly precisely. Take a description of a solar plant in operation. At the popularizing level, an expert is talking to a layman and the aim will be to make the reader *appreciate how the plant works*, perhaps by using analogies or simple diagrams. At the other end of the scale the expert will be addressing fellow solar plant engineers who alone will understand the *complex scientific/mathematical explanations* and formula used. In between there will be several other levels of market. The level of discussion will determine which facts you select, which technical terms you use, which processes you describe, what assumptions you can make.

2 **Remove misconceptions** and clear the ground for fruitful discussion. An article by scientists Sir Fred Hoyle and Professor Chandra Wickramasingh listed some of the mythical origins of the AIDS disease – Haitian pigs, African green monkeys, God, Russians in chemical warfare labs. A psychiatrist noted how readily people (and the media) believed the murderer of members of his adoptive family when he accused his mentally ill sister (also dead) of the crime: 'The mentally ill are mistakenly assumed to be particularly prone to kill others and then themselves. . . .'

3 **Select points and structure carefully**, using plenty of headings. Don't make the texture too dense. In how-to articles of a fair complexity readers will put up with some repetition because it gives them breathers as they busily ingest all the information, as long as there is a steady progression. Notice how the repetition of 'brick' and 'softening', and giving useful examples in this paragraph from a *Building Today* article on basket-weave brick laying (by a lecturer in brickwork), can space out the information so that is it easy to take in:

> When a number of raked cuts have to be completed, as in diagonal basket weave or gable construction, use a softening material under the brick to take the impact out of the blow that a hammer and bolster would create. This decreases the possibility of the brick fracturing. Some good methods of softening are a bucket full of dry sand or a small square of old carpet.

4 **Explain where necessary**. Do not assume that readers know as much as you do. Think of the less knowledgeable readers, but do not make your explanations too conspicuous or you will bore the more knowledgeable. Avoid a pedagogic tone.

Explain things as an extension of your process of selection. Select carefully facts/procedures that may be quite familiar to you, that you take for granted, but which some readers will need to have explained.

5 **Anticipate readers' questions** – as recommended elsewhere in this book.

Why? What? What is the purpose of . . . ? How? So what happened then? Do not just say things are interesting/important. Show how they are.

6 **Illustrate in various ways**: a verbal explanation may not be enough. Figure 19.3 shows a page from the bricklaying article quoted above, showing how the sketches complement the words essential for this kind of article.

Verbal illustration by example, anecdote, or analogy is especially valuable in specialist writing. When discussing calories, it helps to put them into focus if you say that there are 100 calories in three cubes of sugar. The light from the Pleiades started its journey when Shakespeare was seven years old. Sleep to the brain is 'off-line processing'. The lens aperture of a camera is like the pupil of an eye, dilating or contracting in proportion to the light. And so on.

7 **Interpret information and relate it to people.** Identify likely benefits and warn about the possible dangers of discoveries, processes and developments. The education specialist, for instance, considers what effect current education policies will have on employment patterns. Writers on biogenetics warn us about possible political exploitation of developments in cloning, keep readers alert to new theories and developments in the subject area, and to the roles and performance of the Government and other agencies that might have significant effects.

8 **Suggest solutions to problems, or raise the most important questions**, and make intelligent predictions about the future. These are satisfactory ways to conclude an article.

FINDING THE RIGHT LANGUAGE

The care taken to get right the approach to the reader and content, as just outlined, will be undermined by ineffective language.

Chapters 11 and 12 have attempted to draw the 'good writing' map for everybody. But the specialist-turned-writer has special aims that need extra attention. The essential qualities of specialized writing are the three Cs: clarity, conciseness and coherence. There may be a lack of these qualities even if the level of informativeness has been accurately measured to meet the reader's requirements. For words, sentences, and paragraphs must be measured against these requirements as well. Is every word

BRICKS

use the centre of the first brick placed in the setting out procedure as the centre point of the panel (Fig 4).

Stack bond

The popularity of stack bond has increased greatly. It is mainly seen in new buildings, such as supermarkets or offices, specified under and over window openings (Fig 5).

This type of bond consists of multiple soldier courses laid on top of each other, using horizontal and vertical straight joints.

When constructing walling in stack bond it is good practice to construct a maximum of three courses. These courses must be jointed and left to allow the mortar to set (due to the lack of stability inherent in this bond). Continue the remaining courses using the same procedure. Stack bond must be reinforced horizontally with expanded metal on every bed joint.

The jointing or pointing of the brickwork is sometimes completed using two types of joint finish, for example, a flush joint used on the vertical or 'perp' joints, and a raked joint on the horizontal or bed joint. The perpendicular joints can be filled with a coloured mortar that matches the colour of the face brick. This is called 'blinding out'.

Alternatives

There are numerous alternatives to the panelling described in this and the preceding article (Building Today, February 4). Figs. 6, 7, 8 and 9, show four of the lesser known forms of panelling.

Interlacing bond

This is an attractive type of panelling where the smallest cut can be left open for decorative purposes. A typical situation where interlacing bond could be used as a decorative substitute, would be in honeycomb garden wall construction (Fig 6).

Diagonal interlacing bond

This bond is the same as interlacing bond but with the panel at 45 deg. A great deal of cutting is required for this bond, as for all 45 deg. panels (Fig 7).

Raking bond

In this bond the bricks are run in stretcher bond with 75 mm laps, from the centre point in opposite directions. This bond is unfortunately rarely seen in modern building (Fig 8).

Flemish unit bond

This bond is so-called because of the resemblance to the sectional bonding used in one and a half brick thick Flemish bond walling. It can produce an eyecatching effect (Fig 9).   □

Mark Dacey is a lecturer in brickwork at Barry College of Further Education.

Figure 19.3   Line drawings complementing the text: from *Building Today*

necessary, immediately comprehensible? Can every sentence be understood at first reading? Are the sentences and paragraphs in the best order for effective explanation or instruction?

A danger in specialist writing is likely to be jargon, which the *Concise Oxford English Dictionary* defines as: 'unintelligible words, gibberish; barbarous or debased language; made of speech full of unfamiliar terms'.

'Unfamiliar terms' is the definition most relevant to specialist writing. Some technical terms need explanation, but others are readily understood by likely readers from the context. To explain every technical term in the bricklaying article, on the grounds that not every reader will understand every single word, would be absurd, for such a piece would hardly be able to advance. Readers can be assumed to know or be able to work out the meanings of almost all the words in such an article, and to be prepared to use a suitable technical dictionary if necessary.

The bricklaying article contains such unexplained terms as 'soldier course', 'dimension deviation', 'arises', 'rebated'. These terms are irreplaceable.

Jargon words can have different 'ordinary' meanings outside the technical context, as in the above examples, and the writer would have to be sure when this happens that the two meanings were distinct in readers' minds.

It is sometimes difficult to replace jargon without using many more words. This applies to the following jargon words: 'adversarial', 'agribusiness', 'agitprop', 'anarcho-syndicalism', 'biofeedback', 'brainstorming sessions', 'chequebook journalism', 'confrontation', 'credibility gap', 'culture shock', 'docudrama', 'gazump', 'micro-' and 'macro-' compounds (for example, micromarketing and macromarketing).

Many of the 'isms' that abound in jargon are convenient – 'ageism', 'sexism', etc. There is no precise line to be drawn, in fact, between jargon and essential technical terms. It depends on how convenient the usage is for the readers aimed at, and whether the words say something better and clearer than any other words or combinations of words.

Unacceptable jargon

The problem is that subjects, interests, occupations, trades and professions about which specialists write are all the time producing extensive special vocabularies with which only the initiated feel at ease. There is no excuse, however, for such inventions as the National Health's 'bed throughput', 'the efficiency trap', 'the reverse efficiency trap' and 'increased patient activity' (which has nothing to do with pillow-fights).

Writers who are sociologists or social scientists or who read work published by them are in danger of what has been called 'obscurely systemizing the obvious'. Is it necessary to call homosexuals 'affectional preference minorities' or stupidity 'conceptual difficulties'? International agencies are often culprits. The International Monetary Fund has concocted a number of euphemistic 'ities' – 'conditionality', 'additionality', 'mutuality'.

Jargon apart, with high-tech subjects there is not a lot to be done about actual terminology. If you regularly use a computer, the following will be perfectly clear to you. If you know very little about computers, it is unlikely you will understand it:

> Vector graphics are extremely economical on memory, as the image is stored as a series of plotting commands. The straight lines across the screen might require only eight bytes of information in a vector graphics display, two bytes each for the two numbers describing the start of the line and two bytes each for the two numbers marking the end point.

Aiming at clarity

Yet the difficulty with much technical writing is more likely to be in the phraseology than in the choice of vocabulary. Specialists are given to such preambles as: 'If that statement appears obvious to the meanest intelligence, it must be realized that ...' and, 'this had doubtless been said many times in the past, and doubtless will be said many times in the future, but ...'. A paragraph from an article about sales techniques runs:

> Our research project starts from the assumption that communication is central to social life; perhaps nowhere is this more apparent than in selling. In this context interpersonal skills appear to be integral features not only of sales success but also of commercial success in general.

This means that business success depends on good relationships with people. Why the laborious 'in this context', 'integral features'?

An article on the hotel and catering industries gets tenses in a twist:

> Management in the hotel and catering industries tends to be very young. It would be surprising to find so many executives in their twenties if the prospect of going into the industries hadn't been so unfashionable in years gone by.
>
> The image of continental waiters working long hours was a more normal perspective for parents than college graduates, well trained for a worthwhile career. In fact, there are more catering colleges in Britain than in any other EEC country.

This is more clearly expressed: Management ... *is* young because it *has been* an unfashionable career. The image *has been* overworked waiters rather than college graduates. ...

The main discussion in the passage is about the present, and past situations should therefore be seen in relation to the present; in other words the present perfect tense is called for. The clutter of abstract nouns such as 'prospect', 'image', 'perspective' – in any case an image is not a perspective – doesn't help.

Gowers's attack on the language of the civil servants in *The Complete Plain Words* has its counterpart in the USA, where the vice was called 'gobbledegook', the coiner of the term defining it as 'talk or writing which is long, pompous, vague, involved'.

Gibberish or gobbledegook is likely to happen with professional people not used to writing for wide audiences. They tend to assume that writing requires them to display how knowledgeable they are. They think the language of writing is altogether different from the language of speech; that, metaphorically, you dress in formal clothes to do it and choose a heavy pen.

Where there is a weight of special terminology, there is an even greater need for clarity in description and exposition. The language of speech is nearer to this objective.

Samples of specialist style

This extract from 'Keeping Juries in the Dark', by Cambridge University legal tutor Roderick Munday (in *The Observer*) is a good example of an article by an expert clarifying the legal issues involved in a well-publicized case. He says:

> Patrick Reilly was acquitted of the murder of Leonie Darnley. The prosecution case was not particularly strong. However, after returning their verdict of 'Not Guilty', the jury learned that Reilly had previously pleaded guilty to a series of vicious sexual assaults, whose method of commission bore some sinister resemblance to the killing of Leonie Darnley. Two newspapers promptly implied that the jurors' evident distress indicated their shame, once this had been revealed to them, at not having reached a different verdict on the murder charge. Any such suggestion is wholly unfair to the jurors concerned and betrays a bewildering ignorance of English criminal procedure.
>
> The theory underlying English law's desire to conceal a defendant's general wicked character is that it is wrong to give a dog a bad name and hang him. There is a justifiable fear that knowledge of an accuser's disreputable past can prejudice a jury against him and thereby prevent a fair trial taking place. Thus, mere evidence of a defendant's general criminous disposition is inadmissible.
>
> Evidence which indicates only a propensity to commit a certain kind of crime (as emerged in the Reilly case) is, again, insufficient. What the law demands – and quite rightly so – is that evidence may only be admitted of other misdoings committed by the accused if it points unmistakably to his guilt in respect of the offence charged.

Here is another example of effective specialist style from the article 'The Tropical Forests and You', in *Environment Now* (April/May 1988), Norman Myers, a consultant of environment and development, puts into good order his research notes on the use of trees as sources of food and pharmaceuticals:

> So much for tropical forests' capacities to improve existing beverages. How about foods – entirely new foods? As agriculturists investigate more of the abundant stocks of food to be found in tropical forests, we can look forward to an ever-greater selection for our meal tables. In New Guinea alone, over 250 kinds of trees bear edible fruits, only 100 or so of which are consumed by local communities. Only a couple of dozen reach the marketplaces of Southeast Asia, and a mere two or three get to the supermarkets of the wider world beyond. There is plenty of scope for agronomists and other technocrats to develop entirely new, and nutritious and tasty, forms of food.
>
> When we visit our neighbourhood chemist for a medication or pharmaceutical product, there is roughly one chance in five that our purchase owes its manufacture, whether directly or indirectly, to raw materials from tropical forest plants. The product may be an analgesic, an antibiotic, a tranquilliser, a steroid compound or cough drops. The commercial value of these end products now amounts, world-wide, to some £12 billion a year.

SHAPING THE SPECIALIST PIECE

Specialist articles are read by people avid for information, explanation, instruction. Except for the most abstruse kind of academic essay, the content must be organized in such a way that it is easy to take in, refer to, and remember, and should wherever possible be related to human activity.

The problems in structure arise either out of faults in the basic shape, or faults in the sequence of contents. Any article – and this is true of business and technical reports – has to have a logical structure if the writer's material is not to become just a list of facts or observations, beginning with the facts first thought of and ending them with those that happened to crop up last.

Chapter 3 has shown how the feature writer can benefit by devising an outline upon which the presentation of the material can be based. This simply means imposing an order upon the material that has been got together. For professionals to whom writing is a secondary activity, the same approach should be adopted. They must first decide what their article is trying to say – what its thesis or point of view or overall purpose is – and this should come across in the intro.

Next comes the development – the evidence, the bulk of the information, the exposition or argument, that make up the body of the article.

Quotes must be authoritative and seen to be so. Finally comes the ending, which sums up, indicating that what was promised has been achieved.

It has been said already that feature articles requiring a logical progression of points/stages, such as how-to-articles, may benefit from headings or lists of points. These will obviously help in most complex or technical pieces. Have another look at Figure 19.3 to consider the headings of the bricklaying article. These are of the most straightforwardly informative kind. The arrangement allows readers to digest the information at their own speed, to pace themselves as they switch from text to illustration and back again.

Headings as links

Headings of this kind are signposts through the article and are particularly useful in long articles. Readers can see them as a framework of the subject matter. They can pause occasionally to go back and forward in the article to check their bearings. If there are several short sections, the headings provide the linking for you. Otherwise, try to have unobtrusive linking words between paragraphs so that the effect is not jerky.

The pattern common to the outlines in this book is:

Idea
Main facts
Supporting material/quotes/anecdotes
Justification of idea
Conclusion

An article, or a report on a subject, fails structurally:

1 If it fails to arouse the reader's interest in the first few paragraphs.
2 If the material is presented in a disorderly or disconnected way.
3 If parts of the material are irrelevant to the purpose of the article (irrelevant material should be rejected at outline stage).
4 If the writer digresses from the purpose. An article is unsuited to any forms of digression.
5 If the conclusions are unjustified by the material.

This approach will be found to apply to all types of articles, whether discussing the significance of rare archaeological finds in a remote part of the Orkneys, considering the side-effects of steroid drugs, or teaching you how to develop your own colour films.

RESEARCH AND FACT CHECKING

Research for a professional article requires experts on all sides. Dr Le Fanu acknowledges, within an article about cancer, the findings of five researchers/doctors working in particular areas in this field. Checking of facts and quotes is most important for scientific writers, and it is recommended that the writer get the typescript of an article approved by significant interviewees.

Medicine can be a minefield. Direct quotation may constitute a violation of 'medical ethics', so indirect speech and cautious summarizing are the common procedures. 'Cure' and 'breakthrough' and suchlike words should be avoided.

Specialists new to journalism may not be sufficiently aware how much information from apparently reliable sources can be inaccurate. It is worth emphasizing again that errors from cuttings are repeated in newspaper articles for months and years; cuttings are such a convenient source of information, and urgent deadlines can make checking less rigorous than it should be. That is no excuse for the specialist writer, however, who must ensure that there is sufficient time to get it right.

Press releases and material from institutes and other organizations may contain errors of fact and wrong spellings of names, and faulty grammar may make their content unclear. The very jargon of the more technical news release can lead to error as well as impairing the clarity.

Professional organizations

There are professional bodies for professionals-as-writers, and you should join any that exists in your field. As an example of a body and the benefits that can be derived from membership, there is the Association of British Science Writers (ABSW). They give guidance on such matters as making a career of writing in a professional field (addresses are given in Appendix 6).

ASSIGNMENTS

1 Rewrite this paragraph from a Science page article, 'Germ Warfare' by Paul Mango in *GQ*, for *The Sun*. Reduce it by half:

> Ebola is a new virus: it was first discovered in 1976 in Sudan. The Sudanese strain appears to kill about half of those it infects. A second strain, the more fearsome Ebola Zaire, turned up that

same year; it is between 80 and 90 per cent fatal. In the first outbreak in Northern Zaire it infected 358 people, of whom 325 died. Despite intense study we know very little about the virus, except that under a microscope it looks – appropriately – a bit like a question mark. We don't know where it comes from or how it's transferred to humans. It probably hides in a non-human host, but as the World Health Organization noted: 'The source of Ebola virus is completely unknown beyond the simple fact that it is African in origin.

2   Write a 600–700 word article entitled 'Is There a Genetic Answer To Crime?' targeted at *Marie Claire* or *GQ*. Suggest some points to go in a box as well, and two or three ideas for illustrations. Build it around the following paragraph from a student article and the additional points I have listed below:

The argument that genetic research might lead to more effective measures to prevent crime has a limited appeal. It is an inadequate argument anyway. Do we put the criminal-to-be on trial and on probation before he/she ever commits a crime or after? As there are certain causal questions to which genetic research has no answers, then its limitations are clear. The rise in crime over the past 50 years is clearly not genetically caused. In America relaxed gun laws, rising poverty and drug addiction are contributing factors to the dramatic increase in homicide among 14- to 17-year-olds. At the American Association for the Advancement of Science meeting in Atlanta last week it was pointed out that since 1985 the incidence of homicides had doubled among white Americans of this age group and trebled among black Americans of the same age. The reason for this, the criminologists say, has little to do with the urge to commit murder, rather social and environmental conditions have a much larger part to play. These conditions have created a black underclass where homicide is viral and violent crime endemic. Not one delegate at the AAAS had a solution to America's biggest fear – crime. As Steven Rose, the Open University Professor of Biology asks: why look for the roots of crime in genetic make-up when with one fell swoop the removing of 280 hand-guns from the streets of America would show that the US was taking homicide prevention seriously?

Additional points
Select one or two points to develop from the following:

1 Consider Hitler's and George Bernard Shaw's ideas on genetics.
2 Find out what progress has been made in identifying genes that predispose a foetus to deviant, aggressive behaviour.
3 Consider the concept of free will, and the role of social and environmental factors.
4 Do you think that genetic manipulation is going to be commonplace?
5 Consider the right-wing theories of biological determinism that are used to account for the view that increases of expenditure of welfare are a waste of time ('it's all in the genes').
6 Take account of the right to retain our genetic constitution, that is enshrined in the Universal Declaration of Human Rights.

Suggestions

1 Update what the student says by referring to any more recent associations of genetics with criminology.
2 Make the style much less academic, and the connections in the argument clearer.
3 Put the geneticists' argument first, then counter it with the opposers'.

20 THE WORLD OF PUBLISHING

A closer look at the productions of the publishing organizations reveals a great variety of outlets available for the younger feature writer, whether the aim is towards a staff job, full- or part-time freelance activity or the occasional specialist article sent in on spec in the course of professional work. Newspapers, as we have seen, can be national or local, general or specialist. Magazines include a wide variety of weekly, fortnightly, monthly, bi-monthly and quarterly periodicals ranging from general magazines to different types of professional and regional publications.

NEWSPAPERS

We have mentioned that non-specialist newspapers in Britain fall into three main categories – national dailies and Sundays, the provincial dailies and evenings, and the provincial weeklies and bi-weeklies and that there are striking differences within these categories. The questions are:

- What do the publishing organizations look like from the inside?
- How do they think of their business?
- How do they think of their readers?

The qualities – papers such as *The Times, The Sunday Times, The Guardian* and *The Independent* – are broadsheet, or full-sized, papers aiming at a comprehensive coverage of important news and comment for an educated market. The populars – papers such as *The Sun,* the *Daily Mirror, The People* and the *News of the World* – display, at their best, a vigorous kind of journalism in which great skill is used to express the most complex information in language that will be understood by ordinary people. Some of the best and highest paid journalists accept the challenge. These papers concentrate on the sort of factual, human interest content that will appeal to this market, and go for eye-catching display that will make them easy to read. The populars have all adopted a tabloid, or half-sized, format.

Within these two distinct national groups, there are differences in content and social attitudes as well as in the more obvious political orientations. *The Guardian* has a special interest in education, for example. The *Financial Times*, while covering some general news and some very important world news, is more particularly aimed at the business community. The *Daily Mail,* while having a useful coverage of financial matters, as well as of general news, caters strongly for women readers. Although classified among the populars, with the same tabloid format as *The Sun* and the *Daily Mirror*, the middle-brow *Daily Express* and *Daily Mail* contain news and features that are further upmarket.

Provincial varieties

The provincial press is likewise varied. The dailies, or morning papers, are strong on comment and background features, whereas the evenings go for hard news breaking during the day's editions. The bigger provincial dailies and evenings in conurbations such as Liverpool, Manchester and Birmingham carry a good deal of national news, and their local news takes in a wide catchment area. Smaller town evenings, by comparison, can be quite parochial in content. Local weeklies are often highly specialized with agricultural news, and may record minutiae of village life.

Sectional interests are the concern of another group of papers – dailies and weeklies such as the *Jewish Chronicle, The Catholic Herald, The Socialist Worker* and the Communist Party's *Morning Star.*

While the language of news, because of its factual, objective basis, might not vary greatly from one paper to another, the language of features can strongly reflect differences of market and readership taste. Apart from these market differences, some features are aimed at specialized groups within a paper's readers. The arts pages attract a different group of readers, on the whole, from those that follow the sports pages; the women's pages reflect a different world to that of the city pages; the horoscopes have little in common with an article on fishing or a bridge column. The feature writer, and especially the outside contributor, must attune to these differences. An approach to a newspaper of any type needs careful judgement, based, as this book has stressed, upon an analysis of a newspaper's market and content.

It has to be said at this stage that the bigger and more prestigious the newspaper, the bigger and more comprehensive the staff it carries, and

Figure 20.1   A world of opportunities at W.H. Smith's

the fewer are the opportunities open to outside contributors. Such work tends to be solicited on a contract or shifts-worked basis, or is ordered because of some speciality not covered by staff writers. Nevertheless many 'big name' staff feature writers have started on casual assignments as freelance contributors. Conversely, there are successful freelance writers who sell easily to the richer, better paying papers, and earn more than they would in a staff job.

THE MAGAZINE WORLD

Most magazines are heavily dependent on advertising; about two-thirds of the space in a consumer magazine is devoted to it, and the advertising itself is as much part of the reader appeal as the editorial content. Editors and advertising directors work closely together in monitoring their readership markets, and we have noted that the surveys and work put into this means that writers often have access to much information about the tastes and requirements of readers. An intelligent study of the pages remains, however, the best guide.

The study of a magazine should reveal a fairly consistent degree of continuity. Having been launched because a demand has been found to exist, it steers its course carefully by its formula; a subtle shift in direction might be made to increase or hold a circulation, stave off competition or recognize new trends, but only as much as will not disturb the existing body of loyal readers. A new gap in the market will be quickly filled, as happened with computer magazines: those that have come too late may not survive the competition. If a fashion dies, magazines generated by it will fade.

The feature writer, particularly the freelance, becomes familiar with this volatility, and keeps abreast of the trends, matching routine and material to the changing scene.

HANDLING THE MATERIAL

Contributors, staff and otherwise, have to be aware of practices in the handling of text.

Unlike news reporting, where constant updating, the use of multiple sources and the flux of the day's events can result in heavy cutting and revising, a feature article should not need drastic editing. Both in newspapers and magazines, space – often a fixed proportion of the whole – is set aside for features, which are usually ordered, or at least planned in advance. A feature article is invariably longer than a news item, often occupying a page or more, or the best part of a page, and is thus not jostling for space with new items that arrive by the minute.

The length of a feature is usually stipulated in the writer's briefing, so the question of cutting should arise only if there is unexpected advertising to accommodate or if the writer has exceeded the length asked for. If a lot of time has been taken to research a feature on new developments in rocket propulsion and the length is as briefed, cutting would be the result of poor planning by the features editor. A specialist contributor who is insensitively handled might be reluctant to submit copy again.

PLANNING AHEAD

Feature-page planning on newspapers has a longer time-scale than that of the news pages for the following reasons:

1   In order to leave editorial production time free for late-breaking news the features pages have to be made up earlier, during the slacker period of production, when there is more time to attend to the fine detail required in features display. The one late page is that carrying the editorial opinion, political comment or news background, which might need to reflect the latest events. Some national daily features pages are made up the day before (where the content is predictable, such as book reviews and television background material). Forward planning, or pre-allocation of space to expected items, ensures that the features department has its quota of pages ready to slot into the production cycle.

2   Since the briefing and research are more complex than with news and the contributors are often busy freelances, features editors take special care with planning, and make sure that sufficient time is allowed for polished work to be produced.

3   Greater attention is give to the layout of features pages than to news stories. All the typographical devices of page design are employed (discussed below). Time is needed at the planning stage to define and project the material in terms of page design and reader persuasion. Feature presentation in newspapers, as a glance at any newspaper will show, is a good deal more sophisticated than that of the rest of the paper, news being usually simply stories + headlines + picture.

4   Though some features can form background and comment on the day's news and be allocated to late slots, a greater number are predictable seasonally, including, for instance, spring fashions and DIY, holiday features in January and February when bookings are being made, sports features tied to known fixtures, showbiz gossip, arts reviews, silly-season

pieces for July and August, pre-Christmas features, spring books, set-piece interviews . . . the list is long. Planning and production requirements mean having such features ready in advance is common sense. An experienced writer knows that ideas and copy for them should be submitted early. Newspapers, and even more especially, magazines, keep a stock of such feature articles for slack periods, or emergencies. An article may be paid for on acceptance but it might, for these reasons, be quite some time before it appears.

In magazines, which might contain a small amount of news (again reserved for late-produced pages), the production time-scale is even longer, as has been noted in earlier chapters. Some monthlies have been known to keep an article as long as a year, or even two years, before using it.

To sum up, a feature article meeting the requirements of the briefing should fit snugly into the space prepared for it. It is the end product of a process of planning that is not possible on news pages.

DEADLINES

Writers of feature articles, and particularly freelances who are more distant from a publication's production methods than is a staff feature writer, can help to facilitate the editing process and secure good treatment for their texts by observing the following points:

1 Making precise arrangements with the features editor to get hold of any pictures, charts or other graphics to go with the article, either from the publication's own sources or from the writer's, and ensuring that they are delivered with the text. They might be invaluable to the projection that the article requires.
2 Enclosing a list of essential telephone numbers and check sources that might be needed by the subeditor in the case of contentious, complex or legally tricky material.
3 Ensuring, by enquiring in advance, that the copy is submitted and presented in the way most acceptable to the publication – for example, via telephone copy-takers, by script (post or personal delivery), by fax or computer input. Note that publications might use more than one method of input.
4 Writing as close to a required length as possible, or advising at the outset what length is likely, and varying the length only by arrangement with the features editor.
5 Giving their own telephone numbers, times for contact and addresses

where they can be found quickly should there be a production emergency.

6 Delivering copy exactly on deadline or before. There is rarely any slack in a deadline. It has been set to fit production schedules in editing, typesetting, page make-up and plate-making that will produce a final press time essential to the distribution arrangements. These in turn, are arranged by contract with the carriers, either rail or road, and cannot normally be varied. Delay can mean extra cost or result in lost sales. Writers in the media – and new freelances should learn this quickly – are expected to be professional in keeping rigorously to deadlines. Missed deadlines will close the door on contributors, however talented they may be.

EDITING AND PRESENTATION

The main considerations in the editing of articles in both newspapers and magazines are projection and presentation. Cutting, revising and rewriting, which are inescapable in the handling of news pages, are rarely necessary. The subeditors know that interference with the copy can quickly damage what the writers are trying to say.

Features subediting pays the same attention to factual accuracy and grammar as does news subediting, but there the similarity ceases. There is a conscious effort to retain the style and the sequence of argument even when unavoidable cuts in length are necessary. The words used in the headlines and in any adjustment to the text must accord with the writer's style and intentions and must not attribute to the writer concepts and claims that were not intended. Subeditors – if approaching the job properly – think their way into the text so that the projection given to the article harmonizes with the thought processes in the writer's mind. Some well established writers even have special contractual arrangements by which any text changes are forbidden unless their agreement has been obtained.

The point of view, which differentiates the subjective writing of feature articles from news writing, need not always identify with that of the publication. The staff feature writers and editorial comment broadly present this. Most newspapers and magazines will give scope to some of their byline contributors for an individual viewpoint. In fact, a named byline (that is, the author's name) above a feature article is the normal indication that the article under it represents the writer's point of view.

The projection – the use of type and illustrations to give the feature an attractive visual appearance – has to take account of these considerations.

Headlines

The headline might be based upon the title submitted by the writer, or more likely, ideas occurring to the subeditor in the course of handling the story, or even a 'team' appraisal by the features department of a paper or editorial department of a magazine of what the article is saying. The in-house approach to headlines is commoner, since the projection of articles is a sophisticated compound of text, illustrations, typography, visual style and editorial policy. The way it looks to the reader, while closely tied to the writer's view, is an integral part of a publication's 'face', in which the contributor is partaking because of a happy conjunction between the article submitted and the editorial requirements of the publication.

Space and projection

Sacrosanct though the words may be, the space and projection accorded to a feature article, and indeed its choice in the first place, stem from the policy and requirements of the publication, whether it be a Sunday broadsheet or an obscure monthly on coin-collecting.

The subjective content of articles nevertheless allows for a wide variety of approach to headline writing. Thus in *Country Life* a look-back article on house sales in 1918, decorated with evocative pictures, is headlined HOMES FIT FOR HEROES. An article in the monthly magazine *Living* entitles an article on sleep and dreams THE MYSTERIES OF YOUR NIGHT LIFE, and links it to colourful pictures of night attire and a worldly read-me standfirst printed in white on purple. A feature article on *The Times* Spectrum page on the hectic lifestyle of Californians is headlined MINISTRY FOR FEELING GOOD, and is commended to readers with a standfirst which says 'Self-love is something they feel strongly about in California – so strongly that now they have set up a special task force'.

Untrammelled by facts, the features subeditor's approach to headline writing is like the advertising copywriter's use of persuasion. The subeditor also has to identify with the product, which in this case is the writer's words.

Typography

Feature articles being generally longer than news items, typographical devices are used both in newspaper feature pages and in magazines to break up the text to give eye appeal.

Figure 20.2 How display techniques project a feature. Bold pictures are used in this *Sunday Times* travel page to offset a dominant advertisement. The byline is incorporated in the standfirst above the intro, and it is used to explain what the writer is doing. The big capital 'W' at the start of the article is typical of the 'stand up drops' used decoratively in the paper's travel articles

The following devices are to be found:

Strapline: This is an explanatory line of type running above a headline containing introductory material which helps to place the main words in context. Thus a headline THE NEW HOPE OF THE BLACK AFRICAN might have above it the line in smaller type: 'Our correspondent looks at life today in a Johannesburg township'.

Standfirst: This is a more detailed explanation about an article and its writer in special type or in a panel, sometimes as white type on a black background, above the start of the article – hence the name 'standfirst' (see Figure 20.2).

Highlight quotes: These are quotes taken from an article, especially an interview-based one, and set in special type, sometimes within panel rules, and placed within the run of the text to break up excessively long areas of reading matter. They are in fact subsidiary headlines calling attention to specific parts of the text.

Crossheads: One or two-word lines set in special type and used as periodic breakers in a long text. They are usually a key word or phase taken from the paragraph or two following. Their main purpose is as eye-rests but they can help in holding the reader's attention by highlighting evocative words and phrases in the text, thus persuading the reader to carry on reading.

WOBs and BOTs: Type used as white on to black or black on to tint background, or even black on to a coloured background – a device used to highlight headlines, quotes or even a standfirst so that it stands out on the page. This is a common device used on the features pages of many newspapers and in all sorts of magazines.

That visual character

Typography, meaning the use of type, is an essential part of the design of newspapers and magazines, and therefore of the projection of features. Every publication has its own special use of type so that it achieves a visual character that makes it instantly recognizable. There is a great range of types available in today's computerized editing and page make-up systems.

Contributors can gain a better insight into a publication's requirements if they study the way articles are displayed, the way pictures are used and the sort of headline ideas that commend articles to the readers. The very act of publishing an article means that much of the publishing process is concerned with catching the reader's eye, and writers should therefore have a feeling for the visual potential of what is being written, especially when aiming for publications that value display highly.

ASSIGNMENTS

The following can be done as individual assignments, complementary to the cutting and filing you have been advised in this book to do, or as group projects supervised by a tutor. The group can be split into individuals or teams. The resulting write-ups can be reported to the whole group, and this could be followed up by a debate:

1 *Preparation:* Buy two copies of all Sunday papers for four weeks. Cut, paste up and photocopy all feature articles.
  Briefly analyse (about 100 words) each feature, along the lines of the analysis given on pages 20 and 22.

2 Find feature articles in two papers, both national broadsheets, that have been developed out of the same news story. Compare them, indicating what they reveal about the targeted readership, editorial policy, political/social slant, etc. (total 600 words).

3 On another day, as for 2, but one broadsheet, one tabloid.

4 On another day, as for 2, but two tabloid papers.

5 Write a proposal (500 words) for a new magazine: indicate the formula, target readership, frequency, price, likely advertisers, staff and freelancers required, and kinds of articles and other content planned. Create a dummy for the first issue.

21 WRITING INTO THE FUTURE

Figure 20.2 shows how the subediting and layout of feature articles is carefully matched to the writer's ideas. The use of new technology – electronic copy input and editing, made possible by the computer, and the generation of type from type masters within a photosetter by photographic means, or laser beams, instead of the traditional hot metal – does not fundamentally alter what writers and subeditors are trying to do. Text still has to be written, presented, edited and turned into the chosen type to fit the pages.

NEW TECHNOLOGY IN NEWSPAPERS

For most newspapers the new methods mean that instead of using typewriters, writers type their text into word processors, called visual display units (VDUs), from where it is stored in the office computer ready for recall for screen editing and, ultimately, for typesetting and page make-up. The keyboarding, as it is called, is on the same QWERTY keyboard as a typewriter, the difference being that instead of using paper, the machine displays the text on its screen set above the keyboard. Instead of having to retype versions and check and correct with a ball pen on the typescript, the writer corrects, cuts and adjusts on screen by the use of simple keyboard commands which move the cursor, or electronic pen, around the screen until the text is satisfactory. It is then sent at a stroke into the newsroom or features queue, or wherever it is destined for, to await editing. The physical demands of keyboarding are no greater than with typing. The various commands are programmed on to a dozen extra keys. The task of learning and using these keys is nothing compared to the workload of typing and correction that the writer has shed.

The writer's concern with new technology ends at this point. In the all-in systems now in use in newspaper production, however, the writer's keystroke is retained in the computer as an electronic signal which delivers the text on to screen for checking and subediting, and produces the final printed text as it appears in the newspaper. This is what is meant by 'direct input'. It is a world in which printers in the sense of typesetters no longer exist.

The VDUs used for editing have more elaborate controls than those used by the writers. This is to enable texts to be merged or rewritten by the use of split screen, which can display two texts side-by-side, and to allow for the text to be keyed onwards into the typesetters in whatever body size or headline type is required. The keystroke setting the text, however, remains the writer's, adjusted as necessary by the subeditor's cursor according to the requirements of editing.

Page make-up

Today's newspaper and magazine pages are made up electronically from the computer inputs which are used to produce negatives of the pages from which the printing plates are derived. There are two methods of doing this.

First, **cut-and-paste**. Here the pages are put together on cards from the body matter and headlines which are delivered as photographic bromides from the typesetters and pasted into position. These and the pictures and adverts, likewise produced to size as photographic bromides, are arranged according to the editorial page plan until the page is made up. It is then a complete photographic replica of what the printed page will look like. The camera operator next photographs the pasted-up page to produce a negative, from which the final printed plate is derived by a chemical process that transfers the image. From here onwards the page is printed on a web offset press, to produce the same result as under the old hot-metal system – except that metal has played no part in the operation. Even the printing plate that goes on the press is made of polymer.

The second method is called **electronic page make-up**. In this, the ultimate computer system, the entire page is assembled on screen from the edited materials, pictures and graphics which have been entered into the computer. When the page is complete and all the components fitting, it is 'locked' and printed out as a photographic negative which is fed straight into a platemaker.

It is possible to 'wire' pages from a central production plant to be received by electronic signal in a satellite plant at which a decoder feeds the signal into a plate-maker to enable simultaneous production of a newspaper in several centres.

Though writers are not directly concerned with all this, they have become part of the process from the moment articles are set off on their electronic journeys on the keyboards of the VDUs. Having said that, there is still some copy on newspapers that arrives by typewriter or telephone to be edited on typescript and then keyboarded into the system. Another area of 'hard copy' entry is in those magazines where typesetting and printing are being carried out by contract arrangements.

Increasingly, because of these developments, newspaper freelances own a word processor that can be linked to a publication's computer. This is done by means of a modem, which attaches to the telephone, enabling the text to be put on line by simply dialling the newspaper's copy input number. Where author's proofs are needed, they can be provided by computer print-outs. This is a vital facility for contributors where expert vetting of an edited version of the text is called for.

With the more sophisticated and expensive word processors it is possible for the writer to be able to recall edited texts from a publication for checking or even to provide an ordered revision or update, though such systems are not commonly in use. Some newspapers lend out portable word processors or work stations to regular contributors, and village Women's Institute reports and flower show results are beginning to arrive by direct input from local correspondents who a short while ago might have been loading 10p pieces into a telephone box. One regular columnist on a South Coast weekly, who had the misfortune to break a leg, found himself working as hard as ever with his specially provided office work station propped up in front of him in bed.

NEW TECHNOLOGY IN MAGAZINES

While newspapers have opted for direct copy input for their reporters and feature writers, the situation in magazines remains varied. A large group's magazines sharing plant make full use of the new methods, using word processors linked to a central computer for copy origination and they enjoy the full benefits of direct input. Only a few in the middle-range general interest and specialist magazines and periodicals still edit on 'hard' copy, sending text for keyboarding and pictures for processing to a printing plant under contract arrangements. A number of smaller companies, however – and not only school and parish magazines and company newspapers – are produced in-house by cheap typesetting and printing systems referred to collectively as desktop publishing.

There are various types of contract arrangements for the middle-range resulting from multiplicity of ownership, purpose and printing requirements. Under these, text editing and page design are generally carried out at a publication's editorial offices and the text and page layouts taken, or posted, to the typesetters and printers who might be hundreds of miles away.

The consequence for writers is that some editing tends still to be on typescript or printouts since the magazine is not generating type or using direct input. Thus, while VDUs are chattering away at the printers as edited copy is fed in and pages prepared to page plans from pasted-up type bromides, writers are delivering their text to the editorial offices or telephoning it through in the traditional way.

Photocopies of pages, or even of galley proofs of type, are sent by the printers to the editorial offices whenever text has to be adjusted or cut to fit, and photocopies or printouts of text are supplied to writers for checking and proofreading. A senior sub may work at the printers on press day to see to late changes. Otherwise, instructions to printers are posted, sent by messenger, or telephoned. It has to be said that such hybrid arrangements are unlikely to last as economies dictate the full utilization of the computer across the board in copy entry, text editing and page make-up.

Writers should check what printout or proofing arrangements exist as well as the arrangements and deadlines for the delivery of copy, depending on the systems used.

Desktop publishing

Desktop publishing (DTP) can cut printing and publishing costs drastically. New magazine titles have kept up despite the recession because launchers know that by doing their own edition, typesetting and page make-up using DTP they can recoup their setting up costs (of perhaps £10,000 to £20,000) with low production costs thereafter. Contract printers, in contrast, can require substantial 'up front' money for their services, with subsequent high production costs. It is also a relief for the small operator to be able to avoid the constant sending of proofs to typesetters for cuts, checking and rechecking.

Some DTP packages are equipped with an A3 screen on which two pages can be worked on at once. Some freelance journalists have found it worthwhile to equip themselves with an Apple Mac computer with Quark-Xpress software to enable them to take on the production of one or two small magazines on top of their normal writing work.

ELECTRONICALLY SPEAKING

As a writer you need to familiarize yourself with how current technology works.

In particular, the word processor (usually marketed as a personal computer) has replaced the typewriter, allowing correcting, cutting and text to be done painlessly. The word processor frees you from the drudgery of typing repeated drafts or defacing a typescript with corrections.

The facility of printing out from a word processor means that it can do exactly what a typewriter can do anyway as well as generating electronic text. All word processors are marketed with a compatible printer to which they are linked by a lead. If a printout is needed, paper is inserted in sheets or as a continuous roll and once the text has been got ready on screen the machine can simply be commanded to print. No further keying is needed.

One word of warning. Potential purchasers of word processors should check that the machine is compatible with, or has the interface available for, the publications' computers to which it is likely to be linked. Computers and systems do vary but most word processors these days are compatible, or can be made so. Equally, in terms of cost, purchasers should check if the printer that goes with the word processor is part of the package or costs extra.

Horses for courses

Don't assume that the word processor with all its facilities will do the writing for you. On the other hand, nothing is simpler than to ease out verbosity on screen, for you can have second, third or fourth thoughts as you scroll through your text and examine what you have written.

Using a word processor to get things right means that you no longer need submit copy that is second best, though the inveterate tinkerer might be tempted to go on changing the words right up to the copy deadline and beyond. Inveterate tinkering can be almost as big a problem as verbosity.

Writers, in fact, come broadly in two kinds: the tinkerer-as-you-go and the do-several-drafts. For the first sort the word processor is a godsend. Instead of umpteen fresh goes at the first paragraph until it comes right, with lines scored out and arrows and balloons all over the page, you can make it all look neat and simple on screen. If you're a several-drafts exponent on the other hand, you print out a few drafts so that you can see them as a whole before doing most of the correcting. Then you will not have to worry that some gems have escaped into the air.

There are other advantages in printing out drafts. You are writing a 3000 word-article on immigration. There are to be three sections of about, let's say, 1000 words each – a convenient size for what the machine calls a 'document'. Your catchline for the first section is Kinds 1. This is perhaps academically orientated so you make a copy and name it Kinds 2, and edit it as a second version which you perhaps make more anecdotal. You copy either Kinds 1 or Kinds 2, depending on which is going to be closer to the third version and name it Kinds 3. You edit this with perhaps additional quotes.

You can even print out all three versions and play about with them until you have produced a fourth or final one, Kinds 4. When you are happy with this you may want to keep Kinds 1 to 3 as the bases for different articles on the subject for different publications, or perhaps for a longer piece. Thus the facilities to store, retrieve, edit, reorder paragraphs and copy documents by pressing a few keys are made to work for you.

Software writing aids

Computer programs that take some of the labour out of writing are constantly being improved and added to. There are idea processors – for example, IdeaFisher, which is partly a brainstormer and partly an interrogator, and triggers off all sorts of lateral associations to get the ideas flowing. There are grammar and style checkers, and outliners, and research sources. Journalism/writing magazines and the computer pages of the national newspapers, notably *The Guardian*'s, will keep you up to date with what is coming out.

But beware. As you become more ambitious, avoid adding on equipment and software for their own sake; they can get in the way. Upgrade your computer only if you see clearly how the new tools will fit your temperament and ways of working. No machine can do your thinking and writing for you, nor will it give you something to say or tell you if you are saying something badly.

I hope this book has helped you to say better whatever it is you have to say.

APPENDIX 1
SUGGESTED RESPONSES TO ASSIGNMENTS

CHAPTER 1

Try to find time to reduce in length some of the articles and assignments you have written after putting them aside for a day or two. Aim to reduce them by a third or a half – it will help you write more concisely.

Exchange some of them with those of a colleague or fellow-student, and subedit each others'.

CHAPTER 2

Assignment 1

The letter should be written more concisely, avoiding 'I plan to write', 'the intention is to prove', etc. Make sure the angle is fresh; it is a fairly well covered subject. The purpose of the article should be stated earlier than paragraph 3 and more precisely. A clearer idea is needed of why readers of the target publication should be interested.

Give a few facts/figures/cases to whet the appetite; the intro can fulfil part of this job. A better last paragraph would be one simply to give your telephone number(s) and at what times you can be contacted.

CHAPTER 3

Assignment 3

You will need to have removed some of the '*I*s' and the clichés.

CHAPTER 8

'House Husbands: How Well do they Cope?' The jargon includes such phrases as 'reflect this growing trend' and 'maximize our position in the workforce'. References to such films as *Mr Mum* and *Trading Places* need updating, and their relevance to the discussion indicated.

'Research shows. . . .' Indicate research evidence more clearly (for example, giving brief details of any survey that provided evidence), but avoid using the word 'research' for most markets.

An attention-grabbing intro is needed. Facts, figures, case-studies? (Paragraphs 5, 6 and 7 rewritten might serve.)

The formula needed here is:

● Problems (difficulties, disadvantages): consider how to order. The following order suggests itself:

1 The couple's problems as a team.
2 The individuals' problems separately.
3 Others' problems.

● Solutions (compensations, advantages): follow order of problems.
● Conclusion.

Alternatively, the structure of the body could be problem/solution. problem/solution . . . one by one.

The article is long on problems and short on solutions. The conclusion begins too feebly: 'Let's hope that . . . .' How the various people wheeled in at the end (employers, etc.) could change their attitudes and some ideas about what they should be doing should be among the 'solutions' throughout (at least briefly). The Hurd quote at the end is not significant enough for an ending. A way of summing up how attitudes should change or be changed is wanted.

CHAPTER 12

Assignments 1–8

Compare your efforts with the styles of the publications listed. For practice: make notes of a leader, or a short article, or two or three paragraphs in a publication. Then put the publication aside and write from your notes to the appropriate style. Compare.

CHAPTER 16

Assignment 3

Make sure your readers are on the same wave-length, and that you dispel any myths (for example, that magistrates are professional law administrators paid for their work in court).

Among questions to consider are: how far are your local magistrates representative of the area's society? Do they reflect sufficiently ethnic minorities, the younger members, the older, the different classes? What are the different motivations for becoming a JP?

CHAPTER 18

Improve a press release

Get the main selling point up-front. Avoid the hype and the gush and find specific facts of interest to the readership aimed at.

APPENDIX 2
MARKS FOR COPY
PREPARATION AND
PROOF CORRECTION

Extracts from BS 5261 Part 2 by kind permission of the British Standards Institution. Copies of the standard may be obtained from BSI Sales, Linford Wood, Milton Keynes MK14 6LE.

BS 5261C : 1976

UDC 001.816 : 655.255.1

Marks for copy preparation and proof correction

(extracted from BS 5261 : Part 2 : 1976)

Repères pour la préparation du manuscrit et correction sur épreuve

Zeichen für die Manuskriptvorbereitung und Korrektur der Probeabzüge

Notes on the use of the marks
(clauses **4.5, 4.6, 4.7** and **4.8** of BS 5261 : Part 2 : 1976)

1. For each marking-up or proof correction instruction a distinct mark is to be made:

(a) in the text: to indicate the exact place to which the instruction refers;

(b) in the margin: to signify or amplify the meaning of the instruction.

It should be noted that some instructions have a combined textual and marginal mark.

2. Where a number of instructions occur in one line, the marginal marks are to be divided between the left and right margins where possible, the order being from left to right in both margins.

3. Specification details, comments and instructions may be written on the copy or proof to complement the textual and marginal marks. Such written matter is to be clearly distinguishable from the copy and from any corrections made to the proof. Normally this is done by encircling the matter and/or by the appropriate use of colour (see below).

4. Proof corrections shall be made in coloured ink thus:

(a) printer's literal errors marked by the printer for correction: green;

(b) printer's literal errors marked by the customer and his agents for correction: red;

(c) alterations and instructions made by the customer and his agents: black or dark blue.

British Standards Institution

8402-1-4k-JWD

Classified list of marks (Table 1 from BS 5261 : Part 2)

NOTE: The letters M and P in the notes column indicate marks for
marking-up copy and for correcting proofs respectively.

Group A   General

Number	Instruction	Textual mark	Marginal mark	Notes
A1	Correction is concluded	None	$/$	P Make after each correction
A2	Leave unchanged	------ under characters to remain	Ⓙ	M P
A3	Remove extraneous marks	Encircle marks to be removed	✕	P e.g. film or paper edges visible between lines on bromide or diazo proofs
A3.1	Push down risen spacing material	Encircle blemish	⊥	P
A4	Refer to appropriate authority anything of doubtful accuracy	Encircle word(s) affected	Ⓞ	P

Group B   Deletion, insertion and substitution

B1	Insert in text the matter indicated in the margin	⋏	New matter followed by ⋏	M P Identical to B2
B2	Insert additional matter identified by a letter in a diamond	⋏	⋏ Followed by for example Ⓐ	M P The relevant section of the copy should be supplied with the corresponding letter marked on it in a diamond e.g. Ⓐ
B3	Delete	$/$ through character(s) or ⊢———⊣ through words to be deleted	♂	M P
B4	Delete and close up	$\tilde{/}$ through character or ⊢≈≈⊣ through character e.g. chara͜cter chara͜bcter	♂̃	M P

2

Number	Instruction	Textual mark	Marginal mark	Notes
B5	Substitute character or substitute part of one or more word(s)	/ through character or ⊢———┤ through word(s)	New character or new word(s)	M P
B6	Wrong fount. Replace by character(s) of correct fount	Encircle character(s) to be changed	⊗	P
B6.1	Change damaged character(s)	Encircle character(s) to be changed	✗	P This mark is identical to A3
B7	Set in or change to italic	———— under character(s) to be set or changed	⊔⊔	M P Where space does not permit textual marks encircle the affected area instead
B8	Set in or change to capital letters	≡≡≡ under character(s) to be set or changed	≡	
B9	Set in or change to small capital letters	≡≡ under character(s) to be set or changed	≡	
B9.1	Set in or change to capital letters for initial letters and small capital letters for the rest of the words	≡≡ under initial letters and ≡≡≡ under rest of word(s)	≡̄	
B10	Set in or change to bold type	∿∿∿∿ under character(s) to be set or changed	∿	
B11	Set in or change to bold italic type	∿∿∿∿ under character(s) to be set or changed	⊔⊔ ∿	
B12	Change capital letters to lower case letters	Encircle character(s) to be changed	≢	P For use when B5 is inappropriate
B12.1	Change small capital letters to lower case letters	Encircle character(s) to be changed	≠	P For use when B5 is inappropriate

3

Number	Instruction	Textual mark	Marginal mark	Notes
B13	Change italic to upright type	Encircle character(s) to be changed	⬜	P
B14	Invert type	Encircle character to be inverted	↻	P
B15	Substitute or insert character in 'superior' position	/ through character or ʎ where required	⌐ under character e.g. ²⌐	P
B16	Substitute or insert character in 'inferior' position	/ through character or ʎ where required	L over character e.g. L₂	P
B17	Substitute ligature e.g. ffi for separate letters	├────┤ through characters affected	⌣ e.g. ffi	P
B17.1	Substitute separate letters for ligature	├────┤	Write out separate letters	P
B18	Substitute or insert full stop or decimal point	/ through character or ʎ where required	⊙	M P
B18.1	Substitute or insert colon	/ through character or ʎ where required	⊙⊙	M P
B18.2	Substitute or insert semi-colon	/ through character or ʎ where required	;	M P
B18.3	Substitute or insert comma	/ through character or ʎ where required	,	M P

Number	Instruction	Textual mark	Marginal mark	Notes
B18.4	Substitute or insert apostrophe	/ through character or ∧ where required	ʼ	M P
B18.5	Substitute or insert single quotation marks	/ through character or ∧ where required	ʻ and/or ʼ	M P
B18.6	Substitute or insert double quotation marks	/ through character or ∧ where required	ʻʻ and/or ʼʼ	M P
B19	Substitute or insert ellipsis	/ through character or ∧ where required	•••	M P
B20	Substitute or insert leader dots	/ through character or ∧ where required	⟨•••⟩	M P Give the measure of the leader when necessary
B21	Substitute or insert hyphen	/ through character or ∧ where required	⊢–⊣	M P
B22	Substitute or insert rule	/ through character or ∧ where required	⊢—⊣	M P Give the size of the rule in the marginal mark e.g. ⊢1 em⊣ ⊢4 mm⊣
B23	Substitute or insert oblique	/ through character or ∧ where required	⦸/	M P

APPENDIX 3
NATIONAL UNION OF
JOURNALISTS' PROFESSIONAL
CODE OF CONDUCT

NATIONAL UNION OF JOURNALISTS
Acorn House, 314 Gray's Inn Road, London WC1X 8DP

CODE OF PROFESSIONAL CONDUCT

Like other trade unions, formed for mutual protection and economic betterment, the National Union of Journalists desires and encourages its members to maintain good quality of work and high standards of conduct.

Through the years of courageous struggle for better wages and working conditions its pioneers and their successors have kept these aims in mind, and have made provision in Union rules not only for penalties on offenders, but for the guidance and financial support of members who may suffer loss of work for conforming to Union principles.

While punishment by fine, suspension or expulsion is provided for in cases of "conduct detrimental to the interests of the Union or of the profession," any member who is victimised [Rule 20, clause (g)] for refusing to do work . . . "incompatible with the honour and interests of the profession." may rely on adequate support from Union funds.

A member of the Union has two claims on his/her loyalty – one by his/her Union and one by his/her employer. These need not clash so long as the employer complies with the agreed Union conditions and make no demand for forms of service incompatible with the honour of the profession or with the principle of trade unionism.

1. A journalist has a duty to maintain the highest professional and ethical standards.

2. A journalist shall at all times defend the principle of the freedom of the Press and other media in relation to the collection of information and the expression of comment and criticism. He/she shall strive to eliminate distortion, news suppression and censorship.

3. A journalist shall strive to ensure that the information he/she disseminates is fair and accurate, avoid the expression of comment and conjecture as established fact and falsification by distortion, selection or misrepresentation.

4. A journalist shall rectify promptly any harmful inaccuracies, ensure that correction and apologies receive due prominence and afford the right of reply to persons criticised when the issue is of sufficient importance.

5. A journalist shall obtain information, photographs and illustrations only by straightforward means. The use of other means can be justified only by over-riding consideration of the public interest. The journalist is entitled to exercise a personal conscientious objection to the use of such means.

6. Subject to justification by over-riding considerations of the public interest, a journalist shall do nothing which entails intrusion into private grief and distress.

7 A journalist shall protect confidential sources of information.

8. A journalist shall not accept bribes nor shall he/she allow other inducements to influence the performance of his/her professional duties.

9. A journalist shall not lend himself/herself to the distortion or suppression of the truth because of advertising or other considerations.

10. A journalist shall only mention a person's race, colour, creed, illegitimacy, marital status or lack of it, gender or sexual orientation if this information is strictly relevant. A journalist shall neither originate nor process material which encourages discrimination on any of the above-mentioned grounds.

11. A journalist shall not take private advantage of information gained in the course of his/her duties, before the information is public knowledge.

12. A journalist shall not by way of statement, voice or appearance endorse by advertisement any commercial product or service save for the promotion of his/her own work or of the medium by which he/she is employed.

APPENDIX 4
CODE OF PRACTICE
FOR THE PRESS

The Press Complaints Commission is charged with enforcing the following Code of Practice which was framed by the newspaper and periodical industry and ratified by the Press Complaints Commission.

All members of the press have a duty to maintain the highest professional and ethical standards. In doing so, they should have regard to the provisions of this Code of Practice and to safeguarding the public's right to know.

Editors are responsible for the actions of journalists employed by their publications. They should also satisfy themselves as far as possible that material accepted from non-staff members was obtained in accordance with the Code.

While recognizing that this involves a substantial element of self-restraint by editors and journalists, it is designed to be acceptable in the context of a system of self-regulation. The Code applies in the spirit as well as in the letter.

It is the responsibility of editors to cooperate as swiftly as possible in PCC enquiries.

Any publication which is criticized by the PCC under one of the following clauses is duty bound to print the adjudication which follows in full and with due prominence.

1 Accuracy

(i)   Newspapers and periodicals should take care not to publish inaccurate, misleading or distorted material.

(ii) Whenever it is recognized that a significant inaccuracy, misleading statement or distorted report has been published, it should be corrected promptly and with due prominence.

(iii) An apology should be published whenever appropriate.
(iv) A newspaper or periodical should always report fairly and accurately the outcome of an action for defamation to which it has been a party.

2 Opportunity to reply

A fair opportunity to reply to inaccuracies should be given to individuals or organizations when reasonably called for.

3 Comment, conjecture and fact

Newspapers, while free to be partisan, should distinguish clearly between comment, conjecture and fact.

4 Privacy

Intrusions and enquiries into an individual's private life without his or her consent including the use of long-lens photography to take pictures of people on private property without their consent are not generally acceptable and publication can only be justified when in the public interest.

Note – private property is defined as (i) any private residence, together with its garden and outbuildings, but excluding any adjacent fields or park-land and the surrounding parts of the property within the unaided view of passers-by, (ii) hotel bedrooms (but not other areas in a hotel) and (iii) those parts of a hospital or nursing home where patients are treated or accommodated.

5 Listening devices

Unless justified by public interest, journalists should not obtain or publish material obtained by using clandestine listening devices or by intercepting private telephone conversations.

6 Hospitals

(i) Journalists or photographers making enquiries at hospitals or similar institutions should identify themselves to a responsible executive and obtain permission before entering non-public areas.
(ii) The restrictions on intruding into privacy are particularly relevant to enquiries about individuals in hospitals or similar institutions.

7 Misrepresentation

(i)   Journalists should not generally obtain or seek to obtain information or pictures through misrepresentation or subterfuge.
(ii) Unless in the public interest, documents or photographs should be removed only with the express consent of the owner.
(iii) Subterfuge can be justified only in the public interest and only when material cannot be obtained by any other means.

8 Harassment

(i)   Journalists should neither obtain nor seek to obtain information or pictures through intimidation or harassment.
(ii) Unless their enquiries are in the public interest, journalists should not photograph individuals on private property (as defined in the note to Clause 4) without their consent; should not persist in telephoning or questioning individuals after having been asked to desist; should not remain on their property after having been asked to leave and should not follow them.
(iii) It is the responsibility of editors to ensure that these requirements are carried out.

9 Payment for articles

Payment or offers of payment for stories, pictures or information, should not be made directly or through agents to witness or potential witnesses in current criminal proceedings or to people engaged in crime or to their associates – which includes family, friends, neighbours and colleagues – except where the material concerned ought to be published in the public interest and the payment is necessary for this to be done.

10 Intrusion into grief or shock

In cases involving personal grief or shock, enquiries should be carried out and approaches made with sympathy and discretion.

11 Innocent relatives and friends

Unless it is contrary to the public's right to know, the press should generally avoid identifying relatives or friends of persons convicted or accused of crime.

12 Interviewing or photographing children

(i)   Journalists should not normally interview or photograph children under the age of 16 on subjects involving the personal welfare of the child, in the absence of or without the consent of a parent or other adult who is responsible for the children.

(ii) Children should not be approached or photographed while at school without the permission of the school authorities.

13 Children in sex cases

1   The press should not, even where the law does not prohibit it, identify children under the age of 16 who are involved in cases concerning sexual offences, whether as victims or as witnesses or defendants.

2   In any press report of a case involving a sexual offence against a child–
    (i)   The adult should be identified.
    (ii)   The term 'incest' where applicable should not be used.
    (iii) The offence should be described as 'serious offences against young children' or similar appropriate wording.
    (iv)   The child should not be identified.
    (v)   Care should be taken that nothing in the report implies the relationship between the accused and the child.

14 Victims of crime

The press should not identify victims of sexual assault or publish material likely to contribute to such identification unless, by law, they are free to do so.

15 Discrimination

(i)   The press should avoid prejudicial or pejorative reference to a person's race, colour, religion, sex or sexual orientation or to any physical or mental illness or handicap.

(ii) It should avoid publishing details of a person's race, colour, religion, sex or sexual orientation, unless these are directly relevant to the story.

16 Financial journalism

(i)   Even where the law does not prohibit it, journalists should not use for their own profit, financial information they receive in advance of its general publication, nor should they pass such information to others.

(ii) They should not write about share or securities in whose performance they know that they or their close families have a significant financial interest, without disclosing the interest to the editor or financial editor.

(iii) They should not buy or sell, either directly or through nominees or agents, shares or securities about which they have written recently or about which they intend to write in the near future.

17 Confidential sources

Journalists have a moral obligation to protect confidential sources of information.

18 The public interest

Clauses 4, 5, 7, 8 and 9 create exceptions which may be covered by invoking the public interest. For the purposes of this code that is most easily defined as:

(i)   Detecting or exposing crime or a serious misdemeanour.

(ii) Protecting public health and safety.

(iii) Preventing the public from being misled by some statement or action of an individual or organization.

In any case raising issues beyond these three definitions the Press Complaints Commission will require a full explanation by the editor of the publication involved, seeking to demonstrate how the public interest was served.

Comments or suggestions regarding the content of the Code may be sent to the Secretary, Press Standards Board of Finance, Merchants House Buildings, 30 George Square, Glasgow G2 1EG, to be laid before the industry's Code Committee.

APPENDIX 5
SOCIETY OF AUTHORS QUICK GUIDE 1: COPYRIGHT

Copyright and Moral Rights

I Copyright

1. How long does United Kingdom copyright protection last?

(a) Works published during the author's lifetime

The period of copyright protection lasts until fifty years from the end of the calendar year in which the author died. For a published work of joint authorship, i.e. a work by two or more authors in which the contributions of the authors are not distinct, the period of protection runs from the end of the calendar year of the death of the author who dies last.

(b) Works not published, performed in public, offered for sale to the public on gramophone records or broadcast during the author's lifetime

— works not published during the author's lifetime, but posthumously published before 1st August 1989: 50 years from publication.

— works unpublished where the author dies before 1st August 1989: the end of 2039 (1989 plus 50 years).

— works unpublished where the author dies after 1st August 1989: the author's lifetime plus 50 years.

(c) Anonymous and pseudonymous works

The period of protection is fifty years from the end of the calendar year in which the work is first 'made available to the public' unless during that period 'it is possible for a person to ascertain the identity of the author by reasonable enquiry', in which case the period is as under (a) above.

2. Who owns the copyright in letters and how long does protection last?

Letters are entitled to the same protection as other literary works. The letter itself belongs to the recipient, but the copyright in it belongs to the writer and, after his/her death, to the writer's estate.

3. How much may be quoted from a copyright work without permission?

Generally speaking it is an infringement to quote 'a substantial part' of a copyright work without permission. The Copyright Act 1988 does not define what is meant by 'substantial' but in one case 4 lines from a 32-line poem were held to amount to 'a substantial part'. Other legal precedents indicate that the quality of the 'part' and its value to the user must be taken into account as well as its length in determining whether it is 'substantial'. Even a 'substantial' quotation from a copyright work may not be an infringement if it is fair dealing ... for purposes of criticism or review' and provided it is 'accompanied by sufficient acknowledgement'; but the term 'fair dealing' is not defined in the Copyright Act. Some further guidance is given in the Society's *Quick Guide to Permissions*.

There is no copyright in a title, but when a title is distinctive and closely identified in the public's mind with the work of a particular author, that author may be able to obtain an injunction and damages if the title is used by another writer. See *Quick Guide No 2*.

5. Is there copyright in a pseudonym?

What we have said about titles applies here. If an author writes for a periodical under a pseudonym, he/she can, in the absence of agreement to the contrary, use the pen-name elsewhere when he/she ceases to contribute to that periodical.

6. Is there copyright in a plot?

There is no copyright in an idea or in the bare bones of a plot. To succeed in an action for infringement of copyright, the plaintiff would have to show that the combination or series of dramatic events in the allegedly infringing work had been taken from the like situations in the plaintiff's work.

In many cases where judgement has gone against the plaintiff, it is clear that the copying of 'a combination or series of dramatic events' has to be very close indeed before the copyright is held to have been infringed. Proceedings have failed because it has been held that incidents common to two works were stock incidents or revolved around stock characters common to many works. Furthermore, as copyright is not a monopoly, it is a perfectly good defence if a later author can prove that he had no knowledge of an earlier author's work.

7. What formalities have to be complied with in order to acquire copyright protection?

There are no formalities in the United Kingdom or in any country which is a member of the Berne Copyright Union. This Union includes in its membership most of the principal countries of the world, with the important exceptions of the USSR, China and some of the South American republics.

Although copyright is automatically acquired immediately a work is written, authors are advised to establish evidence of the date of completion of each work. One way of doing this is to deposit a copy of the script with your bank and obtain a dated receipt. Another is to post a sealed envelope, containing a copy, to yourself.

8. What is the purpose of the copyright notice © followed by the name of the copyright owner and the year of first publication?

This is the copyright notice prescribed by the Universal Copyright Convention, of which Great Britain and more than sixty other countries are members, including the United States and the Soviet Union (which is not a member of the Berne Union). Works of the nationals of any member state bearing the UCC copyright notice are protected in every other member state, whether or not that state's domestic law requires registration or other formalities.

9. What is the period of copyright protection in the USA?

The US Copyright Act of 1909 provided for two separate terms of copyright: a period of 28 years from publication, followed by a renewal period of a further 28 years.

However, the comprehensive new Copyright Act 1976, which came into force on 1st January 1978, made fundamental changes in the duration of protection for new works, and also contained some complicated transitional provisions as follows:

(a) *Works in their second 28-year period on 1 January 1978:* copyrights, originally registered with the US Register of Copyrights before 1950 and renewed before 1978, are automatically extended by the new Act until 31 December of the 75th calendar year from the original date they were secured. In effect, this means that all existing copyrights in their second term are extended for 19 years. This extension applies not only to copyrights less than 56 years old, but also to older copyrights that have previously been extended in duration under a series of Congressional enactments beginning in 1962.

(b) *Works in the first 28-year period on 1 January 1978:* works originally copyrighted between 1 January 1950 and 31 December 1977 must still be renewed. Application for renewal must be made to the US Register of Copyrights within the calendar year prior to the expiry of the original 28-year term, but under the new Act the renewal period is extended to 47 years, making a total period of 75 years.

Many works by British authors published from 1957 will have acquired their first 28-year term of protection under the UCC, simply by bearing the prescribed copyright notice (see paragraph 8 above). Such works must be registered with the US Register of Copyrights and also renewed during the final year of the first 28-year term, i.e. a work originally published in 1961 will need to be registered (if not already registered) and renewed before 31 December 1989 (1961 + 28) in order to obtain protection for the full 75-year period. If published in 1962, the work will need renewal in 1990, and so on. The necessary forms may be obtained from the Society or from Register of Copyrights, Library of Congress, Washington DC 20559, USA. Registration and renewal applications must be made in the name of the author or the author's heirs.

(c) *Works created on or after 1 January 1978:* works created after the new law came into force are automatically protected for the author's lifetime, and for an additional 50 years after the author's death. For works made for hire, and for anonymous and pseudonymous works, the new term is 75 years from publication or 100 years from creation, whichever is shorter.

(d) *Works in existence but not copyrighted on 1 January 1978:* unpublished works that were created before 1 January 1978, but have neither been published nor registered for copyright, automatically receive protection under the new law. The copyright will generally last for the same life-plus-50 or 75/100 year terms provided for new works. However, all works in this category were guaranteed at least 25 years of statutory protection; the new law specifies that in no case will copyright in a work of this sort expire before 31 December 2002, and if the work is published before that date the term is extended by another 25 years, to the end of 2027.-

II Moral Rights

1. What are an author's 'moral rights'?

There are three moral rights conferred by the Copyright Act 1988:

(a) *the right of paternity* is the right of an author to be identified whenever a work is published, performed or broadcast. In other words, bookwriters, scriptwriters, illustrators, and translators must be properly credited.

(b) *the right of integrity.* This is the right of an author to object to 'derogatory' treatment of a work. Treatment is 'derogatory' if it amounts to 'distortion or mutilation ... or is otherwise prejudicial to the honour or reputation of the author ....'.

(c) *the right not to have work falsely attributed to you.* This is the right of a person not to have a literary or dramatic work falsely attributed to him/her as author.

2. Does an author have to comply with any formalities?

Yes. An author does not benefit from the right of *paternity* unless and until he or she has 'asserted' the right in writing. It is not clear from the Act when the 'assertion' must take place, but we advise authors and agents to include a suitable clause in each publishing contract. A recommended form of wording will appear from time to time in *The Author* and can be given to members on request. The second and third rights do not depend on 'assertion'.

3. How long do moral rights last?

The rights of *paternity* and of *integrity*, like copyright, last until fifty years from the end of the calendar year in which the author died. The right of a person not to have work falsely attributed to him/her expires twenty years after that person's death.

4. When do moral rights not apply?

The rights of paternity and integrity do not apply when work is published in a newspaper, magazine or similar periodical. Nor do the rights benefit authors contributing to an encyclopaedia, dictionary, yearbook or other collective work of reference.

5. Can an author waive his/her moral rights?

Yes. Moral rights cannot be assigned to someone else, but they can be waived by the author in writing. Furthermore, moral rights are not infringed by any act to 'to which the person entitled to the right has consented'.

6. What happens to moral rights when an author dies?

The rights pass to whomever is nominated in the author's will. If no direction is given in a will, the rights pass to the person receiving the copyright. However, the right of a person not to have work falsely attributed to him/her is only actionable by an author's personal representatives.

Revised edition © The Society of Authors 1989
Available free to members (£1 post free to non-members) from
The Society of Authors, 84 Drayton Gardens, London SW10 9SB.

APPENDIX 6
PROFESSIONAL
ORGANIZATIONS

This appendix is a rough guide only to the most useful organizations. For a fuller list, refer to writers' guides such as Macmillan/PEN *The Writer's Handbook, Writers' and Artists' Yearbook* (A & C Black), the UKPG Contact – PRO, and *The Media Guide*, ed. Steve Peak (*The Guardian/ Fourth Estate*) and Hennessy and Hodgson, *Journalism Workbook* (Focal Press, 1995).

Association of British Science Writers (ABSW)
C/o The British Association for the Advancement of Science, Fortress House, 23 Saville Row, London W1X 1AB
Tel: 0171–439–1205

British Association of Communicators in Business
3 Locks Yard, High Street, Sevenoaks, Kent TN13 7LT
Tel: 01732–459–331
Publishes *Editor's Handbook* for editing house journals.

British Association of Journalists
99 Fleet Street, London EC4
Tel: 0171–353–3003

Campaign for Press and Broadcasting Freedom
9 Poland Street, London W1V 3DG
Tel: 0171–731–7795

Works for more accessible and more accountable media, with right of reply, and with portrayal of minorities.

Institute of Journalists
2 Dock Offices, Surrey Quays Road, London SE16 2XU
Tel: 0171–252–1187

Trade union and professional association for writers, journalists and broadcasters.

Institute of Public Relations
Gate House, 15 Northburgh Street, London EC1V 0PR
Tel: 0171–253–5151

The Institute of Scientific and Technical Communicators
Kings Court, Goodge Street, London W1P 1FF
Tel: 0171–436–4425

National Union of Journalists
Acorn House, 314 Gray's Inn Road, London WC1X 8DP
Tel: 0171–278–7916
Works for agreements on salaries, fees and conditions. Trade Union.

PEN
7 Dilke Street, London SW1 4JE
Tel: 0171–352–6303

The English branch of International PEN, which is open to all writers. Concerned with freedom of expression throughout the world.

Society of Authors1
84 Drayton Gardens, London SW10 9SB
Tel: 0171–373–6642

Independent trade union. Advises on negotiations with publishers, film companies, etc.

Writers' Circles:
Jill Dick, Oldacre, Horderns Park Road, Chapel-en-le-Firth, Derbyshire SK11 7SY

Will put you in touch with nationwide network. The Regional Arts Association of your area will put you in touch with local groups if your local library cannot.

Majorie Harris, Secretary, London Writers Circle, 'Bradfield', Leafy Grove, Keston, Kent

You may have to try several before finding one that suits you. Avoid mutual admiration societies, and groups that talk vaguely about 'being a writer' rather than on dissecting specific pieces of work and giving meaningful encouragement and support.

Writer's Guild of Great Britain
430 Edgware Road, London W2 1EH
Tel: 0171–723–8074
Trade Union, affiliated to the Trades Union Congress.

APPENDIX 7
TRAINING

National Council for the Training of Journalists, Latton Bush Centre, Southern Way, Harlow, Essex CM18 7BL
Tel: 01279–430–009

The NCTJ is the main body concerned with the training of newspaper journalists. It accredits colleges, universities, and company training centres to run courses based on its own subject syllabuses. It also provides them with a sequence of preliminary examinations in newspaper journalism, law, public affairs and shorthand.

Direct entrants to newspapers or news agencies study a distance learning foundation course pack over the first six months of employment and then mostly attend a 12-week block release course. Alternatively, there are the full-year NCTJ pre-entry course and graduate diploma courses. Students take all seven preliminary examinations on the course and before entering the industry.

For those trainees unable to attend college full-time the NCTJ has seven different distance learning courses available.

Pre-entry trainees then have eighteen months' and direct entrants two years' on-job training and experience in full-time employment before sitting the NCTJ's National Certificate Examination

Trainees can also gain a government NVQ (national vocational qualification) and SVQ (Scottish) in newspaper journalism and periodical journalism, and can also train as NVQ/SVQ assessors and verifiers.

See your local directory of adult education institutes (in London, *Floodlight*), for courses in feature writing, or creative writing (which sometimes includes article writing). The **National Institute of Adult Education**, 19B de Montfort Street, Leicester LE1 7GE, publishes a list twice yearly of weekend and longer courses (£1 post paid).

There are several reference books that give further education courses, among which you will find some in journalism, media studies, mass communications, etc. Many of these are theoretical and research-based, but there has been an increase in practical journalism courses as modules in university media studies courses and in university departments of continuing education. Consult such directories as *The Potter Guide to Higher Education* (Balebank Books), and *British Universities Guide to Graduate Studies* (Pitman). For various kinds of writing courses, see Macmillan's *Writer's Handbook.*

There are an increasing number of degree courses in journalism available in universities, in their Departments of Continuing Education and in polytechnics. See Macmillan's *Writer's Handbook* for these, as well as writing courses, circles and workshops throughout the country.

Practical courses are provided in-house by some of the large magazine publishing companies, and also by the following schools/institutions:

The City University, Northampton Square, London EC1V 0HN
Tel: 0171–477–8000
Undergraduate and graduate courses in journalism. The Department of Continuing Education organizes several writing workshops, including Writing Freelance Articles for Newspapers and Magazines.

Harlow College, College Square, The High, Harlow, Essex CM20 1LT
Tel: 01279–868000
NCTJ-validated course leading to pre-entry certificate. A full list of accredited NCTJ colleges and universities is available from the NCTJ.

London College of Printing and Distributive Trades, Elephant and Castle, London SE1 6SB
Tel: 0171–514–6500
Pre-entry and postgraduate courses in periodical journalism. Some companies send employees here for daytime release courses lasting four weeks.

The London School of Journalism Ltd, 22 Upbrook Mews, Bayswater, London W2 3HG
Tel: 0171–706–3536
Correspondence and tutorial courses include general and freelance journalism for diploma.

The Newspaper Society, Association of Regional and Local Press, 74 Great Russell Street, London WC1B 3DA
Tel: 0171–636–7014
Holds conferences, exhibitions and seminars every year. Publishes *Reaching the Regions. Regional Newspapers: Facts and Figures.*

Periodicals Training Council, Imperial House, 15–19 Kingsway, London
WC2B 6UN
Tel: 0171–836–8798
Organizes and monitors training. Courses on various aspects of magazine
journalism, arranged for companies in-house.

PMA Training, Administrative Offices, The Old Anchor, Church Street,
Hemingford Grey, Cambridgeshire PE18 9DF
Tel: 01480–300653
Numerous short courses in journalism up to senior levels, held in
Clerkenwell, Central London. Also in-house courses organized. Fully
equipped with Apple Mac and PCs.

The Thomson Foundation, The Bute Building, King Edward VII
Avenue, Cardiff CF1 3NB
Tel: 01222–874873
Courses for experienced journalists from overseas include feature writing.

University of Wales College (Centre for Journalism Studies),
The Bute Building, King Edward VII Avenue, Cardiff CF1 3NB
Tel: 01222–874000
One-year postgraduate course in journalism includes feature writing.

West Herts College, Watford Campus, Hempstead Road, Watford WD1
3EZ
Tel: 01923–257–500
Higher National Diploma course in advertising and marketing communications. Also courses in media studies and creative writing.

APPENDIX 8
USEFUL ADDRESSES

The Advertising Association, Abford House, 15 Wilton Road, London SW1V 1NJ
Tel: 0171–828–2771

Authors' Licensing and Collecting Society (ALCS), 74 New Oxford Street, London WC1A 1EF
Tel: 0171–255–2034

British Association of Picture Libraries and Agencies, 18 Vine Hill, London EC1R 5DX
Tel: 0171–713–1780

British Broadcasting Corporation, Broadcasting House, Portland Place, London W1A 1AA
Tel: 0171–580–4468

BBC External Services, Bush House, London WC2B 4PH
Tel: 0171–240–3456

BBC Television, Television Centre, Wood Lane, London W12 7RJ
Tel: 0171–240–8000

British Library Reading Room, Great Russell Street, London WC1B 3DG
Tel: 0171–412–7676

British Library Science Reference and Information Service, Physical Sciences, 25 Southampton Buildings, Chancery Lane, London WC2A 1AW
Tel: 0171–412–7494/6

British Newspaper Library, Colindale Avenue, London NW9 5HE
Tel: 0171–323–7353

British Standards Institution, 389 Chiswick High Road, London
W4 4AL
Tel: 0181–996–9000

CAM (Communications, Advertising and Marketing) Foundation,
Abford House, Wilton Road, London SW1V 1NJ
Tel: 0171–828–7506
Examinations Board providing examinations (certificate and diploma) for
the PR and advertising professions.

Campaign for Freedom of Information, 88 Old Street, London
EC1V 9AR
Tel: 0171–439–9840

Celebrity Service Inc., 171 West 75th Street, New York, NY 10019
93 Regent Street, London W1R 7TA
Tel: 0171–499–8511
Publishes *Celebrity Bulletin, The Contact Book,* and *Celebrity Register.*

Central Office of Information, Hercules Road, London SE1 7OU
Tel: 0171–928–2345

Cyberia Café, 39 Whitfield Street, London W1P 1RE
Tel: 0171–209–0982
Public access Internet café. Other similar places in London, Kingston-
upon-Thames, Surrey, Edinburgh, and other cities and towns.

Freelance Press Services, Cumberland House, Lisadel Street,
Manchester M6 6GG
Tel: 0161–745–8850

HMSO Bookshop, 49 High Holborn, London WC1V 6HB
Tel: 0171–430–1671
Both telephone and counter service. Agents throughout the country. For
government publications.

Independent Television Commission, 33 Foley Street, London W1P 7LB
Tel: 0171–255–3000

Index on Censorship, 39c Highbury Place, London N5
Tel: 0171–278–2313

National Viewers and Listeners Association, All Saints House, High
Street, Colchester CO1 1UG
Tel: 01206–561–155

Periodical Publishers Association (PPA), Imperial House,
15–19 Kingsway, London WC2B 6JN
Tel: 0171–379–6268

Operates the Periodicals Training Council.

Public Relations Consultants Association Ltd, Willow House, Willow
Place, London SW1P 1JH
Tel: 0171–233–6026

Radio Authority, Holbrook House, 14 Great Queen Street, London
WC2B 5DG
Tel: 0171–430–2724

Writer's Digest Books, 9933 Alliance Road, Cincinnati, Ohio 45242,
USA

BIBLIOGRAPHY

BOOKS

Out of print books may be available through the public library service, or consulted at a national library, such as The British Library. There is a wealth of books on all aspects of writing published in the USA, partly because there are many colleges of journalism. The following bibliography reflects this, even though some of the American books may not be too easy to find. Try Freelance Press Services. Simmonds, 16 Fleet Street, London EC4Y 1AX has more books on journalism, including the American Writer's Digest titles, than most bookshops. Information on other stockists can be obtained by writing to the US Information Service, Reference and Research Library 55–56 Upper Brook Street, London W1A 2LH.

BASIC REFERENCE LIBRARY

The following is a rough guide to a basic writer's reference library. You will want to add many more in time, according to the way your interests and your work develop, from the lists that follow or from your own lists. Much depends on how easy it is for you to get to a well-stocked reference library. Details of the books in the basic list will be found in the lists that follow:

1 English dictionary.
2 *Hart's Rules for Compositors and Readers*, Oxford University Press.
3 *The Oxford Dictionary for Writers and Editors*, OUP.
4 A dictionary of dates.

5 A selection of Penguin dictionaries: politics, economics, religions, twentieth century history, etc.
6 *Writers' and Artists' Yearbook*, A & C Black.
7 *The Writer's Handbook*, Macmillan.
8 *Titles and Forms of Address*, A & C Black.
9 *Whitaker's Almanac.*
10 World atlas and world gazetteer.
11 Atlas and gazetteer of the British Isles.
12 Encyclopaedias. Discover which would be most useful – Chambers, Penguin's, etc. *The New Encyclopaedia Britannica*, thirty volumes, is the most comprehensive.
13 *Pear's Cyclopaedia.*
14 *Fowler's Modern English Usage*, revised by Gowers.
15 Gowers's *The Complete Plain Words.*
16 A concise world history.
17 Dictionary of quotations.
18 Dictionary of modern quotations.

GENERAL REFERENCE

The Advertisers' Annual. Lists advertising rates of publications. Use with NUJ Freelance Guide to determine fees payable. Gives details of trade journals under subject headings.
Benn's Media Directory. Volume 1: UK; volume 2: international. Benn Business Information Services. Gives magazines under subject headings.
Britain: An Official Handbook, HMSO, London, Annual.
Chambers Biographical Dictionary.
Concise Guide to Reference Material, ed. A. J. Walford, Library Association, London.
Dictionary of National Biography.
Directory of Publishing, Cassell/Publishers Association. Annual. Gives all main publishers, organizations and agencies.
Dod's Parliamentary Companion. Annual. Gives names and backgrounds of MPs.
Guinness Book of Records, Guinness Superlatives Ltd.
Hollis Press and Public Relations Annual, Hollis Directories, Sunbury-on-Thames, Middlesex.
International Who's Who, Europa Publications, London. Annual.
International Year Book and Statesman's Who's Who, Kelly's Directories Ltd.
Keesing's Record of World Events.

Kelly's Handbook, Kelly's Directories Ltd. Annual. Royalty, nobility, MPs, etc.

Municipal Year Book. For local government matters.

The Ordnance Survey Atlas of Great Britain.

Oxford Companion of English Literature, current edition Margaret Drabble, OUP.

Research for Writers, Ann Hoffmann, current edn, A & C Black.

The Statesman's Year Book, Macmillan. Annual.

The Statesman's Year Book World Gazetteer, 2nd edition, John Paxton, Macmillan.

The Times Concise Atlas.

The Times Illustrated Road Atlas.

Titles and Forms of Address: A Guide to their Correct Use, current edn, A & C Black.

Whitaker's Almanac, J. Whitaker and Sons Ltd. Annual. Complete edition 1236 pages. Shorter paperback edition 692 pages.

Who's Who, A & C Black. Annual.

Who Was Who, A & C Black. Several volumes.

Willing's Press Guide, Thomas Skinner Directories. Lists UK publications, with a section classified under subject headings for magazines. Lists important publications of other countries.

DICTIONARIES

Look for latest edition.

Bartlett's Unfamiliar Quotations, L. L. Levinson, Allen & Unwin.

Bartlett's Familiar Quotations, Macmillan.

Brewer's Dictionary of Phrase and Fable, concise edition, Cassell, 1992.

Chambers' Dictionary of Dates.

Chambers' Encyclopaedia.

Collins Dictionary and Thesaurus. The thesaurus, in straightforward alphabetical order, takes up the bottom half of each page, so you can make reference to the dictionary at the same time.

The David and Charles Book of Quotations, ed. Robert I. Fitzhenry, David and Charles. Arrangements by subject categories makes it particularly useful for gathering ideas for titles and slants.

Everyman's Dictionary of Dates, J. M. Dent.

Fowler's Modern English Usage, 2nd edn, revised by Sir Ernest Gowers, OUP 1978. The classic on the subject.

Newspeak: A Dictionary of Jargon, Jonathan Green, Routledge & Kegan Paul.

The Oxford Dictionary for Writers and Editors.

The Oxford Dictionary of Quotations.
The Oxford Thesaurus.
The Penguin Dictionary of Quotations and *The Penguin Dictionary of Modern Quotations*, compiled by J. J. and M. J. Cohen, Penguin Books.
Roget's Thesaurus, Penguin. The arrangement by concepts will still appeal to many, in spite of the convenience of the Collins and Oxford version.
Shorter Oxford English Dictionary.
Slang Thesaurus, Jonathan Green, Pan Books.

DIRECTORIES: CONTACTS

Advertisers' Annual, Windsor Court, East Grinstead House, East Grinstead, West Sussex. Tel: 01342 26972.
The Blue Book of British Broadcasting. Tellex Monitors. Over 1500 key personnel, working on programmes.
Contact, International Publishing Corporation Business Press Information Services Ltd. Address as for *Advertisers' Annual.* Useful addresses, particularly for PROs.
Creative Handbook, 100 St Martin's Lane, London WC2.
Hollis Press and Public Relations, Contact House, Lower Hampton Road, Sunbury-on-Thames, Middlesex TW16 5HG.
Information, Press and PR Officers in Government Departments and Public Corporations, Central Office of Information, Hercules Road, London SE1 7OU.
The Spotlight Casting Directory and Contacts, Charles House, 7 Leicester Place, London WC2. Covers the world of entertainment.
Two-Ten Communications, 210 Old Street, London EC1V 9UN. Provides updated lists of editorial contacts in the press and broadcasting.
UKPG News Contact Directory, UK Press Gazette, Maclean-Hunter House, Chalk Lane, Cockfosters Road, Barnet, Herts EN4 0BU.

DIRECTORIES: ORGANIZATIONS

Directory of British Associations, Current British Directories.
Encyclopaedia of Associations, Gale Research Co., Detroit, USA.
Voluntary Organisations: An NCVO Directory, National Council for Voluntary Associations, 26 Bedford Square, London WC1.
Writer's Resource Guide, B Clarke, USA. 1500 sources of research information.

DIRECTORIES: PUBLICATIONS

UK

A to Z of Free Newspapers and Magazines in Great Britain, Association of Free Newspapers.

British Rate and Data, Maclean-Hunter, Maclean-Hunter House, Chalk Lane, Cockfosters Road, Barnet, Herts EN4 0BU. Gives circulation and readership figures, readership profiles, advertisement rates, etc. for newspapers and magazines in the UK.

Current British Journals, David Woodworth, The Library Association, 1970. Denotes level of appeal, for example, popular, student, technical, professional, trade, research, ecclesiastical, society, institution.

Media Directory, Maclean-Hunter.

The Media Guide, a *Guardian* book published by Fourth Estate.

Technical and Specialized Periodicals Published in Britain, Central Office of Information, London, 1974. Still useful; complement with more up-to-date sources.

Whitaker's Books in Print, Book of the Month, Books to Come, Paperback Books in Print, J Whitaker & Sons.

US

Editor and Publisher Year Book, New York. Gives names and departments of regional papers in USA.

Guide to American Directories, 10th edn, Coral Gables, Fla: Bernard Klein, B. Klein Publications, 1980.

International

Travel Writer's Market, USA. Available from Freelance Press Services. Gives some 400 markets for travel articles and photographs, in US, Canada and other parts of the world.

Ulrich's International Periodicals Directory, New York/London: Bowker. Annual.

The Australian Marketing Guide Casebook, University of Queensland Press, 1981.

INDEXES

Many publications produce indexes. Some, like *The Times,* put them into volumes annually. Other annual volumes select from various publications. The following is a sample:

Applied Science and Technology Index. Technical journals.
Architectural Periodicals Index. International periodicals on Architecture.
British Humanities Index, Library Association. Selects from quality news-
    papers, weekly reviews, selected magazines, professional journals.
The Clover Index, General interest/hobby type journals.
The Clover Newspaper Index. The broadsheet newspapers, *The European*
    and *The Economist.* Weekly so up-to-date.
Current Technology Index. Scientific and technical journals.
Design and Applied Arts Index. International journals in design, arts and
    crafts.
Reader's Guide to Periodical Literature, New York: H W Wilson Co.
Research Index. Indexes articles and news items of financial interest in
    national press and business periodicals.
The Times Index.

AUTHORSHIP

The list includes one or two books about how to write non-fiction books
– a natural progression, after all, for some article writers. Others are
surveys of writing techniques, devoting separate chapters to articles, short
stories, novels, plays, etc. Many of such books fill me with suspicion. It is
hard enough to write one kind of thing well, harder still to explain to
others how to write it. The following, however, can be recommended,
especially for budding writers who are unsure which direction to take.

Ashe, Geoffrey, *Art of Writing Made Simple*, Heinemann, 1972. Covers
    the main kinds of fiction and non-fiction and it says too much.
    Nevertheless, it is well worth reading.
Bolt, David, *An Author's Handbook*, Piatkus Books, 1986. Deals clearly
    with the practical things authors need to know – such as the correct
    presentation of manuscripts.
Blackwell, Basil, *Guide for Authors*, Blackwell, 1985.
Doubtfire, Dianne, *Creative Writing*, Hodder & Stoughton, 1983. Fiction
    and non-fiction – in a short book. But it has some telling points to
    make.
Kerton, Paul with Colin Greeland, *The Freelance Writer's Handbook*,
    Ebury Press, 1986. Concise, lively, unstuffy, going straight to the essen-
    tials: fiction, broadcasting, as well as journalism.
Legat, Michael, *Writing for Pleasure and Profit*, Robert Hale, 1986.
    An author/publisher does a skilful job of bridging the gap between
    the two. *An Author's Guide to Publishing*, revised edn, Robert Hale
    1991.

Linton, Ian, *Writing for a Living*, Kogan Page Ltd, 1985. Covers the whole field, but focuses on how to approach and deal with the people who commission work.

Wells, Gordon, *The Book Writer's Handbook*, 2nd edn, Virgin Books, 1991 (first published Allison and Busby, 1989). *The Successful Author's Handbook*, Macmillan Press/Papermac, 1981. *Writer's Questions Answered*, Allison and Busby, 1986. Very useful reference book, though short, covering almost any topic the beginning writer is likely to ask.

BROADCASTING

Boyd Andrew, *Broadcast Journalism – Techniques of Radio and TV News,* 3rd edn, Focal Press, 1994. A profusely illustrated and detailed account.

Hilliard, R. L., *Writing for TV and Radio*, 3rd revised edn, Communication Arts Books, 1976.

Paice, Eric, *The Way to Write for TV*, Elm Tree Books, latest edition.

Tyrell, Roberts, *The Work of the TV Journalist,* Focal Press 1981.

Writing for the BBC, BBC Publications, latest edition.

EDITING

Butcher, Judith, *Copy-Editing. The Cambridge Handbook,* Cambridge University Press, 3rd edn, 1992.

Cheney, Theodore A. Rees, *Getting the Words Right. How to Revise, Edit, or Rewrite,* Writer's Digest Books, Cincinnati, Ohio, 1983. You reduce, you rearrange, and you reword. How to discover the flaws, and how to put things right. Cheney is author, journalist, communication expert, and teacher for many years. One of the best books on editing skills there is.

Hodgson, F. W. *Subediting: Modern Newspaper Editing and Production,* Focal Press, 2nd edn, 1993. The first detailed examination of subbing and editorial production techniques under computerized systems.

Sellers, Leslie, *Doing it in Style*, Pergamon Press 1968. Alphabetical book: practical common sense. *Keeping up the Style*, Pitman, 1975. *The Simple Subs Book*, 2nd edn, Pergamon Press, 1985. The author was production editor of the *Daily Mail*. The third book is subtitled *A Manual for Subeditors (and Would-be Subeditors) on Newspapers, Trade Papers and House Journals*. It has become a classic. The second edition was updated to include new chapters on colour and electronic editing.

FEATURE WRITING

The following list is of books that may cover writing for all kinds of markets – newspapers and magazines. Books specifically dealing with writing for magazines are listed separately.

Campbell, Morag, *Writing about Travel,* A & C Black, 1989.

Dick Jill, *Freelance Writing for Newspapers,* A & C Black, 1991.

Fontaine, André, *The Art of writing Non-Fiction,* Crowel, New York, 1974. Highly readable general guide. Particularly good on different kinds of writing: descriptive, dramatic, explanatory, and so on.

Friedlander, Edward J. and Lee, John, *Feature Writing for Newspapers and Magazines,* Harper and Row, New York, 1988.

Holmes, Marjorie, *Writing the Creative Article Today,* revised edn, The Writer Inc., Boston, 1986.

Hull, Raymond, *How to Write 'How-to- Books and Articles,* Poplar Press, 1982. Covers special problems, responsibilities of the how-to writer and the special organizing and writing skills required. Approaches to editors, use of illustrations, finding an expert to collaborate with: a comprehensive guide.

Knott, Leonard L., *Writing After Fifty,* Writer's Digest Books, 1985. Inspiration to continue your writing career for thirty years or so, as the author has done, or even to start a new career.

Newcombe, Duane, *How to Sell and Resell Your Writing,* Writer's Digest Books, 1987.

Ruehlamann, William, *Stalking the Feature Story,* Writer's Digest Books 1978. Good ideas on how to develop a story.

Raskin, Julie and Males, Carolyn, *How to Write and Sell a Column.* Writer's Digest Books, 1987. Ideas and tips garnered from many kinds of columnists in the US. Useful tips on how to market column ideas.

Samson, Jack, *Successful Outdoor Writing,* Writer's Digest Books, 1979. Fishing, boating, camping, are among the activities; features and columns for newspapers and magazines, and books, are among the products. Due attention is given to photography. Excerpts of well-crafted articles are skilfully analysed.

Schoenfeld, Clarence A. and Diegumueller, Karen S., *Effective Feature Writing,* New York, Holt, Rinehart and Winston, 1982. An organized approach, based on many years of teaching as well as writing. This makes it useful as a reference book. Lavishly illustrated by quotation. Good for specific aspects: titles, intros, endings, etc.

Wells, Gordon, *The Craft of Writing Articles,* Allison and Busby, 1983. Much practical advice for the beginner, without wasting a word, in a slim volume.

Wilbur L. Perry, *How to Write Articles that Sell*, John Wiley, New York, 1981. This informative, no-nonsense book concentrates on finding ideas and marketing them.

Witt, Leonard (ed), *The Complete Book of Feature Writing*. Writer's Digest Books, 1991.

Zinsser, William, *On Writing Well: An Informal Guide to Writing Non-Fiction,* Harper and Row, New York, 1988. Includes self-editing, interviewing, travel. Entertaining and wise about sports writing, and on writing about your job.

MAGAZINE JOURNALISM

Davis, Anthony, *Magazine Journalism Today*, Focal Press, 1988. Deals with all stages of magazine production and all kinds of magazines. Invaluable guide to the editing and production sides of the business as a complement of the books that concentrate on the writing aspects.

Freedman, Helen, Rosengen and Krieger, Karen, *The Writer's Guide to Magazine Markets: Non-Fiction,* New American Library, New York, 1983.

Gill, Brendan, *Here at 'The New Yorker'*, Michael Joseph, 1975. The inside story of one of the world's great magazines.

Graham, Betsy P., *Magazine Article Writing*, Holt, Rinehart and Winston, 1980. Comprehensive: effective use of quotes.

Gunther, Max, *Writing the Modern Magazine Article*, The Writer Inc., 1976. Inside story of successful freelance writer. Analyses some of his best work.

Hines, John, *The Way to Write Magazine Articles*, Elm Tree Books, 1987. A brief, readable survey of the essentials for a beginner.

Mitford, Jessica, *The Making of Muckraker,* Quartet Books, 1981. The experience of twenty years of investigative articles for the top American magazines distilled in a fascinating book. The instruction is contained in a long introduction and in the comments to the seventeen articles printed. Memorable tips on ways of getting people to talk, while still smiling.

Morrison, John, *Freelancing for Magazines,* Bureau of Freelance Photographers, 1991.

Newcombe, Duane, *A Complete Guide to Marketing Magazine Articles*, Writer's Digest Books, 1975. Reselling articles in several ways.

Spikol, Art, *Magazine Writing: The Inside Angle,* Writer's Digest Books, 1979. Wise-cracking, down-to-earth style, but the advice is sound, and at times profound. The author has wide experience as writer and editor.

Wells, Gordon, *The Magazine Writer's Handbook,* current edn, Allison and Busby. Issues of some seventy magazines analysed to reveal editorial policy, readership, and scope for freelances.

STYLE, USAGE AND WRITING TECHNIQUES

Bagnall, Nicholas, *Newspaper Language*, Focal Press, 1993.

Burzun, Jacques, *A Rhetoric for Writers,* Harper and Row, 1975.

Berner, Thomas R., *Language Skills for Journalists*, Howard Mifflin, New York, 1979. Lucid concentration on grammar.

Bernstein, Theodore M., *Watch Your Language,* Channel Press, New York, 1958. Identifying what makes for good newspaper English has not been done better. The author was managing editor the *New York Times.*

Berry, Thomas Elliott, *The Craft of Writing*, McGraw-Hill, 1975. For anyone. Points cogently made, well backed up by quotation.

Ebbitt, Wilma R. and Ebbitt, David R., *Writer's Guide*, 7th edn, Scott, Foresman and Company, Glenview Il., 1982. Aimed at US college students, and academic in tone, but good advice on writing techniques.

Flesch, Rudolf, *The Art of Clear Thinking, The Art of Readable Writing,* and *The Art of Plain Talk*, etc., Macmillan Publishing Co., New York. First published in the 1940s–1950s – reprinted many times. An author whose experience as writer, editor and teacher was distilled into magnificent common sense.

Gowers, Sir Ernest, revised Sir Bruce Fraser, *The Complete Plain Words,* Penguin Books, 1977.

Gunning, Robert, *The Technique of Clear Writing*, McGraw-Hill, New York, 1968.

Orwell, George, 'Politics and the English language' in *Inside the Whale and Other Essays,* Penguin Books, 1966.

Partridge, Eric, *Usage and Abusage*, revised edn, Penguin Books, 1973. To complement Fowler, not to compete with it: less quirkily authoritarian, witty, constructive and humane.

Rivers, William L., *Writing: Craft and Art*, New American Library, 1985. He nails down with humour the essentials for all kinds of effective writing.

Waterhouse, Keith, *On Newspaper Style*, Penguin Books, 1989. An expanded, revised and updated edition of *Daily Mirror Style.* A polemic against tired, shoddy journalese and a plea for fresh workmanlike writing.

Whale, John, *Put it in Writing*, J. M. Dent, 1984. Analysing the merits of top modern writers, the author has lively, helpful approach throughout.

MISCELLANEOUS

Bell, Judith, *Doing Your Research Project,* Open University Press, 1987.

Brady, John, *The Craft of Interviewing,* Writer's Digest Books, 1976.

Burchill, Julie, *Love It or Shove It,* Century Publishing, 1985. Collection of her columns. And you'll either love this or loathe it.

Cassandra (Sir William Neil Connor), *Cassandra at his Finest and Funniest,* Daily Mirror/Hamlyn, 1967.

Cassell, Kay, *The Complete Handbook for Freelance Writers,* Writer's Digest Books, 1983. Lucid and comprehensive about all you could want to know about organizing your fact gathering, writing and finances.

Cattle, Dennis, and Wade, John, *Teach Yourself Public Speaking.* Hodder and Stoughton, 1980. Covers all aspects: the physical and the psychological as well as the writing.

Crone, Tom, *The Law and the Media,* 3rd edn, Focal Press, 1994. All the areas of law with which journalists have to be familiar.

Davies, Hunter, *Hunting People*, Mainstream Publishing 1994. A valuable Introduction summarizes the techniques of some well-known interview specialists – Lynn Barber, Angela Lambert, Valerie Crone, John Mortimer, Ray Connolly – as well as his own. The rest is forty-four of his interviews with the famous covering thirty years.

Diehl, Digby, *Super Talk,* Doubleday, New York, 1974. Interviews with celebrities.

Dobson, Christopher, *The Freelance Journalist.* Focal Press, 1992.

Drewry, John E., *Writing Book Reviews,* Greenwood Press, Westport, Conn., 1974. Lists the questions reviewer should ask of book being reviewed.

Ellis, Alice Thomas, *More Home Life*, Duckworth. A collection of *Spectator* pieces worth preserving in book form.

Evans, Hilary, *The Art of Picture Research. The Freelance Photographer's Market Handbook,* BFP Books. Annual. Lists the markets for the freelance photographer and photographer/writer: magazines, picture libraries, calendar publishers. Useful for any freelance writer.

Finch, Peter, *How to Publish Yourself*, Allison and Busby, 1987.

Greenwood, Walter and Welsh, Tom, *Essential Law for Journalists,* Butterworths, 10th edn, 1988.

Harris, Geoffrey, and Spark, David, *Practical Newspaper Reporting*, 2nd edn, Focal Press, 1993.

Harriss, Leiter and Johnson, *The Complete Reporter*, Macmillan, 1981.

Hattersley, Roy, *Press Gang,* Robson, 1983. The political/personal columnist republishes his *Punch* series, 1981–1983.

Hennessy, Brendan and Hodgson, F. W., *Journalism Workbook.* A manual of tasks and resources. Focal Press, 1995.

Hetherington, Alastair, *News, Newspapers and TV,* Macmillan, 1985. What is news, and how should it be handled? Who makes the decisions? How are they made? By a former editor of *The Guardian.*

Hodgson, F. W., *Modern Newspaper Practice,* Focal Press, 4th edn, 1996. The organization, production and economics of the newspaper business.

Hoffmann, Ann, *Research for Writers,* A & C Black. Yearly.

Hoinville, Gerald, Jewell, Roger et al, *Survey Research Practice,* Heinemann Educational Books, 1978.

Holden, Anthony, *Of Presidents, Prime Ministers and Princes.* Weidenfeld & Nicolson, 1994. An anthology of pieces, including interviews/profiles while features editor of *The Times* and Washington correspondent for *The Observer,* among other things.

Hoover, Hardy, *Essentials for the Scientific and Technical Writer,* revised edn, Dover Publications, 1980.

Hunt, Todd, *Reviewing for the Mass Media,* Chilton Book Co., New York, 1972. Plenty of analysis of quotes, common sense advice.

Jackson, Ian, *The Provincial Press and the Community,* Manchester University Press, 1971. Still valid.

Jones, Graham, *The Business of Freelancing,* BFP Books, 1987. A well established freelance journalist and author, photographer and desktop publishing consultant concisely but comprehensively covers the freelance writing business.

Keeble, Richard, *The Newspapers Handbook,* Routledge, 1994.

Keene, Martin, *Practical Photojournalism,* Focal Press, 1993.

Larkin, Philip, *Required Writing: Miscellaneous Pieces, 1955–82,* Faber and Faber, 1983. The late Philip Larkin's reputation rests on his poetry, but he was reviewer (mainly of poetry but also of jazz music) of wit and insights.

Lewis, Mel, *Writing to Win,* McGraw-Hill, 1987. Insights that come from straddling two fields of journalism and publicity writing. Includes business letters, reports and proposals as well as advertising and press releases.

Metzler, Ken, *Creative Interviewing,* Prentice-Hall, 1977. Good on the psychological aspects of interviewing, and the preparation of questions.

Mortimer, John, *Character Parts,* Penguin Books, 1987. A selection from his interviews, all but one of which appeared in *The Sunday Times.*

Northmore, David, *Freedom of Information Handbook: How to Find Out What You Want to Know,* Bloomsbury Publishing, 1993.

O'Brien, Flann (Myles na Gopaleen), *The Best of Myles,* Picador (Pan Books), 1977. The best of the famous humorous column in *The Irish Times.* His real name was Brian O'Nolan.

Parsons, Tony, *Dispatches from the Front Line of Popular Culture,* Virgin Books, 1995. On music, love and sex, travel, polemic and culture for *New Musical Express, Arena* and *The Face* among magazines; and *The Daily Telegraph, The Guardian, The Sunday Times* and the *Daily Mirror.*

Photographer's Market, Writer's Digest Books. Annual.

Pritchard, John, *The Penguin Guide to the Law,* Penguin, 1982. Over 900 pages. The most comprehensive handbook to the law as it affects the individual ever compiled.

Purcell, Ann and Carl, *A Guide to Travel Writing and Photography.* Harrap Publishing, 1991.

Rigg, Diana (compiler), *No Turn Unstoned,* Arrow Books, 1982. The worst ever theatrical reviews, hilarious reading.

Sherwood, H. C., *The Journalistic Interview,* revised edn, Harper, 1972.

Todd, Alden, and Loder, Cari, *Finding Facts Fast,* Penguin Books, 1990. The essential research techniques.

Turabian, Kate, *A Manual for Writers of Research Papers, Theses and Dissertations.* The essential guide whenever you get into academic areas. The correct forms for referring to everything, from books to Parliamentary Bills. First British edition by John Spink, Senior Lecturer, College of Librarianship, Wales, First published Chicago, 1937, revised British edition, Heinemann, 1982.

Whittaker, Kenneth, *Using Libraries,* 3rd edn, André Deutsh, 1972.

Wells, Gordon, *Low-Cost Word Processing,* Allison and Busby, 1986.

Williams, Paul N., *Investigative Reporting and Editing,* Prentice-Hall, 1978.

Zinsser, William, *Writing with a Word Processor,* Harper & Row, 1983.

Zobel, Louis Purvin, *The Travel Writer's Handbook,* Writer's Digest Books, 1980.

MAGAZINES

ADVERTISING AND PUBLIC RELATIONS

Broadcast, 7 Swallow Place, London W1R 7AA, Tel: 0171–491–9484.

Campaign, Haymarket Publishing Group, 30 Lancaster Gate, London W2 2LY. Tel: 0181–943–5000. Weekly.

Marketing, Haymarket Publishing Group, 30 Lancaster Gate, London W2 2LY. Weekly.

Marketing Week, St Giles House, 50 Poland Street, London W1V 4AX. Tel: 0171–439–4222.

PR Week, Haymarket Publishing Group, 30 Lancaster Gate, London W2 3LP. Tel: 0171–439–4429.

Two-Ten Communications, 210 Old Street, London EC1V 9UN. Tel: 0171–490–8111. Updated lists of editorial contacts in the press and broadcasting.

JOURNALISM/WRITING AND MARKETING

Some magazines in this list are useful for updating your marketing information but nothing replaces your own study of recent issues of any publication you aim to write for.

The Author, 84 Drayton Gardens, London SW10 9SB. Tel: 0171–373–6642. Quarterly.
British Journalism Review, edited by Geoffrey Goodman, BJR Publishings, c/o Cassell plc, Villiers House, 41–47 Strand, London WC2N 5JE. Quarterly. Perceptive comment on larger issues.
Freelance Market News. See samples (pages 306 and 311). Freelance Press Services, Cumberland House, Lisadel Street, Salford, Manchester M6 6GG. Tel: 0161–745–8850. Eleven times a year.
The Journalist, National Union of Journalists, 314 Gray's Inn Road, London WC1X 8DP. Monthly newspaper of the NUJ. Tel: 0171–278–7916.
Press Gazette, Maclean-Hunter House, Chalk Lane, Cockfosters Road, Barnet, Herts. EN4 0BU. Tel: 0181–975–9759. The journalists' weekly trade/professional paper. Formerly *UK Press Gazette*.
The Writer, 8 Arlington Street, Boston, Ma 02116. Monthly.
Writer's Digest, 9933 Alliance Road, Cincinnati, Ohio 45242. Monthly. The best.
Writers' Monthly, 29 Turnpike Lane, Haringey, London N8 0EP. Gives useful updates, for example, movements of editors, and regular market surveys including overseas markets. Tel: 0181–342–8879.
Writers' News, PO Box 4, Nairn IV12 4HU Scotland. Tel: 01667–54441. Monthly.

INDEX